The Modern Language Review

JANUARY 2014   VOLUME 109   PART 1

General Editor
PROFESSOR DEREK CONNON

English Editor
PROFESSOR ANDREW HISCOCK

French Editor
DR ALISON WILLIAMS

Italian Editor
PROFESSOR JANE EVERSON

Hispanic Editor
PROFESSOR DEREK FLITTER

Germanic Editor
PROFESSOR KATRIN KOHL

Slavonic Editor
DR KATHARINE HODGSON

Assistant Editor
DR JOHN WAŚ

MODERN HUMANITIES RESEARCH ASSOCIATION

The Modern Humanities Research Association

was founded in Cambridge in 1918 and has become an international organization with members in all parts of the world. It is a registered charity number 1064670, and a company limited by guarantee, registered in England number 3446016. Its main object is to encourage advanced study and research in modern and medieval European languages, literatures, and cultures by its publication of journals, book series, and its Style Guide.

Further information about the activities of the Association and individual membership may be obtained from the Hon. Secretary, Dr Barbara Burns, School of Modern Languages and Cultures, University of Glasgow, Glasgow G12 8RS, UK, email membership@mhra.org.uk, or from the website at www.mhra.org.uk

The Association's publications, including most back volumes, are available in print or electronically. Full details are available from www.mhra.org.uk

The Modern Language Review

The *Modern Language Review* is one of five journals available to members of the Modern Humanities Research Association in return for a composite membership subscription payable in advance through the Assistant Treasurer. (Associate membership is open to graduates for four years after their first degree, and postgraduate membership is also available.) Some other publications of the MHRA are available to members at special rates.

The *Modern Language Review* and other journals published by the MHRA may be ordered from JSTOR (http://about.jstor.org/csp).

ISSN 0026–7937 (Print)
ISSN 2222–4319 (Online)

© 2014 The Modern Humanities Research Association

All rights reserved. No part of this publication may be reproduced in any material form (including photocopying or storing it in any medium by electronic means) without the prior written permission of the copyright owner, except in accordance with the provisions of the Copyright, Designs and Patents Act 1988, or under the terms of a licence permitting restricted copying issued in the UK by the Copyright Licensing Agency Ltd, Saffron House, 6–10 Kirby Street, London EC1N 8TS, England, or in the USA by the Copyright Clearance Center, 222 Rosewood Drive, Danvers, Mass. 01923. Application for the written permission of the copyright owner to reproduce any part of this publication must be made to the General Editor.

DISCLAIMER

Statements of fact and opinion in the content of the *Modern Language Review* are those of the respective authors and contributors and not of the journal editors or of the Modern Humanities Research Association (MHRA). MHRA makes no representation, express or implied, in respect of the accuracy of the material in this journal and cannot accept any legal responsibility or liability for any errors or omissions that may be made.

TYPESET BY JOHN WAŚ, OXFORD

Guidelines for Contributors to *MLR*

The *Modern Language Review* publishes articles and book reviews in English on any aspect of modern and medieval European (including English and Latin American) languages, literatures, and cultures (including cinema). The journal does not publish correspondence. We are glad to receive general and comparative articles as well as those on language-specific topics. We encourage submissions from postgraduates. Articles should be submitted to the appropriate section editor in one typescript copy together with an identical electronic copy sent as an email attachment. Articles should conform precisely to the conventions of the *MHRA Style Guide*, 3rd edn, 2013 (ISBN 978-1-78188-009-8), obtainable from www.style.mhra.org.uk, price £6.50, US$13, €8; an online version of the *Guide* is also available from the same address. Authors should provide an abstract of their articles with keywords highlighted in bold type. This abstract should not exceed 100 words. At the end of articles and reviews contributors should include, in this order, their affiliation or location; name as it is to be printed; name and postal address for correspondence; and email address. Simple references should be incorporated into the text (see *MHRA Style Guide*, 10.2). Double spacing should be used throughout, including quotations and footnotes, which should be in the same large size of type as the rest of the article. Articles are typically about 8000 words in length including footnotes, but longer and shorter ones are also welcome. Quotations and references should be carefully checked. Quotations from languages covered by the journal, and from Latin and Greek, should be given in the original language. Latin and Greek passages should normally be translated or at least paraphrased; usually this is not required in the case of modern languages, though it may be helpful where dialects or early forms of the language are cited. However, since the journal has a broad readership, please provide translations or paraphrases of quotations within comparative or general articles (except for modern French). If in doubt, consult the appropriate section editor.

The *Modern Language Review* regrets that it must charge contributors for the cost of corrections in proof which the Editor in his or her discretion thinks excessive. Contributors should keep a copy of their typescript. Typescripts not accepted for publication will not normally be returned. If your article is accepted, you will be asked to supply a definitive version of it both in hard copy and as an email attachment. Authors should ensure that there is no discrepancy between the computer file and the printout.

It is a condition of publication in this journal that authors of articles and reviews assign copyright, including electronic copyright, to the MHRA. *Inter alia*, this allows the General Editor to deal efficiently and consistently with requests from third parties for permission to reproduce material. The journal has been published simultaneously in printed and electronic form since January 2001. Permission, without fee, for authors to use their own material in other publications, after a reasonable period of time has elapsed, is not normally withheld.

On publication of each issue of the journal authors will receive, by email, the finalized PDF of their contribution as it appears in the printed volume. Physical offprints are not supplied. Authors of articles will also receive a complimentary copy of the printed issue in which the article appears.

Articles and books for review should be sent to the Editor concerned:

General and Comparative. Professor Derek Connon, Department of French, Swansea University, Swansea, SA2 8PP (d.f.connon@swansea.ac.uk).

English and American. Professor Andrew Hiscock, School of English, Bangor University, Bangor, LL57 2DG (mhraassistant@bangor.ac.uk)

French. Dr Alison Williams, Department of French, Swansea University, Swansea, SA2 8PP (a.j.williams@swansea.ac.uk).

Italian. Professor Jane Everson, School of Modern Languages, Literatures and Cultures (Italian), Royal Holloway, University of London, Egham, TW20 0EX (j.everson@rhul.ac.uk).

Hispanic. Professor Derek Flitter, School of Modern Languages, Queen's Building, University of Exeter, Exeter EX4 4QH (d.w.flitter@exeter.ac.uk).

German, Dutch, and Scandinavian. Professor Robert Vilain, School of Modern Languages, University of Bristol, 17 Woodland Road, Bristol, BS8 1TE (robert.vilain@bristol.ac.uk).

Slavonic and Eastern European. Dr Katharine Hodgson, School of Modern Languages, Queen's Building, University of Exeter, Exeter EX4 4QH (k.m.hodgson@exeter.ac.uk).

CONTENTS

ARTICLES
PAGE

'Tolle lege': Epiphanies of the Book
By Theodore Ziolkowski 1

Lacunary Knowledge in Sebald and Proust
By Edward J. Hughes 15

'P.S.': The Dangerous Logic of the Postscript in Eighteenth-Century Literature
By Richard Terry 35

Ruins and Visions: Stephen Spender in Occupied Germany
By Florian Alix-Nicolaï 54

Henri-Georges Clouzot's *L'Enfer*: Modern Cinema at the Crossroads of the Arts
By Marion Schmid 75

Michel Tournier and the Virtual Essay
By Christy Wampole 96

The Power of Woman's Words, the Power of Woman's Silence: How the *Madrastra* Speaks in the Thirteenth-Century Castilian *Sendebar*
By Andreea Weisl-Shaw 110

What Do We Say When We Say 'Juan Gelman'? On Pseudonyms and Polemics in Recent Argentine Poetry
By Ben Bollig 121

Hölderlin on Tragedy and Paradox: 'Die Bedeutung der Tragödien [. . .]'
By Charles Lewis 139

'Das Land, in dem das Proletariat [nur] genannt werden darf': The Language of Participation in Heiner Müller's *Der Lohndrücker*
By Michael Wood 160

'Long Live Poland!': Representing the Past in Polish Comic Books
By Ewa Stańczyk 178

Looking for the Creator: Pelevin and the Impotent Writer in *T* (2009) and *Ananasnaia voda dlia prekrasnoi damy* (2011)
By Sally Dalton-Brown 199

REVIEWS

Author, Reader, Book: Medieval Authorship in Theory and Practice, ed. by Stephen Partridge and Erik Kwakkel (Venetia Bridges) 219
Larissa Tracy, *Torture and Brutality in Medieval Literature: Negotiations of National Identity* (David Matthews) 220
Desire in Dante and the Middle Ages, ed. by Manuele Gragnolati and others (Ruth Chester) 221
Vital Matters: Eighteenth-Century Views of Conception, Life, and Death, ed. by Helen Deutsch and Mary Terrall (Andrew Wells) 223
Tropen und Metaphern im Gelehrtendiskurs des 18. Jahrhunderts, ed. by Elena Agazzi (Orsolya Kiss) 224

Stefano Villani, *George Frederick Nott (1768-1841): un ecclesiastico anglicano tra teologia, letteratura, arte, archeologia, bibliofilia e collezionismo* (FABIO CAMILLETTI) 226
Rosa Mucignat, *Realism and Space in the Novel, 1795-1869: Imagined Geographies* (ARI J. BLATT) 228
David Palumbo-Liu, *The Deliverance of Others: Reading Literature in a Global Age* (LOUIS LO) 229
Hans Ulrich Gumbrecht, *Atmosphere, Mood, Stimmung: On a Hidden Potential of Literature*, trans. by Erik Butler (PIERPAOLO ANTONELLO) 231
Mari Hughes-Edwards, *Reading Medieval Anchoritism: Ideology and Spiritual Practices* (REBECCA PINNER) 234
The Collected Works of John Ford, vol. I, ed. by Gilles Monsarrat and others (LESEL DAWSON) 235
Literary Community-Making: The Dialogicality of English Texts from the Seventeenth Century to the Present, ed. by Roger D. Sell (RENZO D'AGNILLO) 236
Hal Gladfelder, *Fanny Hill in Bombay: The Making & Unmaking of John Cleland* (CAROLYN D. WILLIAMS) 238
Nancy Easterlin, *A Biocultural Approach to Literary Theory and Interpretation* (GAVIN MILLER) 239
Hemingway in Africa, ed. by Miriam Mandel (WILLIAM BLAZEK) 240
Kevin J. Hayes, *A Journey through American Literature* (MICHAEL J. COLLINS) . . . 242
H.D., *Bid Me to Live: A Madrigal*, ed. by Caroline Zilboorg (ALICE KELLY) 243
Alan Robinson, *Narrating the Past: Historiography, Memory and the Contemporary Novel* (DAVID JAMES) 245
Thomas Hinton, *The 'Conte du Graal' Cycle: Chrétien de Troyes's 'Perceval', the Continuations and French Arthurian Romance* (AD PUTTER) 246
Sara E. Melzer, *Colonizer or Colonized: The Hidden Stories of Early Modern French Culture* (MICHAEL HARRIGAN) 248
La Librairie de Montaigne: Proceedings of the Tenth Cambridge French Renaissance Colloquium, 2-4 September 2008, ed. by Philip Ford and Neil Kenny (JEAN BRAYBROOK) 249
Penser l'ordre naturel, 1680-1810, ed. by Adrien Paschoud and Nathalie Vuillemin (NICK TREUHERZ) 250
Benoît Jullien, *Un commerce pour gens ordinaires? La Rochelle et la traite négrière au XVIIIe siècle*; Annick Notter and others, *Être noir en France au XVIIIe siècle (1685-1805)*; *La Rochelle, l'Aunis et la Saintonge face à l'esclavage*, ed. by Mickaël Augeron and Olivier Caudron (ROGER LITTLE) 252
Friedrich Melchior Grimm, *Correspondance littéraire*, VII: *1760*, ed. by Sigun Dafgård Norén (DEREK CONNON) 253
Germaine de Staël: Forging a Politics of Mediation, ed. by Karyna Szmurlo (JOANNE WILKES) 254
Claire Lozier, *De l'abject et du sublime: Georges Bataille, Jean Genet, Samuel Beckett* (DAVID HOUSTON JONES) 256
David Platten, *The Pleasures of Crime: Reading Modern French Crime Fiction* (LUCY O'MEARA) 257
Helena Sanson, *Women, Language and Grammar in Italy, 1500-1900* (FRANCESCO SBERLATI) 258
Dante's 'Commedia': Theology as Poetry, ed. by Vittorio Montemaggi and Matthew Traherne (JULIA BOLTON HOLLOWAY) 261
Davide Dalmas, *Il saggio, il gusto e il cliché: per un'interpretazione di Mario Praz* (ILARIA MALLOZZI) 262
Amit Thakkar, *The Fiction of Juan Rulfo: Irony, Revolution and Postcolonialism* (OLIVIA VÁZQUEZ-MEDINA) 264

Contents

Judith Ryan, *The Cambridge Introduction to German Poetry* (IAN COOPER) 265
Die Lebenszeugnisse Oswalds von Wolkenstein: Edition und Kommentar, IV: *1438–1442, Nr. 277–386*, ed. by Anton Schwob and Ute Monika Schwob (ALMUT SUERBAUM) . 266
Johann Joachim Eschenburg und die Künste und Wissenschaften zwischen Aufklärung und Romantik: Netzwerke und Kulturen des Wissens, ed. by Cord-Friedrich Berghahn and Till Kinzel (ROGER PAULIN) 268
Hilary Brown, *Luise Gottsched the Translator* (JOHN L. FLOOD) 269
Elke Pfitzinger, *Die Aufklärung ist weiblich: Frauenrollen im Drama um 1800* (STEFFAN DAVIES) 271
Ludwig Tieck: Leben — Werk — Wirkung, ed. by Claudia Stockinger and Stefan Scherer (BRIAN HAMAN) 273
Peter Goßens, *Weltliteratur: Modelle transnationaler Literaturwahrnehmung im 19. Jahrhundert* (ANNA GUILLEMIN) 274
Michael James White, *Space in Theodor Fontane's Works: Theme and Poetic Function* (JEFFREY L. SAMMONS) 277
Christopher D. Johnson, *Memory, Metaphor, and Aby Warburg's Atlas of Images* (RITCHIE ROBERTSON) 279
Claudia Hillebrandt, *Das emotionale Wirkungspotenzial von Erzähltexten: Mit Fallstudien zu Kafka, Perutz und Werfel* (ERNEST SCHONFIELD) 280
Kafka und die kleine Prosa der Moderne/Kafka and Short Modernist Prose, ed. by Manfred Engel and Ritchie Robertson (RONALD SPEIRS) 282
Heimo Schwilk, *Hermann Hesse: Das Leben des Glasperlenspielers* (OSMAN DURRANI) 283
Catherine Gouriou, *Du 'fatum' au divin: le mythe dans l'œuvre d'Alfred Döblin (1935–1957)* (DAVID MIDGLEY) 285
Joseph Roth: Europäisch-jüdischer Schriftsteller und österreichischer Universalist, ed. by Mira Miladinović Zalaznik and Johann Georg Lughofer (ANDREW BARKER) . . . 286
Thomas Mann, *Briefe*, III: *1924–1932*, ed. by Thomas Sprecher and others; Thomas Mann, *Bekenntnisse des Hochstaplers Felix Krull: Der Memoiren erster Teil*, ed. by Thomas Sprecher and Monica Bussmann (RITCHIE ROBERTSON) 287
Klaus Mann, *'Lieber und verehrter Onkel Heinrich'*, ed. by Inge Jens and Uwe Naumann (KARINA VON LINDEINER-STRÁSKÝ) 290
Bloch-Wörterbuch: Leitbegriffe der Philosophie Ernst Blochs, ed. by Beat Dietschy and others (CATHERINE MOIR) 292
Memorialization in Germany since 1945, ed. by Bill Niven and Chloe Paver (DORA OSBORNE) 293
Thomas Krämer, *Die Poetik des Gedenkens: Zu den autobiographischen Romanen H. G. Adlers* (HELEN FINCH) 295
German and European Poetics after the Holocaust: Crisis and Creativity, ed. by Gert Hofmann and others (KIRSTIN GWYER) 296
New Directions in German Cinema, ed. by Paul Cooke and Chris Homewood (SEÁN ALLAN) 298
Translating Sholem Aleichem: History, Politics, and Art, ed. by Gennady Estraikh and others (LEAH GARRETT) 299
Susan Broomhall and Jennifer Spinks, *Early Modern Women in the Low Countries: Feminizing Sources and Interpretations of the Past* (JANE FENOULHET) 301
Anna Schur, *Wages of Evil: Dostoevsky and Punishment* (SARAH J. YOUNG) 302
Tolstoy on War: Narrative Art and Historical Truth in 'War and Peace', ed. by Rick McPeak and Donna Tussing Orwin (W. GARETH JONES) 304
Lydia Ginzburg's Alternative Literary Identities: A Collection of Articles and New Translations, ed. by Emily Van Buskirk and Andrei Zorin (SARAH PRATT) 305

Soviet and Post-Soviet Identities, ed. by Mark Bassin and Catriona Kelly (VICTORIA DONOVAN) 307

Abstracts of Articles, Vol. 109, Part 1 (January 2014) 309

'TOLLE LEGE': EPIPHANIES OF THE BOOK

'Epiphany' as a Term

Since the mid-1940s, according to Google's Ngram Viewer, occurrences of the term 'epiphany' in English (and also in German), which had remained few and virtually flat since 1800, have increased sharply. The frequency of usage coincides essentially with the publication of James Joyce's *Stephen Hero* (1944),[1] where the author first introduced the word (which was subsequently dropped from *Portrait of the Artist as a Young Man*). The term, hitherto 'little-noticed', was picked up immediately by Joyce scholars,[2] and its use escalated in the decades following publication of Joyce's *Epiphanies* in 1956,[3] as it rapidly became a staple of Joyce criticism and literary theory generally.[4] The phenomenon, with or without the designation 'epiphany', was soon detected in other literary works: among such European contemporaries as Hugo von Hofmannsthal, Robert Musil, and Rainer Maria Rilke;[5] in such later English-language writers as Virginia Woolf, Thomas Wolfe, and William Faulkner;[6] and, more broadly according to one author's Bachelardian phenomenology, in such earlier writers as Shakespeare, Alexandre Dumas, and Jane Austen,[7] or Wordsworth, Tolstoy, and Pater.[8] Some scholars of English literature now trace its origin back to Wordsworth's 'spots of time'.[9]

Inevitably a term with such a mystical theological aura, having been broadly secularized, could not long be restricted to literary criticism. In the history of science Galileo's discovery of Jupiter's four largest moons is called, on the editorial page of the *New York Times*, 'an epiphany that began to upend the given

---

I am grateful to my son, Professor Eric J. Ziolkowski, for his suggestions in connection with this essay.

[1] James Joyce, *Stephen Hero*, ed. by Theodore Spencer (New York: New Directions, 1944; new edn 1955); subsequent references to this edition will be given in the text identified by the abbreviation *SH*.

[2] Irene Hendry, 'Joyce's Epiphanies', *Sewanee Review*, 54 (1946), 449–67 (p. 449).

[3] *James Joyce: The Epiphanies*, ed. by O. A. Silvermann (Buffalo: Lockwood Memorial Library, University of Buffalo, 1956).

[4] See, for instance, the bibliography in Morris Beja, 'Epiphany and the Epiphanies', in *A Companion to Joyce Studies*, ed. by Zack Bowen and James F. Carens (Westport, CT: Greenwood, 1984), pp. 707–25.

[5] Theodore Ziolkowski, 'James Joyces Epiphanie und die Überwindung der empirischen Welt in der modernen deutschen Prosa', *DVjs*, 35 (1961), 594–616.

[6] Morris Beja, *Epiphany in the Modern Novel* (London: Peter Owen, 1970).

[7] Janice Rosen, *Epiphanies in Literature* ([n.p.]: Madcap Press, 2012).

[8] Martin Bidney, *Patterns of Epiphany: From Wordsworth to Tolstoy, Pater, and Barrett Browning* (Carbondale: Southern Illinois University Press, 1997).

[9] Ashton Nichols, *The Poetics of Epiphany: Nineteenth-Century Origins of the Modern Literary Moment* (Tuscaloosa: University of Alabama Press, 1987), p. xi.

view of the universe';[10] and the expression has been applied to various other scientific insights ever since Archimedes cried out 'Eureka!' in his bathtub or the apple fell on Newton's head. The word has been appropriated by psychologists to designate, most generally, 'sudden and abrupt insights and/or changes in perspective that transform the individual's concept of self and identity'[11] and, more narrowly, the discovery of lesbian and bisexual identity.[12] On the Internet, the 'BusinessDictionary.com' includes 'epiphany' to designate 'a sudden realization about the nature or meaning of something'. In Woody Allen's film *To Rome, with Love* (2012) the character played by Allen remarks at one point: 'I'm having a breakthrough… an epiphany.' As a further sign of its popularization, the rock groups Staind and Bad Religion both brought out popular songs entitled 'Epiphany'.

By now the term has been trivialized so radically and so wholly distanced from its original theological meaning or from Joyce's specific understanding that it is taken to refer to virtually any sudden burst of insight. So it may be worthwhile, some seventy years after the beginnings of its popularization, to look back at the origins of the term and, in the attempt to bring some precision and clarity to its usage, to determine some distinctions among its various applications. In that connection I shall propose a qualification of the general term—'epiphany of the book'—to designate a very specific type of the sudden insight known as 'epiphany'.

The ancient Greeks were acquainted with what they called ἐπιφάνεια or 'showing forth' (from ἐπί and φαίνω) to designate the manifestation of a deity in a vision or during a ritual process.[13] The vocable, most frequent in Hellenistic times, occurred in epic, mythic, fairy-tale, and legendary contexts, and also in the practice of divine cults.[14] But the term has become familiar in Western culture primarily through its theological use in Christianity, where it was applied to the Twelfth Night or Feast of the Epiphany, the celebration of the moment when the Three Magi 'rejoiced exceedingly with great joy' when, seeing that the star of the East had come to rest over the house where Jesus lay, they went in and discerned in the seemingly unpretentious baby the future divine saviour (Matthew 2. 9–11).

From that time forth, the moments associated with epiphany in Chris-

---

[10] 'The Starry Messenger', *New York Times*, 19 January 2013, p. 16.

[11] Matthew G. McDonald, 'The Nature of Epiphanic Experience', *Journal of Humanistic Psychology*, 48 (2008), 89–115 (p. 90).

[12] Karol L. Jensen, *Lesbian Epiphanies: Women Coming Out in Later Life* (New York: Harrington Park Press, 1999).

[13] Fritz Graf, 'Epiphany', in *Encyclopaedia of the Ancient World*, ed. by Christine F. Salazar, IV (Leiden: Brill, 2001), 1122–23.

[14] See especially the exhaustive entry 'Epiphanie' in *Paulys Realencyclopädie der classischen Altertumswissenschaft*, suppl. IV (Stuttgart: Metzler, 1924), pp. 277–323.

tian legend are mostly characterized by light (the φάος or φῶς at the root of ἐπιφάνεια): the star that leads the Magi; the moment of transfiguration on the mountain when Jesus's face 'shone like the sun' for Peter, James, and John while his garments became 'white as light' (Matthew 17. 2: λευκὰ ὡς τὸ φῶς); the voice of God who tells the disciples that his beloved Son is 'like a lamp shining in a dark place' (II Peter 1. 19: ὡς λύχνῳ φαίνοντι ἐν αὐχμηρῷ τόπῳ); the 'light from heaven' (Acts 9. 3: φῶς ἐκ τοῦ οὐρανοῦ) that flashes upon Saul as he approaches Damascus; the 'light of confidence' ('lu[x] securitatis') that infused St Augustine's heart, driving out the darkness of doubt, when he took up the Bible and read (*Confessions*, VIII. 12. 29);[15] the lightning bolt that threw Martin Luther to the ground, like a frightful summons from heaven ('de caelo terroribus'), and led to his vow to become a monk and enter the monastery.[16]

Joyce's 'Lightnings of Intuition'

It is precisely this 'light' (*claritas*) characterizing Thomas Aquinas's definition of beauty that Joyce (1882-1941) appropriated. In the famous statement from *Summa theologiae* (Ia. 39. 8) Aquinas writes:

Nam ad pulchritudinem tria requiruntur. Primo quidem integritas, sive perfectio, quae enim diminuta sunt, hoc ipso turpia sunt; et debita proportio sive consonantia; et iterum claritas, unde quae habent colorem nitidum pulchra esse dicuntur.

Three things are required for beauty. First, integrity or completeness—for those things that are incomplete are ugly by dint of that very fact; then proper proportion or harmony; and finally brightness, whence things that have a bright colour are said to be beautiful.[17]

In *Stephen Hero* the protagonist, in his conversation with Cranly, paraphrases the passage: 'You know what Aquinas says: The three things requisite for beauty are, integrity, a wholeness, symmetry and radiance' (*SH*, p. 212)—an idea that he hopes some day to expand into a treatise. Stephen goes on to define *claritas* more specifically:

After the analysis which discovers the second quality the mind makes the only logically possible synthesis and discovers the third quality. This is the moment which I call epiphany. First we recognise that the object is *one* integral thing, then we recognise that it is an organised composite structure, a *thing* in fact: finally, when the relation of the parts is exquisite, when the parts are adjusted to the special point, we recognise that it is *that* thing which it is. Its soul, its whatness, leaps to us from the vestment of its appearance. The soul of the commonest object, the structure of which is so adjusted, seems to us radiant. The object achieves its epiphany. (*SH*, p. 213)

[15] Cited from Augustine, *Confessiones/Bekenntnisse*, ed. by Joseph Bernhart (Munich: Kosel, 1955).
[16] Among the many discussions of Luther's conversion see, for instance, Erik H. Erikson, *Young Man Luther: A Study in Psychoanalysis and History* (New York: Norton, 1958), pp. 90-95.
[17] Saint Thomas Aquinas, *Summa theologiae*, Latin text and English translations, 61 vols (London: Blackfriars; New York: McGraw-Hill, 1964-81), VII (1976), p. 132 (my own translation).

In *Portrait of the Artist* Stephen discusses the same passage, this time citing it in a condensed version of the Latin original but omitting the word 'epiphany' in his own definition: 'Aquinas says: *Ad pulchritudinem tria requiruntur: integritas, consonantia, claritas.* I translate it so: *Three things are needs for beauty, wholeness, harmony and radiance.*'[18] After analysing as an example a butcher boy's basket, Stephen concludes: 'You see that it is that thing which it is and no other thing. The radiance of which he speaks is the scholastic *quidditas*, the *whatness* of a thing' (*P*, p. 166).

The extent of Joyce's knowledge of Aquinas is uncertain. According to one authoritative source, 'Joyce made little formal study of St. Thomas's works during his student days' but presumably worked further on the texts privately.[19] If so, he may have come across various passages in which Aquinas identifies beauty with light: for instance, 'lux pulchrificat, quia sine luce omnia sunt turpia' ('light beautifies since without light all things are ugly').[20] In any case, for Joyce 'radiance'—that is to say, the traditional *lux* or φάος—is usually associated with those moments of illumination that in *Stephen Hero* he calls 'epiphanies': 'a sudden spiritual manifestation, whether in the vulgarity of speech or of gesture or in a memorable phase of the mind itself'—those 'most delicate and evanescent of moments' (*SH*, p. 211) that he regarded it as the duty of the man of letters to record.

Joyce scholars have defined these moments more or less broadly, comparing them, for instance, to Proust's technique in *A la recherche du temps perdu*[21] or equating them with revelations generally.[22] And the interpretations have only increased over the years. In every case, Joyce's epiphanies are triggered by a word or incident or object in earthly reality and are accompanied by that flash of light—the 'lightnings of intuition' (*P*, p. 136)—sometimes symbolized by the light bulb appearing over the head of figures in cartoons or by the phrase captured in the popular song 'I'm beginning to see the light'.

Here, however, we want to consider epiphanies of a different sort: not simply 'one way of deriving meaning from experience in the modern world' or a 'literary epiphany' in which 'the poet is trying to make something happen in the reader'[23] but, on the contrary, those that are triggered specifically

---

[18] James Joyce, *A Portrait of the Artist as a Young Man* (New York: Signet, 1948), p. 165; subsequent references to this edition will be given in the text identified by the abbreviation P.

[19] William T. Noon, SJ, *Joyce and Aquinas* (New Haven: Yale University Press, 1957; repr. Archon Books, 1970), p. 9.

[20] Saint Thomas, *Comment. in Psalm.*, Ps. 25. 5; cited by Jacques Maritain, 'Art and Scholasticism' with Other Essays, trans. by J. F. Scanlan (London: Sheed & Ward, 1930), p. 24. In this connection see also Umberto Eco, *The Aesthetics of Thomas Aquinas* (1970), trans. by Hugh Bedin (Cambridge, MA: Harvard University Press, 1988), pp. 64–121 ('The Formal Criteria of Beauty').

[21] Harry Levin, *James Joyce: A Critical Introduction*, rev. edn (New York: New Directions, 1960), p. 28.

[22] Hendry, 'Joyce's Epiphanies', p. 451.

[23] Nichols, *The Poetics of Epiphany*, p. 31.

by a passage in a book and that we can characterize as epiphanies because they also signify sudden insight and usually involve the traditional 'light' or 'radiance'. In these cases, in contrast to the delicacy and evanescence that characterize Joyce's epiphanies, the insight is powerful and lasting and not restricted to the individual but exemplary for the more general transformation of an epoch. (I find the term 'epiphany' more appropriate for such insights triggered by something in the real world than 'revelation', which normally implies communication by a deity or some other supernatural being.)

Augustine in the Garden

To this end let us look back to Saint Augustine (354–430) and his conversion at a moment when, he tells us (*Confessions*, VIII. 7. 16), the thirty-two-year-old Manichaean philosopher and rhetorician found himself 'filthy, deformed and sordid, stained and ulcerous' ('quam turpis essem, quam distortus et sordidus, maculosus et ulcerosus'). One day, in this mood of dejection and bearing with him his copy of the Pauline Epistles, he went into the garden with his friend Alypius (VIII. 8–12) and there, weeping beneath a fig tree, he heard a voice singing 'tolle lege, tolle lege' (VIII. 12. 29).

In his assumption that he was being advised by a divine spirit to take up and read the 'codex of the apostle' that he had left behind with his friend, he was encouraged by the life of Saint Anthony, which he had only recently (VIII. 6. 14) heard for the first time from his African countryman Ponticianus, who described Anthony's conversion, and which Augustinus now recalls (VIII. 12. 29). The wealthy young man happened to go into a church where the Gospels were being read and heard the passage (Luke 19. 22) in which Jesus tells the rich ruler: if you wish to be perfect, then 'sell all that you have and distribute it to the poor, and you will have treasure in heaven; and come, follow me'. Thereupon Anthony sold his possessions, placed his sister in a nunnery, and went off into the Egyptian wilderness to become an anchorite.

Returning to his friend, Augustine picked up the volume (VIII. 12. 29), opened it at random, and read the first passage upon which his eyes fell and which he cites (with a few textual liberties) in Latin: '[let us conduct ourselves becomingly as in the day,] not in revelling and drunkenness, not in debauchery and licentiousness, not in quarrelling and jealousy. But put on the Lord Jesus Christ, and make no provision for the flesh, to gratify its desires' (Romans 13. 13–14). He read no further, he tells us, for instantly, 'as though my heart were infused with the light of assurance' ('quasi luce securitatis infusa cordi meo'), all shadow of doubt vanished. This moment, with its sudden illumination in a flash of light, is an epiphanic insight in Joyce's precise sense: but an epiphany triggered not by any external word or gesture or phenomenon but specifically by a passage read in a book. This 'epiphany of the book', moreover, resulted in a profound life-change inasmuch as it marked Augustine's conversion from classical antiquity to Christianity—a shift that recapitulated the 'age of rapid and dramatic change' of which Augustine was a prime representative.[24] It is this epochal significance that distinguishes 'epiphanies of the book' from mere 'epiphany' or the similar phenomenon of bibliomancy.

Bibliomancy

Augustine is utilizing the Pauline Epistles here in a form of bibliomancy allegedly familiar among his Roman contemporaries—notably Hadrian and other emperors—from the so-called *Sortes Vergilianae* or 'Virgilian lots': the practice of opening the works of Virgil at random, placing one's finger on a passage, and then reading it as prophetic.[25] The practice was so widespread by the Renaissance that Rabelais could ridicule it in *Gargantua and Pantagruel*, citing at one point (Book III, Chapter 10) several ancient examples of those who learnt their fates by opening the works of various poets at a certain page, as when, for instance, 'par sors Homericques souvent on a rencontré sa destinée' or, 'avecques l'ongle les [sc. œuvres de Virgile] ouvrans', discovers 'le sort futur de vostre mariage'.[26] Pantagruel urges Panurge to consult Virgil about his marital destiny (Book III, Chapter 12). But when Panurge does so, all three passages turn out to be open to an unfavourable interpretation: that Panurge's wife will beat, rob, and cuckold him.

We find what may well be a more recent example in the life of the nineteenth-century Swiss legal historian and anthropologist Johann Jakob Bachofen. In the inaugural lecture that the twenty-six-year-old scholar delivered in 1841 when he assumed the chair of Roman Law at the University of Basel, on the current dispute between natural law and historical law ('Das Naturrecht und das geschichtliche Recht in ihren Gegensätzen'), Bachofen urged his listeners, in making their own decision in the matter, to follow the advice given to Aeneas (*Aeneid*, III. 96) by the oracle of Apollo at Delos: 'antiquam exquirite matrem' ('Seek out the ancient mother').[27] In the light of that statement it is difficult not to believe that the passage from the *Aeneid*, through a kind of personal *Sors Vergiliana*, inspired what turned out to be Bachofen's

---

[24] Peter Brown, *Augustine of Hippo: A Biography* (1966; Berkeley: University of California Press, 2000), p. ix. See also Brown's discussion of the conversion episode on pp. 98–102.

[25] See *The Virgilian Tradition: The First Fifteen Hundred Years*, ed. by Jan M. Ziolkowski and Michael C. J. Putnam (New Haven: Yale University Press, 2008), pp. 829–30. Bibliomancy of the Bible, in contrast, was regarded as sinful by many Christians. See A. Dorner, 'Bibliolatry', in *Encyclopaedia of Religion and Ethics*, ed. by James Hastings, 13 vols (New York: Scribner, 1910), II, 615–18.

[26] François Rabelais, *Œuvres complètes*, ed. by Pierre Jourda, 2 vols (Paris: Garnier, 1962), I, 441.

[27] Johann Jakob Bachofen, *Urreligion und antike Symbole*, ed. by Carl Albrecht Bernoulli, 3 vols (Leipzig: Reclam, 1926), III, 49–70 (p. 62).

major life-work, *Das Mutterrecht* (1861), in which he developed the theory of matriarchy that made a huge impact on many subsequent thinkers.

Curiously enough, we owe the career of one of the finest twentieth-century classical scholars to a case of *Sors Vergiliana*. The late Bernard Knox liked to relate the story of his own turn to the classics.[28] Following what he admits was a middling degree at Cambridge, where he was active in the Socialist Club, Knox went to Spain to fight with the International Brigades against the Fascists. Later, having moved to the United States, he entered the US army and was soon selected for officer training. After service with the OSS behind enemy lines in France, Knox was sent to Italy to work with the partisans there. In one of those actions he took cover in a ruined house, where, in the debris, he saw 'a handsome, gilt-edged book lying under a patina of brickdust and broken glass. One word of its long title was legible: MARONIS'. Remembering medieval legends about the *Sors Vergiliana*, 'I opened the book and stabbed my finger at a line. What I got was not a prophecy; it was a cry of agony—the last lines of the first Georgic', which lament the reversal of right and wrong in the world with its many wars and faces of evil. 'These lines, written some thirty years before the birth of Christ, expressed, more directly and passionately than any modern statement I knew of, the reality of the world I was living in.' As he left the ruin and crawled through the rubble, Knox resolved: 'If I ever get out of this, I'm going back to the classics and study them seriously'—which, fortunately for his students, friends, and readers, he did.

The similarity of these examples to Augustine's experience is clear; but there is a major difference. The *Sortes Vergilianae*, like bibliomancy generally, normally apply only to the individual consulting the text; but epiphanies of the book have a broader significance. In the case of Augustine, his conversion marks symbolically the epochal shift from the classicism of late antiquity to the Christianity of the early Middle Ages.

Petrarch on the Mountain

Paradoxically, another famous epiphany of the book involves Augustine's *Confessions*, a work that, Petrarch says, changed him to a significant extent ('is liber me mutavit eatenus').[29] In the account of his ascent of Mont Ventoux (*Familiarum rerum libri*, IV. 1) Francesco Petrarch (1304–1374) describes his own spiritual experience.[30] On 26 April 1336, almost a thousand years after

[28] As in the Introduction to his *Essays Ancient and Modern* (Baltimore: Johns Hopkins University Press, 1989), pp. xi–xxxv (pp. xxx–xxxii).

[29] From his *Epistolae de rebus senilibus*, VIII. 6; quoted by Bortolo Martinelli, *Petrarca e il Ventoso* (Bergamo: Minerva Italica, 1977), pp. 154–55.

[30] I cite the text according to the edition—Francesco Petrarca, *Die Besteigung des Mont Ventoux*—by Kurt Steinmann (Stuttgart: Reclam, 1995), which appends notes as well as an informative afterword and materials.

Augustine's birth, the thirty-two-year-old poet and his brother Gherardo set out to climb the mountain in south-eastern France that is renowned for its spectacular view over the Rhône valley. He recorded the experience that same evening in a long letter addressed to his teacher, Dionigi da Borgo San Sepolcro, who had introduced him to the works of Augustine and presented him with a pocketbook copy of the *Confessions*. Petrarch writes that, ever since childhood, he had longed to ascend the mountain that is visible from every direction—motivated purely, he says, by the desire to see this unusually lofty place ('sola videndi insignem loci altitudinem cupiditate', § 1). (The word *cupiditas*, which in the Middle Ages was regarded as a sin, is repeated later, where Petrarch confesses that his curiosity was enhanced by the old shepherd's warning: 'crescebat ex prohibitione cupiditas', § 8.)[31] Finally he was stirred by a passage in Livy about King Philip of Macedonia and his ascent of the Thessalian Mount Haemus, from which it was rumoured that one could see both the Adriatic and the Black Seas.

In his opening paragraphs Petrarch provides details of the ways and byways of the climb. When they finally reach the summit, he stands there 'like someone struck senseless' ('stupenti similis steti', § 17), gazing down upon the clouds at his feet—a view, he writes, that enabled him for the first time to understand the legends about Mounts Athos and Olympus. When his gaze shifts east towards Italy, he is struck by a longing for his homeland, and he reflects on the ten years since he completed his studies at the University of Bologna—reflections that call to mind a sentence from the *Confessions* (II. 1. 1) in which Augustine summons up his past iniquities and the carnal corruption of his soul. As he thinks about the past ten years he looks to the west, towards the Pyrenees and Spain, and then again towards Lyon in the north and the Gulf of Marseille in the south—a perfect example of what has been called Petrarch's new 'horizontality' in contrast to Dante's medieval 'verticality' of view.[32]

While he is admiring these various scenes and taking pleasure in terrestrial beauty, as illuminated by the brilliant sunshine, it occurs to him to look at the copy of the *Confessions* that Dionigi had given to him. The passage upon which his eyes first fall is the one (X. 8. 15) in which Augustine writes that men go forth to admire the heights of the mountains and the mighty currents of the sea and the broadest flow of the rivers and the circulation of the ocean and the orbits of the constellations—only to lose themselves ('et relinquunt se ipsos'). At this, Petrarch confesses himself astounded: 'Obstupui, fateor' (§ 28). He closes the book, angry with himself for admiring earthly things—he who should have learnt from the ancients that nothing is admirable except the soul

---

[31] On *curiositas* see especially Martinelli, *Petrarca e il Ventoso*, pp. 158–59.

[32] Karlheinz Stierle, *Francesco Petrarca: Ein Intellektueller im Europa des 14. Jahrhunderts* (Munich: Hanser, 2003), pp. 34–36.

('nichil preter animum esse mirabile'). Satisfied that he has seen enough of the mountain, he turns his inner eyes upon himself ('in me ipsos interiores oculos reflexi', § 29) and, without saying another word, returns to the world below.

Along the way he recalls the passage in which Augustine described his own conversion, as well as the incident from Saint Anthony's life mentioned by Augustine in the moment before his own *tolle lege*. (By Petrarch's time Evagrius's *Life of Saint Anthony*, in the Latin translation by Athanasius, had become a popular work of devotional literature.) As he glances back from time to time at the mountain's summit, Petrarch thinks to himself how puny its height now seems in comparison with the height of human contemplation ('et vix unius cubiti altitudo visa est pre altitudine contemplationis humane', § 33). With such thoughts and emotions he reaches their peasant abode for the night, where he immediately writes his letter to Dionigi.

This letter has been widely interpreted.[33] Petrarch did not, of course, retreat into a medieval mindset but, rather, emerged from his experience as one of the earliest Renaissance humanists. Ever since 1860, when Jacob Burckhardt called Petrarch 'one of the first truly modern men' because he recognized 'the significance of nature for a receptive spirit',[34] the letter has been regarded by historians of philosophy as a landmark—a 'boundary between two worlds':[35] between the medieval concern with salvation and the modern turn to the outside world, between the medieval orientation around Christian belief and Renaissance humanism. At least one prominent scholar has taken the letter to be essentially a rhetorical tour de force, written not in the night following the climb but years later, in 1353, in conscious imitation of Augustine.[36] Regardless of one's view of Petrarch's precise position in this conflict between verticality and horizontality, between *memoria* and *curiositas*, between time and space,[37] what matters in our present context is the fact that his awareness of the epochal tension was triggered not by his experience of the landscape itself but by a subsequent epiphany of the book that resulted in a total change of perception that, as in the case of Augustine, reflected the spirit of the times.

Kleist's 'Kant Crisis'

A remarkable parallel to Petrarch's letter is evident three-and-a-half centuries later in another letter recounting a 'crisis of consciousness'[38] produced by a

[33] For a summary of views see Steinmann's 'Nachwort' to his edition, pp. 39–67. For full discussions see Martinelli, *Petrarca e il Ventoso*, pp. 149–215; and Stierle, *Francesco Petrarca*, pp. 318–43, where he calls the letter an *experimentum crucis*.
[34] Jacob Burckhardt, *The Civilization of the Renaissance in Italy*, trans. by S. G. C. Middlemore, rev. edn (New York: Phaidon, 1950), p. 179.   [35] Steinmann, 'Nachwort', p. 39.
[36] Giuseppe Billanovich, 'Petrarca e il Ventoso', *Italia medioevale e umanistica*, 9 (1960), 389–401.
[37] Hans Blumenberg, *Die Legitimität der Neuzeit* (Frankfurt a.M.: Suhrkamp, 1966), p. 338.
[38] The term is used by Tim Mehigan, *Heinrich von Kleist: Writing after Kant* (Rochester, NY:

book. This letter, written by the German dramatist Heinrich von Kleist (1777–1811) on 22 March 1801, was addressed not to a teacher but to his fiancée, Wilhelmine von Zenge, whose moral education he sought carefully to guide; it was composed not after a mountain climb but following a foot journey from Potsdam back to Berlin; but the spiritual crisis was again evidence of a major upheaval in intellectual history: not from antiquity to medieval nor from medieval to Renaissance but from the certainties of Enlightenment rationalism to Kantian scepticism. In his letter, which he calls 'diese[ ] Geschichte meiner Seele' ('this history of my soul'),[39] Kleist tells his fiancée that he recently became acquainted with what he labels 'd[ie] neuere[ ] sogenannte[ ] Kantische[ ] Philosophie' ('the newer so-called Kantian philosophy').

If people had green glasses instead of eyes, he explains, they would have to conclude that the objects they see through them are themselves green: 'und nie würden sie entscheiden können, ob ihr Auge ihnen die Dinge zeigt, wie sie sind, oder ob es nicht etwas zu ihnen hinzutut, was nicht ihnen, sondern dem Auge gehört' ('and they would never be able to decide whether their eye is showing them the things as they are or whether it is adding something to them that belongs not to them but to the eye'). It is the same with human reason, he continues. 'Wir können nicht entscheiden, ob das, was wir Wahrheit nennen, wahrhaft Wahrheit ist, oder ob es uns nur so scheint' ('We cannot determine whether that which we call truth is truly truth or whether it only appears so to us'). Earlier in the letter Kleist had proclaimed that 'Bildung' seemed to him the single goal worth striving for and truth the only wealth worth possessing. Now he feels deeply wounded within his most sacred self: 'Mein einziges, mein höchstes Ziel ist gesunken, und ich habe nun keines mehr' ('My sole, my loftiest goal has sunk, and I no longer have one'). Since reaching this conviction—'daß hienieden keine Wahrheit zu finden ist' ('that no truth is to be found here on earth')—he has not touched another book, and whenever he wanted to force himself to work, 'ein innerlicher Ekel überwältigte meinen Willen' ('an inner disgust overcame my will').

This turning-point in Kleist's spiritual and intellectual life, including debate about the work that precipitated it, has provoked at least as much critical discussion as has Petrarch's letter.[40] It was long known—since the 1905 edition of Kleist's works by Georg Minde-Pouet—and still is for the most part, as his 'Kant crisis' ('Kantkrise') and was thought to have been provoked by

Camden House, 2011), p. 16. Mehigan provides the most complete recent discussion of Kleist's 'Kant crisis' (pp. 15–46).

[39] Heinrich von Kleist, *Sämtliche Werke und Briefe*, ed. by Helmut Sembdner, 2 vols, 2nd edn (Darmstadt: Wissenschaftliche Buchgesellschaft, 1961), II, 630–36, especially p. 634.

[40] For a recent discussion of the various theories see Michael Mandelartz, 'Von der Tugendlehre zur Lasterschule: Die sogenannte "Kantkrise" und Fichtes "Wissenschaftslehre"', *Kleist Jahrbuch* 2006, pp. 120–36. Mandelartz regards it as 'gesichert' ('certain') that Fichte's *Bestimmung* triggered the crisis.

Kleist's reading of Kant's *Kritik der reinen Vernunft* (*Critique of Pure Reason*, 1781) or, perhaps, his *Kritik der Urteilskraft* (*Critique of Judgement*, 1790). But subsequent studies have suggested other sources: notably Johann Gottlieb Fichte's more recent and accessible work on the 'purpose' or 'determination' or 'destiny' of humankind (*Die Bestimmung des Menschen*, 1800). Others maintain that what appeared to be an abrupt break was actually the result of a continuity of development, since Kleist had already been reading Kant for some months.[41] It has even been suggested, as in the case of Petrarch's letter, that it was what amounted to a rhetorical exercise to prepare his fiancée for his refusal to accept a government position—her father's condition for their marriage—and, instead, to undertake the career of an independent writer.[42] But no one denies the significance of the Kantian experience in Kleist's life.[43] That the underlying shattering emotional experience was genuine is reinforced by the fact that Kleist repeated his description of the experience in a letter to his sister on the following day (23 March) and in virtually the same words.

What matters in our context is not the specific work but the fact that the epiphany was triggered by a book, whether by Kant or by Fichte. Kleist's crisis—the realization that we cannot know external reality with any certainty and that objects have no existence independent of the experiencing subject— could have been precipitated by the so-called 'Copernican turn'—the view that our perception of external reality is always qualified by the categories of our own reason—in various writings by either Kant or Fichte. According to Kant's transcendental analysis, 'liefern uns die Kategorien vermittelst der Anschauung auch keine Erkenntnis von Dingen' ('the categories [of our reason] provide us by way of contemplative experience with no knowledge of things') but serve only the possibility of 'empirische Anschauung' ('empirical experience').[44] In other words, we never know reality as such but only what the categories of our reason tell us about it. Similarly, Fichte concludes that 'das Bewußtsein eines Dinges außer uns absolut nichts weiter ist, als das Produkt unsers eignen Vorstellungs-Vermögens' ('the consciousness of a thing outside of us is absolutely nothing further than the product of our own power of imagination').[45] Either of these statements would have sufficed to shatter Kleist's earlier Enlightenment faith in our knowledge of an objective reality accessible to human reason. Again, then, we find an epiphany—one

---

[41] Ilse Graham, *Heinrich von Kleist: Word into Flesh. A Poet's Quest for the Symbol* (Berlin: de Gruyter, 1977), pp. 58–77 (p. 58).

[42] Johannes Hoffmeister, 'Beitrag zur sogenannten Kantkrise Heinrich von Kleists', *DVjs*, 33 (1959), 574–87.

[43] Mehigan, *Heinrich von Kleist*, pp. 15–16.

[44] *Kritik der reinen Vernunft*, I. 2. 22, in Immanuel Kant, *Werke in zehn Bänden*, ed. by Wilhelm Weischedel (Darmstadt: Wissenschaftliche Buchgesellschaft, 1968), III, 146.

[45] Johann Gottlieb Fichte, *Die Bestimmung des Menschen*, ed. by Theodor Ballauff and Ignaz Klein (Stuttgart: Reclam, 1962), p. 93.

that reflects a generational shift from rationalism to doubt—produced by a book, even though it is accompanied here not by a flash of light but by a temporary sense of frustration and despair until Kleist was illuminated, early the following year when he began his first drama, *Die Familie Schroffenstein*, by the realization that he could cope with the new reality in literary and poetic form.

Mill's Awakening

A quarter-century later and across the Channel another young writer experienced an epiphany remarkably similar to Kleist's, marking the shift *mutatis mutandis* from Enlightenment certainties to nineteenth-century scepticism. John Stuart Mill (1806–1873) tells us in his autobiography that his early education had been 'in a certain sense, already a course of Benthamism'.[46] 'The Benthamic standard of "the greatest happiness" was that which I had always been taught to apply.' In addition to Bentham, his studies led him to Locke and 'into the higher branches of analytic psychology' (*AOW*, p. 43). These were the ideas that in the winter of 1822–23 informed the Utilitarian Society that he founded: a group of 'young men agreeing in fundamental principles—acknowledging Utility as their standard in ethics and politics' (*AOW*, p. 49). From that time forward, he continues, 'I had what might truly be called an object in life; to be a reformer of the world' (*AOW*, p. 80) in the eighteenth-century, pre-Revolutionary sense of the word.

But the time came, in the autumn of 1826, when the twenty-year-old 'awakened from this as from a dream' (*AOW*, p. 80). Asking himself if he would be happy if all his objectives in life were realized—'if all the changes in institutions and opinions which you are looking forward to, could be completely effected' (*AOW*, p. 81)—he realized that the answer was clearly negative. 'At this my heart sank within me: the whole foundation on which my life was constructed fell down.' He began to understand that the pleasures associated by reason and logic with things beneficial to the great whole were artificial and casual and that 'the habit of analysis has a tendency to wear away the feelings' (*AOW*, p. 83). The thought that his whole education had been misdirected produced, in 'the melancholy winter of 1826–27', a sense of profound dejection. Despite the successes and distinction that he had achieved, he now felt that he had 'to begin the formation of my character anew' (*AOW*, p. 84).

The shift was triggered, as in the cases of Augustine, Petrarch, and Kleist, by a book: the *Mémoires* (1792–94) of Jean-François Marmontel, which he was

[46] John Stuart Mill, *'Autobiography' and Other Writings*, ed. by Jack Stillinger (Boston: Houghton Mifflin, 1969), p. 41; subsequent references to this edition will be given in the text identified by the abbreviation *AOW*.

reading 'accidentally' (*AOW*, p. 85). He came upon the passage in which the author describes his father's death and the family's distress, 'and the sudden inspiration by which, then a mere boy, he felt and made them feel that he would be everything to them—would supply the place of all that they had lost'. Moved to tears by the scene—by this epiphany of the book that was accompanied even by the traditional illumination: 'a small ray of light broke in upon my gloom'—Mill realized that he was no longer without hope, that he had discovered within himself the capacity for happiness: not the analytically planned happiness of the whole but a happiness that was attained as the indirect result of some other action. 'Those only are happy (I thought) who have their minds fixed on some object other than their own happiness' (*AOW*, p. 85). Now, for the first time, Mill turned his thoughts to 'the internal culture of the individual' (*AOW*, p. 86)—what Kleist called 'Bildung'—and began to understand the role of art and literature as 'instruments of human culture' (*AOW*, pp. 86-87). It was this insight that catalysed Mill's shift from the utilitarianism of Bentham—that utility is the basis of universal happiness and morality—towards the modified doctrine, later explicated in his *Utilitarianism* (1861), with which he is today identified and which took into account various kinds and degrees of individual pleasure as described, for instance, in his essays 'What Is Poetry?' and 'The Two Kinds of Poetry' (both 1833). Again, however, it is not the details of Mill's theory that concern us but, rather, the fact that his epiphany was triggered by a passage in a book.

Re-Joyce

At this point it is appropriate to return briefly to Joyce. As we have seen, what I call 'epiphanies of the book' are quite different from the fleeting moments of insight that Joyce portrays in his works. But it is worth noting that Joyce's initial insight regarding epiphanies was itself triggered by a book: Aquinas's *Summa theologiae*, which is the source for his famous definition. Paradoxically, then, his own intellectual shift—from traditional nineteenth-century narrative style to a twentieth-century literature of epiphanic moments—was an epiphany of the book. While the epiphanies that he describes are fleeting moments, the insight that he received from Aquinas changed the entire nature of his experience and writing.

Epiphanies of the Book

The five cases we have considered display certain characteristic similarities. First, the individuals who experienced these epiphanies were all young adults of respectively twenty (Mill, Joyce), twenty-three (Kleist), and thirty-two (Petrarch and Augustine) years. These are neither childhood incidents nor affairs of mature seniority; the individuals are all still youths at the crucial stage in their development when major changes in focus and goal can still occur.[47] Second, in all five cases the individual was living at what is known in German as an 'Epochenschwelle'[48]—the threshold between two historical epochs: late antiquity and the Christian Middle Ages (Augustine), the Middle Ages and the Renaissance (Petrarch), Enlightenment rationalism and post-Kantian scepticism (Kleist and Mill), and nineteenth-century realism and twentieth-century consciousness (Joyce). Third, the insight is not fleeting but wholly changes the individual's life and, unlike bibliomancy, reflects a broader epochal shift. Finally, the fact that the epiphany is triggered by a book and not by a mere word or gesture is significant because the book exemplifies the intellectual mindset that characterizes the various epochs in the history of philosophy and culture.

Readers can of course be profoundly moved at any age and at any point in history by insights from their reading, as in bibliomancy. But what I have termed 'epiphanies of the book' are memorable because they symbolize through specific cases profound transformations of personal perception that simultaneously reflect epochal shifts taking place in their cultures as a whole. To that extent they differ markedly from the 'epiphanies' as illustrated by the various usages cited at the outset. The phenomenon is not triggered by a commonplace incident such as Joyce's word or gesture; but it is worth noting and defining as a specific type of 'epiphany' because the individuals with whom it is associated exemplify major shifts in cultural history—shifts whose effects we all experience. It has not been my aim here to offer new readings of these renowned works or to make a contribution to Joyce studies in particular but, rather, to identify certain common elements among five works rarely treated together and, in the process, to provide a precisely defined category into which other examples that occur to readers may be fitted.

PRINCETON UNIVERSITY   THEODORE ZIOLKOWSKI

[47] See in this connection the chapter 'The Novel of the Thirty-Year-Old', in Theodore Ziolkowski, *Dimensions of the Modern Novel: German Texts and European Contexts* (Princeton: Princeton University Press, 1969), pp. 258–88.

[48] The term was coined by Blumenberg in *Die Legitimität der Neuzeit*, but it has become standard usage; see Reinhart Koselleck, *Epochenschwelle und Epochenbewußtsein* (Munich: Fink, 1987).

LACUNARY KNOWLEDGE IN SEBALD AND PROUST

> About the early sixteenth-century painter Matthias Grünewald [. . .] we know hardly anything at all, apart from his pictures [. . .]. These lacunae of ignorance [. . .] were sufficient somehow for me to move into this territory.   (W. G. SEBALD)[1]

> [Q]uelle richesse, quelle variété, cache à notre insu cette grande nuit impénétrée et décourageante de notre âme que nous prenons pour du vide et pour du néant.
> (MARCEL PROUST)[2]

Maurice Merleau-Ponty prefaces *Sens et non-sens*, his series of essays on art, philosophy, and politics, with an observation on how, in the work of art, expression and communication function in a space marked by risk and fallibility: 'ni pour l'artiste ni pour le public le sens de l'œuvre n'est formulable autrement que par l'œuvre elle-même; ni la pensée qui l'a faite, ni celle qui la reçoit, n'est tout à fait maîtresse de soi'.[3] The limits that are thus placed on intelligibility and knowingness prompt Merleau-Ponty to reflect that expression is never complete and that the work of art is 'comme un pas dans la brume, dont personne ne peut dire s'il conduit quelque part'.[4] Jean-Yves Tadié's psychoanalytical study, *Le Lac inconnu: entre Proust et Freud*, draws the image in its title from a view expressed in *A la recherche du temps perdu*, that heightened emotion finds not the language one consciously seeks but rather 'une phrase tout autre, émergée d'un lac inconnu où vivent ces expressions sans rapport avec la pensée et qui par cela même la révèlent'.[5] In Proust's oxymoron, revelation arrives via 'ce magnifique langage', which is seemingly accidental and yet efficacious. As Malcolm Bowie observes in his own comparative reading of Proust and Freud, language may work away from

---

An earlier version of the material contained in this article formed the basis of a memorial lecture given at Queen's University Belfast in March 2011 in honour of Richard Bales.

[1] Sebald's words are taken from Eleanor Wachtel, '"Ghost Hunter": An Interview with W. G. Sebald', in *The Emergence of Memory: Conversations with W. G. Sebald*, ed. by Lynne Sharon Schwartz (New York: Seven Stories Press, 2007), pp. 37–61 (p. 42).
[2] Marcel Proust, *A la recherche du temps perdu*, 4 vols (Paris: Gallimard, 1987–89), I, 344. Subsequently abbreviated to *RTP*, with accompanying volume and page numbers.
[3] Maurice Merleau-Ponty, *Sens et non-sens* (Paris: Nagel, 1966; repr. Paris: Gallimard, 1996), p. 8.
[4] Ibid.
[5] Jean-Yves Tadié, *Le Lac inconnu: entre Proust et Freud* (Paris: Gallimard, 2012), p. 9. The work forms part of Gallimard's 'Connaissance de l'Inconscient' collection. Tadié draws his quotation from *RTP*, IV, 401.

deeply embedded emotion but can also provide 'a surreptitious return route to the libidinal substratum'.[6]

The endorsement of the oblique and the unplanned contrasts with those better-known moments in the *Recherche* when a resourceful narrator confidently coins metaphors for the representation of the life of the mind. In *Le Temps retrouvé* the adult Marcel, travelling along Parisian streets, is transported in memory to when, as a boy, he accompanied Françoise to the Champs Élysées: 'Et, comme un aviateur qui a jusque-là péniblement roulé à terre, "décollant" brusquement, je m'élevais lentement vers les hauteurs silencieuses du souvenir' (*RTP*, IV, 437). Elsewhere in the novel, when confronted with the contradiction between the memory of Albertine alive and the knowledge of her death, he concludes: 'j'étais un homme, un de ces êtres amphibies qui sont simultanément plongés dans le passé et dans la réalité actuelle' (*RTP*, IV, 114). Memory's metaphors are also varied in the work of W. G. Sebald, who observes that 'memory is [...] what qualifies us as emotional creatures, psychozootica or however one might describe them'.[7] Whether aviators, amphibians, or psychozootica, we are, for both writers, marked by our preoccupation with the past. Richard Bales explores the connections between memory and writing in both authors, drawing on the image of 'the immense edifice of memory' in Proust's madeleine episode, in which the spontaneous recall of a distant past is triggered by the senses.[8] As the narrator reflects, 'après la mort des êtres, après la destruction des choses, seules [...] l'odeur et la saveur restent encore longtemps, comme des âmes, à se rappeler, à attendre, à espérer, sur la ruine de tout le reste, à porter sans fléchir [...] l'édifice immense du souvenir' (*RTP*, I, 46). Notwithstanding the analogy forged between the souls of the departed and the somatic memory triggers of taste and smell, Proust's expansive image conjoins an alternative scenario, that of destruction of the past as signalled in the language of ruins. Memory's would-be miraculous availability cannot, then, erase a sense of precariousness and a propensity to lapse into oblivion. Indeed, for both Sebald and Proust a melancholy unknowingness often acts as a key narrative driver. Observations made by the seventeenth-century scientist Thomas Browne, among them the view 'Der Mohnsamen geht überall auf' ('The iniquity of oblivion blindly scatters her poppyseed'), provide a framing for Sebald's *The Rings of Saturn*.[9] The text, which constructs a legacy

---

[6] Malcolm Bowie, *Freud, Proust and Lacan: Theory as Fiction* (Cambridge: Cambridge University Press, 1987), p. 68.   [7] Wachtel, '"Ghost Hunter"', p. 56.
[8] Richard Bales, '"L'Édifice immense du souvenir": mémoire et écriture chez Proust et Sebald', in *Mémoire. Transferts. Images*, ed. by Ruth Vogel-Klein (= *Recherches germaniques*, suppl. IV-2 (2005)), pp. 129–37 (p. 130). See also a follow-up article in which the comparative reading of the two authors is extended: Richard Bales, 'Homeland and Displacement: The Status of the Text in Sebald and Proust', in *W. G. Sebald: Schreiben ex patria/Expatriate Writing*, ed. by Gerhard Fischer (Berlin: Rodopi, 2009), pp. 461–74.
[9] W. G. Sebald, *Die Ringe des Saturn* (Frankfurt a.M.: Fischer, 1995), p. 36; *The Rings of Saturn*,

of ruins, draws much of its persuasive power precisely from the forces of cognitive doubt and loss. Todd Samuel Presner argues that in sharp contrast with the Hegelian model of the progress of World Spirit, 'Sebald's narrative is a disorienting, compressed, and peripatetic journey through Suffolk, which takes decline and destruction as its organizing principles: "On every new thing there lies already the shadow of annihilation [...] (*The Rings of Saturn*, pp. 23–24)"'.[10] In the same volume the narrator, reflecting on the experience of being airborne, observes 'Wenn wir uns aus solcher Höhe betrachten, ist es entsetzlich, wie wenig wir wissen über uns selbst' (*Die Ringe des Saturn*, p. 114: 'if we view ourselves from a great height, it is frightening to realize how little we know about our species' (*The Rings of Saturn*, p. 92)), while in the closing pages of *A la recherche* the narrator writes of a dizzying verticality that renders retrieval of one's past a fragile enterprise: 'J'avais le vertige de voir au-dessous de moi, en moi pourtant, comme si j'avais des lieues de hauteur, tant d'années' (*RTP*, IV, 624).

The characterization of knowledge as lacunary is thus present in both authors, and we can extend to Sebald the capacity for 'dramatic portraiture of mental process' which Malcolm Bowie attributes to both Proust and Freud.[11] The risk in which artistic expression and communication are seen to be accomplished by Merleau-Ponty finds an echo in *Austerlitz*.[12] There, Sebald's eponymous hero draws on the procedures of photography to capture the delicate, fallible functioning of memory:

Besonders in den Bann gezogen hat mich bei der photographischen Arbeit stets der Augenblick, in dem man auf dem belichteten Papier die Schatten der Wirklichkeit sozusagen aus dem Nichts hervorkommen sieht, genau wie Erinnerungen, sagte Austerlitz, die ja auch inmitten der Nacht in uns auftauchen und die sich dem, der sie festhalten will, so schnell wieder verdunkeln, nicht anders als ein photographischer Abzug, den man zu lang im Entwicklungsbad liegenläßt.[13]

In my photographic work I was always especially entranced, said Austerlitz, by the

---

trans. by Michael Hulse (London: Vintage, 2002), p. 24. I am greatly indebted to Eric Robertson for his generous guidance in working with Sebald's texts in the original German. For an exploration of how Sebald's German versions 'have in some respects a noticeably different character from that of the English versions' see Mark R. McCulloh, 'Introduction: Two Languages, Two Audiences. The Tandem Literary Œuvres of W. G. Sebald', in *W. G. Sebald: History—Memory—Trauma*, ed. by Scott Denham and Mark McCulloh (Berlin: de Gruyter, 2006), pp. 7–20 (p. 8). Published translations are sometimes lightly adapted in the present article.

[10] 'Auf jeder neuen Form liegt schon der Schatten der Zerstörung' (*Die Ringe des Saturn*, p. 35). Todd Samuel Presner, 'Hegel's Philosophy of World History via Sebald's Imaginary of Ruins: A Contrapuntal Critique of the "New Space" of Modernity', in *Ruins of Modernity*, ed. by Julia Hell and Andreas Schönle (Durham, NC: Duke University Press, 2010), pp. 193–211 (p. 202).

[11] Bowie, *Freud, Proust and Lacan*, p. 88.

[12] Merleau-Ponty argues that mastery is denied both to the thought which produces the work of art and to that which receives it: 'On verra par l'exemple de Cézanne dans quel risque s'accomplit l'expression et la communication' (*Sens et non-sens*, p. 8).

[13] W. G. Sebald, *Austerlitz* (Frankfurt a.M.: Fischer, 2001), p. 117.

moment when the shadows of reality, so to speak, emerge out of nothing on the exposed paper, as memories do in the middle of the night, darkening again if you try to cling to them, just like a photographic print left in the developing bath too long.[14]

'Clinging to the memory' is a risk that similarly confronts Proust's narrator. He asks in his account of the madeleine episode: 'Arrivera-t-il jusqu'à la surface de ma claire conscience, ce souvenir [. . .] qui sait s'il remontera jamais de sa nuit?' (*RTP*, I, 46); and in appealing in the same context to the Celtic myth of the transmigration of souls, he cautions dramatically that for many, the moment of reconnection with these souls never comes (*RTP*, I, 44). These metaphors of the night connect with what Martin Klebes observes of Sebald's later works generally, namely that 'the inaccessibility of psychic interiors is a striking, recurrent theme'.[15]

Memory's precariousness is signalled in the epigraph to the first of the four autofictional life-stories that make up *The Emigrants*, 'Dr Henry Selwyn': 'Zerstöret das Letzte die Erinnerung nicht' ('And the last remnants memory does not destroy').[16] The lapidary pronouncement inaugurates a series of interconnected perspectives on memory. Thus, the troubled past of refugee painter Max Ferber (who is Max Aurach in *Die Ausgewanderten*) leaves him confronting 'die Lagune der Erinnerungslosigkeit' (*Die Ausgewanderten*, p. 259: '[the] lagoon of oblivion' (*The Emigrants*, p. 174)), while the author-narrator's Aunt Fini believes that her uncle Adelwarth's tales of travel in exotic locations suggest that he was suffering from Korsakov's syndrome, a disease in which deficient memory is replaced by fantastic creations of the mind. In fact memory's obliteration is something actively sought by Ambros Adelwarth, who had been manservant and lover to the wealthy Cosmo Solomon. Long after the latter's death, a desolate Adelwarth undergoes electro-convulsive therapy in an attempt to erase consciousness of his past, the psychiatrist who treated him, Dr Abramsky, suggesting to the narrator that what motivated his uncle was 'die Sehnsucht [. . .] nach einer möglichst gründlichen und unwiderruflichen Auslöschung seines Denk- und Erinnerungsvermögens' (*Die Ausgewanderten*, p. 167: '[his] longing for an extinction as total and irreversible as possible of his capacity to think and remember' (*The Emigrants*, p. 114)). Commenting on this scene, Sebald draws on Dante's notion that 'nothing is as horrendous as imagining the times of happiness from an environment which is that of hell'.[17] The perspective of a willed oblivion similarly informs Proust's nar-

---

[14] W. G. Sebald, *Austerlitz*, trans. by Anthea Bell (London: Penguin, 2002), p. 109.
[15] Martin Klebes, 'Sebald's Pathographies', in *W. G. Sebald*, ed. by Denham and McCulloh, pp. 65–75 (p. 70).
[16] W. G. Sebald, *Die Ausgewanderten* (Frankfurt a.M.: Fischer, 1994), p. 5; *The Emigrants*, trans. by Michael Hulse (London: Vintage, 2002), p. 1.
[17] Wachtel, '"Ghost Hunter"', p. 55.

rator's reflection as shaped by Marcel's experience in relation to the departed Albertine: 'l'oubli seul finit par amener l'extinction du désir' (*RTP*, IV, 34).

In the diary of Sebald's great-uncle Adelwarth, which is part historical document and part fictional recreation, memory is evoked as 'eine Art von Dummheit. Sie macht einen schweren, schwindligen Kopf, als blickte man nicht zurück durch die Fluchten der Zeit, sondern aus großer Höhe auf die Erde hinab von einem jener Türme, die sich im Himmel verlieren' (*Die Ausgewanderten*, p. 215: 'a kind of dumbness. It makes one's head heavy and giddy, as if one were not looking back down the receding perspectives of time but rather down on the earth from a great height, from one of those towers whose tops are lost to view in the clouds' (*The Emigrants*, p. 145)). For Ambros Adelwarth, memory of travels in 1913 with Cosmo Solomon to exotic, early twentieth-century, Western tourist locations (Constantinople, Jerusalem) can only heighten the desolation which separation from that past and from Cosmo triggers. Cosmo himself, far from the battlefields of the First World War, becomes nevertheless one of its victims, for, traumatized by knowledge of what trench warfare entails, he succumbs to melancholy, eventually entering a sanatorium in Ithaca, New York, and falling into terminal decline. Decades later, Adelwarth chooses to be admitted to the same institution, where he 'stets den Eindruck [erweckte], als sei er von einem heillosen Leid erfüllt' (*Die Ausgewanderten*, p. 162: 'always gave the impression of being filled with some incurable grief' (*The Emigrants*, p. 111)), in the words of Dr Abramsky. If in Sebald's narrative the great-uncle's lost love is oppressive and isolating—the private person in Adelwarth is described as ceasing to exist: 'er [bestand] nur mehr aus Korrektheit' (*Die Ausgewanderten*, p. 144: 'nothing was left but his shell of decorum' (*The Emigrants*, p. 99))—the very end of *Le Temps retrouvé* throws up stages of mourning that are no less daunting and yet also transient: 'après la mort le Temps se retire du corps, et les souvenirs [. . .] sont effacés de celle qui n'est plus et le seront bientôt de celui qu'ils torturent encore, mais en qui ils finiront par périr quand le désir d'un corps vivant ne les entretiendra plus. Profonde Albertine que je voyais dormir et qui était morte' (*RTP*, IV, 624). As with Adelwarth, Albertine's depth and death are synonymous with her ultimate unknowability.

Alongside memory thus stand the cognate states that are hypermnesia, amnesia, apathy, and oblivion. The melancholic Austerlitz observantly identifies memory's capacity to occlude reality, conceding that his cultivation of erudition over decades constituted a form of compensatory memory. But as he concludes, 'diese Selbstzensur meines Denkens' (*Austerlitz*, p. 206: 'this self-censorship of my mind' (*Austerlitz*, p. 198)) leads to mental collapse.

For both Sebald and Proust, then, the ingrained reflex of retrospection is variously feared, repressed, celebrated, and sabotaged. In interviews on his work Sebald stresses that the past holds 'something terribly alluring'.[18] Thus the narrative of *Austerlitz* is worked around the eponymous protagonist's eventual discovery of his childhood origins and the wider trauma of the Second World War. The memory trigger is the disused Ladies' Waiting Room in the old Liverpool Street station in London, which, nearly fifty years on, Austerlitz finds himself inside, a few weeks before its demolition. For Sebald's rootless character, the condemned building becomes, applying Proust's metaphor, the 'édifice du souvenir'. Yet with its imposing, complex architecture, it is a site of faintly glimpsed, fragmented knowledge. Indeed, *Austerlitz* may be read as belonging to the category of epistemological drama which Malcolm Bowie identifies in Proust's Albertine cycle.[19] And if another critic questions the link specifically to Proustian involuntary memory, preferring to see in the station's infrastructure an externalization of Austerlitz's buried memory, an alternative parallel within the *Recherche* might be the sombre architecture-memory coupling present in the evocation of the departed Albertine: 'Maçonné par la contiguïté des souvenirs qui se suivent l'un l'autre, le noir tunnel sous lequel ma pensée rêvassait depuis trop longtemps' (*RTP*, IV, 115).[20]

In the micro-psychological world of *Albertine disparue*, with its claustrophobic focus on Marcel's conflicted attachment to Albertine, a process of refraction allows nevertheless for significant moments of connection with wider, national obsession. Working to come to terms with Albertine's death and the reality of their conflicted relationship, the narrator moves without transition from private aggression to the war of 1870. In this apparent digression, the quest for self-knowledge is obliquely accessed via an excursus on history. The narrator's contention is that war comes to seem natural to populations whose perspective it wholly dominates:

Ceux qui ont vécu pendant la guerre de 1870, par exemple, disent que l'idée de la guerre avait fini par leur sembler naturelle, non pas parce qu'ils ne pensaient pas assez à la guerre, mais parce qu'ils y pensaient toujours. Et pour comprendre combien c'est un fait étrange et considérable que la guerre, il fallait, quelque chose les arrachant à leur obsession permanente, qu'ils oubliassent un instant que la guerre régnait, se retrouvassent pareils à ce qu'ils étaient quand on était en paix, jusqu'à ce que tout à coup sur ce blanc momentané se détachât, enfin distincte, *la réalité monstrueuse que depuis longtemps ils avaient cessé de voir*, ne voyant pas autre chose qu'elle. (*RTP*, IV, 115, emphasis added)

---

[18] Ibid., p. 57.
[19] Bowie, *Freud, Proust and Lacan*, p. 56.
[20] Russell J. A. Kilbourn rejects the linkage to the madeleine episode in his 'Architecture and Cinema', in *W. G. Sebald: A Critical Companion*, ed. by J. J. Long and Anne Whitehead (Edinburgh: Edinburgh University Press, 2004), pp. 140–54 (p. 146). On the metaphor of the tunnel, the terms used by Hell and Schönle in their study of the place of destruction in modernity are applicable: 'The ruin's dialectic between absence and presence, fragment and whole, is also one between the visible and the invisible' (*Ruins of Modernity*, ed. by Hell and Schönle, p. 7).

Explaining dialectically the maieutic exposure of war's 'monstrous reality'—'il arrive pour toutes les idées trop constantes, qui ont besoin d'une opposition pour s'affirmer' (*RTP*, IV, 115)—Proust reinforces the homology between individual aggression and loss and public catastrophe. Significantly, the psychological dynamic leading to the discovery of truth recalls Proust's 'lac inconnu' (*RTP*, IV, 401) considered earlier. As Bowie points out, the epistemological predicament facing Marcel in love sees 'general questions of intellectual method assume [an] organising role' in the Albertine cycle.[21]

In a related way, investigation of the grounds of knowledge in Sebald assumes a dialectical character. The hero Austerlitz's history works metonymically to the extent that private memory and the inscription in history collide. Of his desire to probe the past, Sebald insists that it is far removed from indulgence in nostalgia: 'it is to my mind an attempt to provide something like critical historiography'.[22] Blindness in the face of the catastrophic impact of war is a central motif in the author's work, most notably in *Luftkrieg und Literatur*, where, analysing the period 1930 to 1950, he controversially describes the attitude of his fellow countrymen as 'ein Hinsehen und Wegschauen zugleich' ('looking and looking away at the same time').[23] Referring to the Allied bombing of Germany in the last years of the Second World War, Sebald writes of 'dieser ungeheuren Verwüstung' (*Luftkrieg und Literatur*, p. 43: 'this monstrous destruction' (*On the Natural History of Destruction*, p. 36)).[24]

The First and Second World Wars were central concerns of Proust and Sebald respectively. In preparatory drafts for his novel Proust often demonstrates a strong engagement with ideological issues which was to become diluted in the final version of *A la recherche*.[25] The circumspection signalled by the technique of filtering the impact of catastrophe contrasts with Sebald's outspoken characterization of a German national will to suppress memory of its mid-twentieth-century history. Ironically, the observation in *A la recherche* regarding the circumstances in which awareness of 'la réalité monstrueuse' of the Franco-Prussian War of 1870 comes to crystallize forms part of the Albertine cycle, much of which was drafted during the First World War, the analepsis doubtless allowing Proust to evoke an atmosphere of military

---

[21] Bowie, *Freud, Proust and Lacan*, p. 53.
[22] W. G. Sebald and Gordon Turner, 'Introduction and Transcript of an Interview Given by Max Sebald (Interviewer: Michaël Zeeman)', in *W. G. Sebald*, ed. by Denham and McCulloh, pp. 21–29 (p. 24).
[23] W. G. Sebald, *Luftkrieg und Literatur* (Frankfurt a.M.: Fischer, 2001), p. 6; *On the Natural History of Destruction*, trans. by Anthea Bell (London: Penguin, 2004), p. ix.
[24] Although he was born in 1944 in the Allgäu Alps in southern Germany, away from the centres of wartime destruction, Sebald writes of being subliminally burdened by the unspoken weight of the historical moment.
[25] See Marion Schmid, 'Ideology and Discourse in Proust: The Making of "Monsieur de Charlus pendant la guerre"', *MLR*, 94 (1999), 961–77.

destruction and mental numbing while shielding him from any suspicion of defeatism in relation to the conflict of his own day.

That same sense of obliquity is at work when, writing about the contemporaneous destruction of the First World War, Proust's narrator proposes a geological model of understanding: 'la querelle prenait des formes immenses et magnifiques, comme le soulèvement d'un océan aux millions de vagues qui essaye de rompre une ligne séculaire de falaises, comme des glaciers gigantesques qui tentent dans leurs oscillations lentes et destructrices de briser le cadre de montagnes où ils sont circonscrits' (*RTP*, IV, 351). The annihilating capacity of war is thus worked via the circumlocutory choice of metaphors drawn from oceanography and geology. A variant on this oblique evocation of the conflict comes when Saint-Loup suggests the Wagnerian-style beauty formed by German air raids over Paris in the same conflict (*RTP*, IV, 337–38).

Sebald was forthright in rejecting the recourse to aesthetics in the representation of war. In his Zurich lectures of 1997 he surveys post-war German literature and protests that to construct what he terms a pseudo-aesthetic from a world in ruins threatens literature itself.[26] The uncompromising reflection on ethics and poetics is aimed at highlighting the tacit consensus that '[der] wahre Zustand der materiellen und moralischen Vernichtung, in welchem das ganze Land sich befand, durfte [. . .] nicht beschrieben werden' (*Luftkrieg und Literatur*, p. 17: 'the true state of material and moral ruin in which the country found itself was not to be described' (*On the Natural History of Destruction*, p. 10)). A more veiled form of dissent is voiced by Proust's narrator in *Le Temps retrouvé* in relation to the insistence of some nationalist writers (most notably Barrès) that literature had to act in the service of the nation and narrow patriotic endeavour (*RTP*, IV, 467).

How both authors assess the representation of catastrophe thus throws up important contrasts alongside points of connection. Yet in Proust and Sebald not only does the private merge with the collective, but the collective is worked on to a planetary scale. Evoking an early-evening, Parisian scene in the First World War, Proust's protagonist looks towards the Trocadéro and likens the view of the sky to a seascape:

Mer en ce moment couleur turquoise et qui emporte avec elle, sans qu'ils s'en aperçoivent, les hommes entraînés dans l'immense révolution de la terre, de la terre sur laquelle ils sont assez fous pour continuer leurs révolutions à eux, et leurs vaines guerres, comme celle qui ensanglantait en ce moment la France. (*RTP*, IV, 342)

Planetary scale, as a foil for catastrophic human destruction, is thus proposed as a vehicle of intelligibility. This anticipates the overarching metaphor signalled in Sebald's title, *The Rings of Saturn*. Reflecting that the planet's rings are the vestiges of an interplanetary collision, Peter Fritzsche argues that the

[26] *Luftkrieg und Literatur*, p. 59; *On the Natural History of Destruction*, p. 53.

image signals a disturbing naturalization of history, a move, Fritzsche adds, which Sebald himself regularly opposes.[27] In *The Rings of Saturn* Sebald aligns human patterns of activity and the Earth's revolutions, dwelling on the arresting image of how, progressively around the globe, the whole of the human race, responding to night falling, lays itself down to sleep. More precisely, the spectacle of sunset on the Suffolk coast prompts the narrator to retrieve the seventeenth-century perspective of Thomas Browne:

> In Amerika [. . .] stehen die Jäger auf, wenn die Perser gerade eintauchen in den tiefsten Schlaf. Gleich einer Schleppe wird der Nachtschatten über die Erde gezogen, und da nach Sonnenuntergang fast alles von einem Weltgürtel zum nächsten sich niederlegt, so fährt er fort, könnte man, immer der untergehenden Sonne nachfolgend, die von uns bewohnte Kugel andauernd voller hingestreckter, wie von der Sense Saturns umgelegter und geernteter Leiber erblicken—einen endlos langen Kirchhof für eine fallsüchtige Menschheit. (*Die Ringe des Saturn*, p. 97)
>
> The huntsmen are up in America [. . .] and they are already plunged in their deepest sleep in Persia. The shadow of night is drawn like a black veil across the earth, and since almost all creatures, from one meridian to the next, lie down after the sun has set, so, [Thomas Browne] continues, one might, in following the setting sun, see on our globe nothing but prone bodies, row upon row, as if levelled by the scythe of Saturn—an endless graveyard for a humanity struck by falling sickness. (*The Rings of Saturn*, pp. 78–79)

An echo of Browne's phantasmagoria is audible in *Austerlitz*, where the nocturnal perambulations through London of the disturbed eponymous hero set him apart from the conformism of 'Londoner jeden Alters, [die] in ihren Betten liegen, [. . .] das Gesicht vor Furcht gegen die Erde gekehrt, wie einst bei der Rast auf dem Weg durch die Wüste' (*Austerlitz*, pp. 186–87: 'Londoners of all ages [who] lie in their beds [. . .] stretched out with their faces turned to the earth in fear, like travellers of the past resting on their way through the desert' (*Austerlitz*, pp. 178–9)). The image of a prostrate humanity thus forms part of Sebald's paradigmatic use of planetary movement as a backcloth to consideration of human mortality. In *A la recherche*, well beyond the initial images of a recumbent Marcel ('Longtemps je me suis couché de bonne heure' (*RTP*, I, 3)) and a narrator puzzling over the world of dream, we find in *Le Temps retrouvé* an exploration of the workings of a *vis sciendi* in those whose urge, always to be frustrated, is to know what sleep entails and who remain powerless to influence 'le maître qui étend ses esclaves avant de les mettre à une besogne précipitée [. . .]. Et depuis tant de siècles nous ne savons pas grand'chose là-dessus' (*RTP*, IV, 295). In the iterative act of laying out and anaesthetizing human bodies, abortive attempts to dispel ignorance of the workings of sleep acquire a millennial character. Proust as much as Sebald is drawn to what

---

[27] Peter Fritzsche, 'W. G. Sebald's Twentieth-Century Histories', in *W. G. Sebald*, ed. by Denham and McCulloh, pp. 291–99 (p. 291).

the latter calls 'Die Unsichtbarkeit und Unfaßbarkeit dessen, was uns bewegt' (*Die Ringe des Saturn*, p. 29: 'the invisibility and intangibility of that which moves us' (*The Rings of Saturn*, p. 18)). If the planetary scale favoured by both authors dwarfs human cognition, their predilection for large-scale temporal perspective generates explanatory models that stress the inchoate character of human knowledge.

The effect of defamiliarization regularly sought by Proust and Sebald may be read alongside Merleau-Ponty's assertion made specifically in relation to the art of Cézanne and cited earlier: 'dans quel risque s'accomplit l'expression et la communication. C'est comme un pas dans la brume.'[28] In *The Rings of Saturn* the narrator, awakening from the effects of anaesthesia in a Norwich hospital, dwells longingly on the speculation of Thomas Browne, who, reflecting on the anatomy lesson as depicted by Rembrandt, wonders:[29] 'Vielleicht war es der weiße Dunst, von dem er [. . .] behauptet, daß er aufsteige aus der Höhle eines frisch geöffneten Körpers, während er, so Browne im selben Zug, zu unseren Lebzeiten unser Gehirn umwölke, wenn wir schlafen und träumen' (*Die Ringe des Saturn*, pp. 27–28: 'Perhaps [. . .] it was the white mist that rises from within a body opened presently after death, and which during our lifetime, so he [Thomas Browne] adds, clouds our brain when asleep and dreaming' (*The Rings of Saturn*, p. 17)). Proust's narrator likewise combines fallible perception and the workings of corporeality when he speculates that sleep might function as 'cette brune obscurité où la réalité est aussi peu translucide que dans le corps d'un porc-épic et où la perception quasi nulle peut peut-être donner l'idée de celle de certains animaux' (*RTP*, III, 629).

In these examples, the sceptical turn of mind is consistently predicated on the defectiveness of the senses. Descartes observes in the first of his *Méditations métaphysiques* that 'nous ne pouvons pas même distinguer la veille d'avec le sommeil'.[30] The confrontation in Proust with the opaqueness thrown up by sleep likewise functions epistemologically. As his narrator speculates, 'Mais il est peut-être d'autres mondes plus réels que celui de la veille' (*RTP*, III, 629–30). Sebald prizes Thomas Browne's explanation that white mist clouds the brain as we sleep, while in a no less expansive manner Proust's narrator sees the emotion rapidly aroused by erotic dream as being triggered by 'des piqûres intraveineuses d'amour' invented by 'quelque docteur miraculeux' (*RTP*, IV, 490). Significantly, the narrator looks not just to modern medicine

---

[28] Merleau-Ponty, *Sens et non-sens*, p. 8.

[29] The reference is to Rembrandt's *The Anatomy Lesson* (1632), now housed at the Mauritshuis Museum.

[30] René Descartes, '*Discours de la méthode*' *suivi des* '*Méditations métaphysiques*' (Paris: Flammarion, 1908), p. 65, quoted in English translation in Stanley Cavell, *The Claim of Reason: Wittgenstein, Skepticism, Morality, and Tragedy* (New York: Oxford University Press, 1979), p. 130. Reflecting on scepticism and the existence of the world, Cavell sees in the opening pages of Descartes's *Méditations* a classical formulation of 'the reasonableness of doubt'.

to deliver dream analysis, for he adds that emerging from such a dream often entails a profound sense of loss, which he articulates in art-historical terms:

quelque chose de plus précieux se dissipe [. . .], tout un tableau ravissant de sentiments de tendresse, de volupté, de regrets vaguement estompés, tout un embarquement pour Cythère de la passion dont nous voudrions noter, pour l'état de veille, les nuances d'une vérité délicieuse mais qui s'efface comme une toile trop pâlie qu'on ne peut restituer. (*RTP*, IV, 490)

The developed pictorial dimension (the melancholy sensuousness of Watteau's *L'Embarquement de Cythère* (1717) provides the ironically transparent reference point for this dispersal of oneiric emotion) shows how with Proust, as with Sebald, the reflection on dream finds an essentially cultural mediation. Moreover, works of art may themselves hold an evasive, unformulated, alluring quality. In these examples of the dream-life drawn from both authors, we see it linked to seventeenth-century medical science, Rococo painting, intravenous medicine, and modern anaesthesia.

Geology provides an additional dimension to this turning away from waking consciousness. In 'Max Ferber' the mother of the eponymous hero observes in her memoirs how, at school in early twentieth-century Germany, the timeline they draw to indicate successive geological eras functions to the exclusion of humanity: 'Unser ganzes Leben wäre auf dieser Linie nicht einmal der allerwinzigste Punkt' (*Die Ausgewanderten*, p. 305: 'Our entire lives would not even show as the tiniest dot on that line' (*The Emigrants*, p. 204)). If the remark carries its own pathos when read retrospectively within the narrative of decline and catastrophe that is the Lanzberg family story, it also signals how in Sebald geological time can occlude memory of human disaster.

These images of human invisibility and obliteration provide an instructive contrast with Proust's 'édifice immense du souvenir'. The formulation, as we have noted, derives from Proust's heavily anthologized madeleine episode, in which the jaded adult Marcel digs down in his mind. Sebald may be nodding playfully in Proust's direction when in *Vertigo* (the German original, *Schwindel. Gefühle.*, conveys the idea of a hoax) he describes the folk tradition of eating small Seelenwecken rolls to mark the Christian days of memory at the beginning of November, All Saints and All Souls. The Seelenwecken and the madeleine tap into cultural memory (the madeleine recalling the scallop shell, the emblem of pilgrimage to Santiago de Compostela). For both authors, these everyday material signs not only serve to sustain a culture of memory working both privately and collectively but also function epistemologically. Yet as Proust's adult protagonist observes: 'Il est clair que la vérité que je cherche n'est pas en lui, mais en moi' (*RTP*, I, 45), a conclusion that we might infer is also Sebald's, given the ironic distancing from the image of the child, wooden spoon in hand, digging in the flour barrel kept in his grandparents' bedroom in the naive belief that the material contents of the receptacle will satisfy the search for revelation.[31]

While the food link proposed here is speculative, a direct borrowing from Proust which Sebald leaves unattributed is identified by Richard Bales.[32] It occurs when Austerlitz, an inveterate reader and writer, falls into a state of exhaustion and the ability to articulate thoughts in writing deserts him. Looking back on this loss of the power of memory and language, Austerlitz, in conversation with the narrator, articulates his sense of paralysis:

> Schon spürte ich hinter meiner Stirn die infame Dumpfheit, die dem Persönlichkeitsverfall vorausgeht, ahnte, daß ich in Wahrheit weder Gedächtnis noch Denkvermögen, noch eigentlich eine Existenz besaß, daß ich mein ganzes Leben hindurch mich immer nur ausgelöscht und von der Welt und mir selber abgekehrt hatte. Wäre damals einer gekommen, mich wegzuführen auf eine Hinrichtungsstätte, ich hätte alles ruhig mit mir geschehen lassen, ohne ein Wort zu sagen, ohne die Augen zu öffnen, so wie hochgradig seekranke Leute, wenn sie etwa auf einem Dampfer über das Kaspische Meer fahren, auch nicht den leisesten Widerstand an den Tag legen, falls man ihnen eröffnet, man werde sie jetzt über Bord werfen. (*Austerlitz*, p. 182)

> [...] some soul-destroying and inexorable force had fastened upon me [...]. I already felt in my head the dreadful torpor that heralds disintegration of the personality, I sensed that in truth I had neither memory nor the power of thought, nor even any existence [...]. If someone had come then to lead me away to a place of execution I would have gone meekly, without a word, without so much as opening my eyes, just as people who suffer from violent sea-sickness, if they are crossing the Caspian Sea on a steamer, for instance, will not offer the slightest resistance should someone tell them they are about to be thrown overboard. (*Austerlitz*, pp. 173–74)

The wording replicates the formulation used by the narrator in *Le Temps retrouvé* to record the nullifying of mental faculties experienced by an ageing Marcel, who has been stumbling when out and about in Paris:

> quand je fus rentré, je sentis que je n'avais plus ni mémoire, ni pensée, ni force, ni aucune existence. On serait venu pour me voir, pour me nommer roi, pour me saisir, pour m'arrêter, que je me serais laissé faire sans dire un mot, sans rouvrir les yeux, comme ces gens atteints au plus haut degré du mal de mer et qui, traversant sur un bateau la mer Caspienne, n'esquissent même pas une résistance si on leur dit qu'on va les jeter à la mer. (*RTP*, IV, 616)

Highlighting Sebald's unattributed quotation, Bales makes the link to another moment in *Le Temps retrouvé*, when the narrator, referring to the workings of intertextuality, likens the book to a cemetery where most of the inscriptions on the tombs are no longer visible.[33] For J. J. Long, 'the ethics of quotation [in Sebald] are irreducibly ambiguous', and the critic considers a range

---

[31] W. G. Sebald, *Schwindel. Gefühle.* (Frankfurt a.M.: Fischer, 1994), p. 74; *Vertigo*, trans. by Michael Hulse (London: Harvill, 2000), pp. 64–65.
[32] Bales, 'Homeland and Displacement', pp. 463–64.
[33] Bales, '"L'Édifice immense du souvenir"', p. 136.

of categories in his handling of Sebaldian composition, among them 'empathic identification', 'illegitimate appropriation', and embedded quotation.[34] Sebald himself deals with techniques of montage and borrowing in an essay on Jan Peter Tripp, identifying in the painter's patient compositions an aura of remembrance which converts the objects represented into melancholy mementoes.[35] In the same essay Sebald invokes Proust, stressing the linkage between memory and death, with ephemeral moments being suspended in Proust as in the works of Tripp. He returns to the twinning of memorialization and human mortality, showing how in one of Tripp's interiors lost time, remembrance, and death form a memorial shrine.[36] And in a specific link between textual and pictorial composition, Sebald argues for the link between remembrance and quotation, explaining that the incorporation by montage of a quotation into a painting or a text tests the reader's/viewer's knowledge of the world, by drawing us into the time of culture. Such time signals engagement with, and attentiveness to, cultural production. Seen in this light, the unattributed transposition of Proust's lines about the nauseous victims of the Caspian Sea creates an effect of textual embedding. The unmarked borrowing, while appearing to suggest autonomy rather than influence, thereby becomes a form of oblique memorial tribute, remembrance indeed consisting in a mere quotation, to use Sebald's formulation.[37]

Within the time of culture, as Merleau-Ponty comments in his preface to *Sens et non-sens*, works of art and scientific enquiry themselves deteriorate, albeit more slowly than within 'le temps de l'histoire et du monde physique'.[38] For both Proust and Sebald, the time of culture, captured in the image of the book as an accumulation of blurred burial inscriptions in *Le Temps retrouvé*, facilitates the often melancholic endeavour to retrieve knowledge. If intertextuality draws us into the time of culture, as Sebald, invoking Umberto Eco, suggests, we see a pictorial instantiation of the phenomenon in the *Recherche*. As Kazuyoshi Yoshikawa has demonstrated, however replete Proust's novel may be with references to the works of painters, some sources remain concealed even when textual transpositions of them are provided—paintings by

[34] J. J. Long, 'W. G. Sebald: A Bibliographical Essay on Current Research', in *W. G. Sebald and the Writing of History*, ed. by Anne Fuchs and J. J. Long (Würzburg: Königshausen & Neumann, 2007), pp. 11–29 (p. 19).

[35] W. G. Sebald, 'As Day and Night, Chalk and Cheese: On the Pictures of Jan Peter Tripp', in *Unrecounted: Poems by W. G. Sebald; Lithographs by Jan Peter Tripp* (New York: New Directions, 2004), p. 92. The principal contents of *Unrecounted* are thirty-three 'micropoems' by Sebald and thirty-three lithographs by Jan Peter Tripp.

[36] W. G. Sebald, 'As Day and Night', p. 93.

[37] J. J. Long argues that the stylistic uniformity present in Sebald's texts points to their modernist character, and he contrasts this with the collage-like appropriation more characteristic of postmodern literature (*W. G. Sebald: Image, Archive, Modernity* (Edinburgh: Edinburgh University Press, 2007), p. 172).

[38] Merleau-Ponty, *Sens et non-sens*, p. 8.

Chardin, for example, in *A l'ombre des jeunes filles en fleurs*: 'Les tableaux cachés', Yoshikawa concludes in relation to these moments of oblique ekphrasis, 'ouvrent ainsi la voie à une recherche plus vaste [. . .] sur la genèse des descriptions dans le roman de Proust.'[39] Likewise, Proust's earlier, enthusiastic work in the field of literary pastiche signals the author's technique of working with, and through, the voices of influential nineteenth-century predecessors.[40] Here again, living in the time of culture enacts a form of memorialization in the field of literature and art.

Social mimesis in both Sebald and Proust, which is often worked via the construction of tableaux, can similarly open onto the quest for knowledge and intelligibility. We see the effect of pictorialization in *The Rings of Saturn*. Curious about local culture, Sebald's reflex in this story of travel and pilgrimage is to work back in time in a move that suggests the author's will to give the past, in Peter Fritzsche's words, 'a nostalgic luster and richness'.[41] We read how in the summer of 1914, on the occasion of a charity ball held at the White Pier building in Lowestoft, ordinary folk excluded from the fashionable event rowed out in small craft to the end of the pier. If their position on the moving waters of the harbour suggests a mobile vantage-point, the narrative of Sebald's informant in 1992 (Frederick Farrar, by then an old man) as he looks back to the days just before the First World War generates a sfumato effect:

so sehe ich alles wie hinter wehenden weißen Schleiern: die Stadt von der Seeseite her [. . .] der Vater mit ein, zwei anderen Herren mit aufgekrempelten Hosen voraus, die Mama allein mit dem Parasoleil, die Schwestern mit ihren gerafften Röcken und dahinter die Dienstboten mit dem Eselchen, zwischen dessen Tragkörben ich meinen Sitz hatte. Einmal, vor Jahren, sagte Frederick Farrar, hat mir von diesem Bild sogar geträumt, und unsere Familie ist mir vorgekommen wie einst der kleine Hof Jakobs des Zweiten in der Verbannung an der Küste von Den Haag. (*Die Ringe des Saturn*, p. 65)

[. . .] it is as if I were seeing everything through flowing white veils: the town like a mirage over the water [. . .] Father walking ahead with one or two gentlemen whose trousers are rolled up, Mother by herself with a parasol, my sisters with their skirts gathered in one hand, and the servants bringing up the rear with the donkey, between whose panniers I am sitting on my perch. Once, years ago, said Frederick, I even dreamed of that scene, and our family seemed to me like the court of King James II in exile on the coast of The Hague. (*The Rings of Saturn*, p. 48)

Consistent with the oneirographic dimension that memory can assume in his work, Sebald's *belle époque* dream sequence, mediated through white veils, recalls the earlier reference in Thomas Browne to the 'white mist [. . .] which

---

[39] Kazuyoshi Yoshikawa, *Proust et l'art pictural* (Paris: Champion, 2010), p. 269.

[40] See Marcel Proust, *Pastiches et mélanges*, in *'Contre Sainte-Beuve' précédé de 'Pastiches et mélanges' et suivi de 'Essais et articles'* (Paris: Gallimard, 1971).

[41] Fritzsche, 'W. G. Sebald's Twentieth-Century Histories', p. 298.

during our lifetime, [. . .] clouds our brain when asleep and dreaming' (*The Rings of Saturn*, p. 17). Farrar's dream triggers another seventeenth-century narrative, a story of royal exile. As the domestic world of wealthy Edwardians freely mutates, the effect is not dissimilar to the evocation of Marcel's family in Proust's novel, where the daily routine of middle-class life—centred around the living habits of Tante Léonie—in small-town Combray is specifically likened to day-to-day living in the court of Louis XIV (in the opening dream sequence of the novel, Marcel similarly believes himself to be the rivalry between François I and Charles V). If the effect of allochronism is to attenuate the contemporary, Farrar's dreamscape is overlaid in Sebald's text with the grainy, black-and-white photograph of Lowestoft Central station taken in the late twentieth century.[42] As photorealism, historiography, and oral testimony converge, the social-class configuration provided in the image of Edwardian leisure acquires the form of a mystical, melancholy-laden collage energized by the cultivation of doubt. In 'Dr Henry Selwyn' Sebald again dwells on the alignment of social classes by wondering about the configuration of interior spaces within which domestic staff ghost along corridors and are cordoned off from their bourgeois masters; once more, the effect is to render precarious the grounds of social knowledge.[43] Indeed 'patchy knowledge of the past', to quote from 'Paul Bereyter' (*The Emigrants*, p. 54: 'die von blinden Flecken durchsetzte Vergangenheit' (*Die Ausgewanderten*, p. 80)), is integral to Sebald's attempted excavation. The author's work of retrieval in relation to the past and the wonder and loss associated with it recall the dimension of mourning which Michel de Certeau sees in historiography: 'Quelque chose s'est perdu qui ne reviendra pas. L'historiographie est une manière contemporaine de pratiquer le deuil.'[44]

Early twentieth-century leisure and conspicuous consumption, which are evoked in the account of Ambros Adelwarth's work in the service of Cosmo Solomon, convey a form of melancholy grandeur, the Grand Hôtel des Roches Noires in Deauville reflecting emblematically *belle époque* exuberance. That same culture features in Proust's evocation of what for him is contemporaneous life at Balbec. As with Farrar's account of Edwardian England, *A l'ombre des jeunes filles en fleurs* provides a scene of class juxtaposition and reciprocal spectatorship in descriptions of the dining-room of Balbec's Grand Hotel (*RTP*, II, 41–42). With its glass frontage operating melodramatically as a social-class interface between the wealthy on the inside and a spectating multitude on the outside, sociality is transformed into exotic spectacle. If the effect produced is, to borrow from Jacques Dubois, one of social reverie, an

---

[42] Johannes Fabian, *Time and the Other: How Anthropology Makes its Object* (New York: Columbia University Press, 1983), p. 143.

[43] *Die Ausgewanderten*, p. 16; *The Emigrants*, p. 9.

[44] Michel de Certeau, *La Fable mystique*, I: *XVIe–XVIIe siècle* (Paris: Gallimard, 1982), p. 21.

atmosphere of whimsicality and imprecision prevails.[45] In an analogous way, the retrieval of collective memory for Sebald often mutates into chimerical, affect-laden imagination.

Beyond early twentieth-century cultures of leisure set against the North Sea, Venice likewise holds an important oneirographic function in both Proust and Sebald. In *Albertine disparue* Proust's narrator, describing time there with his mother, who is still in mourning for her deceased mother, speaks of the city as an enchanted space and likens his evening walks to those of a character in *Les Mille et Une Nuits* (*RTP*, IV, 229). Marcel is surprised at one point to see that having followed a maze of tiny streets, he should come across 'un vaste et somptueux *campo*' (*RTP*, IV, 229), one of those architectural configurations, the narrator says, on which, in other cities, streets converge. Yet on the following morning Marcel searches in vain for this beautiful square, prompting the narrator to conclude:

> Comme il n'y a pas entre le souvenir d'un rêve et le souvenir d'une réalité de grandes différences, je finissais par me demander si ce n'était pas pendant mon sommeil que s'était produit, dans un sombre morceau de cristallisation vénitienne, cet étrange flottement qui offrait une vaste place entourée de palais romantiques à la méditation prolongée du clair de lune. (*RTP*, IV, 230)

The free rein given to the sense-led exploration of Venice in Proust feeds a sceptical imagination which exuberantly discards 'the claim of reason'.[46]

The sensation of an 'étrange flottement' between reason and fantasy is likewise explored in *Vertigo*. Dreaming in Venice, the narrator sees the hospital island of La Grazia on which 'als befänden sie sich auf einem großen, davonfahrenden Schiff, Tausende von Irren herausschauten' (*Schwindel. Gefühle.*, p. 75: 'thousands of madmen were looking out, as though they were aboard a great ship sailing away' (*Vertigo*, pp. 65–66)). And when a very seasick and mournful Kafka (Dr K.) arrives in the city in 1913, long after reaching what is presented as the precarious land that is Venice, he continues to feel the waves breaking within him.[47] If Kafka's mournfulness leaves him reluctant 'sich hinauszuwagen unter diesen Wasserhimmel, unter dem selbst die Steine zerflossen' (*Schwindel. Gefühle.*, pp. 162–63: 'to venture out beneath this watery sky under which the very stones dissolved' (*Vertigo*, p. 147)), a scenario of Venetian disintegration similarly features in *A la recherche* when

---

[45] For consideration of 'la rêverie sociale' see Jacques Dubois, *Pour Albertine: Proust et le sens du social* (Paris: Seuil, 1997), p. 14. An exploration of the new sociality spawned by *fin de siècle* leisure in Proust's novel is provided in Chapter 4 of my study *Proust, Class, and Nation* (Oxford: Oxford University Press, 2011), pp. 111–55.

[46] Cavell, *The Claim of Reason*. Proust's often-cited opening line to the so-called *Contre Sainte-Beuve*, 'Chaque jour j'attache moins de prix à l'intelligence', signals the young author's sceptical orientation ('Contre Sainte-Beuve' précédé de 'Pastiches et mélanges' et suivi de 'Essais et articles', p. 211).

[47] *Schwindel. Gefühle.*, p. 162; *Vertigo*, p. 146.

an emotionally distraught Marcel ceases to recognize the city ('cette Venise [...] irréelle' (*RTP*, IV, 232)) as his mother prepares to leave for Paris without him: 'Les palais m'apparaissaient réduits à leurs simples parties et quantités de marbre pareilles à toutes autres, et l'eau comme une combinaison d'hydrogène et d'azote, éternelle, aveugle, antérieure et extérieure à Venise, ignorante des doges et de Turner' (*RTP*, IV, 231). The removal of the accretions of aesthetics and historiography signals what Leo Bersani, in an argument suggestively entitled 'Fantasies of the Self and the World', characterizes as 'a kind of ontological crisis, a sudden deprivation of self'.[48]

In *The Rings of Saturn* Sebald describes visits made to the Suffolk coast by the Victorian poet Swinburne, a troubled writer, Sebald reflects, who saw in the slow erosion of the North Sea coast 'die allmähliche Selbstauflösung des Lebens' (*Die Ringe des Saturn*, p. 193: 'the gradual dissolution of life' (*The Rings of Saturn*, p. 160)). Swinburne imagines seeing, floating on the sea, the ancient palace of Kublai Khan which was built on a site later to be occupied by Peking.[49] This expansive lyricism which projects away from contemporaneity is as integral to Sebald's work as it is to Proust's. Late in *A la recherche*, the adult narrator describes feelings experienced on his return to Combray, the site of childhood security. With darkness falling as he goes out to socialize, the retrospective self-portrait is highly romanticized: 'Il arrivait que Gilberte me laissait aller sans elle, et je m'avançais, laissant mon ombre derrière moi, comme une barque qui poursuit sa navigation à travers des étendues enchantées' (*RTP*, IV, 267). A landlocked Combray, then, launches Marcel's enchanted navigation. Another return to the region of one's birth is described by the first-person narrator in *Vertigo*. He visits the tiny chapel in Krummenbach with its mid-eighteenth-century Stations of the Cross in which there was barely room for a dozen worshippers:

Draußen vor dem winzigen Fenster trieben die Schneeflocken vorbei, und bald kam es mir vor, als befände ich mich in einem Kahn auf der Fahrt und überquerte ein großes Wasser. Der feuchte Kalkgeruch verwandelte sich in Seeluft; ich spürte den Zug des Fahrtwinds an der Stirn und das Schwanken des Bodens unter meinen Füßen und überließ mich der Vorstellung einer Schiffsreise aus dem überschwemmten Gebirge hinaus. (*Schwindel. Gefühle.*, p. 195)

Outside, snowflakes were drifting past the small window, and presently it seemed to me as if I were in a boat on a voyage, crossing vast waters. The moist smell of lime became sea-air; I could feel the spray on my forehead and the boards swaying beneath my feet, and I imagined myself sailing in this ship out of the flooded mountains. (*Vertigo*, p. 179)

Readers of Proust will recall both the description of the church in Com-

---

[48] Leo Bersani, *Marcel Proust: The Fictions of Life and Art* (New York: Oxford University Press, 1965), p. 28.
[49] *Die Ringe des Saturn*, p. 193; *The Rings of Saturn*, p. 160.

bray, seen as a triumphal vessel travelling across the centuries, and Marcel's entrance into it: 'je m'avançais dans l'église [. . .] comme dans une vallée visitée des fées' (*RTP*, I, 60). Likewise, the streets of Combray exist 'dans une partie de ma mémoire si reculée' and are 'plus irréelles encore que les projections de la lanterne magique' (*RTP*, I, 48). As with Sebald's Krummenbach chapel, the abandonment of realism sees the workings of a near-hallucinatory visualization and of narrative grounded in heightened affectivity.

A literal conversion of landscape into waterscape features in *Austerlitz* with the evocation of a Welsh valley flooded in order to form a reservoir in 1888. Imagining the now submerged village of Llanwyddn, where the family of Austerlitz's foster father had previously lived, the protagonist still manages to think of life carrying on below in the wake of what is presented as a form of biblical deluge.[50] When reminded that he had been described as a ghost-hunter, Sebald accepted the designation: 'I think that's pretty precise. It's nothing ghoulish at all, just an odd sense that in some way the lives of people who are perhaps no longer here—and these can be relatives or people I vaguely knew, or writer colleagues from the past, or painters who worked in the sixteenth century—have an odd presence for me.'[51]

The cultural matrix formed by literature occasions intense absorption in both Proust and Sebald. Just as Marcel, in his futile policing of Albertine, issues orders to his household in *La Prisonnière* as though he were enacting Racine's *Esther*, so too his mother and grandmother find in the work of Mme de Sévigné a seductive template that facilitates their mutual communication. Indeed, Marcel's mother inhabits the time of culture in a radical way, for when she reads in Mme de Sévigné's letters the words 'ma fille', 'elle croyait entendre sa mère lui parler' (*RTP*, III, 168). In *Austerlitz* the narrator recalls his delightful immersion in a book as night falls (*Austerlitz* (German), p. 180; *Austerlitz* (English), pp. 171–72), while in *Vertigo* the narrator's acquaintance Salvatore Altamura reports on his evening recreation after the stress of the world of work: '[ich] rette mich [. . .] in die Prosa wie auf eine Insel' (*Schwindel. Gefühle.*, p. 144: 'I take refuge in prose as one might in a boat' (*Vertigo*, p. 128)).[52] These characters' dispositions serve to corroborate Bales's argument that literature and art more generally constitute a 'homeland' for both authors.[53]

Literature's memory, functioning, as Sebald reminds us, within the time of culture, releases a procession of authors, among them Casanova, whose *Histoire de ma fuite des prisons de la République de Venise qu'on appelle les Plombs écrite à Dux en Bohème l'année 1787* features in *Vertigo*. The prison in

---

[50] *Austerlitz* (original German edition), p. 80; *Austerlitz* (English translation), p. 72.
[51] Wachtel, '"Ghost Hunter"', p. 42.
[52] The shift in translation from 'island' to 'boat' is noted by McCulloh, 'Introduction', p. 15.
[53] Bales, 'Homeland and Displacement', p. 473.

question, positioned at the top of the ducal palace in Venice, drew its name from the material of its construction, I Piombi. Stiflingly hot for inmates in the summer, it was desperately cold in the winter. For Proust, I Piombi stands as another of the edifices of memory and metaphorically conveys the sense of arduous access to knowledge of the past. As we read in *Albertine disparue*, 'Parfois au crépuscule en rentrant à l'hôtel je sentais que l'Albertine d'autrefois, invisible à moi-même, était pourtant enfermée au fond de moi comme aux "plombs" d'une Venise intérieure, dont parfois un incident faisait glisser le couvercle durci jusqu'à me donner une ouverture sur ce passé' (*RTP*, IV, 218). Memory's constriction thus foregrounds the presence of lacunae that are integral to Marcel's search for emotional knowledge, a search which, he reflects longingly, 'un médecin de l'âme' (*RTP*, IV, 114) would have facilitated.

While the lure of 'autrefois' energizes both Proust and Sebald, historiography is self-evidently a more developed feature of the latter's work. Yet in *Combray* looking out onto the street allows the housebound Tante Léonie to read 'la chronique quotidienne *mais immémoriale* de Combray' (*RTP*, I, 51, emphasis added). Likewise, the Albertine cycle, as we have seen, involves connections, both direct and tangential, with social and literary history. Albertine becomes 'Albertine-Esther' (*RTP*, III, 606); likewise, Marcel's battles with her recall, not in any superficial sense, the Franco-Prussian War, the effect being to link the mental numbing of a nation's population and the failure of self-knowledge. If these appeals to cultural and historical memory indicate the work of grieving that is Marcel's, Sebald's texts are themselves replete with references to the veiling and misting of the past. Crossing disciplines, one sees the pertinence of Michel de Certeau's argument that historiography is a contemporary practice of mourning. 'L'historiographie', he explains, '[...] s'écrit à partir d'une absence et elle ne produit que des simulacres, si scientifiques soient-ils. Elle met une représentation à la place d'une séparation.'[54]

In his scrutiny of contemporary history in *Le Temps retrouvé*, the narrator complains about a cultural turn which sees a diversion of attention away from literature: '"plus de style, avais-je entendu dire alors, plus de littérature, de la vie"' (*RTP*, IV, 461). The 'life, not literature' prescription is one that a disbelieving narrator ridicules:

Car tous ceux qui n'ont pas le sens artistique, c'est-à-dire la soumission à la réalité intérieure, *peuvent être pourvus de la faculté de raisonner à perte de vue sur l'art*. Pour peu qu'ils soient par surcroît diplomates ou financiers, mêlés aux 'réalités' du temps présent, ils croient volontiers que la littérature est un jeu de l'esprit destiné à être éliminé de plus en plus dans l'avenir. (*RTP*, IV, 461, emphasis added)

Proust and Sebald demonstrate that—to return to metaphors explored at the beginning of this article—for the human psychozooticon, for the amphibian

[54] Certeau, *La Fable mystique*, I, 21.

negotiating the terrains of both past and present, the emotion of memory is inescapable. Literature and the time of culture which accommodates it provide a medium for exploration of these states and for the always partial excavation of 'cette grande nuit impénétrée [. . .] de notre âme' (*RTP*, I, 344). 'La faculté de raisonner' which Proust's contemporaries advocate runs counter to his sceptical view of knowledge as partial and elusive. Yet just as the narrator in *Le Temps retrouvé* is suspicious of an exuberant progressivism which envisages the demise of literature, so part of the achievement of both Sebald and Proust is to sustain a European literary tradition in which unknowingness has its place within epistemological narrative. Their works thereby exemplify the modern literary category, signalled by Maurice Merleau-Ponty, of '[ces] grands livres [. . . qui] ont exprimé la révolte de la vie immédiate contre la raison'.[55]

QUEEN MARY, UNIVERSITY OF LONDON   EDWARD J. HUGHES

[55] Merleau-Ponty, *Sens et non-sens*, p. 7.

'P.S.': THE DANGEROUS LOGIC OF THE POSTSCRIPT IN EIGHTEENTH-CENTURY LITERATURE

The Cunning of Postscripts

Tormented by his wife Margery's amorous fascination with the rake Horner, Mr. Pinchwife, the jealous husband in William Wycherley's *The Country Wife* (1675), dictates to her a letter breaking off the affair, with a view to this being dispatched to her defeated lover. The ensuing sequence of events, however, follows the pattern of a familiar stage trick, with Mrs. Pinchwife taking advantage of her husband's momentary absence from the room in search of sealing wax to draft an alternative epistle to her 'Dear, Sweet, Mr. *Horner*', entirely reversing the sentiments of Mr. Pinchwife's brusque note. She subscribes it as being from Horner's 'most Humble Friend, and Servant to command 'till death, *Margery Pinchwife*' and folds it ahead of sealing, though not without adding, in Wycherley's suggestive expression, 'a hint at bottom': in other words, a postscript appended to the letter.[1] It matters to the dramaturgy of this scene and the following one that Margery reads out, and so transmits to the audience, the contents of the body of the letter but not the postscript, the content of that being left dangling for a few hundred lines more.

The next scene finds Pinchwife, secure in his misapprehension about the actual letter received by Horner, glorying in his rival's public exposure and dashed sexual ambitions. Horner, for his part, struggles unsuccessfully to reconcile Pinchwife's triumphalist taunts with the letter's actual import. What rescues him from his bafflement, of course, turns out to be Mrs. Pinchwife's 'hint at bottom', to which his gaze eventually descends:

HORNER But what should this mean? stay the Postscript.
Be sure you love me whatsoever my husband says to the contrary, and let him not see this, lest he should come home, and pinch me, or kill my Squirrel.
(IV. 3. 276–79)

It should be noted here that the dramatic effect requires Horner to stumble belatedly upon the postscript, rather than noticing its presence immediately through the visual layout of the letter. Moreover, it falls to him actually to read it out, though of course no real-life reason, as distinct from the logic of stagecraft, compels that Mrs. Pinchwife should voice the main body of the letter but not the postscript, and that the letter's recipient, Horner, should verbalize its postscript but not the rest. In any event, this division of dramaturgical labour allows the audience to encounter the postscript (not altogether unfittingly) as temporally removed from the main body of the letter, whereas

---

[1] William Wycherley, *The Country Wife*, IV. 2. 153–71, in *The Plays of William Wycherley*, ed. by Arthur Friedman (Oxford: Clarendon Press, 1979).

the two had in fact been drafted in close succession. The stage function of the postscript is to resolve Horner's immediate confusion by tipping him off that the letter he has just perused differs from the one Pinchwife believes him to have been reading.[2]

The whole dramaturgic effect here depends on an interplay between three elements: the letter-text that Pinchwife understands Horner to have received; the actual text that has been surreptitiously interposed by Mrs. Pinchwife; and the letter's postscript, its contents initially withheld from the audience, that eventually allows Horner to make sense of the general confusion. Without the postscript the rest of the subterfuge would very likely have come to grief. The role played by this particular postscript in abetting an adulterous intrigue can be seen as consistent with a more general view, albeit a cynical one, of the usual motives behind adding postscripts to letters. Francis Bacon, for example, includes postscripts in his essay 'Of Cunning' among other slippery verbal techniques by which we can maximize our advantage across all our different communications with others. The true art of the postscript lies, in his view, in its author's consciously misleading a letter's recipient by putting 'that which was most material in the postscript, as if it had been a by-matter'.[3] While this is not exactly what Mrs Pinchwife does, she, as much as Bacon, has evidently grasped the potential of the postscript as a way of managing a communicative act, especially one involving the deception and exploitation of another party.

Postscripts in Eighteenth-Century Letters

This article addresses the use of postscripts in letters by some eighteenth-century authors as well as their incidence in plays and novels in the period. My intention is to try to connect epistolary conventions concerning postscripts with the way in which the device gets exploited for theatrical or novelistic effect, as well as showing in general how correspondents deployed postscripts as a creative resource. My main assertion is that the temporal lag between a letter and its postscript helped eighteenth-century writers conceptualize ways of manipulating narrative time. In the Preface to the first edition of *Clarissa* Richardson sets down that 'Letters on both Sides are written while the Hearts of the Writers must be supposed to be wholly engaged in their Subjects [. . .] So that they abound, not only with critical Situations; but with what may be

---

[2] There has been little work on the use of letters as stage properties in English drama of the Restoration period. However, for an illustration of this type of approach see Alan Stewart, *Shakespeare's Letters* (Oxford: Clarendon Press, 2008).

[3] Francis Bacon, 'Of Cunning', in *Essays*, ed. by Michael J. Hawkins (London: Dent, 1994), pp. 58–60 (p. 59).

called *instantaneous* Descriptions and Reflections.'[4] How best to create within narrative an impression of instantaneous reflection, of an act of writing virtually concurrent with the very event or thought-process that provides its content, posed itself as a significant technical dilemma for eighteenth-century novelists as diverse as Richardson and Sterne. Writing inevitably occupies its own temporal space: the more you write, the more you distance yourself from the event or reflection that provoked you to write in the first place. However, the stop–start effect of inserting a postscript, in either a real or a novelistic letter, allows the correspondent, as it were, to rejoin the present, to recapture the 'instantaneous' moment so much prized by Richardson. Postscripts, or even merely the idea of writing in temporal stages, thus offered a sort of novelistic solution, but not entirely without a negative element: my treatment of the subject also draws in a loose way on Derrida's notion of the supplement, seeing a postscript as aiding a letter (by adding to it), yet also displacing it through superseding it in time.[5] However, before developing these ideas, I want to begin with the properties of postscripts in general.

Postscripts can be defined in terms of both time and space. For the purposes of this article I will use the term variably, either to mean an instalment of a letter evidently written subsequent to the rest of it, or merely to refer to the part of a letter-text placed after the complimentary close and signature, regardless of whether this text was actually penned on a later occasion than the rest. It might be added that I attach no importance here to whether a postscript is indicated by an actual 'P.S.' or not. Postscripts form part of the complex visual and rhetorical grammar of eighteenth-century letters, consisting of the opening salutation, the body of the letter, the complimentary close, the signature, and the 'significant' space inserted between the different component parts. The presence of unused space in a letter, generated, for example, by the visual drop from the signature to the postscript, could indicate the affluence of the sender or suggest a tone of deference towards the addressee in an epistolary culture in which letters tended to be crowded with writing, given the cost of running to an additional sheet.[6]

The addition of a postscript would have registered itself differently within this epistolary culture from the effect it perhaps has nowadays, mainly because of the strong sense of finality and polite ceremony registered by the traditional complimentary close. Take the ending of one of the century's most famous

---

[4] Samuel Richardson, *Clarissa; or, The History of a Young Lady*, 7 vols (London: printed for S. Richardson, 1748), I, p. v.

[5] For Derrida's idea of supplementarity see *Of Grammatology*, trans. by Gayatri Chakravorty Spivak (Baltimore: Johns Hopkins University Press, 1976).

[6] See Jonathan Gibson, 'Significant Space in Manuscript Letters', *Seventeenth Century*, 12 (1997), 1–9.

letters, that from Johnson to Chesterfield on the publication of the *Dictionary* in 1755:

> Having carried on my work thus far with so little obligation to any favourer of Learning, I shall not be disappointed though I should conclude it, if less be possible, with less, for I have been long wakened from that Dream of hope, in which I once boasted myself with so much exultation, My lord, Your Lordship's Most humble, most obedient Servant,
>
> S.J.[7]

The letter complies with the standard canons of epistolary etiquette in concluding with a complimentary subscription, but the entire sentence, within which the compliment fits, has the effect of cancelling it out, as a style of words that might have characterized Johnson's deference to Chesterfield *in the past*—but not any longer. Of more general note, though, is simply that the letter generates a strong sense of closure by virtue of the way that the compliment itself gets swept up syntactically within the rhetorical climax, and had Johnson thought fit to add a postscript (which luckily he did not), this would necessarily have had to register its presence against that powerful competing note of finality.

The addition of a postscript might answer to any number of particular epistolary requirements, with postscripts being used in eighteenth-century letters for all of the following reasons: to transmit the compliments *of* someone other than the letter's signatory or *to* someone other than the letter's recipient (this is perhaps the most common cause); to prompt the recipient to a timely reply; to apologize for errors or visible hastiness in the letter just completed or for impolite brevity or excessive prolixity; to apologize for sending the letter unfranked and so transferring the cost of postage onto the recipient; to respond to some specific point, not considered germane to the whole, in the letter to which the author is replying; to disclose information about the author's state of health or enquire after that of the addressee; to acknowledge some gift received from the addressee; to suggest or arrange a meeting with the addressee; to detail an event, or course of events, occurring after the signing of the letter; to annex to the letter material penned by a second hand; or, in general, to add any extra remark by way of afterthought.

As a general rule, postscripts were viewed as informal features of letters rather than part of the standard epistolary apparatus consisting of salutation, complimentary close, and so on. They are exemplified only infrequently in letter-writing manuals and tend not to be encouraged. John Hill's *The Young Secretary's Guide* (7th edn, 1696) countenances them only as part of what he calls '*Mixed Letters*', these being idiosyncratic letters 'suited to the humour

---

[7] Letter of 7 February 1755, in *The Letters of Samuel Johnson*, ed. by Bruce Redford, 5 vols (Oxford: Clarendon Press, 1992), I, 96–97.

of the Writer', and thrown together from 'Incoherent Matter'.[8] Letters of this kind would naturally be made up of unconnected sections, and within this context of epistolary disjointedness he permits that 'if the different part requires not many Lines, it may be under-written, by way of Postscript, &c'.[9] Because postscripts were most often used to convey compliments, the most common criticism concerning them was the neglect and impoliteness implied by the author's omitting to include the compliments in the main body of the letter:

Begin your Letter about two Inches below the Top of your Paper, and leave about an Inch Margin on the Left-Hand, and what Compliments, or Services, you send in the Letter, insert them rather in the Body or Conclusion of it than by Way of Postscript, as is too often done, but is neither so affectionate or polite, for it not only savours of Levity to your Friends, but has the Appearance of your having almost forgot them.[10]

These remarks make clear the extent to which the visual layout of letters, including the expensive white space afforded by generous margins, contributed to an overall sense of epistolary politeness and decorum. Postscripts, potentially hinting at inattention in the letter itself, could puncture that crafted impression. It was for this reason that they came to be all the more strongly discouraged when the addressee was of higher social rank than the author. *The Complete Letter Writer; or, Polite English Secretary*, for example, asserts unqualifiedly that 'When you write to your Superiors, never make a Postscript'. The addition of a postscript, even of a complimentary kind, risked being viewed as disrespectful by people who 'expect to be treated with Deference'.[11]

How correspondents actually used postscripts was inevitably impinged on by the larger rhythms of epistolary correspondence, these in their turn being influenced by the commercial and logistical realities of the postal system.[12] All letters that form part of correspondences, as most familiar letters did, could be seen in themselves as being postscripts, as coming after letters previously sent and received and as accordingly mediating, or setting in an ever so slightly altered perspective, all the foregoing letters in a series. After the innovations made to the postal system by Ralph Allen in the 1720s and 1730s, vastly expanding the reach and efficiency of the network, postal deliveries became more frequent. Yet, as Sarah Haggarty has pointed out, a role still existed

---

[8] John Hill, *The Young Secretary's Guide; or, A Speedy Help to Learning. In Two Parts*, 7th edn (London: printed for H. Rhodes, 1696), repr. in *British and American Letter Manuals 1680–1810*, ed. by Eve Tavor Bannet, 4 vols (London: Pickering & Chatto, 2008), II, 1–12 (p. 12).

[9] Ibid.

[10] Anon., *The Complete Letter Writer; or, Polite English Secretary*, 12th edn (London: printed for Stanley Crowder and Benjamin Collins, 1768), repr. in *British and American Letter Manuals 1680–1810*, ed. by Tavor Bannet, I, 8–13 (p. 9).

[11] Ibid., p. 10.

[12] See Howard Robinson, *The British Post Office: A History* (Princeton: Princeton University Press, 1948).

for foot-posts and private carriers to convey mail away from the main postal routes, and for a host of personal arrangements to be put in place for letters to be carried from the post office to the addressee's own door.[13] In a postscript of early 1742, for example, William Shenstone tells his correspondent Mrs Knight how pleased he would be to receive his next letter from her at the very moment of his setting off for London the following week, the letter being put into his hand precisely (as he imagines) 'as I put my Foot into the Stirup'.[14]

This unpredictability of deliveries made it very common for the drafting of a letter to be broken in upon either by the arrival of another letter from the same addressee, or by other correspondence occasioning some revision or updating of the letter in hand. Postscripts were of course especially useful in the face of epistolary exigencies of this kind. Also influencing the prevalence of postscripts was the pricing of letters by the sheet. Where the protocols of deference could be set aside, letter-writers became very adept at cramming the maximum wordage onto the page. The need to fill the single sheet, but not to spill over on to an additional one, inevitably placed an artificial check on epistolary flow, requiring a major sustaining—or conscious renewal—of momentum for the author to go beyond it. We can see this, for example, with another of Shenstone's postscripts, this time to Lady Luxborough, penned on 6 June 1749 and tagged onto a letter begun three days earlier:

> I did think to have sent ye former sheet this morning; which having neglected to do, I will endeavour to make some Amends for my Delay by adding another; as an Author now & then throws you in a dull appendix *gratis* in order to attone for his dilatory Publication of a duller Piece.[15]

Shenstone had presumably penned and signed the letter the previous day, coming to a natural halt when he had filled up the sheet. Having neglected to send it off the following morning, however, he embarks on a long postscript, which once more reaches its entirely artificial point of conclusion at the foot of the second sheet: 'Thus has my Pen run on 'till It has cover'd another Sheet'.[16]

Letters written by eighteenth-century authors, like other literary works of the period, straddle the divide between text as artefact and text as process. Shenstone's letters, for example, seem to want to realize themselves as a process unfolding in time, with the postscript representing not just an afterthought so much as an afterthought specifically about the foregoing letter. His postscripts therefore depict him as not just a writer, but also a reader of his own correspondence: 'Upon revisal I am asham'd to send this stupid Letter'; 'I

---

[13] Sarah Haggarty, '"The ceremonial of Letter for Letter": William Cowper and the Tempo of Epistolary Exchange', *Eighteenth-Century Life*, 35 (2011), 149–67 (pp. 152–56).

[14] Letter XXVII, in *The Letters of William Shenstone*, ed. by Marjorie Williams (Oxford: Blackwell, 1939), p. 50.

[15] Ibid., Letter LXXXVIII, p. 198.

[16] Ibid., p. 199.

think on a revisal I am too censorious'.[17] Many of his letters are composed in instalments, with the stages of composition nakedly in evidence or formally divulged either in the body of the letter or very often in the postscript: "Tis now *Oct.* 18th—but this Letter was wrote, in order to have been sent last Week.'[18] His postscripts seem particularly of a piece with the self-reflexive and quixotic spirit of his correspondence: 'This is a random Letter, and ought to be written over again, but [. . .] I love Letters written at different Periods.'[19]

Postscripts were also inevitably bound up with an author's self-consciousness about concluding or failing to conclude, and in this way can be seen as momentary enactments of the anxieties attendant on all forms of human leave-taking and ending.[20] As Johnson notes in his penultimate *Idler* essay: 'There are few things not purely evil, of which we can say, without some emotion of uneasiness, "this is the last".'[21] Postscripts can have the effect of tapering an ending, softening it, or dissipating its sense of climax. This interplay between competing impulses to end or to continue past the end is evident in a letter from Thomas Gray (who styles himself in a postscript elsewhere as 'by trade a Finisher of Letters') to Horace Walpole on 12 June 1750:

I have been here at Stoke a few days (where I shall continue good part of the summer); and having put an end to a thing, whose beginning you have seen long ago, I immediately send it you. You will, I hope, look upon it in the light of a *thing with an end to it*; a merit that most of my writings have wanted, and are like to want, but which this epistle I am determined shall not want, when it tells you that I am ever

Yours,

T. GRAY.

Not that I have done yet; but who could avoid the temptation of finishing so roundly and so cleverly in the manner of good queen Anne's days.[22]

The postscript runs on for another few sentences, with the whole passage being wryly alive to the problematics of closure. Gray, a naturally slow and diffident composer, has enclosed with the letter a copy of the 'Elegy written in

[17] Ibid., Letter XCIX, p. 221; Letter CVIII, p. 254.
[18] Ibid., Letter CXXI, p. 291.
[19] Ibid., Letter CXVII, p. 281.
[20] On the nature of literary endings in general see Frank Kermode, *The Sense of an Ending: Studies in the Theory of Fiction* (New York: Oxford University Press, 1967); Barbara Hernstein Smith, *Poetic Closure: A Study of How Poems End* (Chicago: University of Chicago Press, 1968); and Pat Rogers, 'The Parthian Dart: Endings and Epilogues in Fiction', *Essays in Criticism*, 42 (1992), 85–106.
[21] *Idler*, 103 (5 April 1760), in *'The Idler' and 'The Adventurer'*, ed. by W. J. Bate and others, The Yale Edition of the Works of Samuel Johnson, 2 (New Haven: Yale University Press, 1963), 314.
[22] Letter 153, in *Correspondence of Thomas Gray*, ed. by Paget Toynbee and Leonard Whibley, 3 vols (Oxford: Clarendon Press, 1935), I, 326–27. The reference to 'queen Anne's days' indicates nostalgia for a more elegantly formal style of complimentary close associated with the turn of the century. For Gray's styling himself a 'Finisher of Letters' see ibid., Letter 85 (14 May 1740), pp. 152–55 (p. 154: postscript to a letter from Horace Walpole to Thomas Ashton).

a Country Churchyard', stressing that it is a '*thing with an end to it*', presumably so as to discourage any suggestions for further revisions. He dramatizes the poem's now finished and perfected state by summarily moving to the closure of his own letter, a closure he immediately unravels by appending a postscript. However, the tension between the ended and the *infinito* lodges itself also in the complimentary close ('ever Yours'), as well as expressing itself in Gray's decision lower down to add a formal close to the postscript (albeit without a signature), a decision sensitive to the general epistolary dilemma not just of how to finish a letter but equally of how actually to conclude a postscript.

Postscripts in Literary Works

The use of postscripts in everyday correspondence was not merely unexceptional in itself, but also allowed for the inclusion of material, such as expressing compliments to a third party or acknowledging a gift, often considered too banal or formulaic for inclusion in the main body of the letter. When we turn to letters written specifically by authors, however, these often show a heightened sensitivity to the literary possibilities or dramatic effect of postscripts. Shenstone, for example, ends a gossipy letter to his friend Richard Jago with a plangent one-line postscript: 'Write soon. It is this moment reported that Pope is dead.'[23] The effect generated is complex, partly produced by the sudden insertion of immediacy ('It is this moment') combined with the jolt the reader gets from receiving such momentous tidings through a postscript.[24] The reader is left in no doubt that Shenstone has deployed the postscript to produce a particular epistolary effect.

Postscripts featuring in novels or plays can be seen as observing conventions that relate to letters in general but also more specialized ones specific to the realm of literature. They tend to flourish most in amorous correspondence, as especially facilitating secret affairs or elopements, and as belonging to an epistolary territory over which women were the acknowledged rulers. In *The Life, Travels, and Adventures of Christopher Wagstaff* (1762), for example, postscripts are listed as part of the more general paraphernalia of love letters, here advertised as articles for sale:

All plain, common, prose *love-letters*, with a reasonable quantity of *protestations*, *tears*, *sighs*, and *groans*, &c. fit for country-gentlemen, or reputable tradesmen, (and their

---

[23] Letter XLVI (30 May 1744), in *The Letters of William Shenstone*, ed. by Williams, p. 89.

[24] Shenstone is one of relatively few eighteenth-century writers to have his correspondence published during his own century. *Letters to Particular Friends* came out in 1770, seven years after his death.

answers) shall be furnished at three-pence a line;—and *postscripts*, not exceeding two lines, shall be allowed the purchaser.²⁵

Postscripts nestle alongside 'tears', 'sighs', and 'groans' as a related symptom of amorous distraction. That the lover's postscript tends to be more intense, or more emotionally abandoned, than the main body of their accompanying letter is evident from Eliza Haywood's amatory fiction. In her *History of Jemmy and Jenny Jessamy* (1753), for example, Jemmy is on the receiving end of just such a heart-wrenching postscript in which his lover declares herself languishing and 'distracted' until she has the opportunity of telling him all that her 'soul is full of'.²⁶ Such emotionally volatile postscripts, however, were not the exclusive preserve of female lovers. In Haywood's later novel *The Fruitless Enquiry* (1767) it is Bellazara's 'devoted slave', Antonius, whose heart spills over in his desperate postscript:

Oh! If your gentle heart as yet has ever guessed what it is to love and to despair, believe my labours in the pangs of both, and in compassion to my woes, afford an answer to these distracted lines.²⁷

The postscript here marks the boundary between reason and unreason, between self-control and emotional abandonment. The heart spills out from its confines at the same time as the letter spills out beyond its formal close.

Whereas in such instances the postscript records the mutation of love into distraction, on other occasions it captures the movement from romance into intrigue. Many stage or fictional postscripts serve the lovers in the planning of trysts or even elopements, with the 'P.S.' acting as a sort of cordon sanitaire between the romantic and the purely logistical elements of the communication. In Aphra Behn's *The Rover* (1677) Florinda uses the cover of a masque to convey to her lover Belvile what he describes to his cavalier comrades as 'the softest letter'. Yet while he lets his friends peruse this letter, its exact content remains withheld from the audience, though Belvile paraphrases its purpose as a gentle invitation for him to assist in Florinda's flight from the controlling authority of her brother. Belvile then hands the letter to Willmore for him to relay to the group, as well as to the overhearing audience, the exact words of the postscript: 'At ten at night—at the garden gate—of which, if I cannot get the key, I will contrive a way over the wall—come attended with a friend or

---

²⁵ Anon., *The Life, Travels, and Adventures, of Christopher Wagstaff, Gentleman, Grandfather to Tristram Shandy: Originally Published in the Latter End of the Last Century* [. . .], 2 vols (London: printed for J. Hinxman, 1762), II, 58.
²⁶ Eliza Haywood, *The History of Jemmy and Jenny Jessamy*, 3 vols (London: printed for T. Gardner, 1753), II, 268.
²⁷ Eliza Haywood, *The Fruitless Enquiry: Being a Collection of Several Entertaining Histories and Occurrences, Which Fell under the Observation of a Lady in her Search after Happiness*, 2nd edn (London: printed for T. Lowndes, 1767), p. 118.

two.'²⁸ What Belville cherishes as the 'softness' and 'kindliness' of the main body of the billet seems entirely absent from the postscript, with its bossy, hard-headed plotting, even to the point of Florinda's asking that Belvile enlist his friends to add numbers to the enterprise.

Postscripts need to do something different from the main letter, or to adopt a different tone or register, to merit being postscripts at all. One way of comprehending the relation between the two elements is that postscripts can be seen as forms of reaction against the preceding letter's status as text or discourse. The postscript exudes a greater worldliness than the main text, joining the sentiments of the letter to the imperatives and constraints of real-world situations. The letter enters and touches the world through the funnel of its postscript. In Haywood's *Betsy Thoughtless* Betsy's friend Miss Forward receives a passionate letter from her distracted lover, who dedicates himself as her 'most grateful adorer, And everlasting slave, R. WILDLY'. The sentimental flourish of the close, however, dissolves into sober practicality in the ensuing postscript, in which, as Miss Forward reports, 'he told me, that he would be in the church-porch in the afternoon, hoping to receive my answer'.²⁹ It is as if the romantic ardour expressed in the letter can achieve agency in the world only through the practical offices afforded by the postscript. This sense of a bathetic drop of tone from the nobly sentimental in the main letter to the officiously pragmatic in the postscript figures in a number of fictive postscripts in post-Restoration literature. It also notably exists in real letters written by Laurence Sterne to his friend and probable lover Catherine (Kitty) Fourmantel. In April 1760 he writes to her a touching letter from London, where she was currently staying. 'You are a most engageing Creature; and I never spend an Evening with you, but I leave a fresh part of my heart behind me', he confides to her, before descending in the postscript to the logistics of their next liaison: 'I will be with You soon after two o'Clock—if not at two—so get yʳ Dinner over by then.'³⁰

Although in the letters just quoted postscripts feature as textual auxiliaries to be called upon by both male and female lovers, their usage became viewed in some quarters as particularly characteristic of female letter-writers. Such an association may have been rooted in the fact that female correspondents of elevated social rank were more likely than men to have had their letters scribed by secretaries, and so to have added holograph postscripts as a personalizing touch.³¹ The particular office performed by women's postscripts

---

[28] Aphra Behn, *The Rover; or, The Banish'd Cavaliers*, in *'Oroonoko', 'The Rover' and Other Works*, ed. by Janet Todd (London: Penguin, 1992), pp. 155–248 (pp. 171–72).

[29] Eliza Haywood, *The History of Betsy Thoughtless*, 4 vols (London: printed by T. Gardner, 1751), I, 152.

[30] Letter 54, in *The Letters*, ed. by Melvyn New and Peter de Voogd, The Florida Edition of the Works of Laurence Sterne, 7–8 (Gainesville: University Press of Florida, 2009), VII, 142.

[31] See James Daybell, *Women Letter-Writers in Tudor England* (Oxford: Oxford University Press,

is discussed in Richard Steele's *Spectator*, 79 (31 May 1711), which, through the moral dissection of 'a Billet or two which came from Ladies', aimed to show women's particular weakness and self-deception in the face of amorous temptation. Steele cites the following letter and afterword as evidence of his case:

Mr. SPECTATOR,
I AM Young, and very much inclined to follow the Paths of Innocence; but at the same time, as I have a plentiful Fortune, and am of Quality, I am unwilling to resign the Pleasures of Distinction, some little Satisfaction in being Admired in general, and much greater in being beloved by a Gentleman, whom I design to make my Husband. But I have a mind to put off entring into Matrimony 'till another Winter is over my Head, which (whatever, musty Sir, you may think of the Matter) I design to pass away in hearing Musick, going to Plays, Visiting, and all other Satisfactions which Fortune and Youth, protected by Innocence and Virtue, can procure for,
   SIR,
  Your most humble Servant,
                    M.T.

'My Lover does not know I like him, therefore having no Engagement upon me, I think to stay, and know whether I may not like any one else better.'[32]

By their postscripts may you know them; or, as Steele observes, quoting his fictitious friend Will. Honeycomb, '[a] *Woman seldom writes her Mind but in her Postscript*'. The deplorable M.T., as the Spectator views her, uses the body of her letter to set out the merits of the sort of gadding life of pleasure that might be pursued, within the bounds of innocence, by an unattached, monied, and attractive young woman. What she confides within the deeper confessional of the postscript, though, is her giddiness and amorous promiscuity, leading the Spectator to comment that 'There is no end of Affection taken in at the Eyes only.'[33]

There are various elements of gender stereotyping on display here. Postscripts are adduced as a female epistolary device partly because they provide a vehicle for intrigues, in the arts of which women were seen as being especially adept. Furthermore, they seemed to epitomize the inveterate contrariness of the female mind, such that the portion of a letter that ought to contain the most incidental matter instead gets used to convey its most important business. That this was a feature of women's epistolary technique is a regular source of comment in fictional works of the period. The eponymous heroine

---

2006), p. 109. This convention is an interesting example of postscripts being used partly to add secondary content to the letter but also to provide authentication along with the signature itself. There is in fact a case for associating postscripts with the domain of the signature rather than the letter-text.
 [32] Repr. in *The Spectator*, ed. by Donald F. Bond, 5 vols (Oxford: Clarendon Press, 1965), I, 338–39.
 [33] Ibid., p. 339.

of Elizabeth Griffith's *The Story of Lady Juliana Harley* (1776), for example, observes to her friend Maria that 'the men say that the purport of a lady's letter is always contained in the postscript'.³⁴ Such a perception may have arisen in part from the related observation, as reported, for example, in *An Apology for the Life of George Anne Bellamy* (1785), that 'a woman's postscript is generally longer than the letter itself', a phenomenon associated in its turn with women's supposed predilection for adding postscripts to postscripts.³⁵ In *The History of Lady Bettesworth and Captain Hastings* (1780), when her eponymous Ladyship reaches the concluding postscript of a letter from a female correspondent, she cannot help exclaiming: 'What, another Postscript! Right woman's letter.'³⁶

Postscripts and Novelistic Immediacy

Postscripts were recognized as belonging mainly to so-called 'familiar' letters, informal letters exchanged between friends or loved ones, and their use accordingly has a general relevance to debates about the proper composition of letters of this kind.³⁷ The very concept of epistolary 'familiarity' lent itself to what nowadays might seem bewildering extremities of idealization. James Howell, for example, in a poem 'To the *knowing* READER, touching Familiar or Letters-*missive*' stationed at the front of his regularly reprinted *Epistolae Ho-Elianae* (1645), celebrates such letters as the 'life of Love, the Loadstones that by rare | Attraction, make souls meet, and melt, and mix'. Elsewhere, he claims that '*Letters* Ideas are, | Of the informing soul, they can declare, | And shew the inward Man.'³⁸ This idealized claim that familiar letters allow for a pure converse between souls, making the contents of the soul readily available and legible to the letter's recipient, exercises a significant influence on those seeking to legislate on the proper conduct of familiar correspondences. In a famous pronouncement Thomas Sprat stated that it was characteristic of

---

³⁴ Elizabeth Griffith, *The Story of Lady Juliana Harley: A Novel in Letters*, 2 vols (London: printed for T. Cadell, 1776), II, 59.

³⁵ George Anne Bellamy, *An Apology for the Life of George Anne Bellamy, Late of Covent-Garden Theatre. Written by Herself*, 6 vols (London: J. Bell, 1785), VI, 120.

³⁶ E.M., *The History of Lady Bettesworth and Captain Hastings in a Series of Letters*, 2 vols (London: printed for F. Noble, 1780), I, 10.

³⁷ On familiar correspondence, see Howard Anderson and Irvin Ehrenpreis, 'The Familiar Letter in the Eighteenth Century: Some Generalizations', in *The Familiar Letter in the Eighteenth Century*, ed. by Howard Anderson and others (Lawrence: University of Kansas Press, 1966), pp. 269–82; Bruce Redford, *The Converse of the Pen: Acts of Intimacy in the Eighteenth-Century Familiar Letter* (Chicago: Chicago University Press, 1986); and, more generally, Clare Brant, *Eighteenth-Century Letters and British Culture* (Basingstoke: Palgrave Macmillan, 2006).

³⁸ James Howell, 'To the *Knowing* Reader', in *Epistolae Ho-Elianae* (London: printed for H. Moseley, 1645), sig. A1^r–2^v.

such letters that in them 'the Souls of Men should appear undress'd'.³⁹ Sprat's remark epitomizes a paradoxical strain in the theorization of the familiar letter in which the materiality of the letter, its status as a physical medium between sender and addressee, tends to get discounted. What replaces it, in the minds of such commentators, is the ideal of a pure non-mediated transfer of interiority between author and recipient.

Much of the discussion surrounding familiar letters in the eighteenth century can be reduced to a division between those wanting, on the one hand, to acknowledge, or, on the other, to deny, the letter's mediating role as a textual genre and material entity within such correspondences.⁴⁰ One highly developed view insisted that familiar letters be seen as essentially proxies for conversation between the parties, with the skill of epistolary composition being judged in terms of its ability to reproduce the immediacy and informality of good conversation. In the Preface to his *Letters and Poems, Amorous and Gallant* (1692), one of the most important early collections of authorial correspondence, William Walsh proposed that 'The Stile of Letters ought to be free, easy and natural; as near approaching to familiar Conversation as possible.'⁴¹ The term that was most often used to capture this epistolary technique was 'undress' (as employed by Sprat earlier), which conveyed a sense both of the nakedness and transparency of such correspondence and also its informality and artless negligence, as when Pope assures his addressee John Caryll that 'my letters are scribbled with all the carelessness and inattention imaginable' so that 'my style, like my soul, appears in its natural undress before my friend'.⁴²

While Pope is endorsing relatively common precepts about the composition of familiar letters, it would be wrong to assume these necessarily enjoyed universal approbation. Another school of thought was inclined to cast doubt on the extent to which letters ought to model themselves on conversation: as John Dennis puts it, the purpose of familiar letters was rather 'to supply Conversation, and not to imitate it'.⁴³ Dennis, in fact, was one of a number of commentators to doubt that familiar letters could be reduced to a single

---

³⁹ See Sprat's 'Account of the Life and Writings of Mr. Abraham Cowley', in *The Works of Mr. Abraham Cowley* (London: printed for Henry Herringman, 1668), sig. D1ʳ.

⁴⁰ I am indebted to the discussion of this and related issues in the section on 'Reading Epistolary Fiction', in Tom Keymer, *Richardson's 'Clarissa' and the Eighteenth-Century Reader* (Cambridge: Cambridge University Press, 1992), pp. 1–15.

⁴¹ William Walsh, Preface to *Letters and Poems, Amorous and Gallant* (London: Jacob Tonson, 1692), sig. A2ᵛ.

⁴² Letter to John Caryll (19 November 1712), in *The Correspondence of Alexander Pope*, ed. by George Sherburn, 5 vols (Oxford: Clarendon Press, 1956), I, 155.

⁴³ See the 'Advertisement' to *Letters upon Several Occasions: Written by and between Mr. Dryden, Mr. Wycherley, Mr. ———, Mr. Congreve, and Mr. Dennis* (London: Sam Briscoe, 1696), in *The Critical Works of John Dennis*, ed. by Edward Niles Hooker, 2 vols (Baltimore: Johns Hopkins University Press, 1939–43), II, 382.

epistolary style, arguing instead that the style of a letter should rise and fall with the contours of the individual subjects under discussion, it being proper, as Dr Johnson was later to point out, 'to depart from familiarity of language upon occasions not familiar'.[44] Moreover, the idea that stylistic negligence should be singled out as a particular virtue of familiar letters clashed with more exalted notions of epistolary craft. For Johnson, in letters as much as any other form of literary production, 'The pebble must be polished with care, which hopes to be valued as a diamond.'[45]

These debates about the properties of familiar letters matter to my task in hand only in so far as they provide some context for thinking about postscripts as a distinctive property of letters of this kind. The occurrence of postscripts in familiar letters both validates and contests certain views about the aesthetic of epistolary familiarity. If letter-writers were being encouraged towards an unbuttoned, negligent style, the casual addition of a postscript could seem in keeping with this. Yet, at the same time, the impression apparently sought by such letters of being immediate, sincere effusions from the heart could be jeopardized if the postscripts attached to them appeared to qualify the sincerity of the preceding text, or to flourish their own credentials as instalments even more immediate to the reader than the letters to which they were appended. Whatever else, postscripts could hardly fail to remind readers of the textual machinery of the epistolary form, in contrast to the view that the familiar letter, in its most idealistic construction as an authentic discourse of the heart, transcended such material mediation. When Alexander Pope, one of the more avid proponents of familiar letters as unmediated 'Emanations of the Heart', oversaw the publication of his own correspondence, the postscripts were in many instances silently removed, partly no doubt as a tidying-up exercise but also perhaps in recognition of the way that they compromised the sense of artless sincerity that the published letters were intended to convey.[46]

The complex relation of postscripts to epistolary 'undress' can be explored in a postscript attached by Sterne to a letter to the Revd Francis Blackburne in November 1750, mainly concerning an arrangement for substitute preaching. The postscript runs as follows:

PS
Our Dean arrives here on Saturday
My Wife sends her Resp^{ts} to You & Y^r Lady.
I have broke open this Letter, to tell You, That as I was Going with it to the Post, I

---

[44] See *Rambler*, 152 (31 August 1751), in *The Rambler*, ed. by W. J. Bate and Albrecht Strauss, 3 vols, The Yale Edition of the Works of Samuel Johnson, 3–5 (New Haven: Yale University Press, 1969), v, 46.

[45] Ibid., p. 47.

[46] The phrase appears in the preface to the quarto edition of *Letters of Mr. Alexander Pope, and Several of his Friends* (London: printed for J. Knapton, L. Gilliver, J. Brindley, and R. Dodsley, 1737) and is reproduced in *The Correspondence of Alexander Pope*, ed. by Sherburn, I, p. xxxvi.

encounterd Hilyard, who desired me in the most pressing Manner, not to let this Affair Transpire—& that You might by no means be acquainted with it—I therefore beg, you will never let him feel the Effects of it, or even Let him know, You know ought about it—for I half promised him,—tho' as the Letter was wrote, I could but send it for your own Use—So beg it may not hurt him, by any Ill Impression, as he has Convinced ⟨all⟩ It proceeded only from Lack of Judgm^t.[47]

The purpose of the postscript was to bind Blackburne to keep secret his knowledge of the disclosures contained in Sterne's letter to him, this being necessitated by Sterne's chance encounter with another party involved in the affair as he was en route to post the letter. It is not unprecedented among his letters either that the postscript mainly helps Sterne cover his tracks, or that its addition involves the letter actually being broken open and then resealed.[48] Whereas, following the encounter with Hildyard, Sterne might have thought better of sending the letter at all, or put himself to the trouble of redrafting it, his decision instead to attach a postscript allows him to get away with minimum disruption of his plans.

When Sarah Fielding, in the Preface to her *Familiar Letters between the Principal Characters in 'David Simple'* (1747), tries to define the meaning of the stock expressions '*familiar easy Style*' or '*concise epistolary Style*', she decides that what they amount to is nothing other than 'short, abrupt, unconnected Periods', of the sort that 'any Man may write'.[49] Sterne's postscript above, in its breathless, abrupt, and staccato sentences, conforms closely to this definition. It is not just written after the main letter but written in a different style, one consciously drawing attention to its own urgency as well as its higher level of immediacy. The sheer vigour of its 'nowness' makes the rest of the letter already seem dated, even historical. Whereas the main body of the letter depends on a relatively leisurely relation to a larger situation, the postscript represents an up-to-the-moment reaction to unfolding events.

All these factors, as well as the general urgency of its rendered experience, make Sterne's postscript reminiscent of the way the same device figures in Samuel Richardson's novels as part of the narrative technique that the novelist himself termed 'writing to the moment'.[50] In the very first letter of Richardson's earliest fiction, Pamela relates to her devout parents the recent death of her 'Lady' and the gift of four guineas in mourning money bestowed on her by

---

[47] Letter 6, in *The Letters*, ed. by New and de Voogd, VII, 16–17.

[48] See the 'Postscript' to *A Political Romance*, in *A Sentimental Journey through France and Italy by Mr. Yorick, to Which are Added the Journal to Eliza and a Political Romance*, ed. by Ian Jack (London: Oxford University Press, 1968), p. 210.

[49] Sarah Fielding, *Familiar Letters between the Principal Characters in 'David Simple'*, 2 vols (London: A. Millar, 1747), I, p. vii.

[50] For Richardson's self-consciousness about his 'new Manner of Writing—to the Moment' see his letter to Lady Bradshaigh of 9 October 1756, in *Selected Letters of Samuel Richardson*, ed. by John Carroll (Oxford: Clarendon Press, 1964), p. 329.

her new master. She has enclosed these in a pill-box, 'wrapt close in Paper', to be delivered by the letter-carrier. The main body of the letter closes as follows:

> I know, dear Father and Mother, I must give you both Grief and Pleasure; and so I will only say, Pray for your *Pamela*; who will ever be,
>
> *Your most dutiful Daughter.*
>
> I have been scared out of my Senses; for just now, as I was folding this Letter, in my late Lady's Dressing-room, in comes my young Master! Good sirs! How was I frightned! I went to hide the Letter in my Bosom, and he seeing me frighted, said, smiling, Who have you been writing to, *Pamela?*—I said, in my Fright, Pray your Honour forgive me!—Only to my Father and Mother. He said, Well then, Let me see how you are come on in your Writing! O how I was sham'd!—He, in my Fright, took it, without saying more, and read it quite thro', and then gave it me again;—and I said, Pray your Honour forgive me;—yet I know not for what. For he was always dutiful to his Parents; and why should he be angry, that I was so to mine! And indeed he was not angry; for he took me by the Hand, and said, You are a good Girl, *Pamela*, to be kind to your aged Father and Mother.[51]

The postscript runs on for a few more sentences, with Pamela winding up on a note of embarrassment at 'making another long Letter'. Oddly, the one signature follows the postscript, not the main body of the letter, though Pamela admits to having been interrupted by her master in the actual process of 'folding this Letter', at which point the signature would normally already have been applied.

Pamela's remark about 'another long Letter' is deceptive inasmuch as the text subsequent to her first close does not read like that of a letter. Its breathless sentence formation, flurried punctuation, marked in particular (like Sterne's letter above) by a liberal use of dashes, and general tone of self-dramatization make it very different from the preceding letter or from Pamela's customary epistolary style elsewhere in the novel. What conditions the style of the postscript are two relations in which it stands to chronology: it gets drafted after the preceding portion of the letter, but also it differs from the remainder of the letter through being composed in a much more proximate temporal relation to the events it actually describes. Its status as a *post*-text (that is, post-dating the main body of the letter) vies with its aspiration to be nearly contemporary with the events that form its own subject-matter.

Pamela's embarrassment at having her letter scrutinized by Mr. B, and at having her general pretensions to letter-writing uncovered, does not stop her immediately recording the incident in the dashed-off postscript. The writing and sending of the postscript place Mr. B immediately at a disadvantage inasmuch as Pamela, her parents, and the novel's readers are privy to both portions of the letter, whereas Mr. B (unbeknown to him) gets only to see

---

[51] Samuel Richardson, *Pamela; or, Virtue Rewarded*, ed. by Thomas Keymer and Alice Wakely (Oxford: Oxford University Press, 2001), p. 12.

the first part. The postscript, as the device often does, introduces a division of knowledge between the participants. The movement from the body of Pamela's letter to her postscript says much about the range of possible fluctuations in Richardson's narrative technique in general. Whereas the memoir novel can range steeply across the past perfect and past pluperfect tenses, Richardson's fictions unfold in only a shallow past, where small gradations of temporal removal attract great significance. The idea of the postscript, as a sort of textual phantasm of scripted instantaneousness, marking a temporal moment occurring, in Pamela's words, only 'just now', is integral to the formal technique of his novels.

Postscripts occur commonly in *Pamela*: of the heroine's first twenty letters, eight contain some postscripted material placed after the initial close. In accordance with the meta-textual role of many postscripts, in terms of their commenting on the foregoing letter or the conduct of the larger correspondence, both Pamela and Mr. Williams use postscripts to manage the clandestine release of the former's letters, with Williams promising to 'come once every Morning, and once every Evening, after School-time, to look for your Letters'.[52] The postscript here allows such narrowly logistical details to be kept separate from the more general exchange of sentiments, but it also reflects the common understanding of postscripts as a textual space in which to stow the more secretive elements of a correspondence, even where the letter and postscript will inevitably be received and read together. Mr. B himself uses an early postscript to notify Pamela's parents of his discovery of his own servant John's role in smuggling out an earlier batch of letters: 'P.S. I find my Man *John* has been the Manager of the Correspondence, in which such Liberties have been taken with me.'[53] Again, it is assumed that the postscript provides the most fitting place for issues to do with the general management of correspondences.

Postscripts occur less regularly in *Clarissa*, though normally retaining the same connotation as in *Pamela* of a level of discourse more emotionally spontaneous and more strenuously seeking coincidence with the present moment than that confined to the main body of the letter.[54] Clarissa's letter to Miss Howe (Letter 57), for example, consists of an initial instalment of the letter, at the end of which Clarissa lays down her pen, 'having tired myself and I dare say you'; a second section added some time later, albeit not marked as a postscript, concluded with a complimentary close after a sentence indicating

---

[52] Ibid., p. 129.
[53] Ibid., p. 94.
[54] Though an obvious element of Richardson's epistolary (and narrative) technique, his letter postscripts have received less attention than might have been expected. The only systematic analysis seems to have been by Donald L. Ball in *Samuel Richardson: The Theory of Fiction* (The Hague: Mouton, 1971), pp. 116–21, 295.

Clarissa's intention to put the letter in the post directly ('I will deposit thus far'); and then a final instalment scribbled in pencil on the outside of the letter, after Clarissa has discovered a second letter from Anna waiting for her downstairs.[55] The drafting of the letter in discrete stages allows for the process of its composition itself to become dramatic and for variation in Clarissa's mood and epistolary style. In addition, the longer the letter, the greater the extent to which it must inevitably post-date its own narrative starting-point, so the use of instalments or postscripts allows the letter to update itself constantly against the clock, to haul itself back into contemporaneity with the narrative moment.

Particularly in *Pamela*, the frequency of postscripts seems much in excess of what one would expect in conventional correspondence. In Richardson's own exemplary volume of *Familiar Letters on Important Occasions* (1741), from which the idea of *Pamela* first arose, they occur very sparingly, and with no hint of the resource that they provide elsewhere for Richardson in his capacity as a novelist.[56] Of course, the extent to which it is germane to remark on this, and indeed to scrutinize Richardson's fictional letters as specimens of real letters, evincing real epistolary properties, has been subject to some debate. Janet Altman, for example, insists that the letters merely exist to deliver the narrated world, and that Richardson shows little interest in actively exploiting conventions of letter-writing.[57] Such an opinion is broadly in keeping with a long-standing critical view that Richardson chose the epistolary method simply as a device to render the inner processes of the mind in the most complete and intimate manner, with the letters themselves just acting, in Ian Watt's expression, as a 'short-cut, as it were, to the heart'.[58] A corollary of this general issue is the extent to which we should view Richardson's epistolary heroines as, indeed, letter-writers, or as characterized in a significant way by the avidity with which they compose letters or by their distinctive epistolary characteristics. Would it be any more true to view Pamela, for example, as an obsessive letter-writer than to view Hamlet as a compulsive orator? It would follow that if the novel were not asking us to attend to Pamela's letter-writing, neither would it be asking us to take note of her unusually assiduous use of postscripts or to think about those issues of epistolary etiquette or divided selfhood that might be indicated by the regular usage of such a device.

It is probably best that Pamela's postscripts should remain invisible to cri-

[55] Samuel Richardson, *Clarissa; or, the History of a Young Lady*, ed. by Angus Ross (Harmondsworth: Penguin, 1985), p. 244.
[56] For Richardson's attitude towards familiar letters see John's Carroll's introduction to *Selected Letters of Samuel Richardson*, pp. 31–35; and Elizabeth Bergen Brophy, *Samuel Richardson: The Triumph of Craft* (Knoxville: University of Tennessee Press, 1974), pp. 38–49.
[57] Janet Gurkin Altman, *Epistolarity: Approaches to a Form* (Columbus: Ohio State Press, 1982).
[58] Ian Watt, *The Rise of the Novel: Studies in Defoe, Richardson and Fielding* (London: Chatto & Windus, 1957), p. 195.

tical attention, in the specific sense that it would be wrong to read them as indexing her particular proclivities as a correspondent. However, for Richardson the novelist, it hardly goes too far to suggest that the postscript might be seen as the symbol of his fictive method. That tiny interval of lapsed time separating the body-text from its postscript is the space that Richardson's fictions crave to occupy. It is the space in which the mind can return on itself, and in which the postscript's ability to trump the foregoing text with its claim to a higher level of immediacy hints erotically at dizzying vistas of confession and unbosoming. Perhaps, most of all, Richardson's aspiration to the full flow of dramatic immediacy, his 'writing to the moment', could most perfectly be realized by composing, not text, but post-text. It is on its very post-dating of the previous moment of writing that the postscript bases its claim for currency with the narrative instant. Perhaps only two letters exist in the English language plausibly purporting to capture the absolute coincidence of experiential and epistolary time: 'P.S.'.

The most high-profile opponent of the Richardsonian technique, and especially of the laboured artificiality of his attempt at writing to the moment, is of course Henry Fielding. What has received less comment is the extent to which Fielding seems to have associated Richardson's novelistic trademark with the regularity of his use of letter postscripts. In Fielding's *Shamela* (1741) the eponymous heroine, the bawd Mrs Jervis, and Parson Tickletext all hang postscripts on the end of their letters. Having described to her mother her departure from Squire Booby's house, Shamela herself adds the following postscript:

P.S. Just as I was going to send this away a Letter is come from my Master, desiring me to return, with a large Number of Promises.—I have him now as sure as a Gun, as you will perceive by the Letter itself, which, I have inclosed to you.[59]

The art of Fielding's spoof was to insist on noticing aspects of Richardson's text that a more neutral reading would have silently passed over, among which is the egregious epistolary technique of regular use of postscripts. The passage above, with the manipulative Shamela glorying in her proximity to her grand prize, sends up the clumsiness of the 'Just as' moment, so precious to the novelistic technique of *Pamela*. Fielding appreciated just how germane the postscript was to unlocking and discrediting the fictional method of the man who was to be his main professional adversary over the next decade, a point underlined by the way that his own novella ends, or perhaps more accurately, stops: that is, with a postscript.[60]

NORTHUMBRIA UNIVERSITY　　　　　　　　　　　　　　　　RICHARD TERRY

[59] Henry Fielding, *'Joseph Andrews' and 'Shamela'*, ed. by Douglas Brooks-Davies, rev. by Thomas Keymer (Oxford: Oxford University Press, 1999), p. 334.
[60] Ibid. (Letter from Parson Tickletext to Parson Oliver).

RUINS AND VISIONS: STEPHEN SPENDER IN OCCUPIED GERMANY

The English poet Stephen Spender almost missed the opportunity to report on post-war Germany. When he was interviewed for a job on the Allied Control Commission, which would supervise the occupation of the country, he was greeted with a question: 'Your qualifications don't seem very concise. You describe yourself as a writer and a Fireman. What do you mean by that?'[1] Ironically, it is Spender's multi-faceted personality which ensures the interest of his narrative, published in 1946 to critical acclaim under the title *European Witness*. He was eventually granted a six-month assignment as an officer by the Control Commission: he travelled twice through the British zone, first in July and August 1945, then in September and October 1945. He described his mission as follows:

I went to Germany [. . .] to inquire into the lives and ideas of German intellectuals, with a particular view to discovering any surviving talent in German literature. [. . .] Later, I added to the general purpose of this mission the one of inquiring into the condition of libraries.[2]

Spender's account represents one of the first studies of the devastated country to appear in English after the end of the war. In 1947 at least three major texts on the same subject came out. Robert Birley, an educational adviser in the British zone, published a lecture on 'The German Problem and the Responsibility of Britain'.[3] James Stern's *The Hidden Damage* was written in a more literary vein, even though Stern drew on his experience as a member of USBUS, the US Strategic Bombing Survey.[4] Lastly, the socialist activist Victor Gollancz tried to direct public attention to the critical living standards of the occupied in his pamphlet *In Darkest Germany*.[5] Spender struck a middle ground between Birley's and Gollancz's solemn rhetoric and Stern's congenial, reader-oriented war narrative. In part, this article will consider the extent of *European Witness*'s originality, and the reliability of Spender's report on defeated Germany. It will assess Spender's views on witnessing, before examining the purpose and execution of his mission and, finally, the nature of his reflections on German guilt and Nazi propaganda.

---

[1] John Sutherland, *Stephen Spender: The Authorized Biography* (London: Penguin, 2005), p. 298.
[2] Stephen Spender, *European Witness* (London: Hamish Hamilton, 1946), p. 6. Further page references will be given in the body of the text.
[3] Robert Birley, *The German Problem and the Responsibility of Britain* (London: SCM Press, 1947).
[4] James Stern, *The Hidden Damage* (New York: Harcourt, Brace, 1947; repr. London: Chelsea Press, 1990).
[5] Victor Gollancz, *In Darkest Germany* (London: Gollancz, 1947).

The Ethics of Witnessing

The title of Spender's book, *European Witness*, presents the narrative as a testimony, emphasizing his commitment to truthfulness. At this time, Spender travelled in a country that had become almost inaccessible to civilians without a commission. The British military allowed him to speak freely with Germans in pursuance of his duties, a rare privilege in the days of non-fraternization (p. 11). He thus felt all the more the responsibility to report his findings accurately. However, it has been pointed out that Spender does not content himself with relating his experience. He makes a plea for the return of Germany to the European family. He 'takes the witness stand', as Shoshana Felman argues:

> To testify—before a court of law or before the court of history and of the future; to testify likewise, before an audience of readers or spectators [. . .] [is] to *address* another, to impress upon a listener, to *appeal* to a community. To testify is always, metaphorically, to take the witness stand, or to take the position of the witness insofar as the narrative account of the witness is at once engaged in an appeal and bound by an oath. To testify is thus not merely to narrate but to commit oneself, and to commit the narrative to others: to *take responsibility*—in speech—for history or for the truth of an occurrence, for something which, by definition, goes beyond the personal, in having general (nonpersonal) validity and consequences.[6]

Evidently, in writing as a witness Spender subjects himself to high standards of accuracy. From this perspective, any exposed departure from 'truth' would do a disservice to the author's cause. Yet, how far does Spender live up to the ethics of witnessing? If, as Phyllis Frus argues, 'we cannot retrieve the past except from texts',[7] then the validity of Spender's testimony may only be measured against other texts—his own and those of his contemporaries.

One wonders whether Spender's position as a commissioned observer 'contaminated' his narrative. But, at least on the surface, the assignment does not appear to have undermined his critical distance. In the chapter called 'Nausea' he does not mince his words about the evils of Occupation:

> Other people would probably explain the horror—the longing to get away at all costs—which affects the majority of the members of the Forces occupying Germany as a result of the ruined surroundings, the lack of entertainment and the generally depressing atmosphere. But I think that subtler and deeper than this is a sense of hopelessness which is bred of the relationship of Occupiers and Occupied. [. . .] The sense that the Occupying Forces are as helpless as the people who are occupied and that therefore the relationship between Occupiers and Occupied cannot be a good one because it cannot be based on the human impulse to help one's neighbour—that is what is depressing about the Occupation. The relationship can be one of charity, bribery, corruption,

---

[6] Shoshana Felman, 'In an Era of Testimony: Claude Lanzmann's *Shoah*', *Yale French Studies*, 44 (1991), 39–81 (pp. 39–40).

[7] Phyllis Frus, *The Politics and Poetics of Journalistic Narrative* (Cambridge: Cambridge University Press, 1994), p. 229.

looting, black marketing, rape, all sorts of things: anything except free, mutual and creative. (pp. 61–63)

Although Spender eventually overcomes this crisis of self-doubt and resumes the tour, he questions the practices of his employer, the Allied Control Commission. Though, if he criticizes the occupation as a system, he refrains from lambasting anyone in particular. Indeed, when he deals with individuals, his official functions prevent him from dropping his reserve, as may be evidenced by variations between the drafts of *European Witness*.

It is important to note that Spender's text comes in three different versions. The poet kept a journal during his German travels, and started publishing extracts in the literary review *Horizon* in 1945. The articles were then reworked to form part of *European Witness*. However, Spender's journals were later edited as a separate volume, and their content is not quite identical to what appeared in *Horizon*. In general, the author seems to have been more careful in *European Witness*, since he avoided criticizing German officials and intellectuals too harshly. For instance, he mentioned disquieting rumours about Adenauer in his diary:

I am told that a German employed in the *Kölnischer Kourier* [sic] had offered his resignation some days ago. When asked why he wanted to leave he said: 'Because I am on Adenauer's black list.' He maintained that Adenauer kept a black list of employees in the Civil Government who supported politics other than those of the Christian Democrats. He said this was difficult to prove about Adenauer, as people were too frightened to speak.[8]

This passage was not included in *European Witness*. However, it would have explained the persistent tensions between the mayor of Cologne and the British, who would dismiss him in October 1945, arguing that 'all the effort was going into political intrigues'.[9] Adenauer seems to have remembered the episode: when he eventually became the first Chancellor of the FRG, he established a better rapport with de Gaulle than with his opposite numbers across the Channel, and mistrusted London's détente policy towards Russia. Spender's minor omission thus slightly distorts the overall image communicated in his text.

Similarly, the author baulked at confessions that could tarnish his reputation as a lieutenant. A passage in the *Journals* suggesting that the autobiographer indulged in rather innocent black market dealings, for example, was altered in the travel book. The original lines read as a half-confession: 'Whilst I was in Dortmund seeing the Oberburgermeister, he exchanged one cigarette for two

---

[8] Stephen Spender, *Journals 1939–1983* (London: Faber & Faber, 1985), p. 73.
[9] Thomas Kielinger, *Crossroads and Roundabouts: Junctions in German–British Relations* (London: Foreign and Commonwealth Office, 1997), p. 201.

cigars, which seemed good business to me.'[10] In *European Witness* the author attributes the haggling to his driver:

While we were in Dortmund I went to see the Oberbürgermeister for a few minutes. When I came back to the car, I found that my driver had two cigars. He explained to me that he had got these in exchange for one cigarette, which seemed to me an extraordinary black market deal. (p. 209)

The modifications and excisions can be explained by the late publication of the *Journals* in 1985, at a time when Spender could write more freely about the events. However, these ongoing revisions draw attention to the ambiguous genre status of *European Witness*. While the other versions of Spender's report present themselves as clearly non-fictional, the introduction of the 1946 narrative admits the presence of fictional elements: 'In some cases, I have invented characters or incidents in order to convey some impression which could not be conveyed more directly' (p. 6). If this concession apparently runs counter to Spender's commitment to stick to facts as a witness, it also seems inconsistent with his very first sentence, which locates the book in the realm of non-fiction: 'This book is a Travel Book of a conventional kind' (p. 6).

In fact, the writer challenges the codes of literary non-fiction. Barbara Lounsberry defines the genre according to four criteria: documentable subject-matter chosen from the real world, exhaustive research, the scene, and fine writing.[11] Spender's narrative fulfils most of those conditions, yet the third one is clearly open to question. Lounsberry describes 'the scene' in the following manner:

Instead of merely 'reporting' or 'discussing' an object or event, the artist of non-fiction recasts it in narrative form. The remarkable effect of such transformation is that the moment is reprised; it lives again, yet with the subtle lights and shadings of the author's vision. The facts gain life, depth, and subtle reverberation. Often the scene (or scenes) will be only part of the artful form a work of literary non-fiction may take. Nevertheless, the scene is frequently a sign that the form of the work is consciously artful.[12]

The problem lies in the interpretation of the phrase 'recasts it in narrative form'. Does it imply that writers of literary non-fiction have the right to pen composite characters? American 'New Journalism' did not flinch from taking such liberties in the 1960s, but most editors and critics considered them unacceptable when Spender was writing his account. Interestingly, when he published two extracts from *European Witness* in *Vogue*,[13] he assumed the

[10] *Journals 1939–1983*, p. 85.
[11] Barbara Lounsberry, *The Art of Fact: Contemporary Artists of Non-Fiction* (New York: Greenwood Press, 1990), pp. xiii–xv.
[12] Ibid., pp. xiv–xv.
[13] See Sutherland, p. 318.

right to make up events based on his experiences—a claim that would have startled the New Journalists. Gay Talese noted in the preface to his collection *Fame and Obscurity*:

> The new journalism, though often reading like fiction, is not fiction. It is, or should be, as reliable as the most reliable reportage although it seeks a larger truth than is possible through the mere compilation of verifiable facts, the use of direct quotations, and adherence to the rigid organizational style of the older form.[14]

Spender's apparent belief that fiction can sometimes express a feeling better than fact leads him to insist on what he considers typical. Thus, each episode in his narrative must function as a vignette that contributes to the whole: 'The book is simply a collection of impressions, with a view to building up a general picture of what I saw in Germany in 1945. It is the general picture which counts, not the isolated incidents' (p. 6). This method lends coherence to the narrative but sometimes causes the author to lack precision and lapse into clichés. The description of ravaged Cologne, as well as the conversation with Polish displaced persons, in this way belongs to the commonplaces of war literature. In the chapter which Spender devotes to the fate of uprooted Poles, the ill-treatment they received at the hands of the German population serves as an unsurprising leitmotif:

> They talked very bad German, expressing themselves with heavy gestures rather than with words. 'You English are much too kind to these Germans, much too kind,' one of them said. [. . .] 'How do you think they treated us before?' the youngest but one asked. The chorus went on, passing from one to another. (p. 33)

A similar description can be found in James Stern's *The Hidden Damage*:

> The moment we seemed prepared to listen, they all began to talk at once, in a kind of pidgin-German difficult to understand. [. . .] In their various ways they were all attempting to express the same thought—their utter bewilderment at the way Americans had treated a German, to whom they referred as '*dieser Hund.*' With weird gesticulations (punctuated by pouncing on our cigarette butts) they pantomimed how Nazi soldiers would have behaved under similar circumstances.[15]

The close correspondence between the two descriptions demonstrates the overall reliability of Spender's report. Nevertheless, the comparison also shows that by the time *The Hidden Damage* was published in 1947, Polish displaced persons had become a familiar literary topos that Spender had helped to introduce. He does not individualize the Poles, so it is impossible to determine if he describes a precise event or if he reconstructs a scene from similar occurrences that he witnessed. More broadly, he encourages readers to generalize about displaced persons.

[14] Gay Talese, *Fame and Obscurity* (New York: World Publishing, 1970), p. vii.
[15] James Stern, p. 96.

What sets *European Witness* apart is Spender's own tendency to generalize from isolated images and to marshal them into a developing narrative. The quoted section ends with a statement on the Poles' smouldering frustration and compares them to other war-stricken groups: 'I have seen this expression in the faces of the desperate young men of the demobilized Reichswehr, also in those of the French repatriated prisoners and in those of other men and women labelled Displaced Persons' (p. 35). In this instance, parataxis smoothes over the differences between those three groups. Spender thus questions the very process of categorizing, yet his all-embracing statement is clearly distanced from the individuals themselves. This taste for the bird's-eye view means that, on occasion, he is tempted to oversimplify. Nevertheless, Spender intersperses the narrative with single portraits that give the book its remarkable balance. These enable him to question stereotypes that some of his collective portraits convey. When he describes an American officer, for example, he puts the notion of national character into perspective:

> He was quiet in manner, interested in everyone, generous, humorous and prudent. He was a shining example [. . .] of the great American virtues which are as rare among Americans as are the best national qualities among the members of any nation, with the result that the more we see of English, French or Americans, especially when they are away from their homes, the less we see in them their national virtues. (p. 69)

Although friendliness and humour are readily attributed to Americans, Spender mischievously goes against the grain by adding the far less conventional attributes of prudence and unobtrusiveness. He prompts the reader to distrust sweeping assertions about any nation, including the unmentioned Germans. Although the narrative is not devoid of clichés, Spender heightens awareness of them and refrains from caricature. He demonstrates that a strict commitment to non-fiction is not a sine qua non for accuracy, as a comparison with James Stern's approach will show.

In *The Hidden Damage*, Stern's short editorial note merely states that 'some names have been changed: "Mervyn", for example, was actually Wystan— W. H. Auden'.[16] Such minor amendments imply that the book is generally true to life, yet the writer occasionally indulges in caricature to entertain his readership, as in the instance when he depicts the owners of a cheese factory:

> Monsieur (impossible to call him *Herr*, *Herr Baron*, or even *Graf*) with leather motoring goggles under a *chapeau sportif*; and Madame, a bundle half-smothered in an *imperméable*, a wide-brimmed hat flattened down over her ears by a mud-colored motoring veil and tied beneath a vague promontory that must have been Madame's chin. [. . .] There came a jingle-jangle of a bell, the clip-clop of a horse, and into the yard drove Monsieur and Madame Fromage.[17]

[16] Ibid., p. xi.
[17] Ibid., pp. 243–44.

Despite the fact that Spender can also exhibit a sense of humour, the ethics of witnessing would forbid him from thus misrepresenting his subjects for comic purposes. Stern has more freedom of representation than Spender and Gollancz, since he is chiefly engaged in a personal literary project, and does not attempt to submit his testimony before the court of history. The differences between *European Witness* and *In Darkest Germany* also bring to light the former's originality. Gollancz relied on a collection of figures and photographs to carry conviction. He gathered an impressive amount of data on the German population, and was willing to offer his readers considerable detail:

At the [. . .] conference I was given body-weights in the North Rhine Province, as follows. Children from 6–12: in Düsseldorf (I think the Regierungsbezirk, but possibly the town only), normal 81.4%, middle (loss of weight less than 3%) 4.8%, bad (loss of weight more than 3%) 14%.[18]

On the surface, *In Darkest Germany* provides more compelling information and statistics than Spender's report. However, Gollancz's 144 snapshots bring us back to the vexed question of 'truth' in (semi-)documentary narratives. On the one hand, he avails himself of the photographs to authenticate his account: 'I thought that my visible presence would add verisimilitude, and obviate the charge, for instance, that these were really agency photographs taken in China in the year 1932.'[19] On the other hand, when he wishes to alarm the reader, he painstakingly underlines the gap between verisimilitude and elusive reality: 'I find most of my photographs inadequate, because the photographer was such a brilliant artist that he just couldn't help getting an effect of beauty even out of what was disgusting and vile.'[20] Spender's refusal to draw an impassable line between fiction and non-fiction spares him such rhetorical meanderings.

The idiosyncratic combination of a non-fictional core and representative semi-fictional episodes, of aphorisms and detailed portrayals, renders *European Witness* one of the most nuanced British accounts of post-war Germany. The author recasts the ethics of witnessing with the tools of fiction, yet the guiding deontological principle remains unchanged and holds the book together: the writer does not allow himself to stray from exact fact if doing so would distort the bulk of his testimony. Rejecting the fallacy of objective reportage, pointing out the difficulties of testimony but accepting its moral imperative, he offers a persuasive account within the parameters he has set: 'It is the general picture which counts, not the isolated incidents, which, in themselves, may do less than justice to some of the people or things I saw, more than justice to others' (p. 6).

[18] Victor Gollancz, *In Darkest Germany* (London: Gollancz, 1947), p. 47.
[19] Ibid., p. 15.
[20] Ibid., p. 70.

Spender's Missions

Spender frequently confessed doubts over the aims of his trip to Germany and, indeed, acknowledged the absurdity of its main objectives. He was supposed to investigate the intellectual life of Germany, but was presented with closed, run-down universities, isolated professors, and wandering students. The only leading intellectuals with whom he had a conversation are Ernst Robert Curtius and Ernst Jünger. Consequently, he was sometimes obliged to use second-hand information, and he cautiously quotes his sources in order to limit any risk to his testimony:

> Melchers [a librarian] gave me the names of a few German writers living to-day (he thought) in Germany: Friedrich Georg Jünger, the poet, brother of Ernst Jünger; Stefan Anders, a story writer; Werner Bergengruen, novelist and poet; Theodor Haecker, Catholic philosopher [. . .] A friend of mine who met him in Italy tells me that Anders has written a three-volume novel about the Nazi regime. (pp. 56–57)

Spender thus misspells the name of Stefan Andres, who would become one of the most successful German writers in the 1950s, and hesitates concerning his whereabouts (in fact, Andres came back to Germany from Positano only in 1949). However, it is correct that Stefan Andres wrote a long allegory of Nazism, the *Sintflut* trilogy, which would be published between 1949 and 1959. Therefore, despite a few mistakes, Spender imparts significant literary news to his English readership.

Notwithstanding this short list of contemporaries who represent so many glimpses of hope, he implies that most of Germany's cultural dynamism has vanished. The interview with Curtius in the 'Rhineland Journal' includes a direct statement from the Bonn scholar:

> I said that I had come to inquire into the intellectual life of Bonn. C— said that there was almost no intellectual life left in the whole of Germany, but that nevertheless it was important that I should talk to people and excellent that a writer like myself should understand what was happening in Germany.[21]

The interview was almost entirely deleted in *European Witness*, because Curtius had protested that a promise of confidentiality had been broken when Spender published 'Rhineland Journal' without his approval. They had originally befriended each other in the 1930s, and Spender confesses in his diaries that the desire to see Curtius provided a strong motivation for the German tour: 'My private reason [. . .] was to [. . .] concern myself with the fate of my friend from pre-war days, the great scholar and teacher and critic, Ernst Robert Curtius.'[22] As an academic of international standard and a connoisseur of European literatures, Curtius ought to have represented a key source

---

[21] Stephen Spender, 'Rhineland Journal', *Horizon*, 12 (1945), 394–413 (p. 400).
[22] *Journals 1939–1983*, p. 59.

of information for Spender. Instead, the relationship with Curtius throws light on the difficulty of Spender's undertaking: his personal errand failed and led to an estrangement from his former friend; and, moreover, Curtius's declarations (as recorded in 'Rhineland Journal') raise the question of how meaningful it is to assess the intellectual life of a country in a profound crisis.

The English observer also voices concern about another objective of his visit to Germany, namely an enquiry into the condition of libraries, which he undertook in September and October 1945. Initially, logistic and administrative difficulties prevented him from accomplishing this: 'The German library system is very complicated, and I never fully grasped it, as, owing to the fact that my car was nearly always broken down, I was not able to carry out my work and my inquiries into libraries at all satisfactorily' (pp. 149–50). The writer's incomplete knowledge of local conditions and his Kafkaesque driver compound the sense of chaos. In addition, Spender exhibits reluctance to carry out his duties. He reflects on the ethical implications of purging libraries of Nazi books: as a liberal, he has qualms about restricting freedom of expression. In fact, *European Witness* signals his return to the liberalism of his youth after a protracted flirtation with Communism during the 1930s.[23] In the long poem 'Vienna' (1934), he lamented the crushing of the socialist uprising by the Austrian government, and voiced his contempt for the conservative leaders:

> Let no one disagree let Dollfuss
> Fey, Stahremberg [sic], the whole bloody lot
> Appear frequently, shaking hands at street corners
> Looking like bad sculptures of their photographs.[24]

He does not adopt such a militant tone when considering Nazi works in German libraries for *European Witness*. Indeed, his liberal standpoint resembles Lieutenant Arran's, an American officer he meets in Bonn: 'Above all, Arran impressed by his unobtrusive desire to understand everyone's point of view, qualified by a determination not to be taken in' (p. 69).

Even at the peak of his Communist phase, Spender distrusted the idea of a temporary dictatorship for the common good. In his Left Book Club tract *Forward from Liberalism* he remarked that

> dictatorship is a necessary but unpleasant phase, which is abandoned as soon as the new society is firmly established. Dictatorship is not merely unsocialistic in principle, it is also, as the Russians have learned, in many ways an inefficient way of governing.[25]

As an employee of the Allied Control Commission, which ruled over Ger-

---

[23] See Sutherland, p. 261.
[24] Stephen Spender, 'Vienna', repr. in *New Collected Poems* (London: Faber & Faber, 2004), pp. 47–67 (p. 52).
[25] Stephen Spender, *Forward from Liberalism* (London: Gollancz, 1937), p. 287.

many, Spender harboured grave misgivings about curtailing fundamental rights. An uneasy censor, he would much later go on to co-found Index on Censorship in 1971, an organization denouncing cases of censorship all around the world. Nevertheless, even though post-war British authorities were not planning to destroy Nazi books but only to remove them from the shelves, Spender argues that the process might remind German people of Nazi methods. In this context, it is interesting that Gollancz also highlights the occasional abuses of this procedure. It applied not only to Fascist publications but also to any book that 'contained propaganda directed against the United Nations'.[26] Coincidentally, Gollancz visited a Hamburg public library about a year after Spender, so that he was in a position to give a more comprehensive assessment. Among the works that had been removed from the shelves, he found Tagore's *Nationalism* and Lenin's *Imperialism*, which might have caused embarrassment among the British forces at a time when the imperial power was still struggling with the Indian independence movement. Furthermore, the occupation of Germany was similar in some regards to a colonial undertaking, a fact which the two undesirable volumes would only confirm. As Lord Annan, who had served as a young officer in the Control Commission, argued in a 1987 BBC interview: 'Military Government officials resembled civilised and agreeable officers in a rather forward-looking Bedouin country—tending to treat Germans in the beginning very much as intelligent natives.'[27] Little wonder the victors were not keen on circulating essays that showed them in such a light.

Spender overlooks these abuses, but his criticism digs deeper. Even in the case of Nazi literature, he becomes convinced that the purge does not strike at the root of evil. Many librarians had anticipated British demands and put away unwanted volumes, being, it appears, familiar with such practices:

> The Librarians who were closest to the Nazi policy were the quickest to understand and interpret our aims in the most far-reaching way. For example, a librarian in Aachen, said to me, to show how quick she was to understand: '[. . .] You see, throughout the Nazi regime, we kept all the books by Jewish and socialist writers in a special cellar, under lock and key, as having only historical and scientific interest. All we have to do now is to take out these books and put them on our open shelves, while at the same time we lock up all the Nazi books, because now *they* only have historical and scientific interest.' (p. 153)

Spender points out a certain moral relativism, which Hannah Arendt would analyse three years later:

> Perhaps the most striking and frightening aspect of the German flight from reality is the habit of treating facts as though they were mere opinions. [. . .] The average

---

[26] Gollancz, p. 100.
[27] See Kielinger, p. 144.

German honestly believes this free-for-all, this nihilistic relativity about facts, to be the essence of democracy. In fact, of course, it is a legacy of the Nazi regime. The lies of totalitarian propaganda are distinguished from the normal lying of non-totalitarian regimes in times of emergency by their consistent denial of the importance of facts in general: all facts can be changed and all lies can be made true.[28]

How did the NSDAP convey this propaganda? Its main vehicles were mass meetings, radio, and film. Indeed, Goebbels gave priority to the spoken word over the written one, as he explained in *Kampf um Berlin*:

Auch die moderne Propaganda beruht noch im wesentlichen auf der Wirkung des gesprochenen Wortes. Revolutionäre Bewegungen werden nicht von großen Schriftstellern, sondern von großen Rednern gemacht.[29]

Even modern propaganda still relies, essentially, on the impact of the spoken word. Revolutionary movements are not made by great writers, but by great orators.

This reveals another limit of the poet's errand: since the Nazis did not regard books as their preferred means of influencing German citizens, purging libraries was likely to prove an insufficient method of re-education. Despite the efforts of the regime, pro-Hitler pamphlets never reached large numbers of the population. Besides, as Margaret F. Stieg underlines, 'library use was low and, until the end of the 1930s, declining'.[30] Spender implies his awareness of the situation when he presents Goebbels's *Michael* as one of the few Nazi books that continued to be read during the war (p. 192). The attention paid by British forces to Fascist volumes thus seems legitimate, but ineffective in producing a change of heart among the occupied. Spender could not but feel disillusioned with the task he had been assigned. The author remained pessimistic over the Germans' ability to take part in a democracy after the Second World War but, on the whole, he rejected the concept of collective guilt.

Spender on Collective Guilt

In *European Witness* Spender devotes several pages to the responsibility of the German people for Nazi crimes. The question naturally lay at the core of the post-war debate that took place between the occupiers and the occupied, as well as between German exiles and members of the *innere Emigration*. In 1944 and the first half of 1945, proponents of the collective-guilt theory dominated the discussion. During the last months of the war British authorities encouraged radio broadcasts that supported the themes of German responsibility for crimes, or German dishonesty. The wartime BBC grew less willing

---

[28] Hannah Arendt, *Essays in Understanding, 1930–1954* (New York: Harcourt, 1994), pp. 251–52.

[29] Joseph Goebbels, *Kampf um Berlin: Der Anfang* (Munich: Zentralverlag der NSDAP, 1935), p. 18.

[30] Margaret F. Stieg, *Public Libraries in Nazi Germany* (Tuscaloosa: University of Alabama Press, 1992), p. 266.

to draw distinctions between 'Nazis' and 'Germans'.³¹ Distinguished German refugees or German-speaking intellectuals, such as the Swiss psychiatrist Carl Jung, supported this inflammatory chorus. In an article published in the *Schweizer Rundschau* of June 1945 he goes so far as to argue that the Germans had suffered from a hysterical disposition, a condition which, in his eyes, did not remove their collective guilt.³²

Spender reserves a whole chapter to a review of Jung's article, yet expresses strong reservations about it. He refuses to turn the question of guilt into an exclusively German issue, and requests every citizen of the world to look to his conscience and ask himself 'whether he was in any degree indirectly responsible for Nazism and all its consequences' (p. 162). Jung argued that the German rush into the abyss must not be regarded as a separate phenomenon, for it reveals a long-standing European malady, yet Spender, as a committed citizen of Europe, refrained from stigmatizing the Old World and introduced a much more generalized concept of guilt which transcended borders. This was in keeping with Spender's consistent portrayal of himself as an internationalist. His early poem 'oh young men oh young comrades' sounds like an interpretation of the Communist slogan 'Workers of the world, unite!', since the addressees are not shown to belong to any particular nation:

> Oh comrades, step beautifully from the solid wall
> advance to rebuild and sleep with friend on hill
> advance to rebel and remember what you have
> no ghost ever had, immured in his hall.³³

Even in the collection *Ruins and Visions*, published in the middle of the Second World War, Spender never lost sight of his internationalist tenets. It is clear that in a poem such as 'To Poets and Airmen', dedicated to his friend Michael Jones who died while training, he acknowledged the necessity of fighting against Nazism:

> [. . .] Become what
> Things require. The expletive word.
> The all-night-long screeching metal bird.
> And all of time shut down in one shot
> Of night, by a gun uttered.³⁴

Yet, in 'The War God', which immediately precedes this text in *Ruins and Visions*, he shows how victors and vanquished exchange roles in an endless cycle of retaliation:

---

³¹ See Perry Biddiscombe, *The Denazification of Germany: A History 1945–1950* (Stroud: Tempus, 2007), p. 108.
³² Carl Gustav Jung, 'Nach der Katastrophe', *Neue Schweizer Rundschau*, 13 (1945), 67–88.
³³ Spender, 'oh young men oh young comrades', in *New Collected Poems*, pp. 15–16 (p. 16).
³⁴ Spender, 'To Poets and Airmen', ibid., pp. 164–65 (p. 165).

> And not the slain
> Nor the slayer, forgive,
> Nor do wild shores
> Of passionate histories
> Close on endless love;
> Though hidden under seas
> Of chafing despair,
> Love's need does not cease.[35]

The final line can be read as a warning to the Allies. They should beware the 'semen of new hatred' after victory.[36]

More generally, it is important to note that while Spender's internationalism leaves the door open for Germany's return to the *concert des nations*, it does not necessarily reduce the extent of German guilt. Robert Birley pointed out that setting the country apart from the international context might provide its citizens with the excuse of a grim cultural exception:

> There is some danger in continually speaking as if they were a people whose problems are entirely their own. It is liable to foster that exclusiveness, which is one of their weaknesses. Too often they look back with pride to that unfortunate remark of Tacitus, the first of journalists to exploit the German problem, that the Germans were unlike any other people. It will bring a much needed realism in Germany if speakers from other countries, and England in particular, when visiting Germany would speak of the crisis of our civilisation as one affecting other nations also.[37]

Spender does not attempt to exonerate the occupied in any way, but he insists that German responsibility—whose extent remained to be defined—does not authorize the occupiers to treat each German as though he were not an individual, but only a member of a compromised race. As an autobiographer, a lyric poet, and a liberal, it is not surprising that Spender should advocate an individualist approach. Moreover, in view of his origins, he could be expected to plead for fair treatment of the occupied. His maternal grandparents, Ernest and Hilda Schuster, were both of German descent. Hilda was sensitive to German suffering and the plight of refugees after the First World War, directing much of her philanthropy to the cause. Spender would remember her as 'one of the most important influences of my life'.[38] Indeed, he would ponder his German parentage extensively in his 1951 memoirs *World within World*:

> That we were of Jewish as well as German origin was passed over in silence or with slight embarrassment by my family, either because, as with my grandfather, and his brothers Arthur and Felix Schuster, it was taken for granted, or because, with his descendants, it was deliberately ignored.[39]

---

[35] Spender, 'The War God', ibid., pp. 163–64 (p. 164).
[36] Sutherland, p. 292.
[37] Birley, p. 10.
[38] Sutherland, p. 53.
[39] Stephen Spender, *World within World* (London: Faber & Faber, 1991), p. 13.

Understandably, he does not disclose his origins in *European Witness*. Foregrounding his internationalist convictions instead, he is able to obviate charges of bias when he discusses German guilt. In a broader context, his arguments on this topic synchronize closely with the evolution of the debate from the end of 1945 onwards. Indeed, more moderate voices began to make themselves heard on the topic of guilt. Karl Jaspers's *Die Schuldfrage* marked a watershed when it appeared in 1946, and the German philosopher showed striking similarities with Spender's reflections. They were aware of each other's work, since they both delivered a speech on 'the European spirit' at the first Rencontres internationales de Genève, a month before *European Witness* was published.[40] Jaspers distinguishes between four types of guilt: (1) criminal guilt (concerning individuals who have committed crimes punished by law); (2) political guilt (concerning the whole German nation, which placed itself under the Nazi yoke); (3) moral guilt (each individual German is responsible before his own conscience for his actions); and (4) metaphysical guilt (every human being is responsible before God for not having done all he could to save his neighbour from Nazi atrocities).[41]

Spender draws the same line between collective political responsibility and individual moral guilt and, like Jaspers, he mentions a form of guilt which affects mankind as a whole. Both of them understand the importance of establishing distinctions in order to stave off unfair charges. Failure to differentiate between the four categories led the occupiers to issue the well-known posters depicted in *The Hidden Damage*: 'Asking no question, this placard stated a fact. Over clearer, more detailed photographs ran the bold black headline: "THIS TOWN IS GUILTY! YOU ARE GUILTY!"'[42] Jaspers remarks that no signature or source was given, so that the statement was perceived as a bolt from the blue, a quasi-divine ruling:

> Als im Sommer 1945 die Plakate in den Städten und Dörfern hingen mit den Bildern und Berichten aus Belsen und dem entscheidenden Satz: Das ist eure Schuld!, da bemächtigte sich eine Unruhe der Gewissen, da erfasste ein Entsetzen viele, die das in der Tat nicht gewusst hatten, und da bäumte sich etwas auf: wer klagt mich da an? Keine Unterschrift, keine Behörde, das Plakat kam wie aus dem leeren Raum.[43]

> When in summer 1945 the posters hung in towns and villages depicting images and accounts from Belsen and the decisive sentence: You are guilty!, then consciences became restless, then horror seized many, who in fact had not known, and then something rebelled: who is accusing me? No signature, no authorities, the poster came like a bolt from the blue.

It is therefore hardly surprising that the population expressed some bewilder-

---
[40] Sutherland, pp. 318–19.
[41] Karl Jaspers, *Die Schuldfrage* (Heidelberg: Schneider, 1946), pp. 31–32.
[42] James Stern, p. 81.
[43] Jaspers, p. 44.

ment at the sight of the notices. Nevertheless, James Stern was so shocked by the lack of visible repentance among the occupied population that he sometimes adopted the radical position of American authorities:

> Did the Germans express any feeling of guilt? With the exception of such instances as those quoted in the interviews, the answer is definitely no. Our explanation of this phenomenon is simple: that the feeling of guilt among Germans is so colossal they simply cannot face it, much less give it expression.[44]

Since he offers no definition for the word 'guilt', the line between emotional feelings of guilt on the one hand and political or criminal guilt on the other remains unclear, yet the possessive 'Our' signals that Stern sided, at least on occasions, with hard-line American observers in post-war Germany. In Stern's defence, it must be said that even moderate observers such as Robert Birley tended to conflate collective responsibility and personal accountability. In his lecture the educational adviser makes a statement that collapses Jaspers's first three categories: 'We have noted the political immaturity of the people, and what is worse and of greater consequence, their refusal to accept individual responsibility for the action of their statesmen or administrators.'[45] Such instances highlight the originality of Spender's voice in the English-speaking world, at a time when few of his fellow anglophones agreed with the distinctions drawn in Jaspers's essay. None the less, despite the likenesses between *European Witness* and *Die Schuldfrage*, an important difference can be noted. Spender's humanism remains secular: he considers that human beings are accountable to themselves and each other, but not to God. This characteristic sets him apart from the trend of Christian humanism championed by T. S. Eliot or Curtius. Moreover, since Spender was supposed to take part in the screening and purging of librarians, he had the opportunity of putting his theories into practice.

When can a civil servant be considered too compromised by the Nazi regime to retain his office? The question apparently embarrassed Spender even more than cultural denazification, so that he glossed over the problem and passed the responsibility onto his superiors:

> I left it to the Civilian Military Government to decide whether or not Dr. Peters should be retained. He had been a member of the Nazi Party, but he had also been head of [the Volksbibliothek of Düsseldorf] for a great many years. Perhaps I should be ashamed of the fact that I took no pleasure in the thought that he might have to be removed. The reader who thinks as I did when I first came to Germany that the task of de-nazification is simple, will have some grasp of the complexities in this account of the comparatively straightforward question of Dr. Peters. (pp. 154–55)

Here again, Spender's reluctance chimes in with the policies of the British

[44] James Stern, p. 129.
[45] Birley, p. 17.

authorities, who became less stringent when faced with the burdens of occupation, and eventually implemented a 'modest purge'.[46] The author exhibits more harshness towards German intellectuals, because in his opinion they ought to have behaved in an exemplary way and fought against the spread of Nazi ideas. (Relatively speaking, this resembles the attitude which the French government adopted after the Liberation.) In 'Rhineland Journal' Spender finds Curtius's choice of the *innere Emigration* questionable, and supposes that his former friend compromised himself to some extent, since he had not been imprisoned.[47] Spender's disappointment radicalizes his position towards Curtius, and causes him to share Hannah Arendt's opinion: 'The only way in which we can identify an anti-Nazi is when the Nazis have hanged him. There is no other reliable token.'[48] Interestingly, there is no evidence that Spender was aware of Arendt's works at this time, but he would later review her study of the Adolf Eichmann trial.[49]

This English observer also judges the works of Ernst Jünger with severity. The German hero of the First World War described combat as a mystical experience in *Feuer und Blut*. Spender criticizes the book's suggestion that the German army is destined to win, and disapproves of the aestheticization of violence. In retrospect, these comments may seem unwarranted, for after Hitler came to power, Jünger reviewed his published texts and suppressed the ardently nationalistic passages. Later, he justified the process in a witty metaphor: 'In der Inflation zieh[t] man sein Gold zurück'.[50] The last and most radical extract of *Feuer und Blut* quoted by Spender was not taken up in Jünger's final version. However, it is true that former editions remained available during the Nazi era: in fact, Spender found his copy in a public library.

Even *Auf den Marmorklippen*, a Jünger novel regarded as a critical allegory of Nazism by many critics—including the anti-Fascist British scholar F. A. Voigt—aroused Spender's suspicion because it had not been banned by the Nazis. Indeed, after a seemingly neutral report of a conversation, the English diarist fires a parting shot at his German colleague:

I [. . .] asked him to sign my copy of *Auf den Marmorklippen* [. . .] I did not tell him that I had been given this by the librarian of the public library of Aachen, because she did not know whether to keep it on the shelves and because she had more copies than she knew how to deal with. (p. 216)

The author of *European Witness* certainly accentuates his intransigence in

[46] Biddiscombe, pp. 83–117.
[47] 'Rhineland Journal', p. 399.
[48] Arendt, p. 124.
[49] See Sutherland, p. 426.
[50] 'During inflation you withdraw your gold' (Heimo Schwilk, *Ernst Jünger: Ein Jahrhundertleben. Die Biografie* (Munich: Piper, 2007), p. 358).

order to counteract his fascination with the works of the former German officer. He calls *Feuer und Blut* 'one of the best war books I have read, and also one of the most deeply repulsive' (p. 198). This emotionally charged statement prompted the scholar J. P. Stern to mock the alleged naivety of his fellow critic in a monograph on Jünger published seven years afterwards.[51] However, Stern reaches similar conclusions through a more systematic approach. He acknowledges the 'great force and economy' of the German diarist's writing, 'his ability to express something of the tremendous and shattering impact of the experience' when he depicts combat in the trenches. The academic also voiced reservations as to Jünger's cold-blooded attitude to brutal warfare. He compared him to a man under partial anaesthesia, whose language left no room for the expression of pain.

Spender's analysis of *Feuer und Blut* seems to have set the standard for Jünger's reception by the English readership. Unsurprisingly, British authorities forbade publication of his work from 1945 to 1947 after he had refused to answer the questionnaire (*Fragebogen*) widely circulated in the English and American zones.[52] It elicited detailed information about Nazi affiliations.[53] For his own part, Spender seems to have found the subversive power of Jünger's work just as embarrassing as the inflammatory language of Nazi propaganda.

Goebbels and Nazi Propaganda

The irony of Spender's attitude becomes fully apparent when he decides to write a chapter on Goebbels. Instead of determining which books he wants to have removed from the shelves of public libraries, he picks up some of the Nazi volumes that had been put aside and 'reviews' them. At such moments, he performs an important task as an interpreter of texts which had scarcely been read by the British general public. Unlike *Feuer und Blut*, which had been translated into English in 1929 and benefited from a certain success abroad, Goebbels's novel *Michael* still remained unavailable to English speakers. Spender blames his fellow countrymen for having neglected a work of considerable impact on account of its literary worthlessness: 'To protect ourselves from books such as *Mein Kampf* [and] *Michael* [. . .] we need a new branch of criticism, which considers certain books as social phenomena' (pp. 181–82). Accordingly, his analysis of *Michael* throws light upon key aspects of Nazi propaganda.

First of all, he is struck by the childish aspect of the text, the lack of

---

[51] J. P. Stern, *Ernst Jünger: A Writer of Our Time* (Cambridge: Bowes & Bowes, 1953), pp. 21–51.
[52] Schwilk, p. 439.
[53] Biddiscombe, p. 21.

characterization, and the threadbare storyline. As a result of Goebbels's anti-intellectualism, the protagonist even takes pride in his stupidity:

Ich trage nur ein Buch in der Tasche: den Faust. Den ersten Teil lese ich. Für den zweiten bin ich zu dumm.[54]

I carry one book in my bag: Faust. I am reading the first part. I am too stupid for the second.

Michael acts entirely on his impulses, and at the end of the narrative he more or less opts for self-destruction in a mine. Despite the unpromising plot, Spender is mesmerized by other aspects of *Michael*. He stresses the nihilistic frenzy of the hero which overcomes all contradictions. The protagonist's avowed simplicity does not prevent him, for example, from holding forth on political and social issues. He compares statesmen to artists whose raw material would be their people:

Der Staatsmann ist auch ein Künstler. Für ihn ist das Volk nichts anderes, als was für den Bildshauer der Stein ist. Führer und Masse, das ist ebensowenig ein Problem wie etwa Maler und Farbe. Politik ist die bildende Kunst des Staates, wie Malerei die bildende Kunst der Farbe ist.[55]

The statesman is also an artist. To him, the people is exactly what stone is to the sculptor. Leader and mass, it is just as natural as, for instance, painter and colour. Politics is the visual art of the State, just as painting is the visual art of colour.

Michael also develops a love–hate relationship with a Russian student, Iwan Wienurowsky, who tries to convert him to Bolshevism. Goebbels uses this tormented friendship as a pretext to announce a future war between the Soviet Union and Germany, and Spender is fascinated by the prophetic nature of the author's sentences:

Es gibt eine deutsche Idee, so wie es eine russische gibt. Diese beiden werden sich einmal messen um die Zukunft. Russland ist eine Gefahr für uns, die wir überwinden müssen.[56]

There is a German idea, just as there is a Russian one. One day these two will compete for the future. To us Russia is a danger that we must overcome.

The British poet clearly identifies Goebbels's political potential in such empty propaganda slogans. However, he does not draw the reader's attention to Goebbels's occasional 'slips', which show that Hitler's minister of propaganda never achieved absolute control of his ideological material. For example, the hero of *Michael* presents France as Germany's arch-enemy, which, as opposed to Russia, cannot be in the least admired:

[54] Joseph Goebbels, *Michael: Ein deutsches Schicksal in Tagebuchblättern* (Munich: Eher, 1933), p. 10.
[55] Ibid., p. 21.
[56] Ibid., p. 113.

Drüben liegt Frankreich, unser gemeinsamer Feind. Seine Negerarmeen stehen am Rhein.⁵⁷

France is over there, our common enemy. Its Negro armies are by the Rhine.

It is therefore surprising that earlier in the novel, Michael should pronounce in a burst of enthusiasm a set phrase that sounds rather out of place: 'Ich lebe wie Gott in Frankreich.'⁵⁸

In spite of such inconsistencies, Spender's study of *Michael* can be regarded as particularly significant, and has lost none of its interest to the contemporary reader. It provides a useful complement to his notes on *Kampf um Berlin*, Goebbels's 1934 stylized narrative recounting how the National Socialists rose to power in the capital. Here, Spender is clearly shocked by the Nazis' cynical straightforwardness concerning their aims and techniques:

The grossest of Nazi vulgarities is their repulsive confidence trick of taking the reader into their secrets, especially when they are talking about 'propaganda,' a term which is universally accepted (not only by the Nazis) as a kind of honourable dishonourableness. (p. 179)

He goes on to illustrate his remark with a quotation from *Kampf um Berlin*: 'Propaganda has only one goal; and in politics this goal is only one thing: the winning of the masses. Every means which serves this goal is good. And every means which eludes this goal is bad' (p. 179). This analysis enables Spender to uncover the key paradox of Nazi literature, namely 'the combination of most extreme disingenuousness with most extreme frankness' (p. 177). In order to drive the point home, he might have mentioned the opening paragraphs of Goebbels's account, in which the Fascist leader bluntly declares that he has no claims as a historian of the movement because he is judge and jury:

Dieses Buch hat sich zum Ziel gesetzt, die Geschichte der Bewegung in der Reichshauptstadt darzustellen. Es verfolgt dabei allerdings keinerlei historische Zwecke. Die objective Chronologie des Ablaufs ihrer Berliner Entwicklung aufzuzeichnen, wird späteren Geschichtsschreibern überlassen bleiben. Uns fehlt es an der nötigen nüchternen Leidenschaftslosigkeit, um dabei Licht und Schatten gerecht zu verteilen. Der diese Blätter schrieb, ist selbst an dem Ablauf der Dinge maßgeblich und hauptverantwortlich mitbeteiligt gewesen. Er ist deshalb Partei in jedem Sinne des Wortes.⁵⁹

This book aims at representing the history of the movement in the Reich capital. Yet, in so doing, it does not purport to be historical. We leave it to later history-writers to depict chronologically and objectively how the movement developed in Berlin. We lack the objectivity and absence of passion that are necessary to distribute light and shadow fairly. The author of these lines himself took a decisive and leading part in the course of events. He is therefore an interested party in every sense of the word.

---

⁵⁷ Ibid., p. 109.
⁵⁸ 'I live in clover', lit. 'I live like God in France' (ibid., p. 11).
⁵⁹ *Kampf um Berlin*, p. 11.

Though Spender's temperament causes him to baulk at a detailed analysis of Nazi marketing tricks, such an analysis of *Kampf um Berlin* would have provided noteworthy insights into the party's charm offensive. For instance, the book reproduces numerous drawings by the illustrator Mjölnir. Spender merely asserts that they 'repay study' (p. 179), before moving on to general reflections on the fairy-tale side of Hitlerism. Yet, a less cursory glance would have revealed that these illustrations were a pivotal cog in the propaganda machine. Indeed, Goebbels explained the advantages of the caricature over the written word. Satirical drawings escaped censorship laws more easily than newspaper articles, and they made a counter-attack more difficult: 'Wer die Lacher auf seiner Seite hat, der hat bekanntlich immer recht.'[60] The launching of the weekly *Der Angriff* ('The Attack') was thus accompanied by a carefully planned campaign.[61] First of all, posters which merely indicated the journal's title were put up on the Morris columns to tease the passer-by's curiosity. The second version of the posters mentioned a date: 'Der Angriff beginnt am 4. Juli.' The obvious ambiguity of the sentence aroused rumours of a Communist putsch, which enabled the NSDAP to put its main rivals under scrutiny. Goebbels well knew that there was no such thing as bad publicity and contrived to exploit the misunderstanding he had encouraged. By the time he revealed the actual nature of the 'Angriff', the press and the Landtag had already hyped up the mysterious 'attack'. On the whole, a close reading of *Kampf um Berlin* shows that Spender radically underestimated the importance of visual material for Nazi propaganda.

Conclusion

European Witness provided the public with a persuasive overview of post-war Germany, but one that does not aim at faultless accuracy in the details. Spender's subtle combination of non-fiction and semi-fiction links closely with his intellectual undertaking: he abandons claims to objective reportage in favour of a search for relative sincerity. Spender never conceals his occasional despair over the future of Germany, and his difficult situation brings to mind the typical dilemma of British occupation authorities: they set great value on the 're-education' of the country, while they expressed disillusion when confronted with its material and spiritual state. Robert Birley, introduced on the title-page of his printed talk as a former headmaster of Charterhouse, summed up this official position at the beginning of his lecture, advocating the necessary idealism of what he calls 'an educational task':

[60] 'Whoever has those who are laughing on his side is always, as is well known, in the right' (ibid., p. 201).
[61] Ibid., pp. 195–97.

The eventual success of this occupation depends very largely on our readiness to appreciate the real nature of the responsibility we have accepted. That responsibility means that we must attempt to change the spirit of the people we have defeated in battle. It is undoubtedly one of the most difficult tasks we have undertaken in our history.[62]

However, Spender refrained from voicing well-meaning schoolmasterly goals. He resolutely aimed at a growth in knowledge by acting as a mediator between German writers and his English-speaking readership. In this way, he fulfilled his ambitions as a committed European who wished for Germany's return to the Old Continent's fold—even when he considered that these obligations included analysing texts by Goebbels. A Francophile, Spender was also among the first to underline the potential role of France in the reconstruction of Europe, though he also drew attention to that country's moral downfall in his writings.

In conclusion, Spender's position brings to mind Churchill's famous speech 'The Tragedy of Europe', delivered at the University of Zurich on 21 October 1946, a month before the publication of *European Witness*. The Tory politician was aware of the daring novelty of his arguments:

I am now going to say something that will astonish you. The first step in the re-creation of the European Family must be a partnership between France and Germany. In this way only can France recover the moral and cultural leadership of Europe. There can be no revival of Europe without a spiritually great France and a spiritually great Germany.[63]

The coincidence appears all the more striking as Spender's volume contains a direct echo of Churchill's well-known phrase. In the 'Ernst Jünger' section, the poet concluded his reasoning thus: 'We must wait and be patient, realizing that finally Germany must become part of the European family' (p. 214). He may have altered the text at the last minute in the light of Churchill's speech. Whatever the case, it is remarkable that the poet's threefold loyalty to Germany, France, and his native England chimes in with the most liberal pan-European views. Contrary to the wartime prime minister, Spender even wishes Britain to take an active part in the collaborative process, rather than remaining a spectator of the Franco-German reconciliation. This staunch commitment contributes to the undeniable originality of *European Witness*.

UNIVERSITY OF PARIS III-SORBONNE NOUVELLE
QUEEN MARY, UNIVERSITY OF LONDON   FLORIAN ALIX-NICOLAÏ

[62] Birley, p. 7.
[63] Winston Churchill, 'The Tragedy of Europe', speech delivered at the University of Zurich, 19 September 1946 <http://www.ellopos.net/politics/churchill-europe.asp> [accessed 11 February 2013] (p. 3 of 5).

HENRI-GEORGES CLOUZOT'S *L'ENFER*: MODERN CINEMA AT THE CROSSROADS OF THE ARTS

> Le créateur est le catalyseur intuitif de toutes les informations de son temps.
> (VICTOR VASARÉLY)[1]

Henri-Georges Clouzot occupies an ambiguous place in the history of French cinema. Nicknamed 'the French Hitchcock', he made his reputation in the 1940s and 1950s with psychological thrillers such as *Le Corbeau* (1943), *Le Salaire de la peur* (1953), and *Les Diaboliques* (1954), and quickly became one of France's most popular and revered directors (despite being temporarily barred from film-making in 1944 because of his collaboration with the German production company Continental).[2] Yet in the course of the 1950s, together with a host of more traditional directors stigmatized as 'old guard', Clouzot came under attack from the younger generation of film critics (soon to be film-makers) of the burgeoning Nouvelle Vague, who upended the value systems, aesthetics, and production techniques of French cinema.[3] A paragon of 'cinéma de qualité', he represented the type of technically perfect but intellectually and aesthetically unchallenging film-making that critics such as Michel Dorsday and François Truffaut held responsible for what they denounced as the mediocrity of post-war French film.[4] The box office success and Oscar for Best Foreign Film for *La Vérité* (starring Brigitte Bardot) in 1960 confirmed Clouzot as one of France's leading directors, but French cinema's profound mutation under the influence of the Nouvelle Vague increasingly challenged the masterfully controlled type of film-making that had gained him popularity. After a four-year break, the director returned to film-making in 1964 with *L'Enfer*, a film about a jealous obsession which was to demonstrate his unbroken creative potential and rival the best that

---

[1] Quoted in Magdalena Holzhey, *Victor Vasarély, 1906-1997: la pure vision* (Cologne: Taschen, 2005), front flap.

[2] For an excellent recent appraisal of his work in English see Christopher Lloyd, *Henri-Georges Clouzot* (Manchester: Manchester University Press, 2007).

[3] François Truffaut's polemical article 'Une certaine tendance du cinéma francais', *Cahiers du cinéma*, 31 (1954), 15-29, focusing mainly on scriptwriters Jean Aurenche and Pierre Bost, but, through them, on the commercially successful directors of the 'tradition de la qualité', launched an open battle between the old generation of film-makers and the new 'cinéma d'auteur'. For the battles between Old and New Wave see Antoine de Baecque, *La Cinéphilie: invention d'un regard, histoire d'une culture, 1944-1968* (Paris: Fayard, 2003), pp. 147-56, and René Prédal, *50 ans de cinéma français* (Paris: Nathan, 1992).

[4] In his article 'Le Cinéma est mort', *Cahiers du cinéma*, 16 (1952), 55-58, Dorsday declares: 'Le cinéma français est mort, mort sous la qualité, l'impeccable, le parfait — parfait comme ces grands magasins américains où tout est propre, beau, bien en ordre, sans bavures. Si l'on excepte les inévitables vaudevilles et drames pour l'arrière province, on ne fait plus en France que de *bons* films, fabriqués, léchés, présentés avec élégance. Et c'est là le désastre' (p. 55).

European cinema had to offer at the time.⁵ Convinced that film had fallen behind developments in the other arts—and contrary to the Nouvelle Vague, which aspired to establish cinema as an autonomous art form no longer in the shadow of older media such as literature or the theatre—Clouzot explicitly sought to extend film's expressive possibilities through interart dialogue. As Serge Bromberg explains: 'A 56 ans, Clouzot veut que son prochain film soit la somme de ces trente années d'expérience: un film qui inventera un nouveau cinéma, résolument ancré dans la modernité, et qui fera la somme de ce que l'art contemporain et la caméra peuvent apporter l'un à l'autre.'⁶

The prestigious project, with a star cast led by Romy Schneider and Serge Reggiani, quickly ran into problems during production in July 1964: filming ran behind schedule; Serge Reggiani, having been taken ill, hastily left the set; and tensions were rife between the notoriously authoritarian film-maker and his crew. The project came to an abrupt end after only three weeks of shooting when Clouzot suffered a heart attack while directing a scene. *L'Enfer* acquired legendary status as a 'film maudit', but until very recently, it was virtually impossible to see any of the surviving rushes for the film, and thus to form an idea of the new film language Clouzot intended to forge.⁷ The situation changed when the producer and film restorer Serge Bromberg unearthed 185 film containers with the original footage for *L'Enfer* in the French Film Archive, parts of which feature in a fascinating documentary on the film's troubled genesis (directed by Bromberg and Ruxandra Medrea and released in 2010).⁸ This documentary, together with three surviving scripts housed at the Bibliothèque du Film, Paris, now makes it possible to reconstruct what the finished film might have looked like and to appraise its various artistic influences.⁹ This article aims to show that, contrary to the widely held belief that Clouzot could not face the challenges of the Nouvelle Vague,¹⁰ the director was, with

⁵ Stéphane Delorme affirms: 'Il y a aussi la volonté du cinéaste du *Salaire de la peur* (1951) [sic] de se rajeunir, de rivaliser, d'expérimenter, secoué par les productions européennes récentes (Bergman, Fellini)' ('Les Cercles de *L'Enfer*', *Cahiers du cinéma*, 650 (2009), 72–75 (p. 73)).

⁶ Serge Bromberg, *Romy dans 'L'Enfer': les images inconnues du film inachevé d'Henri-Georges Clouzot* (Paris: Albin Michel-Lobster, 2009), p. 12.

⁷ In 1992 Antenne 2 showed ten minutes' worth of remaining rushes in a commemoration of Romy Schneider's death.

⁸ Serge Bromberg and Ruxandra Medrea, *'L'Enfer' de Henri-Georges Clouzot: la légende d'un film inachevé* (2010). The film is accompanied by a richly illustrated book, *Romy dans 'L'Enfer'*.

⁹ The Bibliothèque du Film also holds 356 storyboards for the film. They have been consulted in preparation for this article but have proved less instructive than the rest of the material.

¹⁰ René Prédal's categorical statement in *50 ans de cinéma français* sums up a more widespread point of view: 'La génération de la guerre aura connu une vie artistique très courte. Née au début des années 40, elle s'effondre à la fin de la décennie suivante, incapable de résister ou de s'adapter à la nouvelle vague. Fruits d'un système — la qualité française — [. . .] ces cinéastes ne sauront plus créer dans un autre contexte, ne pourront pas tirer parti d'une nouvelle donne. C'est le cas de René Clément, Henri-Georges Clouzot, André Cayatte, Yves Allégret, Louis Daquin, Jean Delannoy et même Jacques Tati' (p. 140).

L'Enfer, taking French cinema towards a new form of modernity. I will argue that it is precisely the director's openness to other art forms—in other words, his genuinely intermedial approach to cinema—that held the potential to create new forms of cinematic expression. We will first examine Clouzot's borrowings from a work of literary modernity—Proust's *A la recherche du temps perdu*—for his portrayal of jealousy and his unconventional treatment of time and memory. We will then consider how the director assimilated into his project the visual experiments of the historical avant-garde and, more importantly, developments in kinetic art and electro-acoustic music. Finally, we will examine the afterlife of *L'Enfer* in two closely related films: Clouzot's own *La Prisonnière* (1968), which recycles visual and aural elements from the unfinished earlier film, and Claude Chabrol's *L'Enfer* (1993), adapted from Clouzot's script. While the former helps us to visualize the film that never was, comparison with the latter, which pertains more firmly to the mainstream, further throws into relief the modernity of Clouzot's unfinished project.[11]

The Way by Proust's: Jealousy, Time, Memory

Clouzot started his film career as a scriptwriter and adapter in France and Germany in the 1930s. Unlike other directors associated with 'la qualité française', who relied heavily on professional scriptwriters (a practice Truffaut denounced as one of the reasons for the alleged mediocrity of post-war French cinema),[12] he was (co)responsible for most of his screenplays, including those of *L'Enfer* and *La Prisonnière*.[13] Born into a literary family—his father owned a bookshop in his native Niort—and a lifelong impassioned reader, he made many films that are adapted from works of fiction, ranging from Belgian crime writer Stanislas-André Steeman to the Abbé Prévost. In an interview, Clouzot declared that his own experience of insomnia and depression triggered the idea for *L'Enfer*, yet the various titles he envisaged for the film also anchor the project explicitly in a literary tradition: first called 'Du Fond de la nuit' (a title that echoes both the Bible and Céline's *Voyage au bout de la nuit*), the film became 'La Ronde' (evoking Schnitzler's scandal-provoking play, adapted by Max Ophuls in 1950) before Clouzot finally settled on the Dantean *L'Enfer*. While structural and thematic affinities with Schnitzler and Dante are evident in the film's cyclical structure and the male protagonist's emotional torments, it is one of Clouzot's favourite authors, Proust,[14] who seems more profoundly

---

[11] One of the criticisms that was raised against Bromberg and Medrea's documentary is precisely that it did not take into account the afterlife of *L'Enfer* in these two films. See Delorme, 'Les Cercles de *L'Enfer*', p. 74.

[12] Truffaut, 'Une certaine tendance du cinéma français'.

[13] Belgian writer Jose-André Lacour helped him polish his initial script for *L'Enfer*.

[14] Clouzot discovered Proust in his late teens (cf. José-Louis Bocquet and Marc Godin,

to have influenced the film's thematic preoccupations, spatio-temporal organization, and exploration of extreme states of human subjectivity.

The names of the two protagonists, Marcel and Odette, combined with the theme of jealous obsession, signal from the outset an intertextual link with Proust's *Recherche*, specifically, the two love narratives that echo one another in the novel: that of Swann and Odette in 'Un Amour de Swann' and of the Narrator (often called 'Marcel' by readers and critics) and Albertine in *La Prisonnière*. This intertextual affiliation is affirmed in Clouzot's final film, *La Prisonnière*, which not only borrows its title from the fifth volume of the *Recherche*, but explicitly alludes to Proust in a pivotal scene in which the gallery owner Stan (Laurent Terzieff) arranges a photograph of his deceased mother on a table so that it faces the sadomasochistic photograph shots he takes with nude models. His instrumentalization of the photograph as a prop in a ritualized staging of transgressive sexualities strongly echoes the famous scene in *Du côté de chez Swann* where Mlle Vinteuil desecrates the photograph of her deceased father by using it in a sadistic sexual game. Yet, as can be seen from the manifest differences between Clouzot's and Proust's *La Prisonnière* and between the director's project for *L'Enfer* and Proust's *Recherche*, Clouzot in no way sought to adapt the Proustian universe to the screen. Rather, as is suggested by the conflation of the two love stories that is effected by the choice of names in *L'Enfer*, Proust's novel seems to have offered him a generic matrix for his project. As a seminal exploration of jealousy in literature and a text which heralds new forms of expressing human subjectivity, the *Recherche* opened up thematic and narrative possibilities of expression for his own cinematic study of a destructive jealousy bordering on madness.

A writer at the threshold of twentieth-century modernism, Proust was the first major novelist to analyse, with peerless acuity and insight, the *mal sacré* of a love that no longer finds transcendence on a higher, spiritual plane, and to explore in unprecedented detail the ontological condition of the jealous male subject. Both Swann and the Narrator suffer from an all-consuming passion, condemning them to an existence of insecurity and anguish and prompting them to survey and interrogate their female partners persistently in an attempt to contain and control their supposed infidelities with other men and women. In the emotional abyss experienced by both lovers, inner and outer realities, their anxious projections and the proofs they seek in the material world, frequently clash, leaving them (and the reader) in an unnerving state of unknowing and insecurity. Proust presents love, desire, and, by extension, jealousy as a *cosa mentale*, a mental expenditure that eventually invades the lover's entire being, driving him to the limits of human

Henri-Georges Clouzot cinéaste (Paris: La Sirène, 1993), p. 10), and he exerted a lifelong influence on his work.

reason and cognition and opening up a psychic underworld of pulsions, existential tremors, and emotional torments that borders on pathology and madness.[15] Through the jealous subject, the author probes extreme states of human consciousness and explores further the subjective workings of perception that are at the core of his aesthetic and philosophical enterprise.

Clouzot recreated the ontologically unstable universe of the jealous subject analysed by Proust in his psychodrama of a man in his forties, Marcel Prieur (Serge Reggiani), who suspects his wife Odette (Romy Schneider) of sexual infidelities. Tormented by a destructive and increasingly delirious jealousy, he begins to spy on her, subjecting her to humiliating interrogations (which never yield any conclusive truth), and eventually imprisoning her in the marital bedroom, chained to the bed like 'une bête dangereuse'. The scripts for the film suggest that he may kill her in a bout of madness, but leave the question a blur. Like Proust, who sounded out the emotional hell of the jealous subject in the disturbingly dissociated, oneiric, and often uncanny *La Prisonnière*, Clouzot seeks to fathom the male protagonist's madness in a film that does not merely represent but functions as delirium. An exemplar of what Deleuze has called 'a cinema of the brain',[16] *L'Enfer* would have assimilated the mental delirium of the male protagonist into the film's very texture, fabric, colour, and sound. As we will see in the next section, the director draws on experiments in the visual arts and music to recreate the monstrous proliferation of thought and the aural and visual distortions to which Marcel falls prey, but it is Proust's novel, with its memory- and sensory-driven conception of time, that seems to have inspired the narrative and spatio-temporal organization of *L'Enfer*.

In a manner strikingly similar to the *Recherche*'s celebrated dual narrative perspective, which oscillates between a prospective and a retrospective movement, Clouzot adopts a double internal focalization technique that allows him to unravel the stages of Marcel's paranoia from the moment of greatest narrative intensity, that is, his possible killing of his wife. The surviving scripts show that the film would have opened with a lengthy credit title sequence which, in a few vignette-style scenes, traces the beginning of the couple's relationship, their marriage, parenthood, and proud ownership of a hotel in provincial France. The striking acceleration and deceleration of time recalls the frequent changes of tempo in the *Recherche* (as well as Proust's theoretical reflections on the subjectivity of temporal perception). Several years of the couple's life are compressed into a few minutes of filmic time, while the night when Marcel chains Odette to the bed and possibly kills her extends

---

[15] For studies of jealousy in Proust see Paul Gifford, *Love, Desire and Transcendence in French Literature: Deciphering Eros* (Aldershot: Ashgate, 2005), Chapter 6, 'The Idolatries of Eros', and Malcolm Bowie, *Freud, Proust and Lacan: Theory as Fiction* (Cambridge: Cambridge University Press, 1987), Chapter 2, 'Proust, Jealousy, Knowledge'.

[16] Gilles Deleuze, *Cinéma 2: L'Image-temps* (Paris: Minuit, 1985), p. 265.

to what seems like an eternity. A shot of Odette showing off a souvenir of a miniature train on the viaduct du Gabarit (a railway bridge built by Gustave Eiffel which would have offered a spectacular backdrop for the filmic setting), overlaid with the menacing siren of a locomotive mingled with the anxious cry of a woman, would have segued into the first images of the actual film, in which Marcel, bloodstained and visibly perturbed, feverishly tries to establish whether or not—as he confusedly seems to remember—he has stabbed Odette with his razor. From this first 'image choc' (a term borrowed from Surrealism, which Clouzot employs several times in the script), the film would have vacillated between images of the present (the bloodstained Marcel in his room) and memories of the past, translated visually in the form of flashbacks, in a structure similar to Proust's criss-crossing between different temporal layers. Clouzot had already used narratives based on flashback in *Manon* (1949), a transposition of *Manon Lescaut* to post-Liberation France, and *La Vérité* (1960), the story of a nonconformist young woman who kills her former lover, but here the technique is radicalized, departing from mainstream cinematic representation, where, for the sake of continuity and readability, past and present must remain clearly delineated entities. In the wake of Proust, who broke free from the strictures of traditional plot order imposed by realist aesthetics, the film would have explored the permeable boundaries between past and present, constantly intermeshing different temporal layers. *L'Enfer* abandons traditional chronology in favour of an associative narrative driven by memory and sensory experience, in which the protagonist (and the viewer) navigates space and time freely. Similar to a technique used by Raoul Ruiz some forty years later in his adaptation of *Le Temps retrouvé* (1999), threshold spaces such as windows and doors become metaphorical portals through which the protagonist is transported back into the past.[17] Just as the images of Combray, taking shape and solidity, sprang into being from the Narrator's cup of tea in *Du côté de chez Swann*, revealingly, as Marcel tries to establish what happened while he lost control over his mind, a recollection image slowly emerges in the window pane: 'Très loin... du fond de la nuit, une image arrive, confuse encore. Elle se précise.'[18] As in the *Recherche*, aural sensations (the rattling of approaching trains, a ringing telephone, the sound of running water, the squeal of car tyres) trigger what Proust calls 'involuntary memories', that is, a form of sensory memory stored not at the level of the intellect, but of the body. Unlike their counterpart, voluntary memory, these embodied memories offer a fuller access to the past in so far as they recreate the rich sensory impressions (perfumes, sounds, odours, colours) that accompanied the initial experience. The division between remembering (Marcel in

[17] For a discussion of Ruiz's adaptation see Martine Beugnet and Marion Schmid, *Proust at the Movies* (London: Ashgate, 2005), Chapter 4, 'Surrealist Proust: Raoul Ruiz's *Le Temps retrouvé*'.
[18] Bibliothèque du Film, Paris, SCEN 0949 (1/2).

the present) and remembered self (the younger Marcel seen in flashback), as in the *Recherche*, is intended above all to facilitate shifts between past and present. Yet, contrary to Proust's novel, in which the Narrator gains greater wisdom and understanding of the world as he reaches maturity, Marcel's paranoia in *L'Enfer* increases with time, and thus neither critical distance through experience nor transcendence through art is possible. The film's ending brings no closure to the hell of jealousy, as is indicated by the three letters 'Etc.' (instead of the habitual 'Fin') that were meant to appear before the end credits.

In filmic terms, we can situate Clouzot's project in the tradition of what Deleuze has called the 'time-image', that is, the modern type of cinema that emerged in the aftermath of the Second World War (notably around directors such as Alain Resnais), eschewing the action and causality-driven plots of the mainstream to embrace more complex phenomena of memory, time, perception, and human consciousness and subjectivity.[19] As has been argued elsewhere, the cinema of the time-image shows many striking resemblances to Proust, whose modernist legacy has had a shaping influence on twentieth-century art cinema.[20] *L'Enfer* evinces further similarities to the *Recherche* in its shared preoccupation with the limits of sensory perception and the frontiers of cognition, especially as experienced by the jealous subject. In Proust's novel, however hard the Narrator scrutinizes the phenomena of the material world and interrogates Albertine and her friends, she remains an *être de fuite*, a stranger who can neither be fully known, nor controlled or contained. Even in moments of greatest intimacy the female 'other' asserts her insurmountable strangeness: thus, in *A l'ombre des jeunes filles en fleurs*, when the Narrator attempts to kiss Albertine, as he approaches her dewy cheeks, her face dissolves into an uncanny assembly of lines; in *La Prisonnière*, the sleeping young woman transforms in turn into a plant, a multiple-faced Janus-like being, or a rigid sculpture made of stone.[21] In a striking echo of these scenes in the script for *L'Enfer*, when Marcel approaches the face of the sleeping Odette, her magnified traits decompose into a Cubist-style tableau, before morphing into an abstract, grotesquely hybrid figure (part human, vegetable, and metal):

Le visage d'Odette a cessé d'être un visage... On reconnaît encore un instant le lobe d'une oreille, l'ourlet d'une lèvre, une aile du nez — puis plus rien. Est-ce un fragment de métal ou de végétal monstrueusement agrandi par le microscope électronique? Ou bien une figuration abstraite, un enchevêtrement de veines, de nervures, de failles qui sillonnent une pente luisante criblée de trous?[22]

---

[19] Gilles Deleuze, *Cinéma 2: L'Image-temps*.
[20] See Beugnet and Schmid, *Proust at the Movies*, Chapter 7, 'The Modernist Legacy'.
[21] Marcel Proust, *A la recherche du temps perdu*, ed. by Jean-Yves Tadié, 4 vols (Paris: Gallimard, 1987–89), II, 660–61, and III, 578–80 and 862.
[22] SCEN 0949 (1/2).

Not only does Marcel's close scrutiny of Odette, as allegorized in this image, entail greater strangeness, his anguished surveillance of her every move is perpetually hindered by outside interference beyond his control: her conversation with a guest whom he suspects of having an affair with her is muted by the sounds of a hammer, her dialogue with her best friend and suspected lover Marylou (Dany Carrel) made unintelligible by a blaring radio, her supposed flirtation with a student, observed through a window, remains silent. Unable either to confirm or to refute his jealous suspicions, Marcel becomes increasingly absent to the world around him, prey to nightmarish fantasies and hallucinations. Gradually, in the flashbacks, the filmic images themselves turn hallucinatory, as is best evidenced in an extended film-in-the-film sequence which marks the turning-point from obsessive jealousy to mental illness: one of the guests, M. Duhamel (André Luguet), screens an amateur film made during his stay at the Hôtel du Lac. The sight of the places where he has secretly followed Odette this very morning plunges Marcel into a delirium whereby the hallucinatory visions of his jealous mind replace the 'real' images that unravel on screen. His mental images supersede those of the camera. Marcel's hallucination culminates in an angst-ridden mental image of his wife's and her suspected lover's (Jean-Claude Bercq) bodies fetishistically fragmented in close-up: a voracious mouth sucking a breast, a male hand impatiently fondling a female belly, a woman's pursed, groaning lips and convulsively rolling eyeballs. Initially, the viewer is drawn into the hallucination, but the contrast between the grainy texture of the amateur film and Marcel's smoother fantasy images—not to mention the clash between the anodyne soundtrack (Duhamel's descriptions) and the eroticized image track (Marcel's hallucinations)—betrays the fabricated nature of the latter. The double *mise en abyme* here, more than just a skilful exercise in visualizing mental delirium, would have raised more profound questions about the ontological status of the cinematic image and the medium's problematic relations with the real. While its analogue function appears to ground the cinematic image in reality, it is of course far from constrained by realist conventions: like the paranoid mind, which invents its own delirious images, cinema's 'powers of the false' make it a miracle maker of simulacra.[23] Just as Marcel recycles images of happier days with Odette in his delirious fantasy, so the cinema, Clouzot seems to remind us, refashions reality in alluring, richly textured images whose truth content we should treat with suspicion.

---

[23] On the 'powers of the false' see Deleuze, *Cinéma 2: L'Image-temps*, pp. 126–55.

Exploding the Limits of Perception: Kinetic Art, Surrealism, and Musical Experimentation

If Proust's anatomy of the jealous mind and his fluid conception of time based on memory and sensory experience offered Clouzot a thematic and narrative foil for his portrait of male insanity, it was to experiments in the visual arts that the director turned in search of the new film language he sought to forge in *L'Enfer*. An amateur painter and collector, Clouzot had a keen interest in contemporary art, and first-hand exposure to recent artistic creation through his friendship with leading artists, including Picasso, with whom he had collaborated on a prize-winning film, *Le Mystère Picasso*, in 1955. His last two films, *L'Enfer* and *La Prisonnière*, were strongly influenced by his encounter with Victor Vasarély, the leader and theoretician of one of the most prominent artistic movements to emerge in post-war France: kineticism.

Kinetic art, or the 'new tendency' as it was also called, was launched by the 'Le Mouvement' exhibition at the Gallery Denise René in Paris in 1955. Harking back to Duchamp's readymades and optical machines, Naum Gabo's *Kinetic Constructions*, Viking Eggeling's abstract film classic *Diagonal Symphony*, and László Moholy-Nagy's *Light Modulator*, all of which Vasarély cited in his exhibition text (commonly referred to as 'The Yellow Manifesto'), kinetic art, as its name suggests, seeks to set art in motion. While kinetic sculpture such as Alexander Calder's mobiles and Jean Tinguely's ludic machines quite literally free the artwork from stillness, the dazzling optical effects in kinetic paintings by artists such as Vasarély, his son Jean-Pierre Yavaral, or the Venezuelan artist Jesús Rafael Soto merely simulate movement through optical illusion (hence the term 'Op Art' for this type of kinetic art).[24] As the art critic Magdalena Holzhey explains, in kineticism the very process of vision becomes the subject of the painting.[25] Kinetic artists' privileging of perception and process entails fundamental changes in the relationship between artwork and viewer. Not unlike what Barthes was to claim some fifteen years later for the process of reading,[26] viewers are no longer relegated to the role of passive consumer, but become active participants in the creation of an artwork poised in a state of permanent becoming. Viewers' changing spatial positions and vantage-point with regard to the artwork unlock the desired optical effects and create an illusion of

---

[24] On kinetic art see Michael Compton, *Optical and Kinetic Art* (New York: Arno Press, 1967); Hans-Jürgen Buderer, *Kinetische Kunst: Konzeptionen von Bewegung und Raum* (Worms: Wernersche Verlagsgesellschaft, 1992); Holzhey, *Victor Vasarély, 1906–1997*; and the excellent article '1955b' in Hal Foster and others, *Art since 1900: Modernism, Antimodernism, Postmodernism* (London: Thames & Hudson, 2004), pp. 379–84.

[25] Holzhey, *Victor Vasarély, 1906–1997*, p. 43.

[26] Cf. Roland Barthes, *S/Z* (Paris: Seuil, 1970).

movement. By provoking an interaction between the 'responsive eye'[27] of the viewer and the artwork, kineticism aims to expand the public's perceptual awareness and to alert viewers to the instability and polysemy of the pictorial space—and, by extension, of the world of appearances—they apprehend.

Clouzot's exposure to contemporary art and conversations with Vasarély, the 'Pope of Op', convinced him that cinema—the kinetic medium *par excellence*—was lagging behind in comparison with the latest developments in the visual arts. Kineticism, he came to realize, with its questioning of a stable notion of vision and its exploration of complex phenomena of perception, held the key to giving visual form to the distortions of reality to which the jealous subject in *L'Enfer* falls prey. Transposed to the cinema, the expanded forms of sensory experience afforded by kinetic art would open up new expressive possibilities for film. An alliance between what he considered one of the most original developments in the visual arts and his own *savoir-faire* as a film-maker—and between the formal innovations of kineticism and the technological possibilities of film—would herald the new cinema, resolutely anchored in modernity, which *L'Enfer* sought to inaugurate. In February 1964, together with a small crew, Clouzot filmed the exhibition 'Formes Nouvelles' at the Musée des arts décoratifs in Paris, a display of kinetic art containing, among others, works by Vasarély and Yvaral, which offered him inspiration for the kinetic effects he sought to apply in *L'Enfer*. Seeking to bridge the gap between cinema and the visual arts, he entrusted two artists at the forefront of kinetic art, Joël Stein and Yvaral, with supervising the visual effects for his film.

Between February and June Clouzot carried out a series of lengthy (and costly) tests at the Billancourt Studios near Paris in preparation for the film. The director was in a truly exceptional position in that he was able to experiment at ease and without financial constraint at the vanguard of what, judging from the remaining rushes, can only be called experimental cinema. Yet his situation was doubly paradoxical: first, contrary to avant-garde and experimental film practices, which tend to be artisanal and low budget, his film was produced by a major American studio, Columbia, and had at its disposal an unlimited budget—a situation unparalleled for a European director working outside the American studio system and unheard of in the context of independent and experimental cinema. Second, he entrusted film professionals seasoned in conventional, mainstream cinema (notably cinematographer Andréas Winding) with carrying out experiments which, even by the standards of experimental cinema, were without precedent. As first assistant Costa-Gavras comments: 'Il est parti dans un monde d'essais complètement inconnu pour le cinéma français. C'était le mystère.'[28]

---

[27] This term is borrowed from the title of a major exhibition of kinetic art at the Museum of Modern Art in New York in 1965.

[28] Cited in Bromberg, *Romy dans 'L'Enfer'*, p. 41.

The Billancourt test shoots unearthed by Bromberg and shown for the first time in the documentary he co-directed with Ruxandra Medrea give a vivid idea of the new film aesthetics the director sought to develop, and help us appraise its manifold artistic influences. It is worth noting that Clouzot's experiments evince a strong affinity with the tricks and techniques of Surrealism, which, like kinetic art, questions the stability of optical vision and challenges perceptual habits. In the tradition of the historical avant-garde of the 1920s and 1930s, the test footage incessantly decomposes and recomposes the human form through visual distortions, split imagery, multiplication, and superimposition. The anamorphic effects to which the actors' faces and bodies are subjected recall André Kertész's experimental photographic series *Distortions* (1933), effected through the use of distortion mirrors, while a series of shots of multiplied eyes echoes Man Ray's famous portrait of the Marquise Casati (1922), whose spectral, multiplied gaze haunts the viewer. Refractive filters, footage played in reverse, and the expressive use of shadows and lighting help create an oneiric, surreal atmosphere. There can be no doubt that Clouzot, who began his career in the 1930s and had a lifelong interest in literature and the visual arts, had first-hand knowledge of Surrealist experimentation. His exposure to Surrealist trickery would have been enhanced by a more direct influence for *L'Enfer*: Eric Duvivier and Henri Michaux's *Images du monde visionnaire* (1963), a film on the hallucinatory effects of mescaline, which borrows many of its visual effects from Surrealism—the director Duvivier is known above all for his Surreal work *La Femme 100 têtes* (1967), an adaptation of Max Ernst's eponymous collage novel. *Images du monde visionnaire* alerted Clouzot to the expressive possibilities of a light source called 'heliophor', hitherto used mainly in the natural sciences.[29]

If the test shoots thus to a certain extent harked back to earlier experiments in cinema and photography, the collaboration with Stein and Yvaral also generated numerous visual effects derived from kinetic art: pulsating geometrical forms and contracting and extending shapes emulated the retinal illusions triggered by kinetic painting and sculpture (while also recalling Richter and Eggeling's abstract films of the 1920s that count among the predecessors of kineticism); an eight-metre wheel carrying projectors and colour filters helped create iridescent colour effects; glitter and olive oil generously applied to Romy Schneider's face and body and lit by a heliophor light engine recreated the shimmering, *moiré* effects of kinetic paintings on the female body. Experiments with colour grading and colour inversion combined with futuristic blue and green make-up gave life to hallucinatory new visions of the human body. Although the test shoots followed no narrative logic, it is clear that Clouzot sought to exploit kinetic effects and objects to enhance the film's torrid erot-

[29] See ibid., p. 24.

icism: among the most sexually explicit images of the tests is that of a naked Romy Schneider playing with a spiral (an object Clouzot had discovered at the MOMA, New York) which sensually leaps up and down her body, caressing her breasts and nestling between her legs. Even seemingly abstract experiments with colour and geometrical patterns, by means of visual analogy, became erotically charged (assistant cinematographer William Lubtschansky recalls the 'coïts visuels' he produced by means of accelerated pulsating forms).

Audiences and film professionals alike have been stunned by the recovered test shoots, which, almost forty years on, have lost none of their daring.[30] Given their preparatory status, one does of course wonder—and this is a question asked repeatedly in Bromberg and Medrea's documentary—what role they would have played in the actual film. The surviving footage of the outdoor shooting carried out in the Cantal region in July 1964 yields little insight. On the contrary, compared with the Billancourt tests, the few scenes of marital life and of Marcel stalking his wife that remain are surprisingly conventional. Did the extravagant tests Clouzot carried out during pre-production prove simply incompatible with the film he had scripted, or would he have drawn on them at a later stage of production, either during the several months of interior shots he had planned at the Billancourt studios or in the editing process? To shed light on the place given to visual experimentation in the filmic project we need once again to turn to the remaining scripts for *L'Enfer*. The first of the three scripts housed at the Bibliothèque du Film is a continuity script—that is, it merely gives the action and dialogues. However, a shooting script annotated by Clouzot himself offers more precise indications as to the editing, camera work, special effects, and soundtrack. Finally, another shooting script, annotated by Serge Reggiani's dresser, contains yet more detail on planned visual and aural effects.[31]

The affinity with Surrealist effects present in the test shoots is further tangible in the shooting scripts. A scene towards the beginning of the film, in which Marcel surprises Odette watching slides with his suspected rival Martineau, is a case in point. According to the script, the emotional shock to which the jealous husband is subjected was to be visualized through a sudden freeze of the moving image and a series of grotesquely distorted photographs of Odette and her suspected lover, punctuated by stroboscopic light effects.

---

[30] Interestingly, Romanian cinematographer Mihai Malaimare has recently stated that he was strongly influenced by Clouzot's test shoots for his new collaboration with Francis Ford Coppola, *Twixt* (2012). See 'Des ultraviolets d'enfer', *Cahiers du cinéma*, 677 (2012), 24–28 (p. 26).

[31] There are three remaining scripts held at the Bibliothèque du Film, Paris: the first one, catalogued as SCEN 0949 (1/2), is complete, but is purely narrative (i.e. without any instructions as to camera work or visual/aural effects). The other two are shooting scripts, but are incomplete (they both end at the scene where Marcel follows his wife and Martineau, who are water-skiing on the lake). The one annotated by Clouzot is catalogued CJ0504-B63; the second one, marked 'Y Bonnay' and annotated by Reggiani's dresser, is catalogued SCEN 951 B 287.

The recourse to photography in a feature film immediately brings to mind Chris Marker's 1962 experimental science fiction film *La Jetée*, which consists entirely of still photos; yet, in purely technical terms, Clouzot here, as a note in the screenplay indicates, once again finds inspiration in the experiments of the historical avant-garde and their actualization in Duvivier and Michaux's *Images du monde visonnaire*:

> Cette série de photos pourrait être réalisée, après expérience, suivant le procédé d'Eric Duvivier, celui de Man Ray ou par alternance d'images positives ou négatives, etc., etc. Toute la série traversée de points lumineux qui doivent causer aux spectateurs un effet stroboscopique.[32]

What the director seems to have in mind here are Man Ray's rayographs (negative imaging created by placing objects directly on a sheet of photographic paper and exposing it to light) and Eric Duvivier's aforementioned experiments with heliophor light. Other Surrealist effects of defamiliarization are traceable in a scene in which a batch of envelopes start dancing before Marcel's eyes as he feverishly searches for a letter Odette seeks to hide from him. Not only do the dancing objects recall one of the first masterpieces of Surrealist film, Hans Richter's *Ghosts before Breakfast* (1927), featuring a rebellion of the object world against its owners, but the wording in the script, 'les enveloppes dansent [. . .] un étrange ballet abstrait',[33] echoes another classic of experimental cinema, Fernand Léger and Dudley Murphey's *Ballet mécanique* (1924). Furthermore, the use of hyperbolic mirrors to distort reality in an extended sequence where Marcel follows Odette across a market is reminiscent of the visual tricks first explored in Surrealist film and photography. Yet unlike his predecessors of the historical avant-garde, who used visual trickery to reveal the inherent strangeness of reality and signal its capacity for mystery and anarchy, Clouzot seems to assimilate special visual effects into a more realist project of characterization: spectators are encouraged to attribute the visual distortions to which the cinematic image is subjected to the male character's jealous insanity. Stripped of their anarchic and ludic power, the subversive—often purely formal—experiments of the avant-garde are recuperated for a modern cinema of subjectivity.

A similar narrative recuperation of artistic experimentation can be found in the director's borrowings from kineticism. Vasarély's kinetic sculptures and paintings had sensitized Clouzot to an art form that unsettles habitual perception by making it physiologically impossible for the eye to decide between different hypotheses. Indeed, a feature of kineticism is precisely its capacity to construct a polysemic pictorial space where different interpretations of a visual phenomenon become possible depending on the

[32] SCEN 951 B 287.
[33] Ibid.

vantage-point of the viewer and his or her movement in space. By dispensing with binary opposites (convex/concave, still/mobile, form/pattern, etc.) and foregrounding the pluridimensional, kinetic art compels the viewer to explore the complexity of perceptional and emotional experience.[34] As the art critic Michael Compton explains, kineticism seeks to 'set off optical effects and so to create powerful visual equivalents of emotions and physical phenomena of the highest energy'.[35] Vasarély himself speaks of the 'emotional shocks' to which kinetic art subjects the viewer, and describes its function as making phenomena that can be barely fathomed perceivable by sensory experience: 'Dans mes tableaux, je rends sensible quelque chose qui, même sur le plan de la connaissance, est à la limite de l'inexprimable.'[36]

It is precisely kineticism's potential to cast doubt on the dependability of perceptual experience that interests Clouzot in his portrayal of the paranoid mind in *L'Enfer*. The third screenplay testifies to the extensive borrowing the director made from kinetic art in his quest for visual effects that could convey Marcel's hallucinations: in one of the first scenes, the tiles in the bathroom where he believes he may have killed his wife start to oscillate before his eyes; on the bedroom window, under the battering rain, strange patches of light which advance, retract, and fuse as in a kinetic painting appear on the screen; the letters of the 'Hotel' sign dissolve into a series of verticals and horizontals, multiply, shift, and recompose so as to form the name 'Odette'; later, during accesses of jealous insanity, solid landscapes dissolve and dematerialize before his eyes. These are only a few examples of the ways in which Clouzot would have used optical effects derived from kineticism to convey the disconcerting distortions of reality to which the male protagonist is prey. Once again, the director does not altogether relinquish the imperatives of realist aesthetics: a clear colour coding would have allowed spectators to distinguish between objective reality (filmed in black and white) and Marcel's hallucinations (filmed in dazzling, non-naturalistic colours).[37] As with his appropriation of Surrealist effects, there is a marked discrepancy between the original purpose of kinetic art and Clouzot's use of kinetic effects in his film. His collaborator Stein explains that, contrary to kinetic artists, who wanted 'un art complètement froid, complètement rationnel, vidé d'une interprétation littéraire', the director was interested in kinetic effects as a means to give visual form to

[34] Vasarély himself comments on his 'Black and White' series in the following terms: 'J'en ai déduit philosophiquement parlant, que les signes blanc et noir, l'antinomie inéluctable des idées du passé, comme "jour et nuit", "ange et diable", "bien et mal", sont en réalité des complémentarités, idée androgyne et féconde. Accoupler l'affirmation et la négation de l'unité, c'est rendre la connaissance intégrale. Quelle perspective!' (cited in Holzhey, *Victor Vasarély, 1906-1997*, p. 55).
[35] Compton, *Optical and Kinetic Art*, p. 2.
[36] Jean-Louis Ferrier, *Entretiens avec Victor Vasarély* (Paris: Belfond, 1969), p. 56.
[37] Bromberg, *Romy dans 'L'Enfer'*, p. 59.

his protagonist's mental affliction.[38] At first sight, then, Clouzot's approach to visualizing madness may seem not dissimilar to that of Hitchcock, who masterfully exploited visual effects in films such as *Spellbound* (1945) and *Vertigo* (1958).[39] What distinguishes the two directors is that while Hitchcock kept special effects localized to particular scenes (most notably the dream sequence in *Spellbound*, made in collaboration with Salvador Dalí), in *L'Enfer* the entire filmic form would have been tainted by the theme of paranoia: indeed, increasingly, for Clouzot form and content had become inseparable entities.

Before moving on to the afterlife of *L'Enfer* in two later films, we must briefly look at the sound effects for the project, which, together with the visual experimentation, would have constituted one of its major innovations. As explained by assistant set designer Jacques Douy, the experiments of electro-acoustic music, especially around figures such as Stockhausen and Boulez, were part of the cultural environment of the 1960s and of considerable interest to Clouzot.[40] The director entrusted sound engineer Jean-Louis Ducarme and composer Gilbert Amy, one of the leading figures of electro-acoustic music, with the responsibility of creating an experimental soundtrack that would convey the gradual dissolution of the male protagonist's mind. Prefiguring the experiments of Nathalie Sarraute, who developed a comparable double postulation of the self in her autobiographical novel *Enfance* (1983), the male protagonist's voice in *L'Enfer* is split into two entities: the 'je' of his interior monologues and a much more unsettling 'tu' (also called 'La Voix') which probes, questions, or reassures the 'je' in a sustained, often frenetic, dialogue.[41] The second shooting script for the film, as well as several loose sheets, contains a complex notation system for the polyphonic interaction between the two voices. Beyond the communicative function of language, particular attention is given to the timbre, volume, rhythm, texture, and density of the voice. As in a Dada, 'Lettriste', or contemporary sound poetry performance,[42] the two voices enter into crescendos and staccatos, abruptly accelerate or slow down, stutter, stammer, and rustle. The only remaining

[38] Bonus 'Ils ont vu l'enfer', on DVD *'L'Enfer' de Henri-Georges Clouzot: la légende d'un film inachevé*.

[39] Other cinema classics that explore madness include Buñuel's *El* (1953) and Nicholas Ray's *Bigger than Life* (1956).

[40] Cf. the interview with Douy in Bromberg and Medrea's documentary, *'L'Enfer' de Henri-Georges Clouzot*.

[41] The juxtaposition of two voices that uncover different states of human subjectivity also recalls Bernard Heidsieck's sound poetry of the 1960s, which, in turn, was influenced by contemporary experiments in the fields of concrete and electronic music. For the history of sound poetry and a close reading of one of Heidsieck's poems see Jean-Pierre Bobillot, 'Bernard Heidsieck, "Poème-partition B2B3 (Exorcisme)"', in *Twentieth-Century French Poetry*, ed. by Hugues Azérad and Peter Collier (Cambridge: Cambridge University Press, 2010), pp. 204–13.

[42] The Lettrist cinema of Isidore Isou and Maurice Lemaître in the 1950s continued the experiments of the historical avant-garde. See, for instance, Isou's experimental film *Traité de bave et d'éternité* (1951).

tape of the sound experiments commissioned for the film, extracts of which are played in Bromberg and Medrea's documentary, reveals how far Clouzot had moved away from any conventional use of sound in his project: words are broken up into their constituent syllables, which are repeated, permutated, or echoed; recorded sentences are played backwards; natural sounds are anamorphosed by means of synthesizers. The amplified sound of objects (a hammer, a saw, a motorboat) would have taken on a menacing presence, and aural hallucinations (most notably Marcel's jealous thoughts, which interfere with and gradually replace the news broadcast on the radio) would have drawn viewers into the protagonist's paranoia. Just like the human body and the material world, whose shapes would have been decomposed by striking visual effects, natural sound is distorted into a monstrous noise, an abstract, angst-ridden music that punctuates the protagonist's paranoia.

Recycling and Adaptation: Clouzot's 'La Prisonnière' and Chabrol's 'L'Enfer'

When Clouzot suffered a heart attack while shooting *L'Enfer*, his career as a director seemed to be over: henceforth no film insurance company would cover him, and thus, finding a producer became virtually impossible. Yet, four years later, he bounced back with what was to be his last film, *La Prisonnière* (1968). This dark portrait of voyeurism and sadomasochistic relationships, while once again entering into dialogue with Proust's novel (from which it borrows its title), also looks back to *L'Enfer*, whose new cinematic techniques inspired by kineticism it recycles and re-enacts in a different social and geographical context (the bohemian world of avant-garde artists in Paris and its suburbs). Shot in the vivid colours of 1960s pop art and exhibiting a highly stylized aesthetic, *La Prisonnière* tends to be considered an oddity among Clouzot's more classical œuvre, yet the recently rediscovered footage for *L'Enfer* and the scripts on which we have drawn throughout this article reveal striking similarities between the two films. As a diptych, *La Prisonnière* and *L'Enfer* illuminate one another: the former gives an idea of what the latter would have looked like, while the latter's experiments in part inform the aesthetics of the former.

With this last film, Clouzot engages more directly with kinetic art, which for him had clearly lost none of its fascination. *La Prisonnière* revolves around the love triangle of Gilbert (Bernard Fresson), a kinetic artist, his partner José (Elisabeth Wiener), a film editor, and the enigmatic Stan (Laurent Terzieff), a gallery owner promoting kinetic art. When she discovers his habit of photographing female nudes in bondage, José becomes fascinated by Stan, agrees to pose for him, and begins a tortuous, self-destructive affair. In a study of sadomasochism that recalls Gilles Deleuze's essay 'Le Froid et le Cruel' (itself based on Sacher-Masoch's *Venus im Pelz*),[43] Clouzot examines the ambiguous relationship between dominator and dominated, pointing to the cerebral nature of sadomasochistic desire and drawing attention to the role of 'educator' held by the male character, who awakens deep-rooted, repressed fantasies of humiliation and subjugation in the female protagonist. The gallery, Gilbert's studio, and Stan's loft (replete with iconic works of twentieth-century art from Bellmer's doll to a neoprimitivist painting by Dubuffet) provide an ultra-modern setting for the melodrama. A striking opening sequence, which follows Gilbert and José from their suburban home into central Paris, visually recreates the perception of the kinetic artist: a series of POV shots taken from the interior of a train in motion evoke Gilbert's decomposition of the material world into a series of vibrating shapes, lines, and colours. The cinematography here, no longer concerned with plot or narrative illustration, conveys the expressive powers of kinetic art, which, by breaking perceptual habit, opens up a more richly sensual take on reality. As Clouzot explains with reference to the Hungarian artist Nicolas Schöffer (one of the fathers of kinetic sculpture), he discovered that simple cinematic techniques such as changes of camera angles could recreate the illusory optical effects of kinetic art:

J'ai pu constater qu'en filmant le simple trajet d'un train de banlieue sous certains angles, en photographiant les caténaires, les rails, les signaux et toutes les structures mécaniques, on retrouvait la même trame que dans certaines œuvres de Schöffer par exemple, et qu'on tirait les mêmes frémissements hallucinatoires.[44]

The extended sequence of the exhibition opening at Stan's gallery serves as a showcase for kinetic art in the film. Set designer Jacques Saulnier modelled the fictional gallery space after the Gallery Denise René and filled it with authentic art works, including a Vasarély painting lent by Clouzot. The footage from the 'Formes Nouvelles' exhibition filmed in preparation for *L'Enfer* was finally recycled in the images of the exhibition, where an array of kinetic sculptures and paintings dazzle a crowd of fashionable spectators (Michel Piccoli makes a cameo appearance alongside other celebrities). The sequence culminates in a psychedelic labyrinth, where, in the distorting and multiplying mirrors of a kinetic installation, José witnesses her husband's advances to a journalist from whom he hopes to secure a favourable review. With its focus on the commercialization of art in the gallery space and the instrumentalization of sexuality for the purposes of personal advancement, the exhibition scene draws the portrait of a generation for whom art, consumption, and love are but one and the same thing. Given the rarefied elite world he himself inhabits, it is difficult to take at face value Stan's opening speech promoting the democratization of art

[43] Gilles Deleuze, *Présentation de Sacher-Masoch: Le Froid et le Cruel* (Paris: Minuit, 2007); Leopold von Sacher-Masoch, *Venus im Pelz* (Frankfurt a.M.: Insel, 1980).
[44] Cited in Bocquet and Godin, *Henri-Georges Clouzot cinéaste*, p. 144.

through the production of 'multiples' (he provocatively announces 'the supermarket of art'). Clouzot critically engages here with Vasarély's 'Yellow Manifesto' (the accompanying text for the 'Le Mouvement' exhibition at the Gallery Denise René, where Vasarély first formulated his vision for the reproduction, diffusion, and integration of art works into the daily lives of twentieth-century citizens), from which much of the speech is borrowed. Convinced that the art work should be repeatable, Vasarély rejected the notion of an original, auratic work of art in favour of mass-produced multiples. He called for cheaply reproduced utilitarian art works available to large sectors of the population: in other words, for a social art, available to all, that would help bridge divisions. In the 'Yellow Manifesto' he states: 'If the art product does not break through the constrictions of an elite of connoisseurs, art is doomed to death by suffocation.'[45] Ironically, it was precisely this infinite multiplication and commercialization of art saturating the market that rang the death knell for kineticism at the end of the 1960s.[46] Clouzot further distances himself from kineticism's theoretical posturing with the dialogue between Gilbert and the journalist, which revolves around the hegemonic struggle between aspiring young artists and the old masters of modernism. The sculptor's disparaging remarks about Picasso, whom he declares 'carbonisé', are all the more ironic in the light of the latter's frenzied activity and unbroken creativity during the last years of his life and the director's own fruitful collaboration with the painter in *Le Mystère Picasso*.

If Clouzot thus seems to adopt a critical stance towards the theories that underpin kinetic art, he none the less freely applies the processes of visual kinetics to the design and cinematography of *La Prisonnière*; in particular, as Christopher Lloyd explains, in the colour and pattern of characters' dress or background objects and their spatial positioning.[47] Parallels with *L'Enfer* are most evident in the film's final sequence, which consists of two sophisticated montages strongly indebted to kinetic art and the historical avant-garde. The first montage comprises a fifty-second flashback (the equivalent of a Proustian instance of involuntary memory) which precedes José's car crash. (Incidentally, her motionless body on the railway tracks resonates with one of the most perversely erotic images from *L'Enfer*, that of a naked Romy Schneider tied to the tracks before an approaching train.) In a series of images each lasting a fraction of a second, the scene of a previous car crash and the faces of Gilbert, Stan, and José, punctuated by coloured screens, each appear in rapid succession. The second, three-and-a-half-minute-long montage simulates the young woman's feverish delirium in hospital as she struggles to regain consciousness. Composed of hundreds of shots, this psychedelic sequence, as Christopher Lloyd

---

[45] Cited in Karl Ruhrberg and others, *Art of the 20th Century*, 2 vols (Cologne: Taschen, 1998), I, 346.
[46] See Foster and others, *Art since 1900*, pp. 381–83.
[47] Lloyd, *Henri-Georges Clouzot*, p. 167.

comments, 'in grossly distorted, fragmented form effectively summarises much of the film, as though José were reliving her experiences at a frantically accelerated pace'.[48] Accompanied by a disturbing cacophony of amplified and electronically distorted sounds (the clicking of a camera mingles with the rattle of an approaching train and with female cries of distress), shots of brightly coloured spirals and contracting and expanding fluorescent cubes punctuate Surrealist images of multiplied eyes and cameras, melding faces and grotesquely distorted body parts. Among the pulsating images, we recognize José in chains, the three protagonists caught in the metal sheets of a kinetic labyrinth, Stan hitting Gilbert with a door. Intercalated shots of Bellmer's doll and a fetish-like sculpture symbolize the sadomasochistic relationship between José and Stan. As was planned for *L'Enfer*, the optical effects here help construct (beyond their purely expressive function) a starkly eroticized atmosphere in which the destructive bearings of human desire and obsession can be explored. With its hallucinated images, the final montage sequence seems to actualize, in the framework of a different but not dissimilar narrative, the planned 'défilé d'images'[49] of *L'Enfer* which would have simulated Marcel's final delirium. In both films (as, indeed, in their tacit hypotext, Proust's *La Prisonnière*), an obsessive male character almost destroys a woman, but in his final film Clouzot shifts from an almost exclusively male perspective to a female one.

On its release in 1968, *La Prisonnière* was coolly received by both the press and the public. With hindsight, we can attribute its failure to please to its atypicality with regard to Clouzot's wider œuvre and its uneasy place in the cinematic landscape of the 1960s. For fans of the classical Clouzot of *Quai des orfèvres* and *Le Corbeau* this hyper-aestheticized portrait of sadomasochism gesturing towards expressive abstractionism[50] was doubtless too unsettling; yet, for younger audiences, compared with more overtly experimental films such as Godard's *Pierrot le fou* (1965) or *2 ou 3 choses que je sais d'elle* (1967)—and given the more liberal environment after May 1968—its still largely narrative-based construction and controlled eroticism must have seemed tame. *La Prisonnière* is virtually never shown today, and apart from Christopher Lloyd's recent appraisal in the first English-language monograph on Clouzot, it seems to be forgotten by film critics. By contrast, Claude Chabrol's more direct reworking of *L'Enfer* in his homonymous 1994 film has generated some critical attention (though not always favourable). Chabrol's film, released thirty years after Clouzot had to abandon his project, is adapted from the continuity (that is, the purely narrative) script for *L'Enfer*. Chabrol kept most of the action and dialogues, but entirely reworked Clouzot's criss-crossing (Proustian) narrative to turn it into a linear, progressive plot. As a director concerned with psy-

---

[48] Ibid., p. 170.
[49] This is the term used in SCEN 0949 (1/2).
[50] See Lloyd, *Henri-Georges Clouzot*, p. 162.

chological motivation and causality, Chabrol considered the memory-based narrative and the kinetic effects of the original a hindrance to the dramatic action. He explains in an interview: 'la construction était formaliste dans le plus mauvais sens du terme et cela détruisait tout le reste. Il [Clouzot] commençait notamment le film par la fin et tout était basé sur des flash-back. C'était influencé par son obsession du moment pour l'art cinétique et Vasarély.'[51] In his own more plot-driven film, the paranoia of the male character gradually taints reality and contaminates it to such an extent that spectators can no longer be certain whether the images they see on screen correspond to an objective reality or are a product of Paul's (François Cluzet) hallucination.[52] Standard cinematic devices for expressing madness and subjectivity—amplified and distorted sound, abrupt changes of camera angle, blurred images, anti-naturalist framing, and marked discontinuity between shots—give visual and aural form to the protagonist's delirium. Internally contradictory shots serve to blur the boundaries between reality and hallucination, most evidently in one of the final scenes, where the camera, in one single shot, moves from the bloodstained Nelly (Emmanuelle Béart) lying on the bathroom floor to Paul, shaving, and into the adjacent room, where we see Nelly (played by a body double) chained to the bed. Complex mirroring techniques are used to similar effect: in a shot of Paul alone facing several mirrors, the shot begins with the fourth mirror reflection of the actor; the camera continues to move between his mirrored simulacra and real silhouette in such quick succession (playing with the inversion of the image) that the spectator loses track of where to situate reality.[53]

With *L'Enfer* Chabrol once again demonstrates his undeniable skill for creating suspense and engrossing spectators in a thriller-like plot. The film does not lack a carefully constructed ambiguity, but its tightly controlled narrative is far removed from the hallucinatory, nightmarish visions Clouzot sought in his project. Ironically, the comparison between Chabrol, a former 'young Turk' of the Nouvelle Vague who quickly turned to a more mainstream, commercial type of cinema, and Clouzot, who in the 1950s and 1960s was discredited as a 'qualité française' director incapable of artistic innovation, throws into relief the latter's creative audacity. While Chabrol skilfully uses cinematic techniques that have been tried and tested (he names Nicholas Ray, Buñuel, and Fritz Lang as influences for *L'Enfer*), Clouzot, by contrast, looks outside the cinema to literature, the visual arts, and music to forge a cinematic language that can give visual and aural form to extreme states of human consciousness. This embracing of and openness towards other arts stands in

---

[51] Cited in Camille Taboulay, 'Chabrol: une saison en enfer', *Cahiers du cinéma*, 473 (1993), 47–55 (p. 48).

[52] In Chabrol's film the protagonists are called Paul and Nelly.

[53] For a detailed discussion of the film see Taboulay, 'Chabrol: une saison en enfer' and her article 'L'Enfer me ment', *Cahiers du cinéma*, 476 (1994), 34–39.

marked contrast to the Nouvelle Vague, which militated to establish cinema as an autonomous art form no longer in the shadow of more established arts, notably literature, the visual arts, and theatre. As Alexandre Astruc postulates in a seminal article that influenced the Nouvelle Vague's *auteur* politics, 'le cinéma est en train tout simplement de devenir un moyen d'expression, ce qu'ont été tous les autres arts avant lui, ce qu'ont été en particulier la peinture et le roman'.[54] In the same article he goes on to dismiss Surrealist cinema, which, he claims, merely transposed its experiments in painting and poetry to film. For Astruc and the *Cahiers du cinéma* critics after him, cinema must distinguish itself from the other arts to become a language in its own right.[55] For Clouzot, by contrast, it is precisely in the dialogue between cinema and the other arts that new forms of cinematic expression may be found.

Clouzot's *L'Enfer* did of course remain unfinished, and it is open to debate whether this ambitious project at the crossroads between the arts was not doomed to fail from the outset. Stéphane Delorme, in an article in *Cahiers du cinéma*, considers both *L'Enfer* and *La Prisonnière* as dead ends in which an ageing film-maker unable to connect with his times had embroiled himself.[56] In Bromberg and Medrea's documentary members of the film crew for *L'Enfer* speculate that Clouzot no longer had control of his project, his heart attack only sealing the fate of a film that was beyond rescue. It could be argued that the project's permeability to other artistic influences and its awkward positioning at the intersection between experimental and mainstream cinema ultimately threw up paradoxes and contradictions that proved insuperable. Yet the fragmented and unfinished form in which we apprehend the film today is perhaps most fitting for the cinematic utopia Clouzot sought to create. Almost fifty years on, the nightmarishly distorted and starkly erotic visions preserved in the surviving rushes continue to gesture, with their expressionist use of colour and plasticity of the visual image, towards a modernity that has lost none of its daring.

UNIVERSITY OF EDINBURGH   MARION SCHMID

[54] 'Naissance d'une nouvelle avant-garde: la caméra-stylo', in Alexandre Astruc, *Du stylo à la caméra... et de la caméra au stylo: écrits (1942–1984)* (Paris: l'Archipel, 1992), pp. 324–28 (p. 325).
[55] See also Bazin's concluding remarks: 'Le cinéaste est, non plus seulement le concurrent du peintre et du dramaturge, mais enfin l'égal du romancier' ('L'Évolution du langage cinématographique', in André Bazin, *Qu'est-ce que le cinéma?* (Paris: Éditions du Cerf, 2002), pp. 63–80 (p. 80)).
[56] 'L'impasse dans laquelle il [Clouzot] s'enferre, et qui sera celle de *La Prisonnière*, est celle du vieux cinéaste essayant de raccorder avec son époque [...] il est permis tout aussi bien de penser que *L'Enfer*, malgré ces beautés, aurait été au final un ratage' (Delorme, 'Les Cercles de *L'Enfer*', p. 73).

MICHEL TOURNIER AND THE VIRTUAL ESSAY

> Mon propos n'est pas d'innover dans la forme, mais de faire passer dans une forme aussi traditionnelle, préservée et rassurante que possible une matière ne possédant aucune de ces qualités.
>
> (MICHEL TOURNIER)[1]

Montaigne could not have anticipated the legacy of his literary attempts in the late sixteenth century, which continue to serve as models of cultural critique and subjective written expression for contemporary writers. While Marielle Macé argues compellingly that the essay was born at its own summit,[2] Montaigne illustrated only one very small subset of possibilities for this kind of writing. The essay prioritizes the process of reaching a conclusion over the conclusion itself, allows room for approximations and digressions, and blurs the boundary between art and science. In the twentieth century new appropriations of the genre, such as the essayistic novel, have materialized, and writers continue to assay the limits of the form. The many recent collections of essays and scholarly works on the essay attest to the vibrancy of the genre in the early twenty-first century.[3]

The French writer Michel Tournier (b. 1924) has experimented throughout his career with various genres, beginning with a focus on the novel, shifting to the short story and novella in the middle years, and dedicating the later years of his textual production to the essay and to polemical, journalistic writing. While such shifts in genre preference are common in writers with long careers, what is significant in Tournier's literary production is his constant trying out of each genre, so to speak, in order to find the best outlet for his philosophical voice that had been stifled when he failed his *agrégation* at the Sorbonne in 1950. The essay is perhaps the most obvious genre suited to digressive reflection, to thought in motion, while formalized philosophy, with

---

I would like to thank Michel Tournier for inviting me to his home in Choisel to discuss his work and to see his garden. Also, a warm thanks to Marielle Macé for her brilliant contributions to the field of essay studies and for her kindness as an interlocutor.

[1] Michel Tournier, *Le Vent Paraclet* (Paris: Gallimard, 1978), p. 195.

[2] 'L'œuvre [*Les Essais* de Montaigne] ici vaut le genre: elle l'a fait naître à son sommet' (Marielle Macé, *Le Temps de l'essai: histoire d'un genre en France au XXe siècle* (Paris: Belin, 2006), p. 13).

[3] These include *Essayists on the Essay: Montaigne in Our Time*, ed. by Carl H. Klaus and Ned Stuckey-French (Iowa City: University of Iowa Press, 2012); G. Douglas Atkins, *On the Familiar Essay* (New York: Palgrave Macmillan, 2009); Kuisma Korhonen, *Textual Friendship: The Essay as Possible Encounter, from Plato and Montaigne to Levinas and Derrida* (Amherst: Humanity Books, 2006); *The Modern Essay in French*, ed. by Charles Forsdick and Andrew Stafford (Oxford: Peter Lang, 2005); G. Douglas Atkins, *Tracing the Essay: Through Experience to Truth* (Athens: University of Georgia Press, 2005); and Cristina Kirklighter, *Traversing the Democratic Borders of the Essay* (Albany: State University of New York Press, 2002).

its emphasis on systems and truths, is perhaps too rigid for the essay's loose form.[4] If Tournier's writing provides any evidence, one might guess that his failure of the *agrégation* had to do with his approximate interpretations of the work of thinkers such as Spinoza, Kant, Descartes, and Husserl. Each of his early novels incorporated various concepts from these thinkers and others, without necessarily explicitly crediting them as the authors of these ideas. In his fictions he consistently sought to access the abstract through the concrete. However, he ultimately gravitated towards the essay, the form *par excellence* of non-systemic meditation. As I will illustrate, Tournier's attraction to the essay form was already foretold in his early fictions.

Tournier's novels, novellas, and short stories are exemplary of what I will call virtual essayism, which entails a two-pronged manœuvre: first, the inclusion of self-sufficient essays or lengthy essayistic parentheses within a fictional frame, and second, the extraction and publication of these essays as the author's own meditations. This is not an occasional tactic in Tournier's œuvre but rather the very means by which it functions. This analysis specifically addresses his fictions and those essays that have been lifted from them, often word for word, and then elaborated and published in subsequent essay collections. Avid readers of his work can confirm that this reiterative poetics creates an uncanny sensation: from book to book, one feels that the themes, images, and theories are vaguely familiar, that they have been encountered somewhere before. These intertextual echoes often include approximative claims based on loose etymological relationships, free association, and imaginative juxtapositions. Unbound by empirical rules of observation and thesis-making, Tournier's essays are often completely virtual in nature; while they follow the formal generic conventions of the essay, the lifted essays remain in essence vestiges of the fictional context in which they were originally fabricated. They simply lack the fictional frame. For this reason, Tournier's virtual essayism is frustrating for readers who might look to the essays as *clés de lecture* for his personal beliefs. The value of the extracted essays as biographical clues is minimal. Instead, they are a hypothetical space in which Tournier plays out the speculations made by his essayist avatar, whose ideas are the culmination of the loose theories of his fictional characters. Reconfiguring accepted ideas about the essay, Tournier recognizes and exercises heretofore unexploited possibilities of the form, seizing the opportunity to run a hypothetical scenario through its full course using the rhetoric of a legitimizing discourse

---

[4] Hugo Friedrich writes of Montaigne, 'One can get a picture of the *Essais* by comparing the book with its extreme contrast, the "system"' (Hugo Friedrich, *Montaigne*, trans. by Dawn Eng (Berkeley: University of California Press, 1991), p. 20); while Adorno claims that the essay is 'the exact opposite of the theological' and of the 'philosophy of absolute knowledge' (T. W. Adorno, 'The Essay as Form', trans. by Bob Hullot-Kentor and Frederic Will, *New German Critique*, 32 (Spring/Summer 1984), 151–71 (pp. 168, 166)).

(comparing and contrasting, speculating about the roots of a problem and its future manifestations, anticipating objections, etc.). This discourse, meant to legitimize, ultimately destabilizes the cogency of the essayist's claims. These essays are not actualities, nor are they fictions, but rather virtualities. In other words, they are almost-essays that still function autonomously; however, they belong ultimately to a virtual world coterminous with ours.

I will begin with an example that clearly shows Tournier's virtualizing manœuvre, and then proceed with an explanation of what I mean by this term. In his novella *Éléazar ou la source et le buisson* (1996), an Irish pastor in the nineteenth century travels across the United States towards California, a new Promised Land. Late in the story, the pastor Éléazar, whose son has been bitten by a snake and is close to death, seeks advice from a Native American chief named Serpent d'Airain. Here, Serpent d'Airain explains the existence of the snake, with short interventions from Éléazar:

> — Le serpent peut être de deux sortes. Il est venimeux ou constricteur. S'il est venimeux, il tue d'un baiser. S'il est constricteur, il tue d'une étreinte. Le premier n'est qu'une bouche, le second n'est qu'un bras. Mais c'est toujours par un geste d'amour qu'il tue. [. . .]
> — L'inversion maligne est sa vocation, reprit l'Indien. A l'origine, il brillait au ciel, comme la plus parfaite des créatures du Grand Esprit. Il rayonnait comme le prince des enfants de Dieu.
> — C'était le plus beau des anges, le Lucifer, le Porte-Lumière, approuva le pasteur [Éléazar].
> — Son orgueil l'a perdu. Il s'est cru l'égal du Grand Esprit. Les soldats de Dieu se sont rués sur lui. Ils lui ont arraché ses ailes, ses bras, ses jambes, son sexe. Ils en ont fait une colonne de cuir terminée par un masque, le serpent. Ils l'ont jeté à terre.
> — C'était l'ange-tronc. Car il est tombé dans les branches d'un arbre, un pommier, et là, Porte-Lumière a enseigné sa sagesse ténébreuse au premier couple humain, Adam et Ève, poursuivit Éléazar. [. . .]
> — Explique-moi la magie de la tête du serpent, demanda Éléazar.
> — La tête du serpent est formée d'os assez lâchement attachés les un aux autres, commença l'Indien. Les mâchoires peuvent se décrocher à volonté. Toute la tête est ainsi démontable. Pour engloutir une proie énorme, par exemple, elle éclate en morceaux, et tout le corps du serpent devient comme une grande chaussette vivante qui s'enfile d'elle-même sur la proie.[5]

This dialogue is a negotiation of the meaning of the snake—as a receptacle of cultural significance—between Serpent d'Airain's tribal tradition and Éléazar's Christian one. The two accounts are compatible and do not contradict one another. In this passage, it is important to note the dialogic structure, a Montaignian signature, which allows both speakers to contribute their individual readings of the snake. Now, compare the nearly word-for-word *reprise* by Tournier from 'Déchiffrement du serpent', an essay published in

[5] Michel Tournier, *Éléazar ou la source et le buisson* (Paris: Gallimard, 1996), pp. 90–91.

Célébrations in 1999. Here, Tournier combines both speakers' assertions into one essay in his own voice. He writes of the snake:

L'inversion maligne définit sa démarche ordinaire. Ainsi l'amour. Il est deux sortes de serpents, les venimeux et les constricteurs. Les venimeux tuent d'un baiser. Les constricteurs tuent d'une étreinte. Les premiers ne sont qu'une bouche. Les seconds ne sont qu'un bras. Mais toujours, c'est par un geste d'amour qu'ils tuent.

La tête du serpent est composée d'os assez lâchement reliés les uns aux autres. Les mâchoires peuvent se décrocher à volonté. Toute la tête est en somme démontable. Pour engloutir une proie énorme par exemple, elle distend ses morceaux, et tout le corps du serpent devient comme une chaussette vivante qui s'enfile d'elle-même sur la proie. [...]

Le serpent, c'est l'ange-tronc, horrible et magnifique.[6]

The rest of this essay develops a myth-based theory about the snake's origins. The juxtaposition of these two texts illustrates the process of virtual essayism: the essayistic 'feel' of many segments of Tournier's novels is confirmed by their subsequent extraction, elaboration, and publication as free-standing essays, as though their 'essayness' were not explicit enough. Every novel and short story written by Tournier has at least one but usually many essayistic theses that are developed and reiterated throughout the narrative's course. These themes are nearly always adapted to a free-standing essay form and published subsequently.[7]

As Richard Norton writes, 'a virtual thing comes to its effectiveness only because an actual thing was established before it as a point of comparison, because the actual thing itself is not in effect, and because the virtual reality is working in place of the actual'.[8] By this definition, Tournier's extracted essays fall into the category of the virtual. In his case, the essay form and its conventions provide a benchmark by which his virtual essays are measured. They seem to meet all of the generic criteria, which explains why readers often believe them to represent Tournier's actual stance on the topics he addresses. Norton continues, 'The virtual event is a whole and acceptable reality between what was supposed to be actually the case and its actual nonexistence caused by failure, neglect, or intent' (p. 500). I claim that Tournier's virtualism

[6] Michel Tournier, *Célébrations* (Paris: Mercure de France, 1999), pp. 49–51.

[7] Here is only a brief list of some of these rearticulated themes: the nomad and the sedentary (one of Tournier's most repeated themes, explored in *Éléazar ou la source et le buisson*, in 'L'Aire du Muguet', in *Le Coq de bruyère*, and in the essay 'Le Nomade et le sédentaire', in *Le Miroir des idées*); image and sign (in the novella *La Goutte d'or*, in 'Le Peintre et son modèle: un épisode inédit de *La Goutte d'or*', in *Petites proses*, and in the essays 'Le Tabor et le Sinaï', in a collection of the same name, and in 'Le Signe et l'image', in *Le Miroir des idées*); the sacred and the profane (in *Éléazar ou la source et le buisson*, in the essay 'La Source et le buisson', in *Le Miroir des idées*); phorie (in *Le Roi des aulnes*, and in the essay 'Le Roi des aulnes', in *Le Vent Paraclet*); the voyage initiatique (explored in *La Goutte d'or*, in 'Amandine ou les deux jardins', and in the interview 'Le sang des fillettes' published in *Le Monde*, 9 December 1977, p. 31); and couplehood (in *Les Météores*, in *Vendredi ou les limbes du Pacifique*, and in the essay 'Les Météores' in *Le Vent Paraclet*).

[8] Richard Norton, 'What Is Virtuality?', *Journal of Aesthetics and Art Criticism*, 30 (1972), 499–505 (p. 499).

is wholly intentional as both an aesthetic and rhetorical gambit, which he deploys consciously as a provoking and destabilizing mechanism.

Tournier dissolves the distinction between the closely related concepts of potentiality and virtuality. Deleuze describes the difference between the two as follows: 'le possible s'oppose au réel; le processus du possible est donc "réalisation". Le virtuel, au contraire, ne s'oppose pas au réel; il possède une pleine réalité par lui-même. Son processus est l'actualisation.'[9] Tournier is clearly familiar with the theme of potentiality as a philosophical concept, although the distinction between the potential and the virtual is not explicitly rehearsed in his writing. He claims, 'le possible ne prolifère nulle part aussi bien que sur les ruines du réel'.[10] Modelling himself after Flaubert, Tournier meticulously researched every place, event, and cultural phenomenon mentioned in his texts, compiling the 'ruins of the real' upon which he would construct his otherworldly narratives. As Pierre Lévy describes in *Qu'est-ce que le virtuel?*, 'Dans la philosophie scolastique, est virtuel ce qui existe en puissance et non en acte.'[11] In *Miroir des idées* (1994) Tournier dedicates a short essay to this very topic entitled 'L'acte et la puissance', which explores both Aristotle's and Plato's views on the actual and the potential, and the concept of potentiality in Leibniz's monadology. He writes:

> Comment préserver l'unité qui persiste entre le vieillard et l'enfant qu'il fut? Il s'agit bien du même individu, mais [. . .] il a changé, voilà tout. Comment retrouver le même dans le changeant? Par la puissance qui est la présence fantomatique du futur dans le présent. Le vieillard était déjà en puissance dans l'enfant. D'année en année, il est passé à l'acte.[12]

Tournier often exploits this theme of potential in his fictions, particularly through the recurrent figure of the child and the *voyage initiatique*. In the above quotation he describes potentiality in terms of latency and the act of becoming, thus forging a provisional definition of the term: the potential is the spectral presence of the future in the present. The old man is one chosen path of himself from boyhood, a potentiality become actuality. Imagine the man were able to create a computer simulation of all the untaken paths in his life. These virtualities would be real in that they have manifested themselves in some form (a digital simulation), but they are never actualized. They remain almost concrete, almost palpable, resembling an actual model but not taking form.

Tournier writes of virtuality explicitly in at least one frequently cited passage, where it is essential to note that the text addresses the virtual in

---

[9] Gilles Deleuze, *Différence et répétition* (Paris: Presses Universitaires de France, 1985), p. 272.
[10] Tournier, *Le Vent Paraclet*, p. 123.
[11] Pierre Lévy, *Qu'est-ce que le virtuel?* (Paris: La Découverte, 1998), p. 13.
[12] Michel Tournier, *Le Miroir des idées*, rev. edn (Paris: Mercure de France, 1996), pp. 161–62.

terms of its relationship to aesthetics. In his debut novel, *Vendredi ou les limbes du Pacifique* (1967), the protagonist Robinson writes in his logbook:

> Mais mes relations avec les choses se trouvent elles-mêmes dénaturées par ma solitude. Lorsqu'un peintre ou un graveur introduit des personnages dans un paysage ou à proximité d'un monument, ce n'est pas par goût de l'accessoire. Les personnages donnent l'échelle et, ce qui importe davantage encore, ils constituent des points de vue possibles, qui ajoutent au point de vue réel de l'observateur d'indispensables virtualités. A Speranza, il n'y a qu'un point de vue, le mien, dépouillé de toute virtualité.[13]

Tournier underscores the necessity of others in order to 'give scale' to existence and to multiply perspectival options. His example hinges on the figure of the painter, whose vocation is to interrogate what is *not* actual. As Norton explains, 'art is not a substitute but an alternative',[14] in other words, art is not a paltry stand-in for things as they are but rather an index of a different state of things. Colin Davis accounts for Tournier's instrumentalization of the possible and the virtual in the following way:

> Ever since *Les Météores* Tournier has insisted upon the virtual coexistence of contradictory states within the work of art. [...] This perception of infinite possibilities informs a more general theory of art. [...] [T]hese 'expressions aussi contradictoires' are possible because the artist captures 'l'élan vital à sa source même, au point où toutes les implications sont encore réunies à l'état virtuel.'[15] All possibilities are simultaneously present; contradictory perceptions arise when the observer focuses upon particular qualities contained within the virtual plenitude of the artwork.[16]

Deleuze, too, had intuited some virtual aspects of Tournier's writing, which he identifies in an essay included in a later edition of *Vendredi* as a closing commentary:

> Le roman de Tournier n'est pourtant pas un roman à thèse sur la perversion. Ce n'est pas un roman à thèse. Ni un roman à personnages, puisqu'il n'y a pas d'autrui. Ni un roman d'analyse intérieure, Robinson ayant fort peu d'intériorité. C'est un étonnant roman d'aventures comique, et un roman cosmique d'avatars.[17]

He then calls the novel 'un roman expérimental inductif' and writes, 'Alors, la réflexion philosophique peut recueillir ce que le roman montre avec tant

---

[13] Michel Tournier, *Vendredi ou les limbes du Pacifique* (Paris: Gallimard, 1967), p. 53.
[14] Norton, 'What is Virtuality?', p. 502.
[15] Michel Tournier, *Les Météores* (Paris: Gallimard, 1975), p. 535.
[16] Colin Davis, *Michel Tournier: Philosophy and Fiction* (Oxford: Oxford University Press, 1988), p. 119.
[17] Deleuze in Tournier, *Vendredi*, p. 261. The third-person narrator describes the arrival of the ship *The Whitebird* in the following terms: 'Chacun de ces hommes était un monde *possible*, assez cohérent, avec ses valeurs, ses foyers d'attraction et de répulsion, son centre de gravité. Pour différents qu'ils fussent les uns des autres, ces *possibles* de Speranza — combien sommaire et superficielle! — autour de laquelle ils s'organisaient, et dans un coin de laquelle se trouvaient un naufragé nommé Robinson et son serviteur métis. [...] Et chacun de ces mondes possibles proclamait naïvement sa réalité. C'était cela autrui: un possible qui s'acharne à passer pour réel' (pp. 238–39).

de force et de vie.'[18] His essay's general theme of otherness allows Deleuze to complicate the relationship between the other, the possible, and the virtual. As he explains, 'autrui comme structure, c'est *l'expression d'un monde possible*, c'est l'exprimé saisi comme n'existant pas encore hors de ce qui l'exprime' (p. 265). He writes also that 'Autrui, c'est l'existence du possible enveloppé' (ibid.). Deleuze's highly intuitive reading of *Vendredi* could be extended to the larger part of Tournier's œuvre, even in the texts that do not manifestly treat the theme of otherness. Most critical theories at hand during the publication of his early successful novels (*Vendredi*, *Le Roi des aulnes*, *Les Météores*)[19] had no stable critical language to accommodate analyses of the avatar, the possible, the potential, and the virtual, which attests to Tournier's prescience. Despite the subsequent advent of a more sophisticated critical discourse, this aspect of Tournier's work has been largely neglected.

Tournier understood that a hypothetical writing practice best accommodates these notions (avatar, virtuality, potentiality, etc.). One often has the sense that he is constantly in the mode of the hypothetical, be it in his fictions or his essays. Of course, all fiction is hypothetical in that it imagines the state of things as they could be, even in the case of science fiction, which often imagines the state of things in another dimension or another universe. I mean rather that Tournier takes that which has already occurred or which someone else has already conceived and recasts it with hypothetical adjustments. From the formal perspective, Tournier follows the conventions of mimetic realism. However, from the conceptual or situational perspective, he often departs on wild deviations from reality, such as in the final pages of *Les Météores* when the character Paul leaks outside his own body, which begins to regulate itself according to meteorological phenomena. Tournier's reflections are often far-fetched and exploratory, yoking together remote ideas, borrowing from literary texts, fables, holy texts, and historical accounts at will. The back cover of the 1978 paperback edition of *Le Coq de bruyère* published by Gallimard describes the collection of short stories in this way:

Comment le Père Noël donnerait-il le sein à l'Enfant Jésus? L'Ogre du Petit Poucet était-il un hippie? Un nain peut-il devenir surhomme? Est-il possible de tuer avec un appareil de photographie? Le citron donne-t-il un avant-goût du néant? A ces questions — et à bien d'autres plus graves et plus folles encore — ce livre répond par des histoires drôles, navrantes, exaltantes et toujours exemplaires.[20]

---

[18] Ibid.
[19] Tournier even inserts himself—an avatar of himself—into his 1975 novel *Les Météores*: 'A 17h19 un souffle d'ouest-sud-ouest découvrit le jupon de la vieille Henriette Puysoux qui ramassait des pommes de terre dans son champ, fit claquer le store du Café des Amis de Plancoët, rabattit brutalement l'un des volets de la maison du docteur Bottereau en bordure du bois de la Hunaudaie, tourna huit pages des *Météores* d'Aristote que lisait Michel Tournier sur la plage de Saint-Jacut' (p. 9).
[20] Michel Tournier, *Le Coq de bruyère* (Paris: Gallimard, 1978), back cover.

This description of the text conforms to the general hypothetical nature of Tournier's œuvre. His refiguration of well-known narratives (the stories of Crusoe, Adam and Eve, the Erlking, the Magi) solicits their reappraisal through alternative contextualizations and hypothetical play. He is entirely possibilitarian in his consideration of the world that surrounds him.[21] Tournier shows to what extent the making of myths is an essayistic process. His hypothetical exercises mirror those of early humans, who sought to explain their surroundings by improvising systems that could account for all of the inscrutable phenomena they encountered. He applies what could be called a loose scientific method, one unbound by the imperative of reality and obeying only the rules of conceivability. For him, the essay is a textual space where he can reiterate and expound upon the thoughts of his characters and narrators, who were not obliged to make plausible assertions. Even though these essays have no fictional narrative frame, Tournier maintains the hypothetical attitude requisite for writing fiction. He often disregards any obligation to plausibility or verisimilitude in the essays and opts instead for arbitrary relationships and a penchant for fantasy. His essays also conspicuously accommodate reason, but a sort of reason that allows for a functional alternation between the actual and the virtual.

Czech novelist Milan Kundera has theorized what he calls the specifically novelistic essay, 'qui ne prétend pas apporter un message apodictique mais reste hypothétique, ludique, ou ironique'.[22] Kundera goes on to explain:

En entrant dans le corps du roman, la méditation change d'essence. En dehors du roman, on se trouve dans le domaine des affirmations: tout le monde est sûr de sa parole: un politicien, un philosophe, un concierge. Dans le territoire du roman, on n'affirme pas: c'est le territoire du jeu et des hypothèses. La méditation romanesque est donc, par essence, interrogative, hypothétique. (p. 101)

He goes on to write, 'une fois dans le corps du roman, la méditation change d'essence: une pensée dogmatique devient hypothétique' (p. 102). Tournier's virtual essayism complicates Kundera's notion of the specifically novelistic essay. Most often, the excised essays have been altered from their original form, but it is not uncommon to find verbatim self-citation. For Kundera, this would mean that Tournier's essays-in-novels lack the hypothetical and ludic necessity of the specifically novelistic essay, since they could be taken seriously as free-standing pieces. However, Tournier manages to maintain

[21] The term *Möglichkeitsmensch* (possibilitarian) is borrowed from Robert Musil's *The Man without Qualities*. The possibilitarian is one who lives 'within a finer web, a web of haze, imaginings, fantasy and the subjunctive mood'. As Musil's narrator explains, 'if he is told that something *is* the way it is, then he thinks: Well, it could probably just as easily be some other way' (Robert Musil, *The Man without Qualities*, vol. I, trans. by Eithne Wilkins and Ernst Kaiser (London: Secker & Warburg, 1953), p. 12).

[22] Milan Kundera, *L'Art du roman* (Paris: Gallimard, 1986), p. 87.

a balance between unfettered hypothetical experimentation and compelling philosophical assertions, whether the essays are embedded in his novel or published as independent pieces.

Tournier's description in his autobiography *Le Vent Paraclet* (1978) of how he shifted from philosophy to fiction, such as his first novel *Vendredi, ou les limbes du Pacifique* (1967), provides perhaps the strongest evidence of his conscious deployment of the essayistic form as a primary expressive method in his fictions. He explains that a text by Paul Valéry, one of his professors at the Collège de France, was his primary model for the kind of books he wished to write: 'Les romans que je cherchais à écrire, [Valéry] en a donné la définition et fourni le modèle avec *Monsieur Teste*.'[23] He goes on to trace a genealogy between Descartes's *Discours de la méthode* and Valéry's unconventional serial publication *Monsieur Teste*, which Tournier describes as follows:

> Il s'agit en somme de raconter une suite de démarches et de découvertes purement cérébrales sans les dégager de leur gangue historique et autobiographique. Fondre l'essai et le roman, la réussite promettant d'être d'autant plus éclatante que l'essai sera plus abstraitement métaphysique et l'affabulation plus aventureusement picaresque. (p. 231)

This explicit acknowledgement of the essayistic novel as aesthetic ideal places Tournier in a genealogy of novelist-essayists such as Marcel Proust, Robert Musil, Hermann Broch, and, of course, Valéry himself. All of these writers experimented and toyed with the tensions and compatibilities of essay and novel. In Valéry's preface to *Monsieur Teste*, he describes the process by which he created this character, whom he calls 'le démon même de la possibilité':[24]

> J'étais affecté du mal aigu de la précision. Je tendais à l'extrême désir insensé de comprendre, et je cherchais en moi les points critiques de ma faculté d'attention.
> Je faisais donc ce que je pouvais pour augmenter un peu les durées de quelques pensées. Tout ce qui m'était facile m'était indifférent et presque ennemi. La sensation de l'effort me semblait devoir être recherchée, et je ne prisais pas les heureux résultats qui ne sont que les fruits naturels de nos vertus natives. C'est dire que les résultats en général, — et par conséquence, les *œuvres*, — m'importaient beaucoup moins que l'énergie de l'ouvrier, — substance des choses qu'il espère. (p. 10)

Readers familiar with Tournier's œuvre can quickly glean from Valéry's preface several defining characteristics of Tournier as a novelist: an emphasis on precision, on the reflective,[25] on artisanal labour, and on writerly craft. He

---

[23] Tournier, *Le Vent Paraclet*, p. 230.
[24] Paul Valéry, *Monsieur Teste*, 32nd edn (Paris: Gallimard, 1929), p. 16.
[25] Regarding the inherently philosophical and reflective nature of his novels, Tournier writes, 'J'avais l'ambition de fournir à mon lecteur épris d'amours et d'aventures l'équivalent littéraire de ces sublimes inventions métaphysiques que sont le cogito de Descartes, les trois genres de connaissance de Spinoza, l'harmonie préétablie de Leibniz, le schématisme transcendantal de Kant, la réduction phénoménologique de Husserl, pour ne citer que quelques modèles majeurs' (Tournier, *Le Vent Paraclet*, p. 179).

is very clear about which of his twentieth-century predecessors influenced him the most when he writes, 'Mon école c'est la NRF, Gide, Valéry, Martin du Gard, Claudel.'[26]

Monsieur Teste is the embodiment of an essayistic thinking process and falls into the same speculative lineage as Robert Musil's possibilitarian Ulrich in *The Man without Qualities*. As Hanna Charney writes, Teste 'is a possibility in conception: an experiment of the author's, an attempt, an "essay"'.[27] In Valéry's *Monsieur Teste* the only section of the book in which Monsieur Teste speaks, or rather writes, for himself is the chapter entitled 'Extraits du log-book de Monsieur Teste'. It is no coincidence that Tournier uses a logbook to report the thoughts of Robinson in *Vendredi*. Jean-Bernard Vray notes, 'Le journal de Robinson, dont le titre Log-book est emprunté à Valéry et renvoie à Monsieur Teste, est truffé de dissertations philosophiques.'[28] These 'dissertations philosophiques' are in many ways the crux of the novel, which relies heavily on the speculative and solitary life. These embodied thoughts emblematize a metaphysical condition with authority over the physical world. Tournier explains, 'Il est donc possible, *il dépend de notre seule force cérébrale* de concevoir des ensembles d'un degré de cohérence supérieur au "reel" et donc d'un degré de réalité plus élevé. Ces ensembles existent: ce sont les systèmes philosophiques.'[29] His writing practice consists in superimposing imaginative and philosophical potentialities of the brain upon verisimilar characters and worlds. Valéry went so far as to create a walking thought, reflection in a human form, an avatar of the speculative self. This project is similar to Tournier's virtual essayist, who abides by the conventions of essayistic writing established by Montaigne.

Tournier's writing is deeply committed to the kind of observational humanism advocated by Montaigne. He explains, 'Je suis un cerveau branché sur le monde extérieur, un observateur [. . .] qui voyage avec des jumelles.'[30] Jean-Bernard Vray is perhaps the first to have recognized a genealogy between Tournier and Montaigne. He notes that in his text *Le Vol du vampire* Tournier erroneously qualifies Montaigne as a novelist.[31] This slip, Vray asserts, could be significant to an analysis of Tournier's œuvre:

[26] Marianne Payot, 'Michel Tournier', *Lire*, 248 (September 1996), 32–40 (p. 40).
[27] Hanna Charney, 'Monsieur Teste and der Mann ohne Eigenschaften: Homo Possibilis in Fiction', *Comparative Literature*, 27 (1975), 1–7 (p. 5).
[28] Jean-Bernard Vray, *Michel Tournier et l'écriture seconde* (Lyon: Presses Universitaires de Lyon, 1997), p. 161.
[29] Tournier, *Le Vent Paraclet*, p. 157.
[30] Payot, 'Michel Tournier', p. 34.
[31] Tournier writes, 'Chaque romancier puise sa substance dans le champ de sa vie personnelle, soit pour la livrer presque à l'état brut à ses lecteurs (Montaigne, Rousseau, Gide) soit pour lui faire subir une distillation qui la rend méconnaissable (Flaubert, justement, mais à des degrés divers dans la *Tentation*, *Salammbô*, *Madame Bovary* ou *l'Éducation sentimentale*)' (Michel Tournier, *Le Vol du vampire* (Paris: Mercure de France, 1981), p. 313).

Montaigne est en effet un peu romancier à la manière de Tournier, poursuivant indéfiniment un propos personnel, 'pilotant' intertextuellement sans cesse 'deçà delà', sans cesse recourant aux récits légendaires, aux 'exemples'. L'œuvre de Tournier pourrait s'intituler aussi *Essais*. [. . .] Tout lecteur de Tournier peut imaginer les titres de ces *Essais* de Michel Tournier qu'on pourrait recomposer en juxtaposant des passages de réflexion sur un même sujet d'une œuvre à l'autre: Du tatouage, Temps et portrait, Inadaptation et suradaptation, Crustacé et vertébré, Le sucré et le salé, Visage, amour et pornographie, De la pureté, De la tyrannie, De la dénaissance, Sexe et société, Des monstres, Photographie et possession, Le monde-vitrine, etc. Ce pôle réflexif, dissertatif existe dans l'œuvre, parfois même avec un peu trop d'insistance.[32]

In addition to the explicit formal connections between the writing of Tournier and that of Montaigne, one must also acknowledge the emphasis of both writers on the dialogic relationship with the reader. The couple in all its forms is for Tournier the most elemental of units.[33] His readers will note immediately to what extent he privileges duality over other epistemological configurations. Nearly his entire œuvre is a product of the juxtaposition of problematic, seemingly oppositional categories. If the essay is a scale that juxtaposes the two sides of a dichotomy (or, in some cases, multiple points of view), it is natural that Tournier would be comfortable weighing his new dichotomies using this apparatus. All of his novels use the dichotomy as an organizing structure, which, upon first consideration, seems a reduction of the world and experience into easily managed, mutually exclusive categories. These categories, however, consistently undo themselves, either through a priori disconcerting pairings, through the upset of dogmatic thought, or through what Tournier calls *inversion maligne* or *bénigne*. Possibly the most synthetic example of Tournier's dichotomies and an excellent summary of many major themes he addresses can be found in his treatise *Miroir des idées*, which he dedicates to the memory of Gaston Bachelard, one of his mentors. This text is of twofold interest, given the allusion above to essay as both metaphorical mirror and scale. The entire text is organized by themes and their opposites, or their reflections, as could be inferred from the title. For example, he opens the book with a chapter called 'man and woman', and continues with standard pairings such as 'cat and dog', 'health and sickness', and 'water and fire'. But this pattern of seeming opposites is soon disrupted by coupled words that do not manifest an oppositional relationship. 'Bull and horse', 'tree and path', 'fear and anguish', and 'action and passion' share some dyadic relationship other than an antithetical one. To intersperse incongruent pairings with more

---

[32] Vray, *Michel Tournier et l'écriture seconde*, pp. 417–18.
[33] The two most cited examples of his obsession with the couple are the Robinson/Vendredi unit in *Vendredi* and the Jean/Paul unit in *Les Météores*. Twinhood, doubling, romantic couplehood, the master/slave dialectic: Tournier analysed all of these configurations in his fictions and his essays. Gilles Deleuze explores the otherness implicit in any two-person unit in his essay 'Michel Tournier et le monde sans autrui', the postface for *Vendredi*.

standard dichotomies is to challenge the facility of juxtaposition and to question the tidy compartmentalization of our *idées reçues*. The job of the reader is to locate the appropriate analogy, to fill in the meaningful space between the two terms. *Miroir des idées* not only serves as a key to Tournier's thematics but also rejects dogmatic thinking in the same way as his novels and essays.

Montaigne's whole essayistic project was largely the result of a need for an interlocutor after the death of his closest friend Étienne de la Boétie. Tournier, too, subscribes to the notion of the reader as interlocutor and as creator of meaning. He states categorically, 'Un livre a deux auteurs, l'écrivain et le lecteur.'[34] The pervasiveness of reader-response theory in the 1960s and 1970s coincided with Tournier's numerous interviews and writings about the centrality of the reader. He is very explicit about the role of the fiction reader, whom he calls 'l'indispensable collaborateur de l'écrivain'.[35] He explains, 'Un livre n'a pas un auteur, mais un nombre indéfini d'auteurs. Car à celui qui l'a écrit s'ajoutent de plein droit dans l'acte créateur l'ensemble de ceux qui l'ont lu, le lisent ou le liront' (p. 12). He elaborates:

s'il s'agit d'un poème, d'un roman ou d'une pièce de théâtre, la présence d'une thèse, exposée explicitement et s'imposant sans ambiguïté, nuit gravement à la valeur de l'œuvre. C'est ce qui condamne à la médiocrité le roman relevant de l'édification religieuse ou du 'réalisme socialiste'. Un roman peut certes contenir une thèse, mais il importe que ce soit le lecteur, non l'écrivain, qui l'y ait mise. (pp. 16–17)

As Colin Davis has noted, Tournier's promotion of the reader as second author seems disingenuous because he often resists readings offered by literary critics. Davis writes:

In theory [...] Tournier relinquishes mastery over his own texts and allows the reader a significant degree of creative freedom. However, all too often Tournier's comments on his own fiction do not accord with his theoretical positions. [...] This desire to defend his fiction against what he regards as deviant readings is accompanied by an aggressive gesture of mastery over other critics.[36]

This duplicity, however, is congruent with my claim that Tournier is a virtual essayist. That his fiction does not accord with the principles set out in his critical writing is not surprising. Always in the mode of the virtual essayist, he is never bound to the stringencies of reason or consistency. While his essays are functional in the sense that they meet all the criteria of the essay as a form, they cannot be relied upon for any cogent statement on his extra-literary beliefs.

A final category that binds Montaigne's project with Tournier's writing is that of play. The essay is a consciously playful form of writing that privileges light-heartedness, discovery, imagination, and a childlike engagement with

[34] Jean-Jacques Brochier, '18 questions à Michel Tournier', *Magazine littéraire*, 138 (June 1978), 11–13 (p. 13).
[35] Tournier, *Le Vol du vampire*, p. 12.
[36] Davis, *Michel Tournier*, pp. 117–18.

one's surroundings. Adorno's assertion that '[l]uck and play are essential to the essay' is equally applicable to Tournier's essayistic writing.[37] Play and humour are one significant impetus for his virtual essayism. In the ludic mode, he is able to rehearse imaginative alternatives without the heaviness and obligation of apodictic discourse. He writes, 'J'espère que l'humour est partout sensible dans tout ce que j'écris.'[38] It is no surprise that in nearly every text Tournier has published there is some manifest form of play, either etymological play (his neologisms such as the *Journal extime*, his puns and nameplay such as Thomas Koussek [*coup sec*] from *Les Météores* and Éléazar [*et les hasards*] from *Éléazar ou la source et le buisson*, and his extraction of new meaning from word roots such as the emphasis on *phorie* in *Le Roi des Aulnes*)[39] or in the form of toying with myths and history (ranging from re-casting Santa Claus as a woman, adding a fourth king to the Magi, and binding Gilles de Rais's perversion to his grieving over the death of Joan of Arc).

Through his conspicuous deployment of the essay and his reiterative poetics, Tournier sets expectations for his readers that he never satisfies. This is not debilitating to his œuvre. In fact, the self-contradiction of his texts and their open-endedness lend an inscrutable appeal, assuring readers that regardless of their best efforts, meaning often remains fugitive. He exercises a politics of clarity in his writing and is over-explicit and insistent on certain recurrent themes. This simplification and recontextualization would seem to increase the manageability of his ideas but often creates the opposite effect. His self-citation and thematic echoes from text to text make it easy for scholars to identify the author's fundamental *idées fixes* but not to reach a definitive conclusion about the significance of those ideas. The inconclusiveness of his œuvre effectuates an intentful subversion of the conventions of literature. The essays serve in many ways as decoys that intentionally destabilize foundational thinking, including neat dichotomies and normative assumptions. In sympathy with Montaigne's legacy, Tournier has followed Valéry's essayistic model in his writing and borrowed the reflective substance from specific European philosophers, never wholly embracing the vocation of novelist. His hybrid texts provide a play space in which he synthesizes philosophical discourse, puns, hypothetical assertions, realist narrative, and explosive mythologies. Tournier forges a second essayist self as his avatar. This avatar, a word that evokes a descended deity in the Hindu faith, has the authorial power of any essayist but remains intact and functional only within the realm of the fictional. He has no authority outside this frame. The membrane that divides his fictional worlds from our world is porous, which leads to confusion about whose ideas belong to whom—to the characters? the narrator? Tournier him-

---

[37] Adorno, 'The Essay as Form', p. 152.   [38] Brochier, '18 questions à Michel Tournier', p. 12.
[39] For more on Tournier's wordplay see Walter Redfern, 'Approximating Man: Michel Tournier and Play in Language', *MLR*, 80 (1985), 304–19.

self? These essays can be read literarily as aesthetic entities, but looking to them for extraliterary insight on his world-view is a largely unavailing endeavour.

Current Tournier scholarship offers a rich body of commentary that assembles the groundwork for other kinds of thinking about this author, who remains one of the most important literary voices of post-war France. Much of this scholarship has focused either on thematic patterns in his texts or on the relationship between his biography and fiction, with a few notable exceptions. My contribution here reorients the focus away from the thematic or biographical level of his work towards the modal complexity of his essayistic fictions and his virtual essays. I take into account his alternative uses of the essay and his enlistment of hypothesis and virtuality as a source for the liberation of new expressive possibilities. Tournier recognizes literature as a tool for the hypothetical reconfiguration of everything, from history to mythology to the entire extant literary corpus. Furthermore, his intuitive forecasting of contemporary epistemological problems and his embracing of the virtual will very likely result in a renewed interest in his work. This departure from Montaigne's original *Essais* attests to the pliability of his early writerly experiments.

Tournier's virtual essayism is significant in that it models an alternative use of the essay form loosened from its defining characteristic: the centrality of an actual meditative subject. He replaces the meditative subject, the essayist, with an avatar who could just as easily exist but who was generated first in a fictional world. Akin to Fernando Pessoa's heteronymic practice of forging invented writerly selves with autonomous biographies, Tournier, too, confounds his own writerly voice with the voices of his dramatis personae. He diverges from Pessoa in his omission of a fictional signature on the free-standing essays. The ideas in his virtual essays are certainly his own—that is, they came from his own mind, though they do not necessarily reflect his own opinions; but they have been filtered through the reflective protagonists who populate his novels and short stories. After this filtering process, Tournier reappropriates the ideas as his own, revealing a sophisticated, polyvocal mesh that conflates fiction and truth. To whom do the thoughts belong in the end? Can he attach his signature to them, or is he plagiarizing the musings of figures who have no autonomous, physical body? Tournier displays for us the virtual nature of thought and of fiction. His practice is an advancement of the essay form and an inverse mirroring of Valéry's Teste experiment. While Valéry seeks to insert the brain in the novel, Tournier seeks to extract the brain from the novel and reframe it in an essayistic format. In toying with the categories of the virtual, he invites and entertains fresh applications of the essay. To borrow his assertation that 'Le vieillard était déjà en puissance dans l'enfant', one could say that, in Tournier's œuvre, 'L'essai était déjà en puissance dans ses fictions'.

PRINCETON UNIVERSITY   CHRISTY WAMPOLE

THE POWER OF WOMAN'S WORDS, THE POWER OF WOMAN'S SILENCE: HOW THE *MADRASTRA* SPEAKS IN THE THIRTEENTH-CENTURY CASTILIAN *SENDEBAR*

Because of the last line of its prologue, the Castilian *Sendebar* was dubbed by its first editor José Amador de los Rios in 1863 as *Libro de los engaños e los asayamientos de las mugeres*. Amador's title is less used nowadays, and for purposes of simplicity as well as in order to keep with the wider textual tradition, the shorter *Sendebar* is preferred.[1] None the less, the reference to 'los engaños e los asayamientos de las mugeres' is very telling, and the structure of the text as a literary construct, as well as the role of the female protagonist within it, warrants further discussion.

The plot is arranged in the traditional format of a frame narrative: twenty-three *exempla* are inserted within an overarching frame which resembles the motif of the wife of Potiphar: the son of King Alcos of Judaea is unjustly accused by one of his father's ninety wives of attempting to seduce her. The Prince, however, is unable to speak in his own defence, because an ominous horoscope has forced him to keep silent for seven days, lest death befall him. Thus the Prince's defence is taken up by his father's seven *privados*, who attempt to temper the king's anger and save the young man's life with the aid of moralizing stories. The *privados* are confronted with the devious *madrastra*, who tells stories in her own turn in order to secure the Prince's conviction. Yet the woman's tales are arguably underdeveloped and of a lesser narrative quality than those of the *privados*, and on the seventh day she even replaces the narrative with a mere threat to commit suicide in order to persuade the King once and for all.[2] In this article, I shall examine the function of the woman's stories within the narrative construct, focusing in particular on their symbolic role as persuasive arguments whose content matters less than their form. I shall argue that, in *Sendebar*, the power of the woman's words resides not in their content but rather in their very utterance, or even in their silence, and by extension that the power of woman herself resides in her ascribed status as an agent of destruction or a troublesome and uncontainable element.[3]

It is important to note that, within the main narrative plot, the evil step-

---

[1] See, for instance, the two recent editions of the text, which both use the shorter title: *Sendebar*, ed. by María Jesús Lacarra, 4th edn (Madrid: Cátedra, 2005), and *Sendebar*, ed. by Veronica Orazi (Barcelona: Crítica, 2006). All references to the Castilian text will be to Lacarra's edition.

[2] I shall be discussing only the Castilian version of the text, not the *Sendebar* tradition as a whole, although I shall draw brief comparisons with the Hebrew version, *Mishle Sendebar*, which would have been widely known around the time the *Libro de los engaños* was composed, and could well date to much earlier. See *Tales of Sendebar/Mishle Sendebar: An Edition and Translation of the Hebrew Version of the Seven Sages Based on Unpublished Manuscripts*, ed. by Morris Epstein (Philadelphia: The Jewish Publication Society of America, 1967), esp. pp. 12–18.

[3] I have already made a similar argument elsewhere, but without engaging in detailed ana-

mother is not the only female protagonist, but rather she is counterbalanced by her radical opposite. Although the critical tradition often overlooks this, the text opens with the tale of a good wife, who is able to advise the King and provide him with a son and heir—precisely the Prince, who will later be accused by the bad wife. We are told that at the beginning, despite all his ninety wives, the king is plagued with sterility and incapable of producing an heir with any of them: 'Estando con todas, según era ley, non podía aver de ninguna dellas fijo' (p. 65). However, with the help and advice of the good wife, he prays to God together with her, and is finally granted the son he so desires. This is the common folk tale of the sterile older man who is granted an heir by the grace of God, which goes back to the biblical story of Abraham and Isaac.[4] Yet, what is interesting here is the figure of the good wife, which counterbalances that of the bad wife who appears later.

The two women could not be further from each other: the good wife is fully devoted to the King while the other is devious and dangerous, first plotting the King's death and then that of the Prince, the only heir to the throne. However, on the surface the two women are still described in similar terms: the good wife is described as 'aquella q'él más quería, e era cuerda e entendida, e avíala él provado en algunas cosas' (p. 65), whereas the bad wife is introduced as 'una muger, la qual más amava e onrávala más que a todas las otras mugeres qu'él avía' (p. 74). Apart from their obvious difference in intention, a few differences are immediately apparent in these descriptions: the good wife is good because she is wise and prudent, and more importantly still because she has been tested by the King. In contrast, the bad wife is described only through the love that the King feels for her and through the primary position in which he places her among his wives. Moreover, the good wife advises the King to turn to God in his distress, thus helping him to obtain a son: 'Yo te daré consejo bueno a esto. Ruega a Dios, qu'Él que de todos bienes es conplido, ca poderoso es de te fazer e de te dar fijo, si le pluguiere, ca Él nunca cansó de fazer merçed e nunca le demandeste cosa que la non diese' (p. 66). The bad wife acts in direct opposition to the King's best interests: she accuses his beloved son of attempting to rape her and, through her stories, she advises

---

lysis. See Andreea Weisl-Shaw, 'The Comedy of Didacticism and the Didacticism of Comedy', *MLR*, 105 (2010), 732–42 (p. 736).

[4] Genesis 17–21. This narrative type comprises two motifs categorized by Stith Thompson: the motif of barrenness, M44 ('Curse of childlessness'); and Q33 ('Reward for saying of prayers'). See Stith Thompson, *Motif-Index of Folk Literature*, 6 vols (Bloomington: Indiana University Press, 1955–58). In her *Motif-Index of Medieval Spanish Folk Narratives* (Tempe, AZ: Medieval and Renaissance Texts and Studies, 1998), Harriet Goldberg lists this tale-type under four different motifs: D1925.3 ('Barrenness removed by prayer. After years of prayer childless couple have child'); T526 ('Conception because of prayer. King and favourite wife have son after much prayer'); T548.1 ('Child born in answer to prayer'); and V57.5 ('Prayers for child answered. Childless couple have baby').

King Alcos to have the Prince put to death: 'Este [. . .] me quiso forçar de todo en todo, e yo non lo tenía a él por tal' (p. 75).

The bad wife is thus guilty of the worst sins women are thought to commit (dishonesty, lasciviousness, and even murder), while the good wife fulfils the role of the perfect subordinated wife, and is presented as the model that all women should follow: 'una mujer llena de virtudes morales, con un fuerte sentido de la fidelidad y, más que nada, de *obediencia al marido* es el recipiente idóneo y adecuado para crear el modelo a seguir por parte de todas las demás mujeres'.[5] However, what is significant here is that, on both occasions, the King immediately believes his wives and acts upon their word. In the case of the first wife, we are told: 'E después que ovo dicho esto, pagóse él dello e sopo que lo que ella dixo que era verdat, e levantárose amos e fiziéronlo así' (p. 67). Later, when the bad wife makes her accusation against the Prince, the King is even quicker to take her at her word and act upon it: 'E el Rey, quando esto oyó, creçiól' gran saña por matar su fijo, e fue muy bravo e mandólo matar' (pp. 75–76). Thus, it does not seem far-fetched to argue that part of the problem here lies with the King himself, and the presence of the two wives clarifies this.[6] The King seems to love and esteem the good wife because he knows her to be good (we are told that he has tested her), but his love for the bad wife seems to have no justification. Without the test of her loyalty, the second wife should not be trusted, and yet the King places his love above his prudence, which therefore leads to bad consequences.[7] His inability to keep his wives (particularly the bad one) silenced and under control triggers the entire sequence of events, and this is revealing for the role that women play within *Sendebar* as a whole.

It is clear that the bad wife is no mean adversary. When she engages in an *exemplum* debate with the *privados*, it takes two stories from each *privado* to determine the King to turn away from her.[8] In contrast, all the *madrastra*

---

[5] José Carlos Vilchis, 'Mujeres "comunes" y "extraordinarias" en *Sendebar*', *Medievalia*, 36 (2004), 43–49 (p. 48, emphasis original). As Vilchis points out, the very fact that this wife is so perfect is problematic in the context of *Sendebar* as a whole, since motherhood stands in stark contrast with the image of woman as 'de naturaleza adúltera y en el peor de los casos perversa' (p. 47). This is only superficially resolved by the immediate disappearance of the good wife from the frame narrative as soon as she gives the King his much-desired son, and, as Vilchis concludes, this avoids any debate 'sobre el hecho de ser mujer y madre al mismo tiempo' (p. 47).

[6] I have already argued that King Alcos proves to be a deficient reader of exemplary tales, which is why he is so prone to being swayed by both his *privados* and the evil wife: Weisl-Shaw, 'Comedy of Didacticism', p. 737.

[7] On the importance of wife-testing see Louise M. Haywood, 'Choosing and Testing Spouses in Medieval Exemplary Literature', in *A Companion to Spanish Women Studies*, ed. by Xon de Ros and Geraldine Hazbun (Woodbridge and Rochester, NY: Tamesis, 2011), pp. 69–80.

[8] The only exception is the third *privado*, who tells just one story; however, the rigorous construction of the text suggests that the third *privado*'s second story might have been lost in transmission: see María Jesús Lacarra, *Cuentística medieval en España: los orígenes* (Zaragoza: Universidad de Zaragoza, 1979), p. 53, and *Sendebar*, ed. by Lacarra, p. 101.

seems to need to do is to tell one single story—and not of the most narratively accomplished—in order instantly to persuade the King that she is right. Throughout the entire text, she tells only five stories in contrast with the advisers' thirteen (or possibly fourteen if, indeed, the third adviser's *exemplum* was lost in transmission).[9]

The *madrastra*'s stories in the Castilian *Sendebar* are underdeveloped in terms of plot, being generally much shorter, sketchier, and less polished than the advisers' tales. In María Jesús Lacarra's edition of the text only two of the woman's stories ('Striges' and 'Fontes') reach the length of two pages, while her shortest tale ('Aper') is barely longer than eight lines, and is shorter than the preamble with which she introduces it. In contrast, the *privados*' stories are all at least one page long in Lacarra's edition, and are on average around two pages long. In fact, even with the presumed fourteenth story by a *privado* missing, their stories total sixteen and a half pages in Lacarra's edition—over twice the length of the bad wife's stories.[10]

Moreover, the exemplary structure of the *madrastra*'s stories is flawed and unconvincing, with the lessons seeming to match the narratives only loosely and by approximation; while this is a general trait of *exempla*, the mismatch is even more pronounced here than usual.[11] The *madrastra*'s first story, 'Lavator', expands upon the moral lesson about the necessity of educating one's children, focusing on the mortal dangers posed to the parents if they fail to do so. Her moral, 'E señor, si tú non te antuvias a castigar tu fijo ante que más enemiga te faga, matarte á' (p. 87), obviously suits her own purposes, but it is far from what might be termed a logical conclusion to the story. The second story, 'Striges', is more narratively interesting, as it deals with a young prince's dangerous encounter with a she-devil; however, it is only barely connected to its moral. The woman introduces her story by accusing the King's advisers of attempting to kill him: 'Señor, estos tus privados son malos e matarte an, así commo mató un privado a un rey una vez' (p. 96). While this introduction is not in itself unreasonable, it does not really match the story itself, within which an adviser features only at the beginning, and not in a very important way. In fact, the *madrastra*'s moralizing reveals quite clearly her awareness

[9] This is slightly different from the *Mishle Sendebar*, where the bad wife tells seven stories, including a double story ('Striga et Fons') on the third day, in contrast to the advisers' fourteen stories, so while there is still a clear imbalance between the woman's tales and those of the advisers, the disparity seems less striking than in the Castilian text: see *Tales of Sendebar*, ed. by Epstein.

[10] This is not so blatantly the case in the *Mishle Sendebar*, for instance, where the bad wife's tales are comparable in length and narrative development to those told by the advisers.

[11] On the loose connection between *exempla* and their morals see e.g. Alexander Gelley, *Unruly Examples: On the Rhetoric of Exemplarity* (Stanford: Stanford University Press, 1995), and Olivier Biaggini, 'Quelques enjeux de l'exemplarité dans le *Calila e Dimna* et le *Sendebar*', *Cahiers de narratologie: récit et éthique*, 12 (2005) <http://narratologie.revues.org/28?lang=en> [accessed 22 July 2013].

that she has failed to manipulate exemplarity to her advantage: 'E, señor, non te di este enxenplo sinon que non te esfuerçes en tus malos privados. Si non me dieres derecho de quien mal me fizo, yo me mataré con mis manos' (p. 98).[12]

While the story of 'Striges' is in itself complex and exciting, the *madrastra* is unskilled in making use of it: not only does she draw an unconvincing lesson from it, but she also fails to notice the much more obvious parallel that the story elicits. As Olivier Biaggini argues, exemplary tales inserted within frame narratives always have at least two possible layers of meaning: the explicit lesson, stated in the moral, and the implicit reading, which emerges by drawing parallels between the story and the overarching frame.[13] Thus, in 'Striges', the she-devil who attempts to deceive the young prince and to make him stray from the right path can be seen to remind us much more of the bad wife herself, and of her attempt at seducing her stepson and plotting the King's death. However, just as the bad wife herself seems to be oblivious to the exemplary potential of her own story, which points the accusing finger back at herself, King Alcos is equally incapable of perceiving the message between the lines, and this allows the debate of *exempla* to carry on.

The rest of the *madrastra*'s tales are equally unconvincing as exemplary constructs. Like 'Striges', 'Fontes' (which she tells on the third day) also points an accusing finger at the woman herself: its complicated plot about the prince who swaps genders with the devil and almost falls prey to the devil's cunning, reminds us of the son of King Alcos, who in a sense has swapped roles with his stepmother: the Prince is now relegated to silence, while the bad wife is free and able to proceed with her false accusations, instead of perhaps the more traditional structure, in which the woman is reduced to silence while the men are in control. The *madrastra* once more fails to draw a proper moralizing message from the story, however, now stressing her reliance on God in order to be saved from her predicament, which here clearly seems to be that of the *exemplum* debate: 'E por ende yo he fiuza que me ayudará Dios contra tus malos privados' (p. 103).

The moral frame to 'Aper' is equally loose, and this is unsurprising given the absurdity of the plot, which features a wild boar which likes to eat figs and which dies when it stops eating them because it waits for a monkey in the fig tree to throw it fruit. The King's reaction at the end of the tale shows that he is more worried about listening to whatever his wife says rather than to reason: 'E quando esto ovo dicho, ovo miedo el Rey que se mataría con el tósigo que tenía en la mano, e mandó matar su fijo' (p. 112). This suggests that, for the second time, the bad wife is trying to kill herself, even though this is never made explicit in the text. And again it becomes clear that the stepmother is

---

[12] This is the woman's first of three threats to commit suicide; I shall return to this issue later.
[13] See Biaggini, 'Quelques enjeux'.

less than confident about her own persuasive powers, so from her introduction to the story she attempts to make the King feel guilty, warning him about her imminent death if he fails to listen to her: 'después que yo sea muerta, veremos qué farás con estos tus consejeros e, quando ante Dios fueres, ¿qué dirás…?' (p. 112).

Finally, the *madrastra*'s last story, 'Simia', seems more logically correct, albeit equally dishonest, in its exemplary message: the wife's lesson here is 'Fío por Dios que me ayudará contra tus malos privados, así commo ayudó al ladrón contra el león' (p. 122). However, once more the parallels that can be drawn between the story and the bad wife's own situation are not as clear-cut as she seems to intend them to be. True enough, on the surface the foolish monkey which attempts to help the lion against the man might be likened to the *privados*. But just as well, the monkey can be compared to the *madrastra* herself, particularly given the way in which the two stories end, one with the castration and death of the monkey and the other with the death of the bad wife herself.

So how can we explain the narrative and exemplary inadequacy of the *madrastra*'s stories? In discussing the smaller number of tales told by the bad wife, María Jesús Lacarra explains this through the woman's position as active character of the main narrative plot, which, as she puts it, 'le impide mantener la serenidad y la objetividad de los privados, meros espectadores'.[14] However, I should like to suggest that this discrepancy is also due simply to the wife's position as a woman who tells stories.[15] From a modern perspective, her narrative inability can be interpreted through Hélène Cixous's discussion of feminine writing, which, according to Cixous, is circumscribed not only by tradition but, even more, by women's own mental blocks: 'writing is at once too high, too great for you, it's reserved for the great—that is, for "great men"'.[16] Moreover, for Cixous, writing (or here, storytelling) is not the only field in which a woman experiences difficulty. The same happens even with the act of speech itself, which represents a brave, but always already doomed, attempt at self-liberation:

Every woman has known the torment of getting up to speak. Her heart racing, at times entirely lost for words, ground and language slipping away—that's how daring a feat, how great a transgression it is for a woman to speak—even just open her mouth in public. A double distress, for even if she transgresses, her words fall almost always upon the deaf male ear, which hears in language only that which speaks in the masculine.[17]

[14] Lacarra, *Cuentística medieval en España*, p. 87.
[15] In making this argument, I am not trying to analyse the bad wife as a real character, but rather I am suggesting that the text itself is constructed on the basis of such an assumption.
[16] Hélène Cixous, 'The Laugh of the Medusa', trans. by Keith Cohen and Paula Cohen, *Signs*, 1 (1976), 875–93 (p. 876).
[17] Ibid., pp. 880–81.

Thus, we could argue, the *madrastra* is, like the good wife at the beginning of the Castilian *Sendebar*, given the right to speak, to tell stories; however, her inferior position and her inability to rise to the occasion are already inscribed within this from the outset.[18]

And yet the argument regarding a woman's inability to speak, or to speak adequately, due to social prohibitions seems to stand in precise opposition to the medieval context. As Richard Howard Bloch incisively puts it: 'If one were to pose the question made famous by Freud at the end of the last century, "What does a woman want?" within the context of medieval antifeminism, the answer would be clear: "A woman wants to speak".'[19] Bloch shows that this stereotype is particularly prevalent within the rhetorical context of antimatrimonial literature of the late Middle Ages. According to Book III of Andreas Capellanus's fourteenth-century *Art of Courtly Love*, women are not only endlessly garrulous, but also obstinately contrary:

Even for a trifle a woman will swear falsely a thousand times. [. . .] Every woman is also loud-mouthed. [. . .] When she is with other women, no one of them will give the others a chance to speak, but each always tries to be the one to say whatever is to be said and to keep on talking longer than the rest; and neither her tongue nor her spirit ever gets tired out by talking. [. . .] A woman will boldly contradict everything you say.[20]

The same misogynist discourse appears in late medieval Spanish texts such as, most notably, Alfonso Martínez de Toledo's *Arcipreste de Talavera*, in which the Archpriest devotes an entire section to mimicking women in order to expose their vices. In every case, women's avarice, disobedience, falseness, envy, or lust emerge in long tirades in which the Archpriest purports to speak like a woman, for whom, he claims, 'El callar le es muerte muy aspera: non podría una sola ora estar que non profaçase de buenos e malos.'[21]

The late medieval image of women as ceaselessly babbling, however, is not what transpires in the *Sendebar*, and the *madrastra*'s *exempla* seems more in tune with Cixous's model of women as inhibited in their linguistic manifestation by an oppressive society. In fact, less at the level of language as such but certainly at the level of their meaning and effect, the *madrastra*'s stories

---

[18] Of course we cannot take this very far, since from the outset the woman is shown to be devious and dangerous, and so her ultimate failure is portrayed as a mere act of justice; however, her lack of skill in furthering her deception is still striking in comparison with male tricksters who engage in *exemplum* debates, such as, for instance, Dimna in *Calila e Dimna*. See *Calila e Dimna*, ed. by María Jesús Lacarra and Juan Manuel Cacho Blecua (Madrid: Castalia, 1984).

[19] Richard Howard Bloch, *Medieval Misogyny and the Invention of Western Romantic Love* (Chicago and London: University of Chicago Press, 1991), p. 54.

[20] Andreas Capellanus, *The Art of Courtly Love*, ed. by John J. Parry (New York: Norton, 1969), pp. 201 and 207, cited in Bloch, *Medieval Misogyny*, p. 54.

[21] Alfonso Martínez de Toledo, *Arcipreste de Talavera*, ed. by Michael Gerli (Madrid: Cátedra, 1998), p. 154.

function like what Robin Lakoff defines as 'woman's language' in modern American society, a language taught to women from their childhood, and which 'submerges a woman's personal identity, by denying her the means of expressing herself strongly, on the one hand, and encouraging expressions that suggest triviality in subject matter and uncertainty about it'.[22]

And yet, despite the poor narrative and exemplary quality of her stories, the *madrastra* manages to uphold the *exemplum* debate for seven days before she is finally defeated. At first glance, her temporary success can be explained in two simple ways. The first explanation could be the narrative necessity of keeping the text going until seven days have passed and the wrongfully accused Prince can finally defend himself—what Federico Bravo calls 'una estrategia de legitimación narrativa'.[23] Secondly, King Alcos is obviously gullible and unable to choose the right course of action, which pushes the story contest to carry on. Nevertheless, I would argue that the mere fact that the *madrastra* can concoct her plot in the first place and uphold it for so long can also be explained through her position as a woman. As Graciela Cándano puts it, 'el saber de la mujer se ligaba a las fuerzas de la naturaleza, a lo misterioso, a lo irracional'.[24] Women's advantage over men, with all the threat this posed, was considered to lie precisely in this feminine knowledge, which was thought to be opposed to reason, natural and instinctive and therefore difficult to combat.[25]

It is thus not difficult to understand why the advisers work so hard to convince the King of the dangers that women pose, and this offers a potential explanation for the fact that the advisers need two stories each time to combat the *madrastra*'s one: one story merely to catch the King's attention and dissuade him from acting rashly, and the second intended to stress, again and again, the cunning of women. This also explains why the women in the

---

[22] Robin Tolmach Lakoff, *Language and Woman's Place: Text and Commentaries*, rev. and expanded edn, ed. by Mary Bucholz (Oxford: Oxford University Press, 2004), p. 42.

[23] Federico Bravo, 'El tríptico del diablo: en torno al libro de *Sendebar*', *Bulletin hispanique*, 99 (1997), 347–71 (p. 366).

[24] Graciela Cándano, 'Mujer frente a saber en las colecciones de "exempla" (Siglo XIII)', in *Edad Media: marginalidad y oficialidad*, ed. by Aurelio González and Lilian von der Walde (México, DF: Universidad Nacional Autónoma de México, Instituto de Investigaciones Filológicas, 1998), pp. 33–58 (p. 42).

[25] This belief was common in the medieval period and frequently found in literary texts: for instance, Cándano quotes the thirteenth-century *Libro de los buenos proverbios* (also translated from Arabic, from a text dating from the ninth century), which instructs men as follows: 'Qui quier aprender la sapiençia guárdese de apoderar las mugeres sobre sí' (Cándano, 'Mujer frente a saber', p. 42). See also F. Regina Psaki's discussion of Boccaccio's representation of feminine knowledge, 'often posited as a corrosive counteragent to the normative knowledge and power of women', which only reveals 'the masculine fear which underlies and generates misogyny as a cultural discourse' ('"Women Make All Things Lose their Power": Women's Knowledge, Men's Fear in the *Decameron* and the *Corbaccio*', *Heliotropia*, 1.1 (2003), <http://www.brown.edu/Departments/Italian_Studies/heliotropia/01-01/psaki.pdf> [accessed 22 July 2013]).

advisers' anti-feminist *exempla* are shown to be so cunning and so persuasive. The women of these stories deceive not only their husbands: in 'Avis', told by the first *privado*, the female protagonist dupes even the husband's spy, a clever parrot which is supposed to watch over her, by pouring water over its cage and using a candle, a mirror, and the noise caused by the movement of furniture in order to persuade it that it is witnessing a storm (pp. 84–85). In other stories women team up against men in order to deceive them; two *exempla*, 'Canicula', told by the fourth *privado*, and 'Pallium', told by the fifth, deal with go-betweens.[26] Moreover, women employ deception even when their intentions are not adulterous, as in the case of 'Elephantinus', told by the sixth *privado*: here a woman lies to her husband in order to cover up the fact that she was robbed of the bread she was taking for him to eat in the fields, and to explain the 'imagen de marfil' that one of the thieves put in her basket 'por escarnio' (pp. 126–27).

In each case, however, the husbands are convinced of the women's good intentions and upright moral behaviour. They would rather disbelieve their spies and even their own eyes in favour of what their wives tell them. For instance, when he becomes convinced that the parrot is lying to him about the storm which obviously never happened, the husband of 'Avis' chastises the bird, accusing it of having attempted to defame his wife by accusing her of adultery: 'En quanto me as dicho es verdat de mi muger así commo esto' (p. 85). Similarly, the husband in the second *privado*'s story, 'Gladius', ends up commending his wife on her good deed (her double adultery, which she has concealed under his own nose by pretending that she was protecting a young man from his master's wrath): 'El marido se tornó a ella bien pagado, e dixo: —Feziste a guisa de buena muger, e feziste bien, e gradéscotelo mucho' (p. 93).[27] And finally, the husband in 'Pallium', who had justly accused his wife of adultery, becomes persuaded of her innocence and actually asks her forgiveness in the end: 'enbió por su muger a casa de sus parientes, e rogóla que l'perdonase, e ella físolo así' (p. 120).

Thus, again and again the *privados* stress the dangers of female cunning, manifested mostly through women's deceptive words, which deprive men of their very senses. If we take this further, however, we can see that the manifest fear expressed in these tales, as in *Sendebar* as a whole, is that women's power resides not only in their stories, that is to say in their words, but in their actions, and even in their very presence. This could be seen to account for the good wife's ability at the beginning of the text to persuade the King that she is right even without telling a moralizing story; it could easily be argued that she is motivated by very personal interests in putting herself forward as the

---

[26] 'Pallium', in *Sendebar*, pp. 118–20; 'Canicula', ibid., pp. 108–10.
[27] 'Gladius', ibid., pp. 92–93.

mother of the King's heir, out of all his ninety wives. This also explains why the bad wife does not always have to offer a clever moral application for her stories, yet her powers of conviction remain as great and as instantaneous.[28]

The *madrastra*'s power over the King is equally clear in her repeated threats of suicide. First, as I have shown already, after telling 'Striges' on the second day, she insists that she will kill herself if the King fails to listen to her. Later, on the sixth day, after telling 'Aper', she threatens to poison herself. As the narrative tells us: 'E quando esto ovo dicho, ovo miedo el Rey que se mataría con el tósigo que tenía en la mano, e mandó matar si fijo' (p. 112). And finally, on the seventh day, the bad wife goes so far as to renounce the stories, but instead commits a symbolic act: she gives all she has to the poor then sits on a pile of wood which is set on fire. As expected, this third threat has the effect that the *madrastra* desires: 'el Rey, quando esto oyó, ante que se quemase, mandó matar al moço' (p. 128).[29] The woman's actions here remind us once again of Cixous, according to whom woman, deprived of the proper right to speak, 'physically materializes what she's thinking; she signifies it with her body'.[30] In this way, it is the very female body which becomes threatening in the text.

The disparity in quality and quantity between the *madrastra*'s tales and those of the *privados*, therefore, as well as the woman's almost inexplicable ability to keep the King under her spell, is not as difficult to explain as might at first appear. Far from being a mere coincidence caused by imperfect textual transmission, this discrepancy reflects the text's own masculine ideology and cultural context.[31] It is significant that, within the overarching frame, the bad wife is not the sole female protagonist, but that she is prefaced by her radical opposite, the epitome of the good wife, who has only the King's interest at

---

[28] For instance, 'Aper' has no moral as such, yet has the instantaneous effect of all the other tales: 'e mandó matar su fijo' (*Sendebar*, p. 112).

[29] In *Mishle Sendebar* the bad wife's threats of suicide come only on the seventh day. First, at the beginning of the day, rather than telling a story, she attempts to commit suicide by jumping into the river; however, when the advisers continue with their stories, she counterbalances these with a new one of her own, 'Fur et luna', which does not appear in the Castilian *Sendebar* but does in fact feature in *Calila e Dimna*, pp. 109-10. Then, when this final story proves ineffective, she again tries to kill herself by ingesting poison and forcing the King to give her some balm to drink in order to save her (*Mishle Sendebar*, pp. 245-71). Thus, arguably, the bad wife of *Mishle Sendebar* uses actions more than words in order to sway the King, whereas the Castilian *Sendebar* places more of an emphasis on the power of the woman's words.

[30] Cixous, 'The Laugh of the Medusa', p. 881.

[31] As we learn from the Prologue, the Castilian *Sendebar* was commissioned around 1253 by the Infante Fradrique, brother of Alfonso X 'el Sabio', so it seems reasonable to suggest that the text pertains to what Hélène Cixous calls 'male writing': as Cixous puts it, male writing is 'a locus where the repression of women has been perpetuated, over and over, more or less consciously, and in a manner that's frightening since it's often hidden or adorned with the mystifying charms of fiction', a locus which 'has grossly exaggerated all the signs of sexual opposition (and not sexual difference), where woman has never *her* turn to speak' ('The Laugh of the Medusa', p. 879, emphasis original).

heart. By using two hyperbolically contoured female figures, the text makes its position on femininity clear. As María Eugenia Lacarra puts it in discussing the figure of the Lady in courtly love:

> Since masculine ideology defined women as naturally inferior to men, it was necessary that the beloved, the *Lady*, be an exceptional woman in the literal sense of the word, that is to say, an exception to the rule. Only by being a unique specimen, could a female be considered worthy of the love of a man.[32]

Or, I should add, only by being truly extraordinary, whether in the positive or the negative sense, could she be worthy of his attention.

None the less, the fear of woman's mysterious powers pervades the text: her words are less important in their content than in their very utterance, and she herself is a distorting element not so much because of her acts, whether these acts be simply storytelling or anything else, but rather through her very presence. And it is because of this danger that, in the end, the good wife disappears from the picture altogether, and the bad wife loses the *exemplum* debate and is punished for her transgression: 'E el Rey mandóla quemar en un[a] caldera en seco' (p. 155). This punishment varies in the other versions of the *Sendebar* tradition, and in the Hebrew *Mishle Sendebar*, for instance, the King ends up forgiving his wife. However, the fact that the announcement of the bad wife's brutal punishment is the last sentence of the Castilian text is very significant: it shows not only the importance this punishment is given within the text as a whole, but also the inability to deal with the danger and mystery of woman in any other way.

UNIVERSITY OF CAMBRIDGE ANDREEA WEISL-SHAW

[32] María Eugenia Lacarra, 'Notes on Feminist Analysis of Medieval Spanish Literature and History', *La Córonica*, 17 (1988), 14–22 (p. 19).

WHAT DO WE SAY WHEN WE SAY 'JUAN GELMAN'? ON PSEUDONYMS AND POLEMICS IN RECENT ARGENTINE POETRY

Juan Gelman is perhaps Argentina's best-known living poet, a Cervantes Prize winner and, like Borges, a name mentioned annually in literary circles as a possible Nobel laureate. His work as a poet and journalist stretches over fifty years and runs to dozens of volumes; his complete works are currently being republished by the Buenos Aires daily *Página/12*, to which he is a contributor; his *Obra reunida* was published in 2011 in Mexico by the Fondo de Cultura Económica and his *Poesía reunida* in a major edition by Seix Barral in 2012. Even his life-story, including political militancy and the tragedy of children murdered by the military junta and a disappeared granddaughter recovered only after years of investigation and struggle, is well known outside Argentina.[1] Gelman's importance as a poet in Argentina has even been noted in the negative: in his sketch of the 'new' Argentine poetry, Martín Prieto notes Gelman's defining role in the direction of 1990s and 2000s poetry, specifically as the subject of an internal debate among the editors of *Diario de Poesía* over whether or not to publish a dossier in homage to him on the thirtieth anniversary of his first book. Prieto suggests that the eventual refusal by the editors was central to the emergence of so-called *objetivista* poetry in Argentina.[2] Subsequently, another argument about the figure and work of Gelman could be identified as a milestone in the separation of the same group in the 1990s in Argentina.[3] Indeed, one might argue that recognition

---

A version of this paper was presented in May 2012 at the University of Cambridge Centre for Latin American Studies as part of their seminar series, and I am grateful to the organizers for their invitation. I would also like to thank Rosemary Cameron for her help in preparing the manuscript.

[1] In the UK, Gelman's case was brought to public attention by, among others, Graham Greene, who wrote a letter to the *Independent* (24 September 1987) supporting Gelman's pleas to return to Argentina to discover the whereabouts of his disappeared relatives; Gelman's letter to Greene requesting his support, with copious annotations by Greene, can be found in the Leeds University Library's Fay and Geoffrey Elliott Collection: see <http://www.leeds.ac.uk/library/spcoll/handlists/148Elliott.pdf> [accessed 7 July 2013] (p. 19 of 32); a transcript is in the author's possession.

[2] Martín Prieto, 'Neobarrocos, objetivistas, epifánicos y realistas: nuevos apuntes para la historia de la nueva poesía argentina', *VOX Virtual*, 23 (July 2009) <www.proyectovox.org.ar> [accessed 28 November 2011].

[3] Prieto recounts the following story: when Gelman was still a wanted man in Argentina, in the 1980s, and his works were largely unobtainable, a homage to him upon his return brought together a number of young writers who formed the magazine *18 whiskies* (named, as it happens, after Dylan Thomas's last, terminal drinking binge). Although many of these writers have little or nothing aesthetically in common with Gelman, one can argue that a central tendency in 1990s poetry in Argentina, *objetivismo*, stems from a meeting inspired by the figure of Gelman. The polemic that emerged in 2000 after one of the younger poets, Daniel Durand, circulated a text entitled 'Gelman asesino', followed by an irate response from another poet, Martín Gambarotta, can almost be taken as a marker for the splintering of that same moment or mode of writing. See Martin Gamboratta, 'Escrache en Balvanera', *Diario de Poesía*, 55.39 (2000), p. 39, and Ana

and controversy both characterize Gelman's figure. Another polemic erupted around Gelman's public role in the 2000s, when the philosopher Oscar del Barco criticized Gelman's status as a 'poet-martyr' as part of a wider critique of the former revolutionary left (of which del Barco had himself also formed part) for a failure to recognize their guilt for violent crimes committed in the name of revolution.[4] Gelman remained silent at the time of the row, but a recent collection, *de atrásalante en su porfía* ('backforward in its stubbornness'), contains pointed lines, after the fashion of Quevedo, directed towards the 'sabios del muy después', those wise long after the event.[5]

As recently as 2011, an acrimonious row erupted, as the poet Santiago Llach accused Gelman of various criminal activities while launching insults against him and his supporters; the editor and poet Daniel Freidemberg robustly took up the case for the defence.[6] Finally, at the time of writing, in the wake of the award of compensation from the Uruguayan government to Gelman's family for the kidnap and clandestine adoption of his granddaughter, Macarena, Gelman was accused (it would seem incorrectly) of double standards by the Uruguayan daily *El país*.[7] All this despite the fact that Gelman has lived, for several decades now, away from Argentina, mostly in Mexico, where he has had his home since the 1980s, and, furthermore, some years after Gelman's investigation of the clandestine adoption of the children of disappeared parents and the role of the Uruguayan government, during and after the dictatorship, in occluding the facts.[8]

Porrúa, 'La *novedad* en las revistas de poesía: relatos de una tensión specular', *Orbis tertius*, 10.11 (2005), 1–10 (p. 4, n. 12).

[4] *Sobre la responsabilidad: no matar. Polémica de la revista 'La intemperie'*, ed. by Pablo René Belzagui (Córdoba: La intemperie, 2007).

[5] Juan Gelman, *de atrásalante en su porfía* (Buenos Aires: Seix Barral, 2009), p. 110.

[6] See, for example, Germán Carrasco, 'Santiago Llach: "Me quedo con la poesía de Facebook antes que con el hijo de puta de Juan Gelman"' <http://www.theclinic.cl/2011/02/12/santiago-llach-%E2%80%9Cme-quedo-con-la-poesia-de-facebook-antes-que-con-el-hijo-de-puta-de-juan-gelman/> (2011) [accessed 6 December 2011], and Santiago Llach, 'Gelmanianos del mundo, haced la autocrítica' <http://monoloingua.blogspot.com/> [accessed 15 February 2011]. Llach repeats a widely circulated but quite unsophisticated reading of the left's supposed guilt in the slaughter of the dirty war, a position not helped by his simultaneous attempt to try to reduce the figure widely held to be the number of disappeared and murdered in the 1970s and claim that there is what amounts to a Peronist cultural and media plot against those like himself who criticize the current left 'establishment'. Coincidentally, Llach, who claims in the interview with Carrasco to have Peronist 'blood in his veins', is the son of the former minister for education in the government of Fernando de la Rua, the collapse of which was a significant factor in the rise of the particular brand of Peronism now in government in Argentina.

[7] See Anon., '¿Qué dirá Juan Gelman?' (Editorial, *El país digital* (Uru)) <http://www.elpais.com.uy/110910/predit-592347/editorial/%C2%BFque-dira-juan-gelman-/> [accessed 6 December 2011], and Gelman's response and clarification (2011), in which he makes it clear that he has, as previously stated, refused all financial compensation ('Qué dirá Juan Gelman' <http://www.pagina12.com.ar/diario/elpais/1-176605-2011-09-12.html> [accessed 6 December 2011]).

[8] Mauricio Rodríguez, *El caso Gelman: periodismo y derechos humanos* (Montevideo: Cruz del Sur, 2006).

The question that this article intends to explore is at once simple and complex: why do polemics and polemicists seem attracted to Gelman, even today? There are, of course, simple biographical and historical answers that one could put forward: his membership of the armed left in the 1970s (often cited by his opponents); the apparently unresolved philosophical and legal question of the supposed 'guilt' of its members;[9] and Gelman's championing of human-rights causes and, on occasions, his public support for the Kirchner and Fernández de Kirchner governments. All of these are perfectly plausible answers; they do not, however, necessarily help us to understand the relationship between the figure of Gelman as a poet (an apparently controversial one at times) and Gelman's poetry.

The position of Gelman as at once a widely respected poet and a polemical figure is further complicated by a tendency in his work which has been present since the 1960s, namely his publication of poems under names other than his own; or that are imagined to have been written by others, sometimes in other languages. In a poem entitled 'Gotán', itself the title of an earlier and well-known collection of poems, Gelman wrote 'yo no escribí ese libro en todo caso | [. . .] me sacaban las palabras',[10] one of many statements that apparently hint at a distancing of poet from poems. His works are sometimes referred to as pseudonymous poems, heteronymous poems, or even, recently, 'alterónimos'; the term 'apocryphal translations' might also be apposite.[11]

One can summarize Gelman's engagement with pseudonymous writing thus: in his 1965 collection *Cólera buey* Gelman included a series of poems attributed to John Wendell, purportedly translated from English into Spanish.

---

[9] This question has been addressed by Pilar Calveiro. Calveiro was a member of the armed left in the 1970s and first came to attention as a sociologist with her 1998 study of the military apparatus, *Poder y desaparición* (with a prologue by Juan Gelman). More recently her volume *Política y/o violencia* details what she calls an 'autoescrache', or self-naming and shaming, which critically analyses the ideology of the armed left. The leader of Montoneros, the group of which she was a member (with Gelman), Mario Firmenich, has been widely accused of being an infiltrator. His political trajectory takes in a background in right-wing Catholic activism, then the Peronist armed left, militarized militancy, and then exile. For a number of years he proselytized from overseas. Calveiro disagrees with the conspiracy theorists. After tracing the militarist and totalitarian logic of the Argentine armed forces, the shift to the right of Peronism and its union bureaucracy in the 1970s, she identifies the impoverished Clausewitzian logic of armed groups and their leaders, who came to mimic the very armed forces they were fighting. In some ways, Calveiro's critique is far stronger than simply saying that Firmenich or others were traitors, or double agents: she argues that the decisions he and those close to him made were so bad, and the consequences for the many rank-and-file militants and their friends and families so lamentably predictable, that no double agent would have dared to make them. See Pilar Calveiro, *Política y/o violencia: una aproximación a la guerrilla de los años 70* (Buenos Aires: Verticales/Norma, 2005), and *Poder y desaparición: los campos de concentración en Argentina* (Buenos Aires: Colihue, 1998).

[10] Juan Gelman, *Cólera buey* (La Habana: La tertulia, 1965; rev. edn Buenos Aires: La rosa blindada, 1971; repr. Buenos Aires: Seix Barral, 2010), p. 31.

[11] Silvina Friera, 'Uno insiste para encontrar el milagro', *Página/12*, 2 December 2011 <http://www.pagina12.com.ar/diario/suplementos/espectaculos/4-23700-2011-12-02.html> [accessed 6 December 2011].

The same collection also included poems written in Spanish, attributed by Wendell to one Dom Pero Gonçalvez. A revised version of the same collection, from 1971, included poems dated as having been written in 1968, which were supposedly translations from a Japanese poet, Yamanokuchi Ando.[12] In the late 1960s, Gelman published a series of poems entitled 'Traducciones, III: Los poemas de Sidney West', poems in the vein of Edgar Lee Masters and his *Spoon River Anthology*, dealing with the deaths of fictional characters in a small US town.[13] This began a tendency towards poems in books by Juan Gelman that are of dubious or questionable attribution, a tendency that lasted up until the 1990s: a series of 'Com/posiciones', works based on poems by early modern Christian mystics, poets of Islamic Spain, and some poems attributed to 'Eliezer Ben Jonon', who, most scholars agree, is a creation of Gelman's and not a real early Spanish or Islamic Spanish poet; as well as two sections in a book of Gelman's poems that are claimed to have been left to Gelman by a disappeared militant poet, and another series by a dead militant poet left to the disappeared poet and which found their way into Gelman's hands (their names are Julio Grecco and José Galván, the initials giving one a clue as to their real author). Finally, in 1994 Gelman published a collection entitled *Dibaxu*, which includes facing-page bilingual poems in a version of Sefardí, a language of the Spanish Jewish diaspora close to medieval Spanish, alongside his own more or less faithful translations into more or less standard Spanish.[14] In interviews, Gelman has also mentioned a collection of sonnets that he wrote while in Italy in the late 1970s, composed in macaronic colloquial Italian. Such a tendency towards an apparent distancing of the poet from the narrative voice might suggest that Gelman is an even less likely candidate for public controversies.

Gelman remarked in an interview with Mario Benedetti that he first started writing apocryphal translations as a means to counter the excessive 'intimismo' of his works in the mid-1960s, the years of his break with the Argentine Communist Party.[15] In particular, Gelman began to write poems by an 'inglés', John Wendell, as a reaction to a moment in which both poetically and politically he felt himself to be stuck in a dead-end street.[16] It is one of these poems that will form the focus of this article. Although Gelman is a linguist and translator, and was familiar with much contemporary writing in other languages, his 'translations' were original poems. It is also worth remembering that, owing to the vagaries of anthologizing, some have come

---

[12] Juan Gelman, '*Traducciones*, I: Los poemas de John Wendell (1965/1968)', in *Cólera buey*, pp. 149–93.
[13] Juan Gelman, *Los poemas de Sidney West* (Buenos Aires: Galeria, 1969).
[14] Juan Gelman, *Dibaxu* (Buenos Aires: Seix Barral, 1994).
[15] Mario Benedetti, *Los poetas comunicantes* (Montevideo: Marcha, 1981), p. 192.
[16] 'Los poemas de John Wendell', in *Cólera buey*, p. 192.

to be republished without any indication of their previous 'pseudonymous' existence. Such is the case with Poem XCI, 'toda poesía es hostil al capitalismo', which in Gelman's anthology *Pesar todo* appears with no indication of the role of 'John Wendell':[17]

XCI

toda poesía es hostil al capitalismo
puede volverse seca y dura pero no
porque sea pobre sino
para no contribuir a la riqueza oficial

puede ser su manera de protestar de   5
volverse flaca ya que hay hambre
amarilla de sed y penosa
de puro dolor que hay puede ser que

en cambio abra los callejones del delirio y las bestias
canten atropellándose vivas de   10
furia de calor sin destino puede
ser que se niegue a sí misma como otra

manera de vencer a la muerte
así como se llora en los velorios
poetas de hoy   15
poetas de este tiempo

nos separaron de la grey no sé qué será de nosotros
conservadores comunistas apolíticos cuando
suceda lo que sucederá pero
toda poesía es hostil al capitalismo[18]   20

The poem opens with a clear and unequivocal statement of position regarding poetry and capitalism. In the opening stanza poetry is presented as a form of refusal to participate or contribute. At the same time, Gelman adopts terms such as 'puede' and subjunctive verbs to suggest poetry as a space of possibilities and conjecture. In the second line, poetry is associated lexically with deprivation ('seca') and difficulty ('dura'), and may 'volverse flaca', or wither. The lexicon—full of words of lack and poverty—associates the poet with the humble, the dispossessed, while at the same time apparently undermining the authorial certainty of the lyric voice ('puede'). Thus, divides are drawn between poetry and capitalism; and between poetry and official riches or wealth: that is to say, poetry is not capitalist, it is unofficial, and, even if it is not necessarily poor, it is by nature not on the side of the rich.

The second stanza proposes poetry as a form of protest and of sharing in the suffering of others. This action takes place as a result of there being hunger ('ya que hay hambre'): that is to say, poetry engages in a direct, causal

[17] Juan Gelman, *Pesar todo: antología* (Mexico City: FCE, 2001), p. 65.
[18] 'Los poemas de John Wendell', in *Cólera buey*, pp. 172–73.

relationship with world conditions, so hunger leads to skinny poetry. Poetry thus reflects its circumstances, and must express the real-world conditions around it. The tone and mood, therefore, are melancholic and lamenting ('pobre', 'flaca', 'penosa', 'dolor'), while the poet is one who feels the 'puro dolor' that exists in the world, and is sensitive to the suffering of fellow man, with pain seen as something held in common between all human beings, perhaps a hint of César Vallejo's presence in Gelman's work. An unmediated triangular relationship thus exists between poet, poem, and world.

Here and in the first stanza, the use of two quatrains suggests the form of the sonnet, which the poem eventually exceeds, after the 'velorios' of line 14; similarly, there are fragments of the *silva* form (eleven- and seven-syllable lines in free combination) and lines that could, with some poetic licence, be read as fourteen-syllable *alejandrinos*, not least the two of the opening. The use of five four-line stanzas reproduces a form employed by Neruda in his *Veinte poemas de amor*, specifically Poem 9, 'Ebrio de trementina', itself a remnant of Darío's *modernismo*.[19] Likewise, there are hints of rhyme ('no [. . .] sino'; 'de [. . .] que') and alliteration ('puede [. . .] de'), all remnants of traditional, accepted poetic forms.

The third stanza presents a sudden change of mood, marked by enjambment from the second stanza and the opening phrase, 'en cambio', to suggest an exuberant overflowing. Still in the subjunctive, poetry is proposed as a surging forth ('abra los callejones'), an animalistic and furious eruption ('las bestias'), as in the Surrealist conception of the links between poetry and the unconscious (one thinks of rearing horses in Salvador Dalí, or Picasso's *Guernica*, or the strange juxtapositions of Enrique Molina's poetry), while the repetition of 'puede ser' underlines the possibility and uncertainty proposed from the outset. The poem thus seems to work through, firstly, socially centred poetry, and then more experimental writing, both of which appear to be suffering under capitalism, and are formally uncertain if not in a state of total collapse. In the fourth stanza, having denied itself at the end of the third, poetry even offers a response to death, either as memory or as expression of pain, a form of memory and mourning that acknowledges and even defeats death, perhaps through its ability to recall that which is lost. In lines 15 and 16 the poem states and repeats its specific contemporary relevance.

In the final stanza poets are separated from the flock ('grey'); they are singled out or victimized, therefore occupying a position of risk, which occurs regardless of political alignment, indeed occurs even to the apolitical. In conclusion, poetry, all poetry, the different models described here (social, experimental, self-denying, or mourning), as is reiterated in the final line,

---

[19] Pablo Neruda, *A Basic Anthology*, ed. by Robert Pring-Mill (Oxford: Dolphin, 1975), p. 5.

is ontologically, 'es', is in essence, at the moment of utterance, oppositional within the capitalist system.

To a certain extent, Poem XCI draws faithfully on Gelman's Communist formation, in particular a reading of Karl Marx. As Boccanera notes, Marx comments in his *Theories of Surplus-Value* that capitalist production does not, in principle and in essence, favour art.[20] If for Marx productive labour is that which produces surplus value, and surplus value is unpaid labour, then unproductive labour is anything that does not produce surplus value. Marx goes on to examine such activities as politics and philosophy, both eminently unproductive, stating:

The educated bourgeois and his mouthpiece are both so stupid that they measure the effect of every activity by its effect on the purse. On the other hand, they are so educated that they grant recognition even to functions and activities that have nothing to do with the production of wealth.[21]

For Marx, poetry, producing no surplus value, would be a form of unproductive labour, and thus economically at odds with capitalism. Gelman said in an interview with Mario Benedetti in 1970 that he felt the contemporary era to be the least favourable to poetry ever, and the level of alienation present in modern society, particularly as a result of advertising, to be more brutal than ever before.[22] Gelman's poem shifts Marx's concepts in time on the basis of an observation of the contemporary period, somewhat simplifying the latter's argument and possibly ignoring the second sentence in the quotation above. At the same time, he argues that poetry is oppositional because of, in short, capitalism's philistine streak. All poets as a result are under threat in the modern age as outsiders, separated from the flock: if poetry is hostile to capitalism, doubtless capitalism will be equally hostile in reply. Gelman's poem makes a plea for solidarity: regardless of political inclination, all those writing poetry are committed already, and must therefore be aware of their high-risk status. Thus poetry is not merely a tool but a *raison d'être*.

We can situate this poem in contemporary controversies about poetry's supposed political function. For writers, the debate, in part sparked by Jean-Paul Sartre's influential essays in *What Is Literature?* over political engagement in writing, became increasingly central in Argentine poetry in the 1960s.[23] This poem is to some extent Gelman's contribution to the debate: a poem

[20] Jorge Boccanera, 'Cinco momentos en la poesía de Juan Gelman', in *Acercamientos a Juan Gelman*, ed. by José Brú (Guadalajara: Universidad de Guadalajara, 2000), pp. 34–53 (p. 42).

[21] Karl Marx, *Theories of Surplus-Value*, Volume IV of *Capital*, trans. by Emile Burns (London: Lawrence and Wishart, 1964), p. 279.

[22] *Los poetas comunicantes*, pp. 189–90.

[23] Jean-Paul Sartre, *What Is Literature?*, trans. by B. Frechtman (London: Methuen, 1947). See also Claudia Gilman, *Entre la pluma y el fusil: debates y dilemas del escritor revolucionario en América latina*, 2nd edn (Buenos Aires: Siglo XXI, 2012).

that contests Sartre's assertion of the impossibility of commitment in poetry. Gelman descries an apparent exit from the impasse in which poetry, as observed by Sartre, would either be uncommitted or else cease to be poetry. Gelman's gesture is to suggest that poetry, by its very act of being, commits an act contrary to the capitalist system, instead of needing to say or do anything to prejudice contemporary social organization. In subsequent writings, Gelman has repeated this and similar points, stating in 1996, for example, that 'la política puede hablar de todo, menos la poesía'.[24] Gelman's position is close to one identified in Walter Benjamin's critique of Charles Baudelaire: if the poet in the age of high capital must stand apart from the interests of his own class, and if the poet is almost of necessity bourgeois, and if at the same time the interests of the bourgeoisie are also those of capital, then poetry is necessarily anti-capitalist;[25] thus, as Boccanera suggests, even a writer infamous for his Fascist affiliations and anti-Semitic writings, Ezra Pound, can be read as an anti-capitalist.[26] Boccanera argues that Gelman is glossing Ezra Pound's Canto XLV, 'With usura', to propose that the practice of poetry is in essence anti-capitalist.[27] Boccanera notes that Pound was one of a number of US poets who, via Raúl González Tuñón, came to interest Gelman. Pound may initially seem a strange choice for a poet of the left, but in an interview cited by Boccanera, Gelman stresses his interest in Pound's critique of capitalism, and his anti-capitalist world-view as expressed in this canto.[28] Pound wrote, 'With usura hath no man a house of good stone | each block cut smooth and well fitting | that delight might cover their face.'[29] This criticism of 'usura' or credit capitalism, seen by many as part of his steady drift towards anti-Semitism and support for Mussolini, is instead reworked by Gelman as a critique of bourgeois capitalism. Gelman's stance thus displays a remarkably catholic optimism regarding the possibility of politically oppositional poetry. In his poetics this is illustrated by his melding of the techniques of what might be called aesthetic and social poetry. Gelman writes clear propositional statements ('todo poesía es hostil al capitalismo'), but does so while breaking up the line, refusing the norms of correct capitalization and running over lines in enjambments that closely echo practices of Surrealist automatic writing; the layout and form seem almost to wrestle with the strictures of traditional poetry (the sonnet or the quatrain, for example), and they constrain the state-

---

[24] Juan Gelman, 'Juan Gelman' [otherwise untitled note in dossier on poetry and politics], *Diario de Poesía*, 36 (Summer 1995–96), p. 11.

[25] Walter Benjamin, *Charles Baudelaire: A Lyric Poet in the Era of High Capitalism*, trans. by Harry Zohn (London: New Left Books, 1973), p. 106.

[26] Boccanera, 'Cinco momentos en la poesía de Juan Gelman', p. 42.

[27] Ibid., p. 45.

[28] Ibid., p. 122.

[29] Ezra Pound, *The Cantos of Ezra Pound* (London: Faber & Faber, 1964), pp. 239–40 (p. 239).

ments being expressed; the poem struggles with several available models of poetic expression.

The presence of Ezra Pound, one of the very many intertexts running through Gelman's œuvre, marked a significant change in his work from the late 1960s onwards. There is a further, less obvious contemporary intertext for Gelman's poem, namely W. H. Auden's words on poetry in the essay 'The Poet & the City':

> Every artist feels himself at odds with modern civilization.
> In our age, the mere making of a work of art is itself a political act. So long as artists exist, making what they please and think they ought to make [. . .] they remind the Management of something managers need to be reminded of, namely that the managed are people with faces, not anonymous numbers, that *Homo Laborans* is also *Homo Ludens*.[30]

It is perhaps unlikely that Gelman was aware of this essay at the time of writing, but the coincidence in date and theme is striking. The poem 'Confianzas', from the 1973 collection *Relaciones*, includes the line 'Con este poema no tomarás el poder' but concludes, resolutely, 'se sienta a la mesa y escribe'. Gelman does quote Auden in his poem 'El tajo', but it is the (in)famous line that 'poetry makes nothing happen' ('La poesía no hace | que algo suceda, dice W. H. Auden') from 'In Memory of W. B. Yeats' (1940) in his collection *Valer la pena* (2001), and the reading is largely critical of Auden's stance. Thus 'Toda poesía es hostil al capitalismo' uses right-wing (Pound) or, perhaps, conservative poetry (the later Auden, of whose position Gelman apparently disapproves) for left-wing purposes. Pound's cosmopolitanism and Marx's anti-capitalism combine to propose a new, open form of literary Communism. The poem, though, is aimed at capitalism and not imperialism, the Argentine Communist Party's enemy of the day, and this marks a clear break from the Communist Party, given their adherence to the Soviet Policy of State Capitalism, as we shall see.

Critical approaches to Gelman's pseudonymous works have generally agreed on the ability of his pseudonymous poems to question the authorial position. For Miguel Dalmaroni, for example, Gelman's poetry is an attempt to deny alienating divides or choices between aesthetic and social poetry, assimilating the lyric subject to social denunciation.[31] But with his poetry of the 1960s, in its search for an epic, for a 'poética politizante y narrativa', in particular in poems dealing with Cuba, the risk emerges of a limit to the truth that can be told with poetry.[32] His break with the Communist Party in the 1960s

---

[30] W. H. Auden, 'The Poet & the City', in *'The Dyer's Hand' and Other Essays* (London: Faber & Faber, 1963), pp. 72–89 (p. 88).

[31] Miguel Dalmaroni, *Juan Gelman: contra las fabulaciones del mundo* (Buenos Aires: Almagesto, 1993), pp. 19, 30.

[32] Ibid., p. 35.

coincides with a search for other forms of expression; rather than the poem being in favour of revolution, the poem itself must be revolutionary.[33] Dalmaroni sees Gelman's translations as an 'alienation technique' in the Brechtian sense, to break with the univocity of social poetry and what seemed to be the apolitical stance of formally experimental poets such as Alejandra Pizarnik and Edgar Bayley. For Geneviève Fabry, Grecco, Galván, Ben Jonon, et al are heteronyms; these allow Gelman a more intimate identification with other life-stories, in particular of those exiled in the past and in other places, or of those members of the armed left who suffered a different fate from Gelman's, namely death and/or disappearance. Gelman's poetry aims to symbolize the experience of loss without turning the symbol into an allegory that could become fetishized, while at the same time allowing *something* to happen to the lyric subject.[34] Similarly, in Sarli Mercado's work on Gelman and Luisa Futoransky, she argues that Gelman uses the 'genre of the self' ('género del yo') to construct a series of geographical spaces, including dialogue with writers and poets from other places and times.[35] Gelman's lyrical 'I' is one that contains millions, or that is another, and techniques such as the use of pseudonyms are one of Gelman's means to 'violentar el lenguaje'.[36]

In her pioneering study of such 'strategies of otherness', Sillato characterized Gelman's poetry as a doubling or displacement of the self or the 'I', in particular through the means of heteronyms, translations, and intertextuality.[37] The 'I' speaks, but at the same time it speaks with the capacity to be an 'other', or several others, at the same time. Sillato, drawing on Hugo Friedrich's ideas in *The Structure of Modern Poetry*,[38] argues that in Gelman's middle and later work we witness a dehumanizing of the lyric 'I' and a distancing from the tradition, most strongly represented in recent poetry by Walt Whitman (but, one might add, taken up by Pablo Neruda), of the poet taking on a collective voice, a tradition, precisely, which Gelman had espoused in his early poetry, especially that written during his membership of the Communist Party.[39]

While such studies draw attention to the importance that unconventional attitudes towards the subject of writing play in Gelman's work, they do not, satisfactorily, hint at an explanation within Gelman's poetry for his ability to provoke intense polemic despite the apparent distancing of Gelman the man

[33] Ibid., p. 40.
[34] Geneviève Fabry, *Las formas del vacío: la escritura del duelo en la poesía de Juan Gelman* (Amsterdam and New York: Rodopi, 2008), pp. 71, 309.
[35] Sarli Mercado, *Cartografías del destierro: en torno a la poesía de J. Gelman y L. Futuransky* (Buenos Aires: Corregidor, 2008), p. 9.
[36] Ibid., p. 167.
[37] María del Carmen Sillato, *Juan Gelman: las estrategias de la otredad. Heteronimia, intertextualidad, traducción* (Rosario de Santa Fe: Beatriz Viterbo, 1996), p. 11.
[38] (Evanston, IL: Northwestern, 1974); English translation of *Die Struktur der modernen Lyrik: Von Baudelaire bis zur Gegenwart* (Hamburg: Rowohlt, 1960).
[39] Ibid., pp. 13–14.

from the poems published under his and others' names. One might suggest, further, that such approaches overstate the radicality of what Gelman is doing.

One must recognize that biographical readings (or, as Todorov calls them, 'aetiological' approaches) are reductive. As Gelman himself notes in one interview, although he recognizes himself in his poems, he does so simply as the one who had written them, 'los leo como poemas de otro'.[40] His pseudonymous writing would seem to want to explore such a relationship between writing and authority. Gelman recognizes, in the same interview, the risks of writing as a well-known political figure, acknowledging that people might approach or reject his work for circumstantial reasons, or 'motivos ajenos a la poesía'.[41] In this sense, one might note that in recent years there seems to have occurred something of a split in Gelman's writing, with overtly political material being reserved for his newspaper columns (he is a contributing editor to the left-wing daily *Página/12*).

Yet the use of pseudonyms both offers Gelman greater room to explore certain themes and paradoxically reinforces the figure of Juan Gelman. More specifically, the poem under discussion demonstrates Gelman's use of a pseudonym to address a very specific political point that was of relevance for him at the time of writing, the moment of his split from the Communist Party of Argentina. The pseudonym, rather than destabilizing the subject, here reinforces it.

My reading follows a line initially indicated by Jorge Boccanera, who argues that Gelman uses, not heteronyms in the fashion of Pessoa, but pseudonyms.[42] Boccanera suggests that Gelman explores a conflict, between the writing of poems as a form of ownership, and writing that comes about as a demand from others and from circumstances, while finding its destination precisely in the uses to which it is put by others, for example when one's poems are turned into anonymous graffiti.[43] Boccanera notes another twin movement, whereby the author is diluted in his pseudonyms while also being reinforced through the naming of 'Gelman', 'Juan', and other variants in the poems themselves, often as a forceful interpellation. Boccanera agrees with other critics in seeing this as a means of escaping 'intimismo' or excessive lyricism in poetry.[44] He quotes an interview with Gelman in which the poet talks of a specific political conjuncture, in the early 1960s, and of his own estrangement from the Communist Party over its alleged conservatism, leading him into an excessive focus on personal problems. His solution, he records, was to

[40] *Conversaciones con la poesía argentina*, ed. by Jorge Fondebrider (Buenos Aires: Libros de Tierra Firme, 1995), p. 257.
[41] Ibid., p. 263.
[42] 'Cinco momentos en la poesía de Juan Gelman', p. 49.
[43] Jorge Boccanera, *Confiar en el misterio: viaje por la poesía de Juan Gelman* (Buenos Aires: Sudamericana, 1994), pp. 207–08.
[44] Ibid., p. 209.

start writing as an Englishman, John Wendell.[45] Apart from the nationalities, however, Gelman's foreign pseudonyms have little in the way of back-story or biography. Something like an exception can be found in the case of his Argentine pseudonyms, in the collection *Hacia el sur*, José Galván, a disappeared militant, and Julio Grecco, a murdered one. Although Boccanera offers Roque Dalton's work as a related example, Dalton gives his creations far more in the way of personal stories. His posthumously published novel *Pobrecito poeta que era yo*[46] creates a series of fictional characters with complex inner lives, all of whom have aspects of personality and biography in common with the author. As Boccanera states, in Gelman 'la transformación del sujeto poético no alcanza a borrar la marca del original'.[47] Furthermore, there is a difference between Juan Gelman and, for example, Rubén Darío, Pablo Neruda, Gabriela Mistral, or even, more recently, Washington Cucurto, in that these writers have all come to adopt legally or de facto a pseudonym for the majority of their creative output.

It is worthwhile comparing the studies of Gelman with other work on heteronyms, in particular those on Fernando Pessoa. Pessoa is acknowledged as a master of heteronymous writing, if not its absolute pioneer. As is well known, Pessoa created a series of figures with names, features, personalities, and lifestories who also write literature, and who engage in a complex exchange of ideas and opinions, all catalogued by Pessoa. Kotowicz argues that when we read the heteronyms, 'each time we seem to be reading a distinctly different poet', and that 'even when Pessoa wrote under his own name he differed just as much'; he created 'disjointed voices belonging to different discourses, written in different languages coming under different names', or, as one of his pseudonyms, Álvaro de Campos, wrote, 'each is an assembly of subsidiary psyches, a badly made synthesis of cellular souls'.[48] Pessoa 'transformed his inner multiple reality into a poetic strategy';[49] 'these imaginary personae were not a disguise, an attempt to conceal the author, the way a pseudonym would';[50] indeed, the heteronyms even gained a certain degree of autonomy, de Campos once writing a letter to a girlfriend of Pessoa's encouraging her to break off with the latter.[51] She replied to Pessoa that she did not really like de Campos. In her study of Pessoa's œuvre Darlene Sadlier argues that 'all of [Pessoa's] intellectual, political, and artistic interests were contradictory',

---

[45] Ibid., p. 201.
[46] (San José, Costa Rica: EDUCA, 1976).
[47] Ibid., p. 212.
[48] Zbigniew Kotowicz, *Fernando Pessoa: Voices of a Nomadic Soul* (London: Menard, 1996), pp. 14–15.
[49] Ibid., p. 40.
[50] Ibid., p. 42.
[51] Ibid., p. 63.

while there is a clear 'structural connection' between the heteronyms.⁵² Pessoa himself argued that they were a product of his own hysterical or schizoid personality; each of the seventy-plus heteronyms, semi-heteronyms, and other characters that Pessoa used for his writing have a tendency both to splinter and to overlap; books composed initially by one heteronym, for example the *Livro de desassossego* or *Book of Disquietude*, change authorship in places. Pessoa himself was capable of composing radically different texts from wholly contradictory standpoints during the same day; none of the heteronyms is necessarily more important or more central than the others.⁵³ 'The heteronyms' "individuality" can be seen in their different stylistic responses to concerns they all share.'⁵⁴ What we have of Pessoa's writings—the reams of paper, piles of notebooks, and discarded snippets found in his famous trunk on his death—are in Barthesian terms a 'text', while the editors who have worked on this legacy since his death are trying—impossibly—to construct the 'work'.⁵⁵

It is not that Gelman compares in some way unfavourably, rather that Pessoa and others are just more exaggerated examples of something that happens with many writers. And, unlike Pessoa, Gelman creates no life-stories, writes no horoscopes for, and conducts no exchanges between his poets. Furthermore, Gelman's texts have all been resolved, paratextually, into a work, in a series of books and anthologies authored by Gelman. Few studies have noted that the names 'Julio Grecco' and 'José Galván', rather than being literary heteronyms, have something in common with the assumed name, or 'nom de guerre', of militants; in part this is a literary practice, but it is also drawn from Gelman's clandestine time in the mid- to late 1970s, when he left and then returned to Argentina under a false name. Just like a militant's cover, these pseudonyms do not imply a different character. There is, as Gelman suggests in an interview included in a documentary film about his work, a long history of both political exile and false passports in his family.⁵⁶

What seems to emerge most strongly from Gelman's pseudonyms, translations, and false names is Gelman, or sometimes Gelman at different stages in

⁵² Darlene J. Sadlier, *An Introduction to Fernando Pessoa: Modernism and the Paradoxes of Authorship* (Gainesville: University Press of Florida, 1998), p. 1.
⁵³ Ibid., p. 5.
⁵⁴ Ibid., p. 47.
⁵⁵ A further contrasting example might be found in the work of Antonio Machado. Machado, who in his *Campos de Castilla* had written a series of highly critical poems about contemporary Spanish life, in particular the provinces, had never in his poetry addressed political projects as such. Through the figure of Juan de Mairena, an apocryphal teacher, Machado was able to explore progressive philosophical ideas while also contributing articles to organs of the Republican cause. Yet Mairena was also given a biography and more developed inner life, one which could not necessarily be attributed wholly to Machado. Meanwhile, a converse example might be found in the case of José Hernández, whose nickname and pseudonym, Martín Fierro, became the name of his most famous character and work.
⁵⁶ *Juan Gelman y otras cuestiones*, dir. by Jorge Denti (Buenos Aires: Página/12, 2005) [on DVD].

his life, and a set of related concerns: memory, exile, loss, and love. Perhaps only one collection stands apart, *Los poemas de Sidney West*, as clearly aiming to distance itself from Gelman. These poems follow a number of years of silence and mark a reconfiguration of Gelman's political position and writing style; to do this they draw heavily on Edgar Lee Masters's 1915 collection *Spoon River Anthology*, which includes a series of laments and odes for the dead of this small, rural American community, and a poem allegedly written by one of the fictional inhabitants about the town, a (mock) epic entitled 'The Spooniad'.[57] While *Sidney West* does stand out from other collections, even these are poems about loss and nostalgia, albeit often in parodic form, and are all still published under his name.

Kate Jenckes argues that there are two tendencies in critical readings of Gelman's work: to read it either as embodying commitment to Argentine leftist politics or as being about autobiographical themes such as exile, religion, or love; in both cases, says Jenckes, the aesthetics of his work is overlooked.[58] In fact, the tendency to separate the aesthetic and the political is one with some basis in Gelman's own later career: he publishes articles in *Página/12* on political themes, particularly on international politics, also lately with a special focus on ecological topics, as well as collections of these prose pieces, while his poetry has become less overtly political. Yet Jenckes's directions are useful: not to overstate either poetry (aesthetics) or politics at the expense of the other, but rather to try and read them dialectically.

Here it is worth setting Gelman's piece in context in order to identify the literary engagements at work in the poem. Changes in the literary landscape of Buenos Aires were well underway in the 1950s. The Perón government of the 1940s and 1950s had maintained a difficult relationship with writers; some intellectuals were jailed, marginalized, or went into exile. Meanwhile, the models of writing that had characterized the avant-gardes and nascent social-realist schools of the 1930s and 1940s seemed to many, by the 1950s, distinctly passé, for both stylistic and, perhaps more importantly, political reasons: by the mid-1950s, with anti-colonial wars taking place in Africa, Asia, and Latin America, but with the horrors of Stalinism made increasingly public, it was clear that manifestos or provocative poetry were not sufficient to change the world, but also that writing in uncritical support of parties or movements brought ethical dilemmas. Many writers sought to use innovations in poetry as a means of exercising political commitment. Gelman and his colleagues in a group around González Tuñón aimed to change poetry in theme, by focusing on the social, the everyday, and political matters; in style, by including colloquialisms, the *voseo* second-person verb form used in

---

[57] First published in *Reedy's Mirror* (St Louis, MO).
[58] Kate Jenckes, 'The Apostrophe of Mourning in the Poetic Work of Juan Gelman', unpublished book chapter (copy in the author's possession).

the River Plate region, and verse forms found in the tango; and in audience, proposing recitals in social clubs and community centres.

We can also situate the poem in a very specific moment in terms of the development of the left in Argentina, with reference to Gelman's relationship with the Communist Party, to which the group of writers around González Tuñón were almost all affiliated, Gelman being no exception.[59] But these were years of increasing schism within the Communist Party and the broad left. The Communist Party's 1963 programme calls for a broad front of the working class and the 'pueblo trabajador' alongside the petite bourgeoisie and the nationalist bourgeoisie, provided that the latter two genuinely desire change, as part of a 'frente democrático nacional, anti-oligárquico, antimperialista [sic] y pro paz [. . .] por un gobierno verdaderamente democrático y popular'.[60] Democracy and pacifism are both stressed, with non-pacific means allowed only if reactionary or imperialist sectors block the democratic route. There is, however, nothing explicitly anti-capitalist in the document; indeed, after an attack on unproductive overseas capital, the programme goes on to stress that non-monopoly foreign capital and national capital will not be expropriated and will actually be protected by law.[61] A plan for a reduction of tax on consumption is also tabled; there are suggestions of some land reform. Links with other socialist countries, through trade, for example, are promoted; more notably, 'coexistencia pacífica' and 'no-intervención' are stated policies of the Communist Party.[62] In a curious discursive move, despite promoting a plan that is progressive, electoral, pacifist, and non-interventionist, there is a brief mention of the importance of Cuba as a model of what can be achieved by a people who fight with determination: 'pueden romper el cerco imperialista y conquistar su libertad e independencia nacional'.[63] It is only after the reference to Cuba that any mention of opposition to capitalism per se appears, namely, that in the wake of the Cuban experience 'el imperialismo y el sistema capitalista se debilitan', although it is not explained by what means this occurs. Thus one can nuance Gelman's much-cited characterization of the Communist Party as 'conservative' by suggesting that its reformist, electoral, and essentially bourgeois capitalist tendencies put it at best in uneasy (pacific) coexistence and at worst in open conflict with the new revolutionary models emerging in Latin America, and leave its nationalism somewhat exposed to

---

[59] Emir Rodríguez Monegal, *Jorge Luis Borges: A Literary Biography* (New York: Dutton 1978), p. 192.
[60] Partido Comunista de la Argentina, 'Programa del Partido Comunista de la Argentina: aprobado por el XII Congreso del Partido, realizado en la Ciudad de Mar del Plata, desde el 23 de febrero al 3 de marzo del 1963' (Buenos Aires: Anteo, 1963), p. 2.
[61] Ibid., p. 4.
[62] Ibid., p. 7.
[63] Ibid., p. 8.

the new continentalist and indeed tri-continentalist models of political action emerging in Latin America.[64]

In his assessment of the development of the left in Argentina, highly critical of the Communist Party, Ramos notes that the Communist Party was proud of its anti-Perón stance, which it saw as consistent with its anti-Fascist position.[65] Communist Party militants who sought links with Peronism were expelled in 1946 and 1953;[66] the Communist Party tended to support elected bourgeois governments (Ramos is particularly scathing of Pablo Neruda's enthusiastic early campaigning and support for the democratically elected and subsequently dictatorial González Videla regime in Chile).[67] The Communist Party, therefore, welcomed the 'Revolución libertadora' coup to depose Perón, in contrast, for example, to revolutionary Socialist tendencies which attempted to arm workers in the defence of democracy.[68] For Ramos, both the orthodox Socialist Party and the Communist Party accepted a broad section of the ideology of the ruling classes (or 'oligarquía terrateniente', to use Ramos's term).[69] There was, Ramos argues, an all too convenient match between the abstract formulae of European Marxism, the 'tactical variations' of Soviet bureaucracy, and the liberal, Mitrista tradition in Argentina, in particular their tendency to look overseas for theoretical solutions to national problems.[70] Ramos goes so far as to describe the Communist Party of the mid- to late 1950s and early 1960s as peopled by 'unitarios stalinistas'.[71]

Gelman's departure from the Communist Party might thus suggest the logical step of a turn towards Peronism. But the anti-capitalism explored in the poem points to another cause for the apparent political dead end detected by Gelman. Communist and Socialist Parties in Argentina had in general opposed Perón, suspicious of his military background and admiration for Mussolini. But at this stage, with an actual Peronist government still fresh in the memory, this poem also demonstrates the difficulties of any left–Peronist rapprochement. In her study of the life of the revolutionary leader

[64] Gelman's complaint against the Communist Party would seem to have contemporary echoes in France, in particular the Althusser–Rancière polemic over the question of student politics; Althusser argued against what he felt were the utopian demands of the student radicals and their '"democratic" illusion of knowledge' (p. 15); Rancière claimed that his former master was simply protecting a position within the apparatus of both the university as an organ of the state and the conservative French Communist Party—in short, a position of political 'timidity': see Warren Montag and others, 'Dossier: The Althusser–Rancière Controversy', *Radical Philosophy*, 170 (November–December 2011), 8–35.
[65] Jorge Abelardo Ramos, *Breve historia de las izquierdas en la Argentina* (Buenos Aires: Claridad, 1990), p. 170.
[66] Ibid., p. 146.
[67] Ibid., p. 15.
[68] Ibid., p. 174.
[69] Ibid., p. 178.
[70] Ibid., p. 179.
[71] Ibid., p. 180.

Mario Roberto Santucho, María Seoane charts the ups and downs of left-wing Peronism in the 1950s and 1960s.[72] In the mid-1950s, in the wake of the 'Libertadora' coup, there emerged the so-called Peronist resistance, and with it the fleeting possibility of a new left that united Peronists with those sectors opposed to the post-Perón settlement. In the late 1950s groups such as Uturuncos, a Peronist *foco*, seemed to suggest a rural guerrilla struggle along the lines of the Cuban model as a strategy for the Argentine radical left.[73] This proved, however, to be abortive. In the early 1960s, despite the return to a form of electoral democracy, the Argentine government continued its repression of left-wing, and in particular Peronist, resistance groups, via the so-called 'Plan Conintes' (='Conmoción interna del estado'). The question of armed struggle continued to raise its head, as both a problem for governments and a contentious point within political groups and parties. After Peronism's fleeting electoral return in 1962, followed by the military's overthrow of Frondizi's government in 1963, the government of Arturo Illia made some gestures towards civil liberties; however, the state was unable to control the progressive radicalization of workers' sectors together with pressure, on the other hand, from the military. The same pressures were felt in the political parties of the left, even once legalized. In 1965 the Communist Party suffered a split, losing a so-called Revolutionary Vanguard, whose members would go on to found the Ejército de Liberación Nacional and to support Ernesto Che Guevara's ill-starred campaign in Bolivia. At the same time the Socialist Party also experienced schism, with the emergence of a Maoist splinter group known as the Vanguardia Comunista.[74]

Perón's disagreements with the cultural world were well known. Leopoldo Marechal was one of the few poets able to find an accommodation within Peronism. Furthermore, and importantly for our poem, Peronism was not an anti-capitalist option; as Karush and Chamosa write, 'the capitalist marketplace constrained the ideological maneuvers of Peronist intellectuals'.[75] In the same volume, speaking more broadly, Plotkin writes that 'Perón never disputed the existence of private property, nor did he ever question capitalism or suggest the possibility of socializing the means of production'.[76]

In this context of a political *huis clos*, Gelman's poem uses the pseudonymous position to address a central concern: what is the contemporary

---

[72] María Seoane, *Todo o nada: la historia secreta y la historia pública del jefe guerrillero Mario Roberto Santucho* (Buenos Aires: Debolsillo, 2009).

[73] Ibid., p. 47.

[74] Ibid., p. 80.

[75] Matthew B. Karush and Oscar Chamosa, 'Introduction', in *The New Cultural History of Peronism: Power and Identity in Mid-Twentieth-Century Argentina*, ed. by Matthew B. Karush and Oscar Chamosa (Durham, NC: Duke University Press, 2010), pp. 1–20 (p. 15).

[76] Mariano Ben Plotkin, 'Final Reflections', in *The New Cultural History of Peronism*, ed. by Karush and Chamosa, pp. 271–86 (p. 274).

relationship between poetry and politics? More specifically, through the use of intertexts from anglophone poetry, particularly anglophone poetry with right-wing political connotations, Gelman attacks simultaneously the capitalist, anti-literary, and anti-cosmopolitan tendency shared by Peronism and the Communist Party. Furthermore, the poem allows him to position poetry as opposed to capitalism almost as if by *force majeure*, though a concrete political option is yet to be identified.

In conclusion, firstly, Gelman's use of pseudonyms is normal: these are just typical avatars of an author's career (one thinks of Borges in 'Funes el memorioso' parodying his own writings, such as *El tamaño de mi esperanza*, of twenty years earlier), and their use should not stand in the way of an examination of the connections and discontinuities of Gelman's work over the years. Secondly, Gelman uses the pseudonym, or alternym, as one might call it, to resolve specific questions about the relationship between literature and politics and, even more specifically, about his own political role as a poet; in relation to this, the creative and literary possibilities of poetic forms associated with the avant-gardes, social poetry, and contemporary anglophone poetry are explored in relation to the search for a position, anti-capitalist and cosmopolitan at once, that exceeds the local contemporary political and literary spheres.

When reprinted today, as happens with relative frequency, Gelman's poetry thus stands at odds with two tendencies that can be detected in contemporary Argentine culture. The first is what Pizarro Cortes calls the 'decentring of the historical subject';[77] the second is the assault on the lyric subject that one finds in much contemporary poetry, not least the work of Martín Gambarotta or Washington Cucurto (Santiago Vega). Here, in this early poem, one might argue, we can detect *in nuce* the elements of his work that make Gelman the poet a frequently controversial figure. Furthermore, the call for anti-capitalist poetic solidarity is at odds with the factionism and *ad hominem* attacks of which he is so often, sadly, the victim.

ST CATHERINE'S COLLEGE, OXFORD   BEN BOLLIG

[77] Carolina Pizarro Cortes, 'The Decentring of the Historical Subject in the Contemporary Imaginary of the Independence Process', *Journal of Latin American Cultural Studies*, 20 (2011), 323–42.

HÖLDERLIN ON TRAGEDY AND PARADOX: 'DIE BEDEUTUNG DER TRAGÖDIEN [. . .]'

Hölderlin's theoretical writings command attention as the reflections by a great poet on the nature and significance of his craft.[1] However, they also give rise to formidable problems of interpretation. There are a number of reasons for those difficulties, often varying according to the text in question. In several cases the essays are fragmentary or unfinished, and appear sometimes to be rapid drafts in which the poet's thoughts are caught on the wing.[2] In other cases the texts are carefully composed, but appear to have a hermetic or riddling quality, as in the so-called *Pindar-Fragmente* (MA, II, 379–85). In many cases a theoretical text has to be considered in the context of a poetic work for which it may provide a commentary or a programme.[3] In others its status as a commentary may be explicit, but that form developed in novel and surprising ways. The only theoretical texts that Hölderlin himself saw into print were his 'Notes' to two plays of Sophocles: the *Anmerkungen zum Oedipus* (MA, II, 309–16) and *Anmerkungen zur Antigonä* (MA, II, 369–76). Like the *Pindar-Fragmente*, those *Sophokles-Anmerkungen* are presented as commentaries on Hölderlin's unorthodox translations of the respective Greek works, while transcending the limits normally assigned to philological commentary. And the *Pindar-Fragmente* themselves defy any easy categorization as poetry, translation, or theoretical reflection.

Even where a full understanding cannot yet be achieved, it may still be possible to characterize the context and shape of Hölderlin's argument, while guarding against oversimplifications that may not do justice to the difficulty of the texts. It is in that spirit that I propose to consider one of the shortest,

I am grateful to the anonymous reviewer, whose comments enabled some deficiencies to be remedied.

[1] Unless otherwise indicated, references to Hölderlin will be to the 'Münchner Ausgabe' of his works: *Friedrich Hölderlin: Sämtliche Werke und Briefe*, ed. by Michael Knaupp, 3 vols (Munich: Hanser, 1992–93), abbreviated MA. For the theoretical works see also the 'Frankfurter Ausgabe': *Friedrich Hölderlin: Sämtliche Werke. Historisch-kritische Ausgabe*, ed. by D. E. Sattler, 20 vols (Frankfurt a.M: Roter Stern; Basel: Stroemfeld and Roter Stern, 1976–2008), XIV: *Entwürfe zur Poetik*, ed. by Wolfram Groddeck and D. E. Sattler (1979), this volume abbreviated FHA; *Johann Christian Friedrich Hölderlin: Theoretische Schriften*, ed. by Johann Kreuzer (Hamburg: Meiner, 1998); *Friedrich Hölderlin: Essays and Letters*, ed. and trans. by Jeremy Adler and Charlie Louth (London: Penguin, 2009), pp. 223–339 (the essays are translated by Adler).

[2] Lawrence Ryan rightly points to 'the constant reformulation of thoughts that often do not find their final expression': see his review of *Friedrich Hölderlin: Essays and Letters on Theory*, ed. and trans. by Thomas Pfau (Albany: SUNY Press, 1988), in *German Quarterly*, 63 (1990), 557–59 (p. 558).

[3] The essay 'Die tragische Ode [. . .]' (MA, I, 865–78) is clearly intended as a basis for Hölderlin's unfinished drama *Der Tod des Empedokles*, and is often referred to under the title of its third section, 'Grund zum Empedokles'. Arguably the essay 'Das untergehende Vaterland [. . .]' (MA, II, 72–77) is similarly to be so understood: see Ernst Mögel, *Natur als Revolution: Hölderlins Empedokles-Tragödie* (Stuttgart: Metzler, 1994), pp. 58–74.

but in some ways most representative, of Hölderlin's theoretical writings. This consists of a single paragraph beginning with the arresting statement that 'Die Bedeutung der Tragödien ist am leichtesten aus dem Paradoxon zu begreifen' (MA, II, 114). I shall refer to this untitled text as 'Die Bedeutung der Tragödien [. . .]', abbreviated to 'Bedeutung'. It consists of only five sentences, and a number enclosed in square brackets below will designate the corresponding sentence. The text (as edited in both MA and FHA) reads as follows:

[1] Die Bedeutung der Tragödien ist am leichtesten aus dem Paradoxon zu begreifen. [2] Denn alles Ursprüngliche, weil alles Vermögen gerecht und gleich getheilt ist, erscheint zwar nicht in ursprünglicher Stärke nicht wirklich sondern eigentlich nur in seiner Schwäche, so daß rechteigentlich das Lebenslicht und die Erscheinung der Schwäche jedes Ganzen angehört. [3] Im Tragischen nun ist das Zeichen an sich selbst unbedeutend, wirkungslos, aber das Ursprüngliche ist gerade heraus. [4] Eigentlich nemlich kann das Ursprüngliche nur in seiner Schwäche erscheinen, insofern aber das Zeichen an sich selbst als unbedeutend=0 gesezt wird, kann auch das Ursprüngliche, der verborgene Grund jeder Natur sich darstellen. [5] Stellt die Natur in ihrer schwächsten Gaabe sich eigentlich dar, so ist das Zeichen wenn sie sich in ihrer stärksten Gaabe darstellt=0.

The difficulties involved in interpreting this text should already be apparent. Hölderlin begins by referring to 'paradox': but is he referring to a specific paradox, or rather to 'paradox' in the sense of a more general category of paradoxical utterance? The manuscript shows that he did indeed begin by referring to the specific paradox 'daß alles Ursprüngliche [. . .] nur in seiner Schwäche erscheint', before separating the thought into two sentences (FHA, p. 382). In that revision, does the initial 'Denn' of the second sentence preserve the initial meaning, or mark the first step in a more complex argument? Furthermore, in this theoretical fragment, turning as it does on the distinction between 'das Ursprüngliche' (or 'der verborgene Grund') and 'die Erscheinung', what is the significance of the distinctly more poetic term 'das Lebenslicht'? Most mysteriously of all perhaps, what is the null sign ('das Zeichen [. . .] =0'), and how does it relate to the concept of '[die] Schwäche'? When the meaning of a sign is set at zero, how does that enable the 'hidden ground' to display itself? Is that zero degree of meaning merely an acute form of 'weakness'? Another difficulty centres on the concept of 'presentation': what is the relation between the notions of 'erscheinen' and 'sich darstellen'? And how does each relate to the idea that, in tragedy, 'das Ursprüngliche' is 'gerade heraus'?

Although 'Bedeutung' was originally assigned by its editors to the period of Hölderlin's first stay in Homburg vor der Höhe (1798–1800), the scholarly consensus now places it in the final phase of his poetics that followed his return from Bordeaux in 1802. It has been suggested, in fact, that it belongs with the *Sophokles-Anmerkungen* published in 1804. In addition to those 'Notes' to his translations of *Oedipus Rex* and *Antigone*, Hölderlin had promised his publisher an 'Introduction' to the tragedies, and it is possible that the text is the only surviving remnant of the latter.[4] That hypothesis would suggest that it is a fragment of a larger whole. On the other hand, despite the difficulty of the thought expressed, the argument appears to be self-contained, comprising a series of deductive steps leading to a definite conclusion. While I shall follow other commentators in referring to 'Bedeutung' as a 'fragment', that qualification should be borne in mind.

In support of the later dating, Hölderlin's more recent editors cite lexical and other similarities to manuscripts of that period, in particular the use of the term 'das Lebenslicht' in the letter to Casimir Ulrich Böhlendorff of November 1802 (MA, II, 920-22) as well as in a manuscript of the elegy 'Brod und Wein'. The expression also figures in other poetic manuscripts of the same period.[5] But part of the fascination of the fragment is the bridge it provides between those two phases of Hölderlin's poetics: between his first Homburg period (the 'Homburg poetics') and the final phase of his thought that followed his return from Bordeaux.[6]

One recent commentator, Ernst Mögel, continues to attribute the fragment to the first Homburg period, linking it in particular to Hölderlin's reflections on the basis for his tragedy on the death of Empedocles. That might give us pause, since Mögel also offers what is perhaps the single most convincing interpretation of one aspect of the text.[7] On the other hand, he does not address all the arguments for the later dating (including paper-type and handwriting), and nor are his considerations based on the usage of 'das Lebenslicht' wholly convincing.[8] Again, the very possibility of this debate illustrates the centrality of the fragment, seeming as it does to connect the thought-world of the Homburg poetics with that of the Sophocles translations.

If 'Bedeutung' has the form of a deductive argument, one way of reading it would be to focus on its conclusion, interpreting the text in the light of the final sentence. This appears to turn on the contrast between two modes of 'presentation', each involving a different aspect of 'die Natur': '[5] Stellt die Natur in ihrer schwächsten Gaabe sich eigentlich dar, so ist das Zeichen wenn sie sich in ihrer stärksten Gaabe darstellt=0.' Here 'die Natur' is to be taken as 'Nature' as an all-encompassing whole, rather than the individual

[4] See the second letter to Friedrich Wilmans from December 1803, MA, II, 926-27 (p. 927).

[5] See MA, III, 402, citing MA, I, 413, MA, II, 921, and MA, III, 213; and see also MA, III, 254. See further *Friedrich Hölderlin: Sämtliche Werke und Briefe*, ed. by Jochen Schmidt, 3 vols (Frankfurt a.M.: Deutsche Klassiker Verlag, 1992-94), II (1994), 1252-53 (this edition, with its extensive commentary, is referred to below as 'Schmidt'); and Wolfram Groddeck, *Hölderlins Elegie 'Brod und Wein' oder 'Die Nacht'* (Frankfurt a.M.: Stroemfeld, 2012), pp. 268 and 316.

[6] Cf. Anja Lemke, *Konstellation ohne Sterne: Zur poetischen und geschichtlichen Zäsur bei Martin Heidegger und Paul Celan* (Munich: Fink, 2002), pp. 61-62, n. 4.

[7] Mögel, pp. 78-81, discussed further below.

[8] On those additional arguments for the later dating see FHA, p. 379, and on 'das Lebenslicht' see further below.

natural things referred to in the immediately preceding sentence ('[4] der verborgene Grund jeder Natur'). For that reason I shall capitalize the term in what follows. Nature is being considered in two distinct aspects, that of its greatest strength (or 'strongest endowment') and that of its greatest weakness (or 'weakest endowment'). Hölderlin can be read as saying that a distinct kind of presentation corresponds to each: in its aspect of weakness Nature can present itself 'truly' or 'properly' ('eigentlich'); in its aspect of strength a more oblique kind of presentation seems to be required, since use must be made of what Hölderlin calls 'das Zeichen [. . .] =0', the zero or null sign. And the latter case is precisely that of the presentation of 'the tragic', since '[3] Im Tragischen nun ist das Zeichen an sich selbst unbedeutend'.

However, that is by no means the way in which the fragment has most frequently been read. A more usual way of reading [5] is to see 'das Zeichen [. . .] =0' as an instance of the 'weakest endowment' referred to in the first half of the sentence. The 'so' in 'so ist das Zeichen' would then have the sense of 'so similarly' rather than 'so conversely'. For the moment, I will merely observe that such a reading is hard to reconcile with the wording of the immediately preceding sentence, which seems to imply that the presentation that is achieved by the medium of 'das Zeichen [. . .] =0' is distinct from the mode in which 'das Ursprüngliche' appears 'in seiner Schwäche'. As Mögel puts it, the argument has the form of '[ein] Umkehrschluss' (p. 79). And the distinction between modes of presentation is supported by the use of the two terms 'erscheinen' and 'sich darstellen'. The latter would seem to be the more general concept, since it can cover the case of both the 'strongest' and 'weakest' aspects of Nature, whereas the term 'erscheinen' in [2] and [4] seems to relate specifically to the aspect of weakness.

We also need to consider how the notions of 'erscheinen' and 'sich darstellen' are related to the idea that (in tragedy) 'das Ursprüngliche ist gerade heraus' ([3]). On the one hand, 'gerade heraus' seems to convey the idea of something manifesting itself directly, without the mediation of an 'appearance' or a (meaningful) 'sign'. That is the interpretation given by Schmidt: 'Erst wenn das "Zeichen", mit dem das Ursprünglich-Elementare erscheinungshaft vermittelt war, als "unbedeutend=0 gesetzt wird" [. . .], löst sich das Elementare aus dem Vermittlungszusammenhang und bricht *unmittelbar* durch: es "ist gerade heraus".'[9] But on the other hand, Hölderlin refers none the less to a 'sign', and therefore presumably to the presentation of 'das Ursprüngliche'

---

[9] Schmidt, II, 1253 (emphasis original). Note that Hölderlin originally wrote 'Nun erscheint zwar in Tragödien das Ursprüngliche gerade heraus', but then amended the text to read '[. . .] das Ursprüngliche ist gerade heraus' (FHA, p. 382). This may be because the notion of 'appearance' implies a consciousness to which something appears, whereas the emergence of the hidden ground of Nature is an event that is liable to eclipse consciousness, at least when considered from the point of view of the tragic protagonist: see MA, II, 373: '*unendlich*, das heißt in Gegensäzen, im Bewußtseyn, welches das Bewußtseyn aufhebt' (emphasis original).

through the medium of that sign. Unless of course 'das Zeichen [. . .] =o' is less a particular sign than a marker for the absence of any sign: as it were, the abolition of language.

In the most general terms, the fragment is concerned with how 'das Ursprüngliche' or 'die Natur' can manifest itself, whether in the form of 'die Erscheinung' or in the signs of human language.[10] The relation between nature on the one hand, and the human sphere of culture on the other (the relation between Nature and Art) is a central theme in Hölderlin: see, for example, the programmatic ode of 1800, 'Natur und Kunst oder Saturn und Jupiter' (MA, I, 285). That relation is central also to his thought about tragedy, which is little interested in the moral problem posed by the fate of the tragic hero. Rather than being founded on the idea of moral fault, or of the clash between different ethical principles, the essence of tragedy lies for Hölderlin in the idea of an excessive union with the ground of Nature, or with Nature considered in its unlimited or 'aorgic' aspect ('das Aorgische': MA, I, 868-69). The question arises how such an event can be captured in the medium of poetry, which of course itself belongs to the sphere of Art. How can a poetic work make manifest not only the subjective feelings of the poet—and to that extent the poet's own nature—but also the originating ground of Nature itself? That question forms the starting-point of the essay 'Die tragische Ode [. . .]' (MA, I, 865-78), which begins with an analysis of a lyric genre, the tragic ode (p. 865), before turning to the general problem of tragic drama (pp. 866-68), and finally to the basis for Hölderlin's own tragedy on the death of Empedocles (pp. 868-78). Compared with the lyric, tragedy expresses a deeper inwardness ('die tiefste Innigkeit' or 'eine tiefere Innigkeit'), which must be presented in more extreme distinctions and oppositions: 'die Form muß mehr den Karakter der Entgegensetzung und Trennung tragen' (p. 866). The form of a drama (as opposed to a lyric) allows too a separation between the poet's own subjectivity and the fate of the tragic protagonist, so that the latter can embody a more intense inwardness (p. 867). The idea of a hidden ground of Nature, coming to the surface with destructive consequences, is exemplified by the central image of Hölderlin's play: Empedocles' legendary death in the crater of Mount Etna.[11]

The problem of tragic presentation is also addressed in the third section of the *Anmerkungen zum Oedipus*. There '[d]ie Darstellung des Tragischen' is said to involve a monstrous event in which the human and divine spheres

---

[10] As we have seen, Hölderlin seems to distinguish the special case of 'appearance' from the more general concept of 'presentation'; the idea of a 'sign' belongs with the latter, so that 'die Erscheinung' could itself be regarded as a special case of 'das Zeichen'—as indeed is indicated by the way the latter is introduced in [3].

[11] On the historical background to the legend see Peter Kingsley, *Ancient Philosophy, Mystery, and Magic: Empedocles and the Pythagorean Tradition* (Oxford: Clarendon Press, 1995), pp. 278-83.

are united, and this encounter between 'der Gott' and '[der] Mensch' is characterized as a limitless union of 'die Naturmacht' on the one hand and 'des Menschen Innerstes' on the other (MA, II, 315). As Helmut Hühn has suggested, this may be the sense in which '[3] das Ursprüngliche ist gerade heraus'.[12] An aspect of Nature that is normally hidden, and indeed unbearable when encountered directly, is revealed in the action of a tragedy. And in this context the *Anmerkungen zur Antigonä* again invoke the concept of the 'aorgic': 'wie der Mensch sich dem Aorgischen nähert, in heroischeren Verhältnissen, und Gemüthsbewegungen' (MA, II, 372). But it should be noted that when the *Sophokles-Anmerkungen* refer to the 'presentation' of the tragic, they also insist that this moment of union is followed by a moment of division or separation (MA, II, 315 and 373).

The idea of Nature as an originating (and potentially destructive) force is undoubtedly the context in which Hölderlin's fragment is to be read. Having stated that in tragedy, '[3] das Ursprüngliche ist gerade heraus', he then glosses 'das Ursprüngliche' as '[4] der verborgene Grund jeder Natur'. This is the aspect of Nature that is normally hidden from view, but that in tragedy is 'out in the open'.[13] However, Hölderlin's use of the term 'das Ursprüngliche' can also give rise to confusion. Evidently its primary meaning is that of an originating principle or force, and as such it is identified with '[4] der verborgene Grund'. However, he begins by distinguishing between two aspects of 'das Ursprüngliche': one of 'original strength' and one of 'weakness': '[2] alles Ursprüngliche [. . .] erscheint zwar nicht in ursprünglicher Stärke nicht wirklich sondern eigentlich nur in seiner Schwäche'. And again in [4] he distinguishes 'das Ursprüngliche [. . .] in seiner Schwäche' from 'das Ursprüngliche, der verborgene Grund jeder Natur'. This may be why, in the final sentence of the fragment, he prefers the more general term 'die Natur', while again distinguishing two separate aspects: Nature in its 'strongest' and its 'weakest' endowments respectively. While 'das Ursprüngliche' more readily connotes a primal (and normally hidden) ground of things, it is easier to see 'die Natur' as containing two distinct but complementary aspects, as it were a tranquil surface and fiery depths. From that point of view 'die Natur in ihrer schwächsten Gaabe' is not a deficient form of Nature, as the term 'weakest' might otherwise

---

[12] Helmut Hühn, *Mnemosyne: Zeit und Erinnerung in Hölderlins Denken* (Stuttgart: Metzler, 1997), p. 215. Hühn also points out that such a case is to be distinguished from '[der] Normalfall', in which '[das] Ursprüngliche' appears 'nur in seiner Schwäche'. Like Mögel (and as argued here), he regards the presentation of the tragic as the converse case: 'in der tragischen Kollision dagegen ist es [. . .] "gerade heraus"' (ibid.).

[13] The expression 'gerade heraus' here is not easy to translate. Adler chooses the highly literal 'straight out' (Adler and Louth, p. 316); the reliable French translation of Denise Naville has 'ressort directement': see *Hölderlin: Œuvres*, ed. by Philippe Jaccottet (Paris: Gallimard, 1967), p. 644; see also Jean-François Courtine, 'De la métaphore tragique', in Courtine, *Extase de la raison: essais sur Schelling* (Paris: Éditions Galilée, 1990), pp. 45–72 (p. 66), who offers 'franchement à découvert'. But it should not, I think, be translated as 'straightforward' (as in Pfau, p. 89).

seem to imply. Rather it is the aspect of Nature that has the virtue of being able to appear, of being bathed in the light of appearance ('[2] das Lebenslicht und die Erscheinung'). This would then be the compensating virtue of Nature considered in that aspect of 'weakness', or in its mild or tender aspect: '[2] weil alles Vermögen gerecht und gleich getheilt ist'. Hölderlin's fragment seems to be interested in both of those aspects, each with its distinct virtue, just as it is interested in the distinct mode of presentation that corresponds to each. Because 'die Erscheinung' attaches above all to the aspect of weakness, it is in this aspect that Nature can present itself 'properly' ('eigentlich'). Conversely, in tragedy the aspect of overwhelming strength emerges into the open, while the sign that allows it to present itself becomes a paradoxical signifier, connoting precisely the opposite of what is presented: '[5] so ist das Zeichen wenn sie sich in ihrer stärksten Gaabe darstellt = 0'.

The analysis above has focused on what seems to be Hölderlin's argument in his two concluding sentences. However, commentators have often taken a different approach, reading those sentences in the light of the preceding ones. The fragment is read as a development of a single 'paradox', namely the paradox that 'original strength' can appear only in the form of 'weakness'. The sign that is without intrinsic meaning or effect, introduced in [3], would then merely be an extreme form of such weakness. That might indeed have been Hölderlin's starting-point when he began to compose the fragment. As we have seen, he initially referred not to '[das] Paradoxon' in general, but rather to the more specific paradox 'daß alles Ursprüngliche [. . .] nur in seiner Schwäche erscheint'.[14] And support for such a reading can also be found in the concept of metaphorical presentation that is so central to the Homburg poetics. Thus rather than considering two distinct modes of presentation, one exemplified by 'erscheinen' or 'sich eigentlich [darstellen]' and another by 'das Zeichen [. . .] =0', the fragment is interpreted in terms of a single concept of metaphorical presentation: here the presentation of 'strength' by means of 'weakness'. The limiting case of 'das Zeichen [. . .] =0' could then be seen either as one in which metaphor as it were falls away, leaving 'das Ursprüngliche' to manifest itself directly ('gerade heraus'). Or alternatively, it could be seen as a similar (but extreme) case of metaphorical expression of strength by weakness.

Accordingly, Charlie Louth, for instance, refers to 'the paradox that the absolute, which Hölderlin identifies here with nature, can only ever appear mediated through something else, that is, it appears "in seiner Schwäche" [in

---

[14] Thus the first version of the text, as constituted by the editors of FHA, reads: 'Die eigentliche Bedeutung aller Tragödien erklärt sich aus dem Paradoxon, daß alles Ursprüngliche, weil alles Gut gerecht und gleich getheilt ist, nicht wirklich sondern eigentlich nur in seiner Schwäche erscheint' ('Konstituierter Text I', p. 382).

its weakness], and not "in ursprünglicher Stärke" [in primal strength]'.[15] In a similar spirit, Peter Szondi explains Hölderlin's thought in the fragment as a 'Dialektik' in which 'das Starke von sich aus nur als Schwaches erscheinen kann und eines Schwachen bedarf, damit seine Stärke in Erscheinung trete'.[16] This interprets 'die Schwäche' as the indirect or metaphorical mode in which Nature, in its 'original strength', appears. And 'weakness' is then identified with 'das Zeichen [. . .] =0', which is in turn equated with the tragic hero, powerless in the face of the primal force of Nature. A similar reading is put forward by Lawrence Ryan, referring expressly to the Homburg poetics of tones:

Es handelt sich im Grunde genommen um eine weitere Anwendung des bekannten Prinzips, wonach ein jeweiliger Grund(ton) sich in seinem direkten Gegensatz äußert; hieraus wird gefolgert, daß 'alles Ursprüngliche... zwar nicht in ursprünglicher Stärke, sondern eigentlich nur in seiner Schwäche' erscheint.[17]

It is true that in the Homburg poetics Hölderlin analyses a poem in terms of the opposed aspects of 'der Grundton' (or 'die Grundstimmung') and 'der Kunstkarakter': the latter is the aspect of the poem that most immediately appears, whereas the underlying 'basic tone' is expressed only indirectly. Furthermore, this notion of indirect expression is described in terms of the concept of 'metaphor'. Thus 'der Grundton' (or 'basic tone') can be expressed only figuratively in 'der Kunstkarakter' (the 'art-character' tone), which expresses the underlying meaning of the poem in the form of a 'metaphor'. The meaning corresponding to the basic tone is accordingly 'eigentlich', whereas that corresponding to 'art-character' tone is 'uneigentlich' or 'metaphorisch' (since it conveys the true meaning only indirectly).[18] This can usefully be compared to the use of the term 'eigentlich' in 'Bedeutung'. But if that comparison is made, it may be difficult to argue that the fragment is solely concerned with a relation of indirect or metaphorical presentation, for example one in which something (say the ground of Nature, or Nature at its highest strength)

[15] Charlie Louth, *Hölderlin and the Dynamics of Translation* (Oxford: Legenda, 1998), p. 77 (bracketed text original).

[16] Peter Szondi, *Versuch über das Tragische*, in Szondi, *Schriften*, ed. by Jean Bollack and others, 2 vols (Frankfurt a.M.: Suhrkamp, 1978), I, 151–260 (p. 162).

[17] Lawrence Ryan, *Hölderlins Lehre vom Wechsel der Töne* (Stuttgart: Kohlhammer, 1960), p. 331 (ellipsis original); and see similarly Helmut Bachmaier 'Theoretische Aporie und tragische Negativität: Zur Genesis der tragischen Reflexion bei Hölderlin', in Bachmaier and others, *Hölderlin: Transzendentale Reflexion der Poesie* (Stuttgart: Klett-Cotta, 1979), pp. 83–145 (p. 133).

[18] See the essay 'Das lyrische dem Schein nach idealische Gedicht [. . .]', MA, II, 102–07 (pp. 102–03): 'Der Gegensaz seiner Grundstimmung mit seinem Kunstkarakter, seines eigentlichen Tons mit seinem uneigentlichen, metaphorischen' (p. 103). On Hölderlin's concept of 'metaphor' see Lawrence Ryan, 'Hölderlins Dichtungsbegriff', *Hölderlin-Jahrbuch*, 12 (1961–62), 20–41 (pp. 29–31), and on his theory of tones generally see Ryan, *Hölderlins Lehre*, and also Charles Lewis, 'Hölderlin and the Möbius Strip: the One-Sided Surface and the "Wechsel der Töne"', *Oxford German Studies*, 38 (2009), 45–60.

appears in the guise of its opposite (say Nature in its greatest weakness).[19] For by the time he reaches his concluding sentence, Hölderlin is willing to say (apparently in more positive terms) that '[5] die Natur in ihrer schwächsten Gaabe [stellt] sich eigentlich dar'. As we have seen, up to this point 'das Ursprüngliche' has been used confusingly in two different senses—namely as including, and as not including, the aspect of 'weakness'. Once that ambiguity has been resolved, the way appears to be open to read 'eigentlich' (in the sense, precisely, of the Homburg poetics) as corresponding to a non-figurative rather than a metaphorical mode of presentation. For in this case the thing that presents itself ('die Natur') is no longer distinct from the mode of its expression ('in ihrer schwächsten Gaabe'). Conversely, when considered as 'das Ursprüngliche', or as 'die Natur [...] in ihrer stärksten Gaabe', the distinction could not be more extreme: here 'das Zeichen [...] =0'.

As I have already observed, that capacity for direct or non-figurative presentation—the capacity to simply 'appear'—might be regarded as the compensating virtue of Nature in its weakness. It is a capacity that 'belongs to' (or is characteristic of) the weakness of every whole.[20] Conversely, it would be characteristic of the strength of the primal ground, or Nature in its 'aorgic' aspect, that its sign '=0'. If that null sign can be taken to be a metaphor, it is a metaphor of the most extreme kind, since greatest strength is presented here by a zero quantity of meaning. But on this interpretation, such nullity is not to be confused with '[5] die Natur in ihrer schwächsten Gaabe'. The latter involves instead a different extreme, that of a purely non-figurative mode of expression. Thus the presentation of Nature in its 'weakest endowment' could be seen as an expression without metaphor, a direct and non-figurative appearance; while the presentation of Nature in its 'strongest endowment' would lie at the opposite extreme, one of non-congruence between sign and meaning. And by the time the fragment reaches its final sentence, Hölderlin is indeed speaking of extremes: 'in ihrer schwächsten [...] in ihrer stärksten'.

Among previous commentators, Ernst Mögel seems to come closest to the approach suggested here. Mögel notes that the fragment describes two contrasting situations, only one of which belongs to the realm of the 'tragic': 'Das Argument [...] beruht darauf, daß Hölderlin zwei einander entgegengesetzte Lebenszustände annimmt: auf der einen Seite einen Zustand des an sich selbst "bedeutenden" [...] "Zeichens" oder "Lebenslichts", auf der andern Seite den Zustand des Tragischen.' The first of those cases stands in direct contrast to the 'presentation' involved in tragedy: 'Bei dem ersten haben wir offenbar

---

[19] Or as Jochen Schmidt puts it: 'In der Erscheinungswelt [...] ist das Ursprünglich-Elementare nur in vermittelter Form da, und das Erscheinen [...], das nur in solch vermittelter und mittelbarer Form möglich ist, ist demnach für das Ursprüngliche [...] seine "Schwäche"' (Schmidt, II, 1253).

[20] Adler (p. 316) mistranslates here: it is not that 'the manifestation of weakness' is part of every whole, but rather that 'appearance' or 'manifestation' attaches to 'the weakness of every whole'.

an einen Zustand der relativen Ruhe zu denken, in welchem die einzelnen Zeichen und Erscheinungen des verborgenen Grundes [. . .] mehr oder weniger in sich selber ruhen und gleichsam in ihrem je eigenen "Lebenslicht" erstrahlen.'[21] We have already seen that the use of the term 'das Lebenslicht' is relevant to the dating of the fragment. But as Mögel suggests, the term may also be a clue to its proper interpretation, indicating that the fragment is not only concerned with the case of tragedy, or presentation in the 'sign= o', but also with the converse case: a state of relative tranquillity in which life stands illuminated by its own light. Indeed, given the use of the superlative of the last sentence, it may be appropriate to speak of 'absolute tranquillity'. As we shall see below, that converse case corresponds to an important strand in Hölderlin's poetics.

As regards the term 'das Lebenslicht' itself, it must be admitted that the parallel usages in Hölderlin are sparse and themselves call for interpretation. The most striking parallel is in the second letter to Böhlendorff, where he describes his impression of southern France at the time of the revolutionary upheavals (MA, II, 920–22). He mentions first the tranquillity of those who live contentedly in the natural world, as compared with the violence of elemental Nature ('Das gewaltige Element, das Feuer des Himmels' as opposed to 'die Stille der Menschen, ihr Leben in der Natur'). But then he turns to the warlike region bordering the Vendée, which had witnessed a counter-revolutionary uprising. There, he says, he was interested by 'das wilde kriegerische [. . .], das rein männliche, dem das Lebenslicht unmittelbar wird in den Augen und Gliedern' (p. 921). For Mögel, such a use of 'das Lebenslicht' casts doubt on the later dating of our fragment, as it does not seem to correspond to the idea of 'relative tranquillity' that Mögel associates with its use there. However, in this letter Hölderlin seems only to be saying that, in exposing himself to the risk of death, the warrior has a heightened and more immediate sense of life, at least as compared with the peaceful shepherds described earlier.[22]

The term is found again in drafts for a poem in the important group of manuscripts known as *Homburger Folioheft*, in the hymn often edited under the title 'An die Madonna' (MA, I, 408–13).[23] It occurs in the following

---

[21] See Mögel 79–80. And as Mögel also observes, presentation in the second case can be seen as involving a particularly pure form of the sign, as it were uncontaminated by the content of experience: 'Indem das Zeichen "an sich selbst als unbedeutend=o gesezt wird", *erfüllt* es also seinen Charakter als Zeichen gerade erst in völliger Reinheit!' (p. 80, n. 48, emphasis original).

[22] Like Mögel, Schmidt interprets 'das Lebenslicht' in the letter to Böhlendorff as connoting the tragic, while drawing different conclusions as to its meaning in the fragment itself (Schmidt, II, 1253). Although the term 'das Lebenslicht' appears to be peculiar to the later period, Mögel notes that a similar expression ('das Flämchen des Lebens') is used in the first stanza of 'Die Muße' (MA, I, 169–70), a poem in hexameters from the period 1797–98. And it is used there in a context that clearly connotes an idyllic state of harmony with Nature (see Schmidt, I, 608: 'Die Wahl des Hexameters entspricht der episch-idyllischen Darstellung').

[23] For a detailed interpretation of the hymn see Anke Bennholdt-Thomsen and Alfredo

context: 'denn es hasset die Rede, wer | Das Lebenslicht das herzernährende sparet' (p. 413). The apposition with 'das herzernährende' suggests that 'das Lebenslicht' is something that gives sustenance to the heart, at once illuminating and vivifying. The wider context is susceptible of different interpretations, but a possible one associates 'das Lebenslicht' with the 'light of love' invoked in the elegy 'Menons Klage um Diotima', and hence with Hölderlin's own love for Susette Gontard.[24] Thus the third stanza of that elegy begins with the apostrophe 'Licht der Liebe!', and both this and the following stanza evoke scenes that are bathed in that light. Of particular interest is the scene depicted in the fourth stanza: that of two loving swans looking down at the surface of the water in which the blue of the sky is reflected, as is the silver of the clouds. For the scene is also apt to evoke the fragility of the lovers' bliss. The swans are looking not at a reality but at a glittering image of the heavens, and also no doubt at their own reflections. Does the light of love attach only to transient appearances, to the captivating illusions of a reflecting surface?

In a well-known article, Karl Eibl has drawn the consequences of such a thought for the interpretation of Hölderlin's poem 'Hälfte des Lebens'.[25] That short lyric is one of a series of nine published poems (the so-called 'Nachtgesänge') that are contemporary with the *Sophokles-Anmerkungen*, and hence with the probable date of 'Bedeutung' itself.[26] The first of its two stanzas depicts an idyllic scene in which a landscape is reflected in water. This is opposed to the second stanza, as a scene of plenitude and beauty is opposed to one of anguish and absence of meaning. But the movement between the two can be interpreted as the breaking of a narcissistic illusion, as the inebriated swans in the poem break the surface of the water: 'Und trunken von Küssen | Tunkt ihr das Haupt | Ins heilignüchterne Wasser.' For our present purposes, 'Hälfte des Lebens' could stand for the thought that the world can be considered as

---

Guzzoni, *Analecta Hölderliniana*, III: *Hesperische Verheißungen* (Würzburg: Königshausen & Neumann, 2007), pp. 179-215. See also Renate Böschenstein, 'Hölderlins allegorische Ausdrucksform, untersucht an der Hymne "An die Madonna"', in *Jenseits des Idealismus: Hölderlins letzte Homburger Jahre (1804-1806)* (Bonn: Bouvier, 1988), pp. 181-209.

[24] MA, I, 291-95 (p. 292), l. 29: see Bennholdt-Thomsen and Guzzoni, pp. 203-04. That interpretation may be supported by reminiscences elsewhere in the hymn of the lovers' journey to Bad Driburg with Wilhelm Heinse: see Schmidt, I, 1064-65. On Susette Gontard and Heinse see further below.

[25] MA, I, 445. Karl Eibl, 'Der Blick hinter den Spiegel: Sinnbild und gedankliche Bewegung in Hölderlins "Hälfte des Lebens"' <http://www.goethezeitportal.de/db/wiss/hoelderlin/haelfte_eibl.pdf> (20 February 2004) [accessed 2 June 2013]; originally published in *Jahrbuch der deutschen Schillergesellschaft*, 27 (1983), 222-35. See further Charlie Louth, 'Reflections: Goethe's "Auf dem See" and Hölderlins "Hälfte des Lebens"', *Oxford German Studies*, 33 (2004), 167-75 (p. 174). Note also that Renate Böschenstein (pp. 206-07) connects the passage from 'An die Madonna' with the problem of captivation by the image of perfection, as found both in an idealized ancient Greece and in the poet's experience of Diotima.

[26] MA, I, 439-46; see the second letter to Friedrich Wilmans of December 1803, MA, II, 926-27 (p. 927).

a world of beautiful appearances, bathed as it were in its own light; but the plenitude of the world of appearances has an intrinsic weakness or vulnerability: it is in danger of tipping into narcissistic captivation and disillusion. That might provide an initial gloss on the statement that '[2] das Lebenslicht und die Erscheinung der Schwäche jedes Ganzen angehört'. But we should at the same time guard against the thought that such 'weakness' has only negative connotations. The world of appearances is after all the only one that we can experience, and is also the world in which aesthetic beauty can be said to reside. And conversely, as 'Bedeutung' itself suggests, an encounter with the hidden ground of Nature is the stuff of tragedy.

In his recent study of 'Hälfte des Lebens' Winfried Menninghaus identifies an important strand of Hölderlin's poetics that is distinct from the poetics of the tragic and the sublime with which he is more often associated. Beginning with an analysis of the poem's metrical signature (the sapphic 'adoneus'), Menninghaus proceeds to demonstrate the significance of the underlying myths of Narcissus and of Adonis:

> Die rituelle Klage um Adonis, in welcher die historische Sappho-Rezeption zugleich die metrische Struktur der sapphischen Strophen-Klausel wiedererkannt hat, ist insofern in der Tat eine Grundfigur der sapphischen Dichtung selbst: der Jüngling [. . .] konnotiert unwiderstehliche Schönheit, aber zugleich Schwäche [. . .] und frühzeitigen Tod.[27]

And if the myth of Adonis is evoked by the poem's metrical signature, that of Narcissus is implied by the image of the drunken swan (pp. 48–51). The fate of an Adonis or a Narcissus is to be distinguished from that of a tragic hero. It reflects a vulnerability that is intrinsic to beauty, or to any perfection belonging to the sensuous world of appearances. And as Menninghaus observes, the figure of Diotima in *Hyperion* can also be seen in this context. Thus, the myth of Adonis is expressly evoked in Hölderlin's novel, where 'Hyperion nimmt [. . .] die Position Aphrodites ein, die gebildete Diotima diejenige des sprachlosen Adonis' (p. 42). And in Hyperion's captivation by Diotima's beauty, the structure of the Narcissus myth is also present (pp. 66–67).

Here we should recall that Diotima's silent and inward quality is one of her most important characteristics in the novel, and her beauty can itself provoke speechlessness (although in both cases this a silence that can speak volumes).[28] It is as if Diotima inhabits a realm of immediate expression, a

---

[27] Winfried Menninghaus, *Hälfte des Lebens: Versuch über Hölderlins Poetik* (Frankfurt a.M.: Suhrkamp, 2005), p. 35; see also pp. 39–47 and 62–68, and in particular p. 56: 'Die Geste des Ins-Wasser-Hängens schreibt so bereits der Imago vollendeter Schönheit die Tendenz auf einen tödlichen Ausgang ein.'

[28] 'Sie schien immer so wenig zu sagen, und sagte so viel' (MA, I, 662); 'Ich kann nur hie und da ein Wörtchen von ihr sprechen. Ich muß vergessen, was sie ganz ist, wenn ich von ihr sprechen soll' (MA, I, 664); 'Sprechen? o ich bin ein Laie in der Freude, ich will sprechen! Wohnt doch

realm of pure 'tones' ('die Töne') rather than linguistic signs.[29] The musical connotations of the latter are obvious, although 'tone' here means music of a particular kind, an immediate expression of the harmony of Nature.[30]

For Hölderlin poetry itself participates in this realm of musical expression, and it is significant that the elements of the poetic calculus described in the Homburg poetics are described as 'tones'.[31] But poetry none the less inhabits the realm of language, not of pure music, and the tones of the Homburg poetics do not simply sound forth in their immediacy, but are rather subject to the rules of 'alternation' or 'modulation' ('der Wechsel der Töne'). As we have seen, those rules themselves involve a relationship described as 'metaphor', in which an underlying 'basic tone' achieves indirect or figurative expression in the corresponding surface or 'art-character' tone. In Hölderlin's conception, therefore, poetry partakes of both realms: the non-figurative realm of music and the figurative realm of language.

I have suggested that the structure of metaphor is present in 'Bedeutung' in the shape of its two opposite and limiting extremes. On the one hand, '[5] die Natur in ihrer schwächsten Gaabe [stellt sich] eigentlich dar': this is as it were the extreme of non-figurative representation. And on other hand, if 'die Natur in ihrer stärksten Gaabe' can present itself by a sign, this is a sign that could not be more different from what is presented, namely 'das Zeichen [. . .] =0'. This is as it were the extreme of poetic figuration. The former case corresponds to the idea of a pure 'tone' rather than a linguistic sign. And it is a case that is described most eloquently in a short piece that belongs to the latest phase of Hölderlin's poetics.

In that piece, the *Pindar-Fragment* 'Vom Delphin', Hölderlin refers to 'Der Gesang der Natur', observing that 'Um diese Zeit giebt jedes Wesen seinen

---

die Stille im Lande der Seeligen, und über den Sternen vergißt das Herz seine Noth und seine Sprache' (MA, I, 655). See similarly MA, I, 656, 666, and 676; and in Diotima's own final letter: 'Stille war mein Leben; mein Tod ist beredt' (MA, I, 748). Note also the ode 'Diotima', which in all three versions begins: 'Du schweigst und duldest' (MA, I, 189, 256, and 327).

[29] 'Wir sprachen sehr wenig zusammen. Man schämt sich seiner Sprache. Zum Tone möchte man werden und sich vereinen in Einen Himmelsgesang' (MA, I, 658); 'seelig vereint, wie ein Chor von tausend unzertrennlichen Tönen' (MA, I, 678; see also 672–73). For a full treatment see Andreas Siekmann 'Die ästhetische Funktion von Sprache, Schweigen und Musik in Hölderlins *Hyperion*', *DVjs*, 54 (1980), 47–57 (pp. 55–56).

[30] See Claudia Alber, 'Allharmonie und Schweigen: Musikalische Motive in Hölderlins *Hyperion*', in *'Hyperion' — terra incognita: Expeditionen in Hölderlins Roman*, ed. by Hansjörg Bay (Opladen: Westdeutscher Verlag, 1998), 161–75 (pp. 169–72).

[31] On Hölderlin's conception of musical tonality see in particular: Hans Joachim Kreutzer, 'Tönende Ordnung der Welt: Über die Musik in Hölderlins Lyrik', in *Hölderlin und die Moderne: Eine Bestandaufnahme*, ed. by Gerhard Kurz and others (Tübingen: Attempto, 1995), pp. 240–79; Gunter Martens, 'Über Handschriften gebeugt: Ein Versuch, Hölderlins Mnemosyne zu fassen', in *Literatur als Erinnerung*, ed. by Bodo Plachta (Tübingen: Niemeyer, 2004), pp. 165–92 (pp. 173–76 and 188).

Ton an, seine Treue' (MA, II, 381).³² This identification of 'der Ton' with 'die Treue' calls to mind the opposite extreme treated in section 3 of the *Anmerkungen zum Oedipus*, in which the action of the tragedy is described as a process culminating in '[die] Untreue' (MA, II, 316). The pure musicality of a 'tone', and the trueness to self connoted by the idea of 'faithfulness', stand at the opposite pole to tragedy. Indeed, the *Pindar-Fragmente* as a whole might be viewed as an anti-tragic counterpart to the *Sophokles-Anmerkungen*, as can be gathered even from their titles: 'Von der Wahrheit', 'Von der Ruhe', 'Die Asyle', etc. And if the term 'Untreue' also figures in the title of what is usually regarded as the first of the sequence, this is surely in a sense opposed to the tragic 'faithlessness' of the *Sophokles-Anmerkungen*: for the full title is 'Untreue der Weisheit', and the commentary describes how true wisdom can reveal itself in adaptability to circumstances.

The *Pindar-Fragment* 'Vom Delphin' expounds a concept of purely musical or non-linguistic expression. The commentary describes a scene in which 'die Trennung' is virtually absent: the only divisions in evidence are those that arise naturally as differences between the natural species, and these are contrasted with those imposed by (human) language. Even the accent of 'need' ('[das] Bedürfnis') is said to be absent, perhaps as the equivalent in the natural world of the divisions created by language. Instead, everything participates in the pure voice of song: 'Nur der Unterschied der Arten macht dann die Trennung in der Natur, daß also alles mehr Gesang und reine Stimme ist, als Accent des Bedürfnisses oder auf der anderen Seite Sprache'.³³ The scene depicted in Hölderlin's commentary, and also expressed in its melodious language, is one of softness, melting and sympathetic echoing: 'Der Gesang der Natur, in der Witterung der Musen, wenn über Blüthen die Wolken, wie Floken, hängen, und über dem Schmelz von goldenen Blumen.' As Bartel observes (p. 110), 'der Schmelz' connotes a melting quality, as well as the lustre of the golden flowers themselves. And as Fink suggests (p. 57), this is a setting in which language (as opposed to song) is notably absent:

Bleibt die 'Sprache' so aus der Harmonie einer Natur, die bei sich selber ist, ausgeschlossen, nimmt der Gesang gerade die Möglichkeit wahr, sich selber darzustellen, d.h. in die Erscheinung zu treten. [. . .] 'Sprache' meint eine unsinnliche Aussageweise,

---

³² The *Pindar-Fragmente*, probably composed at some time between 1803 and 1805, comprise nine pieces, each consisting of a translation of a fragment of Pindar together with a brief commentary; the fragment and commentary form an indissoluble whole. The ordering of the fragments is not certain, since they are found on two different manuscript pages. On the *Pindar-Fragmente* see in particular Markus Fink, *Pindarfragmente: Neun Hölderlin Deutungen* (Tübingen: Niemeyer, 1982); Heike Bartel, *Centaurengesänge: Friedrich Hölderlins Pindarfragmente* (Würzburg: Königshausen & Neumann, 2000); and on the concept of 'Treue' see Schmidt, II, 1293–94.

³³ On language and need see *Hyperion*: 'und über den Sternen vergißt das Herz seine Noth und seine Sprache' (MA, I, 655).

in der ein Wesen sich selber nicht begreift, während 'Gesang' erscheinend sich selber ausspricht.[34]

Fink's commentary here could also serve as an explication of 'Bedeutung'. On the one hand, we have a Nature that can present itself by appearing *as* itself; and on the other, 'eine unsinnliche Aussageweise', which at the extreme is so 'unsinnlich' as to be void or null, an empty signifier ('das Zeichen [. . .] =0'). Nature, in 'song', is able to achieve unmediated expression, as opposed to an expression in the inevitably figurative medium of language. The creatures in the idyllic scene evoked in this *Pindar-Fragment* can remain 'faithful' to themselves, because their self-expression is merely the singing forth of their own natures: 'seine Treue, die Art, wie eines in sich selbst zusammenhängt' (MA, II, 381). And this idea of faithfulness corresponds to Nature conceived as a living and harmonious whole. In Diotima's words in *Hyperion*, 'im Bunde der Natur ist Treue kein Traum. Wir trennen uns nur, um inniger einig zu seyn' (MA, I, 749).

The connection between Diotima and the idea of a purely musical means of expression has already been noted. The figure of Diotima in *Hyperion* is of course of some biographical significance, corresponding as she does to Susette Gontard, wife of Hölderlin's employer in Frankfurt and object of his love. It would no doubt be incorrect simply to identify Susette with the character in the novel.[35] The correspondences are none the less striking, and even uncanny to the extent that Susette came to occupy a place already marked out for her in the novel's early drafts.[36] In the following paragraphs I trace a further connection, both biographical and textual, between Diotima and the figure of the dolphin.

The 'dolphin' in the *Pindar-Fragment* is the sea animal so famously benevolent to mariners, and perhaps also a figure representing the poet Pindar himself (or more generally the poet as singer).[37] But the image also occurs in another context, this time belonging to the period of the composition of *Hyperion*. If that context also provides a connection between the dolphin and Diotima, the mediating figure here is the writer and art critic Wilhelm Heinse (1746–1803).

Ulrich Gaier has shown the importance of Heinse's novel *Hildegard von*

[34] See also the reference in Hölderlin's commentary on '[das] Echo des Wachstums'. For Hölderlin 'echo' can signify a non-linguistic mode of expression, and correspondingly a musical dimension of poetic language that can serve as its proxy: see Hans-Jost Frey, 'Textrevision bei Hölderlin', in Frey, *Der unendliche Text* (Frankfurt a.M.: Suhrkamp, 1990), pp. 77–123 (pp. 78–88).
[35] See generally Valérie Lawitschka, 'Diotima — Susette Gontard', in *Hölderlin-Handbuch: Leben — Werk — Wirkung*, ed. by Johann Kreuzer (Stuttgart: Metzler, 2002), pp. 31–36.
[36] See Jean Laplanche, *Hölderlin et la question du père* (Paris: Presses Universitaires de France, 1969), p. 61.
[37] See Bartel, pp. 107–09. Note that a dolphin also surfaces in the idyllic opening scene of Hölderlin's poem 'Der Archipelagus' (MA, I, 295).

Hohenthal (1795–96) both for the composition of *Hyperion* and for the subsequent development of the poetics of the 'Wechsel der Töne'.[38] Heinse was close to Susette Gontard: his friend Sömmering was the family doctor of the Gontard family in Frankfurt, and Heinse admired Susette for her beauty and cultivation, as well as giving encouragement to Hölderlin.[39] In May 1796 Heinse gave Susette a copy of the second volume of his new novel; both she and Hölderlin will have certainly read the first volume, while Hölderlin had already been impressed by Heinse's earlier novel *Ardinghello*.[40] In 1796 an invasion of French forces seemed to threaten the safety of the Gontard household, and this provided a rare opportunity for the two lovers to travel together. In the course of their flight to Kassel and Bad Driburg, they met up with Heinse. The latter was not only a witness of the love between the two; he also embodied some of the same simplicity and sympathy with Nature that Hölderlin found in Susette: in Erich Hock's words, 'Einfalt, Kindersinn, Heiterkeit'.[41]

Hildegard von Hohenthal opens with a scene that may have helped to justify the author's somewhat scandalous reputation, but is at the same time an evocation of primal innocence. In this scene the musician Lockmann, on a hot day towards the end of May, absent-mindedly takes up a telescope, and in gazing at the surrounding landscape surprises a woman (Hildegard) swimming naked 'like a dolphin':

Unvermerkt drangen seine Blicke unter die Schatten des Lindengewölbes in einem Garten [. . .] wo ein Frauenzimmer sein Morgengewand ablegte, nackend, göttlich schön wie eine Venus, da stand, die Arme frey und muthig in die Luft ausschlug, und […] sich in eine große Wasservertiefung stürzte, darin verschwand [. . .]; dann die ganze zauberische Mädchengestalt wie ein Delphin sich wieder empor warf, und Wasserstrahlen und Schaum von sich schleuderte. (p. 10)

Once she has dried herself 'auf dem grünen Schmelze' (p. 11), Hildegard puts her clothes back on and disappears. We are not far removed from the setting

---

[38] Ulrich Gaier, '"Mein ehrlich Meister": Hölderlin im Gespräch mit Heinse', in *Das Maß des Bacchanten: Wilhelm Heinses Über-Lebenskunst*, ed. by Gert Theile (Munich: Fink, 1998), pp. 25–54 (pp. 43–48); and see also Gaier, 'Wilhelm Heinse', in *Hölderlin-Handbuch*, ed. by Kreuzer, pp. 86–89 (pp. 88–89).

[39] See Hölderlin's letter to his brother of 2 November 1797: 'Heinze [sic], der Verf. des Ardinghello hat bei Dr. Sömmering sich sehr aufmunternd über Hyperion geäußert' (MA, II, 670, italics original).

[40] See Erich Hock, *'dort drüben, in Westphalen': Hölderlins Reise nach Bad Driburg mit Wilhelm Heinse und Susette Gontard*, 2nd edn, augmented by the author, ed. by Alfred Kelletat (Stuttgart: Metzler, 1995), pp. 79–80 and 98; Max L. Baeumer, *Heinse-Studien* (Stuttgart: Metzler, 1966), p. 71.

[41] Hock, p. 96. Page references in the text below are to Wilhelm Heinse, *Hildegard von Hohenthal. Musikalische Dialogen*, ed. (with commentary) by Werner Keil with Bettina Petersen (Hildesheim: Georg Olms, 2002). The *Musikalische Dialogen* are a posthumous publication that appeared in 1805.

of the *Pindar-Fragment*, which is, as Bartel observes, that of a spring day (but also of a scene which is somehow timeless) in which water and vegetation are blended together in a lustrous melting softness ('[der] Schmelz').[42]

A few pages later, we are introduced to Lockmann's ideas on the performance of Allegri's *Miserere*. They echo his previous vision of Hildegard: 'die Töne schmelzen in einander [. . .]. Die Stimmen haben gar keine Begleitung von Instrumenten, nicht einmal der Orgel. Die bloße Vocalmusik ist eigentlich, was in den bildenden Künsten das Nackende ist' (p. 14).[43] This 'naked' music is characterized by simplicity of harmony, and an almost complete absence of rhythm: such as there is arises naturally from words that are sung, and the result is one of immediate impression in which those words themselves disappear (p. 15). Accordingly, to the nakedness of Hildegard in the opening scene there corresponds a species of 'naked' music that appears denuded of metre, or even of the words that give it shape. This is a music of pure tones, corresponding to a world of prelapsarian harmony and beauty: 'Das Zusammenschmelzen und Verfließen der reinen Töne offenbart das innre Gefühl eines himmlischen Wesens, welches sich mit der ursprünglichen Schönheit wieder vereinigen möchte, von der es Schulden trennen' (p. 15). Here we have a purely musical means of expression, at the furthest remove from the divisions instituted by language: and as such, it can be related to the dolphin in the *Pindar-Fragment* as much as to the 'dolphin' in the earlier vision of the naked Hildegard. Indeed, the significance of the latter becomes clear once we learn that Hildegard is a singer. And as we have seen, Diotima herself participates in this realm of musical expression, in which the plenitude of appearance is opposed to the mediation of the linguistic sign. Hölderlin dedicated two of his greatest poems to Heinse: not only 'Brod und Wein', but also (originally) 'Der Rhein', where Heinse is directly addressed in an early version of the final stanza. There his cheerfulness of soul is contrasted with the poet's more agitated dream 'Von des Meergrunds köstlicher Perle' (MA, I, 341). If the reference to Susette Gontard is unmistakable in that dream, those submarine depths are perhaps the ones also evoked in 'Vom Delphin'.[44]

I have been concerned to emphasize Hölderlin's concept of non-figurative

---

[42] Bartel, p. 110; Bartel also makes a connection with the idyllic scene evoked in the first stanza of 'Hälfte des Lebens'.

[43] On the parallel between these two scenes see Werner Keil, 'Heinses Beitrag zur romantischen Musikästhetik', in *Das Maß des Bacchanten*, ed. by Theile, pp. 139–58 (pp. 151–52), and see also Hans-Georg von Arburg, '"Die bloße Vocalmusik ist eigentlich, was in den bildenden Künsten das Nackende ist": Pathosformeln zwischen Literatur, Musik und Malerei bei Wilhelm Heinse', in *Ekstatische Kunst — Besonnenes Wort: Aby Warburg und die Denkräume der Ekphrasis*, ed. by Peter Kofler (Bozen: Edition Sturzflüge, 2009), pp. 145–64 (pp. 149–52).

[44] See Bernhard Böschenstein, '"Was nennnest du Glück, was Unglück?... mein Vater!": Heinse in Hölderlins Dichtung', in Böschenstein, '*Frucht des Gewitters*': *Hölderlins Dionysos als Gott der Revolution* (Frankfurt a.M.: Insel, 1989), pp. 91–113 (p. 101).

presentation—'das Lebenslicht' as the immediate light of appearance—because it is an aspect of his poetics that has tended to be overlooked by commentators on 'Bedeutung'. The question remains whether we are now in any better position to understand the enigmatic concept of 'das Zeichen [. . .] =o'. I have argued that, if the pure music of Nature occupies one pole of Hölderlin's poetics, the empty or 'meaningless' sign must occupy its opposite pole. The former corresponds to an expression that is faithful to the thing expressed, and full of its presence. But the latter corresponds to a limiting extreme of metaphor or indirect expression, one in which any correspondence between literal and figurative meaning has been broken. Or, to use the term that is central to Hölderlin's interpretation of Sophocles, the signifier is now absolutely unfaithful ('untreu') to its signified.

Are there any further contexts that might help to explain this notion of a 'meaningless' sign? At this point, it is difficult to resist citing the version of the late hymn 'Mnemosyne' that begins: 'Ein Zeichen sind wir, deutungslos | Schmerzlos sind wir und haben fast | Die Sprache in der Fremde verloren' (MA, I, 436). As a matter of first impression, the language echoes that of our fragment (compare '[3] das Zeichen [ist] an sich selbst unbedeutend, wirkungslos' with 'Ein Zeichen sind wir, deutungslos'). But the appearance is perhaps deceptive. The theory expounded in 'Bedeutung' is presumably a theory of ancient Greek tragedy. But by the time of 'Mnemosyne' Hölderlin had begun to develop a distinct theory of modern tragedy, and of what the tragic could amount to for contemporary experience. The heroes of Greek tragedy are consumed by a too immediate encounter with the forces of Nature or the divine: in the words of the first letter to Böhlendorff, 'in Flammen verzehrt die Flamme büßen, die [sie] nicht zu bändigen vermochten' (MA, II, 913). By contrast, the tragedy of the modern condition is one of the absence of meaning—as it were too little fate rather than too much.[45] This seems to be the condition evoked at the beginning of 'Mnemosyne'. A similar point can be made about the emptiness of the world described in the second stanza of 'Hälfte des Lebens', which stands in contrast to the plenitude evoked in the first stanza. But the empty signs of the flags (or possibly weathervanes) that clatter in the wind, and the walls that stand 'Sprachlos und kalt', do not signify a hidden ground of Nature that is now exposed to the light. They correspond rather to a state in which both language and feeling have departed.[46]

[45] See MA, II, 374; and see generally Achim Geisenhanslüke, *Nach der Tragödie: Lyrik und Moderne bei Hegel und Hölderlin* (Munich: Fink, 2012), pp. 146–50 and 159–61; as Geisenhanslüke remarks, 'Die Folge "deutungslos" und "schmerzlos" nennt vor diesem Hintergrund eine spezifische Erfahrung der Moderne' (p. 160). As a result, ancient and modern poetry are faced with different tasks: see Lawrence Ryan, '"Vaterländisch und natürlich, eigentlich originell": Hölderlins Briefe an Böhlendorff', *Hölderlin-Jahrbuch*, 34 (2004–05), 246–76 (pp. 262–64).

[46] Cf. Wolfram Groddeck, 'Zahl, Maß und Metrik in Hölderlins Gedicht *Hälfte des Lebens*', in *Weiterlesen: Literatur und Wissen*, ed. by Ulrike Bergermann and Elisabeth Strowick (Bielefeld:

To shed further light on 'das Zeichen [...] =0' it is preferable, therefore, to turn to the *Sophokles-Anmerkungen*. Here several commentators have focused in particular on the notion of 'caesura', described in both the *Anmerkungen zum Oedipus* and the *Anmerkungen zur Antigonä* as a constitutive feature of each tragedy (MA, II, 310 and 369). Thus Hölderlin assigns a particular function to a pause or discontinuity in the action that occurs in the scenes with the prophet Teiresias. He compares the interventions of Teiresias with the 'caesura' in Greek metrics, that is to say the break that divides the rhythm of a line of verse; he also refers to this 'Cäsur' as 'das reine Wort'.[47] For Hölderlin, this is the formal feature that governs the overall shape of the two tragedies (depending on whether the 'caesura' occurs towards the beginning or towards the end). If that formal feature is described in the first section of each set of *Anmerkungen*, Hölderlin returns to the question of form at the beginning of the third sections. And here we can note a correspondence between his accounts of the form and the content of the tragedy. This is particularly clear in section 3 of the *Anmerkungen zum Oedipus* (MA, II, 315). In the first paragraph of that section, the action of a tragedy is described as a process of purification, in which a too close encounter between 'der Gott' or 'die Naturmacht' on the one hand, and the human individual ('[der] Mensch') on the other, is purged by an equally extreme separation ('durch gränzenloses Scheiden'). But in the following paragraph Hölderlin then immediately takes this as the basis for an explanation of the peculiar formal features of the tragedies concerned: the disputatious dialogic exchanges, the tight articulation between dialogue and chorus, and between the larger parts of the tragedy. The formula he uses to sum up these features is particularly interesting for our purposes: 'Alles ist Rede gegen Rede, die sich gegenseitig aufhebt.'

This self-cancelling effect of the form of the tragedy can be compared to the notion of 'das Zeichen [...] =0'. Indeed, there appears to be a connection between the notion of pure form, as a constituent element of a poetic work, and that of such a contradiction. For if the content of what is said is cancelled out, it is precisely the form of the saying that is thrown into relief. And if one interprets 'caesura' in its broadest sense, as meaning any hiatus that signifies by

transcript, 2007), pp. 159–73 (pp. 171–72), making the connection between that second stanza and 'Mnemosyne'.

[47] MA, II, 310. See Monika Kasper, *'Das Gesez von allen der König': Hölderlins Anmerkungen zum Oedipus und zur Antigonä* (Würzburg: Königshausen & Neumann, 2000), p. 28, n. 10: 'Die Zäsur ist offensichtlich das Zeichen, das "=0" ist und das der Natur "in ihrer stärksten Gaabe" zur Darstellung verhilft'; and see similarly Elena Polledri, *'... immer bestehet ein Maas': Der Begriff des Maßes in Hölderlins Werk* (Würzburg: Königshausen & Neumann, 2002), pp. 227–28; Lemke, pp. 68–69; Marion Hiller, *Harmonisch entgegengesetzt: Zur Darstellung und Darstellbarkeit in Hölderlins Poetik um 1800* (Tübingen: Niemeyer, 2008), p. 109. On the original, metrical concept of 'caesura' see Armand D'Angour, 'Metre', in *The Edinburgh Companion to Ancient Greece and Rome*, ed. by Edward Bispham and others (Edinburgh: Edinburgh University Press, 2006), pp. 489–94 (p. 493).

virtue of its pure form, the concept can in fact be found elsewhere in Hölderlin's poetics. As Ryan has noted, just as the *Sophokles-Anmerkungen* borrow the notion of 'caesura' from the poetics of metre, Hölderlin had previously borrowed the notion of tragic 'catastrophe' for the purposes of his doctrine of the 'Wechsel der Töne' in the Homburg poetics.[48] The formal elements of catastrophe and reversal can be found in his analysis of the development of meaning in a poem. Now the 'tones' of the Homburg poetics can be regarded as the constituent elements of poetic meaning, and the rule-governed sequence of tones in the poem corresponds to the progressive development of that meaning. But on Hölderlin's account of those tone sequences, the development is punctuated by a paradoxical moment.[49] At this point, what makes itself felt in the poem is not a particular tone, but rather a reversal in the sequences of tones. This is a reversal that violates the normal rules that generate the sequences, and as a result gives rise to a momentary suspension in the poem's forward progress.[50] Ryan observes that it is by virtue of this reversal that a higher totality is expressed, rather than any of the particular tones that have been sounded so far in the poem: 'in dem Tonschema, das den Verlauf des Gedichts wiedergibt, erhält sie [die Unendlichkeit] keinen eigenen Ton, sondern kann nur als genaue Umkehrung der Zuordnung der Töne fühlbar gemacht werden.'[51] In the absence of any tone giving a determinate meaning, the element of pure form can emerge; and such a moment of paradoxical reversal can be regarded as an example of the caesura, or 'das Zeichen [...] =o'.

Such an interpretation can be contrasted with one often favoured by those commentators who construe 'das Zeichen [...] =o' simply in terms of the fate of the tragic hero: the hero is as it were annulled by that fate. It is true that, in the case of Hölderlin's *Empedokles*-drama, he regards his hero as the embodiment of the opposition between 'Natur' and 'Kunst', and the medium in which their relations are temporarily reversed (MA, I, 870). There is an obvious correspondence here with the moment of reversal in the tone sequences of the Homburg poetics.[52] But that is a different matter from simply equating the fate of the hero with 'das Zeichen [...] =o', especially if it is then implied that the hero exemplifies the 'weakness' referred to in our fragment. For such commentators it seems that the hero's misfortunes are evidence of such 'weakness', as compared with the overwhelming force of a Nature that is 'gerade heraus'. In Szondi's words, 'im Untergang des tragischen Helden,

[48] Ryan, 'Hölderlins Dichtungsbegriff', p. 27; see MA, II, 108.
[49] See MA, II, 88: 'im Karakter eines positiven Nichts, eines unendlichen Stillstands', described by Ryan as a moment of 'Umkehr': 'Hölderlins Dichtungsbegriff', p. 35.
[50] See Lewis, pp. 55–58.
[51] 'Hölderlins Dichtungsbegriff', p. 38; what Ryan refers to in his article as 'die Unendlichkeit' or 'das Unendliche' corresponds to 'das Ursprüngliche' in 'Bedeutung': ibid., pp. 25 and 32.
[52] See Ryan, 'Hölderlins Dichtungsbegriff', pp. 36–37.

wenn das Zeichen=0 ist, stellt zugleich die Natur als Siegerin *in ihrer stärksten Gabe* sich dar'.[53] But as I have tried to argue, that is not necessarily the sense in which 'strength' is opposed to 'weakness' in the fragment. I have suggested rather that the idea of 'weakness' is to be read in terms of a notion of non-figurative presentation. Nature in its 'weakest endowment' can appear directly, reflected in its own light, but is also afflicted with the fragility intrinsic to pure appearance; the governing myths here may be those of Adonis and Narcissus, rather than the tales of the tragic heroes. Conversely, although the tragic sign is is said to be '[3] an sich selbst unbedeutend, wirkungslos', it is not weak. Although it is void of intrinsic meaning or effect, 'das Zeichen [. . .] =0' could rather be said to embody the highest power of language, the power of pure form. That is not to say, however, that the relation between the form and content of the tragedy can be ignored: as we have seen, Hölderlin himself points to a correspondence between the two.

I began this article by commenting on the difficulties facing the commentator on Hölderlin's theoretical works. Many of the factors giving rise to such difficulties are of course present in the case of 'Bedeutung'. Thus we have been trying to understand a text that is (probably) a fragment, taken from a context that is itself unknown (presumably an interpretation of Sophoclean tragedy). There is also evidence that Hölderlin's thoughts developed as he was writing them down. We have noted a shift, in the course of the fragment, from the use of the term 'das Ursprüngliche' to the use of the broader (and perhaps more adequate) term 'die Natur', as well as noting revisions in the manuscript that may reflect the progressive elaboration of his thought. And if a riddling quality is characteristic of some of Hölderlin's later theoretical texts, we can note that 'Die Bedeutung der Tragödien [. . .]' has itself something of the quality of a riddle, in that it expounds the meaning of tragedies in terms of an absence of meaning.

LONDON   CHARLES LEWIS

[53] Szondi, p. 162 (italics original). See similarly Fred Lönker, 'Unendliche Deutung', *Hölderlin-Jahrbuch*, 26 (1988-89), 287-303 (p. 294, n. 11), and Kathrin H. Rosenfield, *Antigone — de Sophocle à Hölderlin: la logique du 'rythme'* (Paris: Éditions Galilée, 2003), p. 163: 'la mort [. . .] qui annule le signe, c'est à dire réduit le héros à rien'. Ryan too sometimes seems to make this assimilation: 'So bezeugt sich das Ganze erst eigentlich im Zunichtewerden des Einzelnen, gleichsam negativ' ('Hölderlins Dichtungsbegriff', p. 25), as does Louth (pp. 77-78 and 227). Hamacher similarly construes the 'das Zeichen [. . .] =0' as an intensification of the idea of 'weakness': '[Das Zeichen lässt] die Sache auch nur geschwächt zur Erscheinung kommen. Wenn aber die Schwäche ins Extrem getrieben und die Erscheinung annulliert wird, kann die Sache [. . .] in ihrer ganzen Gewalt sich darstellen.' See Werner Hamacher, 'Parusie, Mauern: Mittelbarkeit und Zeitlichkeit, später Hölderlin', *Hölderlin-Jahrbuch*, 34 (2004-05), 93-142 (p. 109).

'DAS LAND, IN DEM DAS PROLETARIAT [NUR] GENANNT WERDEN DARF': THE LANGUAGE OF PARTICIPATION IN HEINER MÜLLER'S *DER LOHNDRÜCKER*

In an article published in the East German literary monthly *Neue Deutsche Literatur* in October 1957, the young playwright Peter Hacks considers both the possibility of writing realist plays for a Socialist public and the question of the appropriate form in which to do so. Alongside his recommendation that Socialist Realist theatre must be considered as a new genre altogether, which can be described in terms of neither tragedy nor comedy,[1] Hacks states that the language of the proletariat has both a current shape and a necessary direction to follow. He laments the movement from a poetic language, which is able 'auszudrücken, was das konventionelle Deutsch des Spießers nicht kann',[2] towards the adoption of 'Hochdeutsch' by the proletariat. None the less, he notes that 'Hochdeutsch', the language of the former bourgeois rulers of Germany, can be used to meet the ends of the working classes of the German Democratic Republic (GDR) so long as it has any trace of bourgeois niceties purged from it. He writes:

> Die Sprache derer, die einen Staat und eine unvorstellbar entwickelte Technik beherrschen, kann keine andere sein als die des wissenschaftlichen Zeitalters. Natürlich müssen die toten Elemente des Hochdeutschen ausgeschieden werden: die teuren Worte, die Schul-Konstruktionen, die allzu gerade Korrektheit. Es werden Worte aufsteigen, die eine Sache beim Namen nennen, Satzkonstruktionen, welche einfach sind und praktikabel.[3]

In Hacks's view a simple, hard language, which grasps the complexity of reality and does away with unnecessary nuances, appears to be the new voice of a working class in charge of a new, Socialist state.

Not six months before the publication of this article, Heiner Müller's first play,[4] *Der Lohndrücker*, was published in the May edition of the very same journal. *Der Lohndrücker* depicts the inner workings of a factory in the early

I would like to thank Dr Laura Bradley and Professor Peter Davies (both University of Edinburgh) for commenting on drafts of this article.

[1] Peter Hacks, 'Das realistische Theaterstück', *Neue Deutsche Literatur*, 5.10 (1957), 90–104 (p. 95).
[2] Ibid., pp. 100–01.
[3] Ibid., p. 101.
[4] Questions surrounding the authorship of *Der Lohndrücker*, and the degree to which Müller's then wife Inge Müller played a part in the play's composition, have by no means been conclusively answered. In his 1992 autobiography *Krieg ohne Schlacht* Müller asserts: 'Geschrieben habe ich es allein, und zwar lediglich am Schreibtisch' (Heiner Müller, *Krieg ohne Schlacht: Das Leben in zwei Diktaturen*, in Heiner Müller, *Werke*, 12 vols, ed. by Frank Hörnigk (Frankfurt a.M.: Suhrkamp, 1998–2008) [henceforth W], ix: *Die Autobiographie*, pp. 7–291 (p. 111)). Janine Ludwig, however,

days of the GDR, and the dialogue between the workers is simple in terms of both its grammar and its vocabulary. At first glance, the language of *Der Lohndrücker* may be understood to presage Hacks's essay, by giving a voice to the rulers of the self-proclaimed 'Arbeiter-und-Bauern Staat'. Yet, as I shall argue here, the simple language of the workers in Müller's play does precisely the opposite of giving voice to the proletariat: rather, their language is one which cannot fully express the complexities of social reality, and which demonstrates the fact that they have no voice in the governance of their state. In this sense, Müller can be understood to be engaging with contemporary debates in the GDR in 1956–57, concerning the shape Socialism is to take, and the role and form of democracy in the young Socialist state. As we shall see, while the language of the workers illustrates the silence of public discourse in the political realm, Müller places his hopes for the emergence of a participatory democracy in the theatre audience.

Language and Representation

With the exception of three scenes in the initial editions of the text, the action of *Der Lohndrücker* takes place in a nationalized factory in the GDR, or 'Volkseigener Betrieb' (VEB), in 1948/49. Production is threatened as the kilns required for manufacturing materials are in desperate need of repair. One mason within the factory, Balke, attempts to repair the kilns under very dangerous conditions so that productivity may continue unaffected, and he develops new, more efficient techniques for doing so. Through repairing the kilns, Balke exceeds production norms, becoming the 'bestes Pferd' of the factory's leadership.[5] In increasing production norms, however, Balke also increases the amount of labour required to receive the same wage, causing him and his co-workers to have to work more for less. In the eyes of most of his co-workers, Balke is therefore a 'Lohndrücker' and 'Arbeiterverräter' (p. 126): he receives death threats and a beating, he is bullied in the workplace, and efforts are continually made to sabotage his work.

Balke's story almost exactly matches that of Hans Garbe, a mason at Siemens-Plania in the Lichtenberg district of Berlin, in 1949/50. For his Stakhanovite efforts, Garbe was elevated to the status of 'Held der Arbeit', a personification of the idealized consciousness of the new, Socialist working

presents clear evidence to the contrary in 'Eine Geschichte aus der Produktion: Über die Arbeit am Lohndrücker und die Zusammenarbeit von Inge und Heiner Müller', in *Working for Paradise: 'Der Lohndrücker'. Heiner Müller Werkbuch*, ed. by Peter Kammerer and others (Berlin: Theater der Zeit, 2011), pp. 46–69. The question of authorship does not, however, affect the argument of this article.

[5] Heiner Müller, *Der Lohndrücker*, in *Neue Deutsche Literatur*, 5.5 (1957), 116–41 (p. 125). Hereafter all parenthetical page references in the body of the text will refer to this edition (subsequent editions exhibit textual variants).

class.[6] He became a prominent feature of propaganda to increase productivity, produced by the ruling Sozialistische Einheitspartei Deutschlands (SED).[7] He remained a hero throughout an age in which the 'Aufbau des Sozialismus', announced by Walter Ulbricht in July 1952, continued to be the 'grundlegende Aufgabe' of the East German state;[8] and his story was further projected into national consciousness by literary works such as Eduard Claudius's 1951 novel *Menschen an unserer Seite* and Käthe Rülicke's 1952 collection of interviews with Garbe, *Hans Garbe erzählt*.[9] The paradoxical figure of Garbe as both 'Held der Arbeit' and traitor of the workforce also provided the substance of Bertolt Brecht's unfinished *Büsching* fragment, which served as material for the young Müller.[10]

While the case of Balke offers a rich thematic seam, to which much secondary criticism on *Der Lohndrücker* pays close attention,[11] more consideration must be given to the workers as a whole: it is the workforce, above all, which is represented in the play, and which is to be affected by Balke's actions. This is noted by Helen Fehervary, who writes that the collective stands at the centre of *Der Lohndrücker*, in so far as the text consists of 'Rekonstruktionen jenes dialektischen Prozesses innerhalb einer einzelnen Brigade [...], in denen sich die Probleme der gesamten sozialistischen Gesellschaft widerspiegeln'.[12] Indeed, from the very start the text clearly questions the structures of political power in the young GDR, a matter which is borne out most concretely in the relations between the workers themselves. Almost all of the critical literature examines the text in the context of the first four years of the GDR's existence, from its foundation in 1949 to the Uprising of 17 June in 1953,[13] or in the context

---

[6] Bernhard Greiner, *Von der Allegorie zur Idylle: Die Literatur der Arbeitswelt in der DDR* (Heidelberg: Quelle & Meyer, 1974), p. 65.

[7] Jan-Christoph Hauschild, *Heiner Müller oder Das Prinzip Zweifel* (Berlin: Aufbau, 2003), p. 164. See also Genia Schulz, *Heiner Müller* (Stuttgart: Metzler, 1980), p. 23.

[8] Wolfgang Emmerich, *Kleine Literaturgeschichte der DDR*, rev. edn. (Berlin: Aufbau, 2009), p. 114.

[9] Greiner, *Allegorie zur Idylle*, pp. 70 and 78.

[10] See Wolfgang Storch, 'Brechts Erbe: Die Erdung', in *Working for Paradise*, ed. by Kammerer and others, pp. 70–106.

[11] See e.g. Greiner, *Allegorie zur Idylle*, pp. 60–91; Heinz Hillmann, 'Arbeiterheld oder Lohndrücker? Arbeiter, Dichter, Ökonomen', in *Spiele und Spiegelungen von Schrecken und Tod*, ed. by Paul Gerhard Klussmann and Heinrich Mohr (Bonn: Bouvier, 1990), pp. 201–28; Jonathan Kalb, *The Theater of Heiner Müller* (Cambridge: Cambridge University Press, 1998), pp. 57–68; and Georg Wieghaus, *Zwischen Auftrag und Verrat: Werk und Ästhetik Heiner Müllers* (Frankfurt a.M.: Peter Lang, 1984), pp. 51–74.

[12] Helen Fehervary, 'Heiner Müllers Brigadenstücke', in *Zum Drama in der DDR: Heiner Müller und Peter Hacks*, ed. by Judith R. Scheid (Stuttgart: Klett, 1981), pp. 13–45 (p. 17).

[13] See e.g. Tom Biburger, *Sprengsätze: 'Der Lohndrücker' von Heiner Müller und der 17. Juni 1953* (Pfaffenweiler: Centaurus, 1997); Emmerich, *Kleine Literaturgeschichte der DDR*, p. 159; Fehervary, 'Heiner Müllers Brigadenstücke'; Hauschild, *Heiner Müller*, p. 165; Kalb, *The Theater of Heiner Müller*, p. 66; Wolfgang Schivelbusch, *Sozialistisches Drama nach Brecht* (Darmstadt and Neuwied: Luchterhand, 1974), pp. 96–110; and Schulz, *Heiner Müller*, pp. 23–27.

of international affairs within the Eastern bloc, such as Nikita Khrushchev's so-called 'Secret Speech', delivered at the Twentieth Party Congress of the Communist Party of the Soviet Union, and the Hungarian Uprising, both of 1956.[14] Yet such approaches to the text cannot come close to grasping either why these historical or international moments would have been of particular relevance to an East German author in 1956–57 or, for that matter, to the questions on the minds of the East German audiences for whom *Der Lohndrücker* was written. No attention has been given to the considerable internal conflicts within the GDR in 1956, which informed Müller's textual production and the initial reception of the piece. Indeed, it is in the context of internal conflict within the GDR in the later 1950s that we can recognize the issues highlighted by *Der Lohndrücker* and the questions it may have raised for its contemporary audiences: as we shall see, Müller's text exposes an immense contradiction within the GDR, a Marxist-Leninist state in which parliamentary democracy and the participation of its citizens have been forsaken in favour of a centralized, 'Sovietized' form of governance.[15] While this contradiction was already at the heart of the concerns of the protestors of the 17 June Uprising, in 1956 public platforms were being used to attempt to discuss this issue openly and explicitly, and for the first time.

The joint issues of power and representation are at the centre of *Der Lohndrücker*. The action takes place at a time in which the nationalization of industry stood at the top of the East German political, social, and economic agenda, and the means of production were being wrested from private enterprise. Even before Müller began work on *Der Lohndrücker*, approximately 85 per cent of all industry in the GDR had been nationalized into VEBs between 1948 and 1956.[16] As the term 'Volkseigener Betrieb' suggests, the means of production were now the public possession of the 'Volk', that is, the population of the GDR. Now that the Leninist goal of 'the emancipation of labour from the oppression of capital' had been partially achieved,[17] there was in theory no longer a hierarchy in place, so that the workers were on an equal footing with those ostensibly above them: as Geschke says to the sceptical Stettiner in the very first scene, 'Der Unternehmer ist jedenfalls weg' (p. 116). There is the assumption of equality within the factory: Kolbe advises

---

[14] See e.g. Hillmann, 'Arbeiterheld oder Lohndrücker?', p. 215; Theo Girshausen, *Realismus und Utopie: Die frühen Stücke Heiner Müllers* (Cologne: Prometh, 1981), p. 34; and Grischa Meyer, 'Schwarze Bude im roten Oktober', in *Working for Paradise*, ed. by Kammerer and others, pp. 46–69 (p. 68).

[15] Peter Grieder, *The East German Leadership 1946–73: Conflict and Crisis* (Manchester and New York: Manchester University Press, 1999), pp. 8–9.

[16] Mary Fulbrook, *A History of Germany 1918–2008: The Divided Nation* (Chichester: Wiley-Blackwell, 2009), p. 134.

[17] V. I. Lenin, *The Deception of the People by the Slogans of Equality and Freedom* (London: Lawrence, 1935), p. 21.

Geschke in scene 6b, for example, 'Im Direktorzimmer sitzt ein Arbeiter am Schreibtisch. Du bist auch ein Arbeiter und kannst mit ihm reden' (p. 127). Furthermore, now that the workers apparently jointly own industry, they believe that it is for them to have some say in determining how it is governed, and what the results of their actions may be. In many cases, however, this follows a false logic, epitomized by Lerka's response when Balke challenges him for using damp bricks in their first attempt to rebuild the kiln:

LERKA Tempo oder Qualität. Alles können sie nicht haben.
BALKE Die Minute kostet einen Groschen, Lerka. Aber der Ofen kostet mehr.
LERKA (*nervös*) Wer hat mir was zu sagen? Der Laden hier ist volkseigen, stimmts? Ich bin das Volk, verstehst du.

(p. 121)

Lerka's response betrays a fundamental misunderstanding of his role as an individual worker within a collective: by calling himself 'das Volk', he has committed a Rylesian category mistake of the simplest kind, in that he has presumed 'ich' to belong to the same logical category as 'das Volk', and indeed to be one and the same thing. Yet given the way in which the vocabulary of the VEB functions in giving the workers the impression that a factory belongs to them, it is perhaps most pertinent that Lerka's confusion of 'ich' and 'das Volk' arises here. To cite the philosopher Gilbert Ryle himself, the confusion arises 'from inability to use certain items in the vocabulary',[18] with the vocabulary in question here being of a new, Socialist kind. One thing in particular that Lerka may be said to be misunderstanding is the nature of participation in the GDR, and the degree to which it can be exercised.

As Peter Grieder notes, a 'democratic way to socialism' was enshrined in the SED's charter, yet was received in two conflicting ways.[19] Already during the establishment phase of the SED, the party was split between two views regarding the form democracy was to take in a Socialist East German state: on the one hand, the followers of Walter Ulbricht—then Central Committee member and, as of 1950, General Secretary of the Central Committee of the SED—desired the construction of a state modelled on the Soviet Union; on the other hand, Anton Ackermann, likewise a member of the Central Committee, and his camp recognized the need for a Socialist state qualitatively different from the USSR.[20] None the less, Ulbricht's vision for Socialism on German soil won out, and economic, cultural, and social policies were implemented to shape the infant GDR in the image of its protector superpower. The adoption of Socialist Realism as the state-sanctioned aesthetic for works of art, literature, theatre, and architecture is one such example, although there

---

[18] Gilbert Ryle, *The Concept of Mind* (London: Penguin, 2000), p. 19.
[19] Grieder, *The East German Leadership 1946–73*, p. 10.
[20] Ibid.

was less agreement on what constituted Socialist Realism than in the Soviet Union.[21] Furthermore, a series of economic policies were enacted throughout the 1950s to align the GDR's economy with that of the USSR.[22] Perhaps the most striking example of Ulbricht's desire to emulate the Soviet Union was the decision to move the deadline for a 10 per cent increase in productivity norms in 1953 from 1 June to 30 June, Ulbricht's sixtieth birthday; even the cult of personality à la Stalin was adopted.[23] This in particular is telling with regard to the lack of participation of ordinary East Germans in directing public policy: on 14 June 1953 Rudolf Herrnstadt, then editor of the official daily newspaper of the SED Central Committee, Neues Deutschland, sanctioned the publication of an article criticizing the raising of working norms without the consent of the workers themselves.[24]

In 1956, the year in which Müller began work on Der Lohndrücker, the machinery of East German society and politics came to be questioned in the public realm, as public platforms were being used for overtly criticizing the form democracy appeared to have taken in the GDR. After political unrest in Poland and Hungary, in which popular movements gathered under the banners of democratization and liberalization of political, cultural, and informational machinery, demands were being made for democratization and liberalization within the GDR. For example, a gathering in Erfurt called for a parliamentary democracy modelled on that assumed to be enjoyed by West Germans;[25] a public meeting in Marburg allegedly reached a scale of unrest similar to that of the 17 June Uprising three years earlier;[26] and a student demonstration at the Humboldt University in central East Berlin, initially calling for an end to obligatory courses in Marxist theory and Russian and developing into a demand for greater freedom, was suppressed by a workers' militia.[27]

Ostensibly the GDR was a parliamentary democracy, and much mention was made in public discourse by those within the Politburo of a commitment to democracy. On 29 April 1956 an anonymous article—since attributed to Karl Schirdewan, Ulbricht's then second-in-command in the SED[28]—was

[21] Emmerich, Kleine Literaturgeschichte der DDR, pp. 119-21. For an example of the variety of approaches to Socialist Realism in the GDR in the 1950s see Peter Hacks and others, 'Das Theater der Gegenwart', Neue Deutsche Literatur, 5.4 (1957), 127-34; and Hans Kaufmann, 'Ästhetische Probleme der ältesten und der jüngsten sozialistischen deutschen Literatur', Junge Kunst, 12 (1958), 76-80.
[22] Fulbrook, A History of Germany 1918-2008, p. 162.
[23] Biburger, Sprengsätze, p. 111.
[24] Grieder, The East German Leadership 1946-73, p. 71.
[25] Ibid., p. 108.
[26] Mary Fulbrook, Anatomy of a Dictatorship: Inside the GDR 1949-1989 (Oxford: Oxford University Press, 1997), pp. 188-89.
[27] Grieder, The East German Leadership 1946-73, p. 112.
[28] Ibid., p. 130.

printed in *Neues Deutschland*. The article practised self-criticism on behalf of the party. After condemning the lack of collective leadership in the Politburo, the author goes on to criticize the party's failure to employ democratic measures, writing: 'Nicht immer haben wir mit genügender Schärfe auf die konsequente Wahrung der demokratischen Gesetzlichkeit geachtet.'[29] While 'democracy' is not defined in this context, it would be reasonable to assume that for a party committed to Marxism-Leninism, 'democracy' may be defined in accordance with Lenin's own words as 'the equal right of all to determine the structure and administration of the state'.[30] In this sense, democracy would appear to have a particularly participatory colour. None the less, the SED's own brand of democratic centralism privileged freedom of discussion within the upper echelons of state administration, in essence ruling on behalf of the people.

Müller's text questions the degree to which ordinary East Germans were able to participate in politics and, as a result, determine their social and political reality. While this aspect has not been addressed by criticism of *Der Lohndrücker*, it is at the centre of the text and reflects a key issue in the domestic situation in the GDR in 1956. In the third scene the workers are called together during breakfast to elect a new trade union representative for the factory, and the following dialogue ensues:

DIREKTOR   Also ich schlage den Kollegen Schurek vor, ihr kennt ihn und er kennt sich aus. Habt ihr andere Vorschläge?
ZEMKE   Schurek ist ein Arschkriecher. (*Ab*)
DIREKTOR   Hast du einen Vorschlag, Kollege?
GESCHKE (*zu Stettiner*)   Wer Schurek wählt, ist selber schuld.
STETTINER   Willst dus machen?
GESCHKE (*schweigt*)
STETTINER   Unser Recht kriegen wir nie. Hier nicht. Egal, wer den Bonzen macht.
EIN ANDERER   Wir können nichts machen.
DIREKTOR   Also, wer für Schurek ist, Hand hoch.
   (*Die Arbeiter, auch die Esser und Skatspieler, auch Geschke, heben die Hand, einige mit Frühstücksbrot oder Spielkarte. Wenige Ausnahmen, darunter Karras.*)
KARRAS (*laut*)   Ich kann jetzt nicht, hab die Hand grad in der Tasche.
DIREKTOR (*zählt die Stimmen*)

(p. 120)

In this passage the workers who oppose Schurek's appointment clearly have some grounds for their opposition, but do not present any reasons. Indeed, it may be asked: what will those who vote for Schurek have to blame themselves for? When asked if he would like to stand for the position, Geschke merely answers with silence, rather than affirmation or denial. As the longer stage

[29] 'Die leninistische Geschlossenheit unserer Partei', *Neues Deutschland*, 29 April 1956.
[30] V. I. Lenin, *The State and Revolution*, in *Essential Works of Lenin*, ed. by Henry M. Christman (New York: Bantam Matrix, 1966), pp. 271–364 (p. 347).

direction indicates, Schurek is in fact elected to the position, as there are only a few workers who do not raise their hands. Even Geschke votes in favour of Schurek, despite having already stated in an aside to Stettiner that he would be opposed to the appointment. This apparently contradictory behaviour appears to be the result of lacking commitment to democratic participation: by and large, they seem to be more interested in eating their breakfast and playing skat than in participating in an election. None the less, to read this antipathy as demonstrating that the workers have interests other than voting for a new union representative may be misleading; rather, it seems to be the result of the workers' disaffection with the electoral process: the workers feel that there is nothing they can do to shape their reality, as the comments of both Stettiner and 'ein Anderer' demonstrate. As the real electorate of the GDR would also have found, there was little that casting a vote could do to determine the outcome of an election, as seats within the East German parliament were pre-allotted and policies predetermined.[31]

The election in the third scene is particularly significant because of the way in which a 'democratic' process unfolds. In the face of an official line, such as the promotion of one candidate by the person in possession of authority, little can be done other than affirm that choice: while Geschke votes for Schurek, presumably out of resignation, Zemke merely walks away, and Karras claims that he cannot vote because his hand is in his pocket. The use of the term 'Stimmen' in the stage directions appears, in this light, to approach the ironic. While the German word 'Stimmen' is used in this context to mean 'votes', it also means 'voices', and it is voices which the workers in the VEB lack; they cannot speak up to have their concerns heard or their interests taken into account. Rather, the workers must merely be represented by another, in this case by Schurek. This is perhaps out of the authorities' mistrust that the workforce will actually build Socialism if left to their own devices. As the director complains to Schorn in scene 6a: 'Der Arbeiter hat kein Vertrauen zur Partei. Der Faschismus steckt ihm in den Knochen. Wenn du mich fragst: ich trau keinem' (p. 125). As the play unfolds, it becomes clear that Schurek, who is to represent the interests of the workers, has little trust for them himself. After Lerka's oversight in using damp bricks leads to the failure of the repair of one kiln, Schurek is quick to jump to the worst conclusion: 'Das ist Sabotage. Dafür wirst du bezahlen' (p. 124).

The sham election that takes place does, however, have the semblance of allowing for participation from the workers. 'Democracy' figures here as a whitewash, quickly applied, and revealing the texture of what is going on underneath. This was of particular relevance in 1956, when certain sectors of the East German populace were openly attempting to question the extent

[31] Fulbrook, *A History of Germany 1918–2008*, p. 209.

to which the German Democratic Republic was living up to its name. The image of whitewash is prominent in a poem by Müller from the early 1950s, entitled 'L.E. oder Das Loch im Strumpf', in which Müller tells the story of an activist, Luise Ermisch, who organized efforts to improve the quality of goods produced in a textile factory in 1949:

> Platz: eine Strumpffabrik, vor wenig Wochen
> Von Arbeitern Arbeitern zugesprochen
> Die Tünche auf der Wand war frisch
> In der Kantine. [. . .][32]

Here, the whitewash has been freshly applied, and it is notable that Müller juxtaposes this image with the assertion that the factory had been promised *by* workers *to* workers. The image calls the very foundation of the VEB and nationalized industry in the GDR into question, namely the idea that the *Volk* owns the means of production: the notion that the factory was 'Von Arbeitern Arbeitern zugesprochen' is merely a façade. Furthermore, the very fact that the VEB is promised by a group here places it within an economy of gift-giving, whereby the receiver stands in a symbolic debt to the giver. This is mirrored in the very opening of *Der Lohndrücker*, in which Geschke and Stettiner drink 'Arbeiterbier', 'was der Arbeiterstaat ausschenkt' (p. 116). Providing a workforce with beer appears to be no more than a cynical means of getting the workforce to believe in the political system and work harder.

The naming of both state and beer using the prefix 'Arbeiter-' is part of a rhetorical device employed throughout the play: the word 'Arbeiter' occurs some thirty-five times in the dialogue of the relatively short text, mimicking the rhetoric of the state. While Walter Benjamin designated the Third Reich as 'Das Land, in dem das Proletariat nicht genannt werden darf' in his essay on the 1938 premiere of Brecht's *Furcht und Elend des III. Reiches*,[33] here Müller presents an image of a country in which the proletariat is named with excessive frequency but their rights remain a matter of empty words. While everything is supposedly done in their name, the strict hierarchies involved in statecraft prevent the workers from speaking for themselves and having a voice in their so-called 'Arbeiterregierung' (p. 136). Not only does Müller mimic the rhetoric of the SED, but he also suggests an awareness among the factory leadership of the gulf between the language of the state and social reality. In scene 11 Stettiner,[34] an otherwise unlikely candidate for party membership given his sustained scepticism about the new Socialist reality (see e.g.

---

[32] Heiner Müller, 'L.E. oder Das Loch im Strumpf', ll. 5–8, in *W*, I, 40.

[33] Walter Benjamin, 'Das Land, in dem das Proletariat nicht genannt werden darf: Zur Uraufführung von acht Einaktern Brechts', in *Gesammelte Schriften*, ed. by Rolf Tiedmann and Hermann Schweppenhauser, 7 vols (Frankfurt a.M.: Suhrkamp, 1972–91), II/2: *Aufsätze. Vorträge. Essays* (1977), pp. 514–18.

[34] The name Stettiner may indicate that this character is a migrant from Stettin (now Szczecin),

p. 116), informs the director that he wishes to join the party. In a notably short dialogue, Stettiner utters 'Arbeiter' three times, while also mentioning his past in the SA; once he has gone, the director turns to Schorn and reveals his familiarity with the usual workings of the language Stettiner has deployed: 'Zweimal Arbeiterregierung (*blickt auf die Uhr*) in drei Minuten. Das ist zuviel' (p. 136). Given the discrepancy between the linguistic whitewash applied in the early GDR and the reality it is designed to cover, it is no wonder that Lerka makes the category mistake of confusing himself with the mythological 'Volk', said to rule in the state, and consequently loses his job (pp. 124–25): the rhetoric of the young GDR makes this an easy mistake to make.

The workers' inability to participate in politics is further reflected in the style of their language. Not only do we find long periods of silence in the text, but the dialogue tends to be stilted and consists of a simple subject–predicate–object form, almost completely lacking in subordinate clauses.[35] As we shall see, while this language is shared by the workers, and their fellow proletarians in general, it forbids a direct confrontation with the complexities of reality. In scene 8b, for example, Krüger, an older worker, complains that Balke's plan amounts to no more than exploitation of the workforce. The director replies: 'Krüger, du sagst: Ausbeutung. Du bist dein Leben lang ausgebeutet worden. Jetzt ist dein Junge auf der Universität.' Krüger responds: 'Hab ich ihn auf die Universität geschickt? Ich war dagegen', which is followed by a silence, indicated in the stage directions (p. 131). Krüger gives no explanation here as to why he is against his son being at university (training to be a doctor, as we later discover in scene 12b). Furthermore, he does not directly address questions of exploitation or its relationship to his past or the future(s) of the next generation of GDR citizens. The director's comment offers no direct answer to whether or not Krüger and his colleagues are being exploited, nor does he explain the connection between exploitation and Krüger's son being at university. Rather, much in this scene goes unsaid, leading to disengagement by Krüger, who assents to working with Balke, saying only: 'Wenns sein muß' (p. 131).

The historical situation depicted in *Der Lohndrücker* is one in which contradictions occur regularly: the workers, for example, are said to be living in a state in which they can determine their socio-economic reality, and are emancipated from the exploitative forces of capital; but, as in the case shown

---

which had been awarded to Poland after the end of the Second World War, and that he had been forced to migrate to Germany. This is of relevance with regard to questions of the ethnic and geographical roots of those forced to comply with the East German authorities in the post-war years, and further reminds us of the animosity towards Germans in the Soviet-occupied lands after the capitulation of the Third Reich, but there is no space to consider this detail further here.

[35] Franz Fuhrmann, *Warten auf 'Geschichte': Der Dramatiker Heiner Müller* (Würzburg: Königshausen & Neumann, 1997), p. 71.

above, reality is far more complex and appears to admit exploitation. The language of the workers does not confront this contradiction head-on, rather it is distilled and contains only what is essential. This arises out of their inability to engage in discourse with one another about the contradictory nature of reality. An example of this is the penultimate scene, in which the workers' strike is easily suppressed by the factory leadership. After the majority of the workforce has called for the cancellation of the raised production norm, the following dialogue ensues:

SCHORN (*zeigt auf die zertretene Butter*)   Soll die Butter auch weg? (*Pause*)
EIN ARBEITER   Was hat die Butter mit der Norm zu tun?
SCHORN   Ohne Norm keine Butter.
EIN ARBEITER   Ohne Butter keine Norm.
SCHORN   Wer macht die Preise?
ZEMKE   Uns machst du nicht besoffen.
SCHORN   Das besorgt ihr selber, wie?
DIREKTOR   Geht an die Arbeit.

(pp. 139–40)

This exchange does not serve as dialogue in a constructive sense, as the speakers merely talk past each other. Neither side gives justifications for what they are saying, or explores the complexities of their view in order to present it to the other side for discussion and consideration. This lack of genuine dialogue demonstrates not only an inability to engage in discourse on the part of the workers, but also a disinclination on the part of the authorities to do so: the director and Schorn are able to issue imperatives to the workers that are obediently followed, bringing an end to the strike. As Müller later believed to have been the case with the 17 June Uprising, and no doubt Hungary and the GDR in 1956, popular opposition has been quelled in such a way that any opportunity for dialogue between the state and the masses has been lost.[36]

Language and Participation

While the language of the workers in *Der Lohndrücker* serves to illustrate their inability either to confront the reality they inhabit or to partake in changing their reality through discourse, there is a potential for optimism in Müller's text. Some critics have noted that the simplicity of the language in *Der Lohndrücker* is an attempt on Müller's part to avoid the psychologization of the dramatis personae;[37] while this is clearly important, critics have not yet considered how the language of the text might affect the responses of a theatre audience. In a somewhat different vein, Wolfgang Emmerich states that 'Die

---

[36] Heiner Müller, 'Gespräch mit Bühnentechnikern', in *W*, XI, 44–51 (p. 47).
[37] See e.g. Fehervary, 'Heiner Müllers Brigadenstücke', p. 21; and Schulz, *Heiner Müller*, p. 24.

Sprache ist präzis und gestisch, d.h., die Sprechweise des jeweils Agierenden zeigt, führt vor das für ihn Charakteristische',[38] whereby he notes an affinity between Müller's language and Brechtian *Gestus*. Yet, again, as we shall see, the workers' language in *Der Lohndrücker* appears to be laconic, rather than offering precise, albeit non-psychological, characterizations.

In an article from November 1957, the young East German screenplay writer Lothar Creutz writes that he regards the distillation of the language of the workers as the most promising aspect of the text in comparison with other texts by young Socialist playwrights: 'Da wird ferner zur Sache gesprochen, und nur Sache; drei Zeilen besagen da mehr als in den vorher besprochenen Stücken ein ganzer Akt [. . .].'[39] He goes on to write that the clear goal of Müller's style is one of dividing an audience along lines of those for and those against Socialism.[40] However, while an audience member may indeed be led to affirm or deny Socialism, the text in fact operates in a much more complex fashion.

Müller gives an indication of the role of his target audience in a note at the beginning of the text, the first half of which reads:

Das Stück versucht nicht, den Kampf zwischen Altem und Neuem, den ein Stückschreiber nicht entscheiden kann, als mit dem Sieg des Neuen vor dem letzten Vorhang abgeschlossen darzustellen; es versucht, ihn in das neue Publikum zu tragen, das ihn entscheidet. (p. 116)

A central conflict in the text is one of old versus new, specifically considerations of a capitalist, Fascist history in relation to a new, Socialist reality. This prefatory note demonstrates that Müller posits a role in this conflict for the theatre audience as a collective body. Furthermore, he sets out the rhetorical stance of the play: rather than teaching an audience what to think about what is being presented on stage, he implies that the material in the play is there for the audience members to consider independently. This serves the aim of creating a new public which is qualitatively different from the section of the GDR public depicted in the text.

But, we may ask, how does Müller see this new public coming about? What he is seeking to achieve is to make his audience productive, and the notion of 'Produktion' is indeed key to understanding Müller's aesthetic in *Der Lohndrücker*. When he published the play along with a selection of his texts under the title *Geschichten aus der Produktion* in 1974,[41] Müller was not referring solely to industrial production. As Janine Ludwig notes, the term 'Produktion' must also be read in the Marxian sense of 'die Produktion des Menschen im

---

[38] Emmerich, *Kleine Literaturgeschichte der DDR*, p. 159.
[39] Lothar Creutz, 'Anfänge sozialistischer Dramatik', *Theater der Zeit: Beilage*, 12.11 (1957), 2–8 (p. 8).
[40] Ibid.
[41] Heiner Müller, *Geschichten aus der Produktion 1* (West Berlin: Rotbuch, 1974).

Übergang aus seiner Vorgeschichte in seine Geschichte';[42] that is, producing people who are no longer the objects of history but its subjects, possessing the agency to act in history and alter it. In an East German interview given in 1966, Müller states:

Wenn bei uns [in der DDR] etwas gebaut wird, ein Kraftwerk oder ein Wohnblock, dann wird mehr gebaut als nur ein Kraftwerk oder ein Wohnblock; jede Arbeit bei uns produziert auch Produktivität bei denen, die sie tun, und das Thema wäre die Freisetzung von Produktivität und der Lust an der Produktivität bei Leuten, die hier arbeiten.[43]

For Müller, the building of Socialism cannot begin with people who are already good, committed Socialists, but these people must become so. He writes in 1953: 'Die das neue Neue schaffen, sind noch nicht neue Menschen. Erst das von ihnen Geschaffene formt sie selbst.'[44] That is, the new person can be produced only by what s/he produces. According to Müller, one can become a new person through production because the act of producing itself generates new consciousness. *Der Lohndrücker* offers a potential route out of the impasse: Müller's text grants the possibility for the production of a new audience through the potential for myriad responses to what is depicted. With each individual spectator having the opportunity to produce his/her own response to the play, this act of production is to produce a new collective of individuals, existing within a shared discursive space yet punctuated by difference. This potential audience, therefore, is not homogeneous or committed to the party line, but internally varied, opening the space for dialogue. Rather than saying everything that could be said, albeit in a condensed form, the workers' language produces a degree of silence through what is left unsaid; this may be filled by the audience member, allowing for numerous, nuanced readings of the reality depicted on stage.

In the passages cited above, we can see that the workers' dialogue is more about what is not said than what is said, and provokes more questions than it answers. In the case of the resolution of the strike scene, for example, according to the prevailing economic model both sides of the argument are indeed right to some extent: while a new working norm needs to be established to increase productivity in order to push down the price of consumer goods, without the foodstuffs required for the maintenance of a human body there is little labour that can be achieved without killing off the workforce. Yet, as noted above, both sides here merely talk past each other, and do not engage in discussion of the matters at the heart of the conflict. There is a chasm between these two dialectically opposed positions which invites consideration from an

---

[42] Ludwig, 'Eine Geschichte aus der Produktion', p. 108.
[43] Heiner Müller, 'Gespräch mit Heiner Müller', in *W*, x, 7–34 (p. 9).
[44] Heiner Müller, 'Sieg des Realismus', in *W*, VIII, 52–56 (p. 54).

audience. No doubt an audience member from the time of *Der Lohndrücker*'s stage debuts in Leipzig and Berlin in 1958 would have experienced both the hardship of the early 1950s and the relative success of the SED's economic policies: according to the East German women's magazine *Die Frau von heute*, the price of butter fell by a staggering 79 per cent from DM 65 to DM 14 per 500 g between November 1948 and July 1950;[45] and by the end of the 1950s, the GDR's economy was beginning to challenge that of the Federal Republic.[46] In neither developing their arguments further nor giving full consideration to the other side of the argument, the workers open the floor for debate among the audience members with respect to the methods employed to reinvigorate the economy and the place of the working public in it.

Müller's text further enhances the potential productivity of the workers' language by regularly combining it with silence. At the beginning of scene 8d, for example, while Balke is working in the kiln, Kolbe brings him his lunch and says, 'Gegen den Ofen war der Panzer ein Kühlschrank', to which Balke replies, 'Der Ofen ist kein Nazitank. Du kannst aussteigen' (p. 132). This is followed by an indication in the stage directions that Kolbe 'schweigt'. Here, the language is pared down, stating very simply some differences between sitting in a Nazi tank and working in the Socialist kiln, but the insertion of silence after the exchange encourages the audience to begin considering the histories of the workers in question: both were former Nazis and fought on the side of Capitalism and Fascism, and indeed, only a few scenes previously, Schorn confronts Balke with the accusation that he denounced Schorn for sabotage in a grenade factory (pp. 127–28). Yet now both are apparently committed Socialists, playing their part in the foundation and establishment of Socialism. Furthermore, whereas one was compelled to fight in a tank, Balke seems to advocate the position that it is possible to get out of the oven. However, this raises the question whether he really means that this is a question of choice. And, if it is down to choice, is he claiming that one can depart from the building of Socialism? If so, one clearly has to depart from the GDR altogether, as former union representatives (p. 120) and party secretaries have already done (p. 125).

Some commentators have noted that the use of pauses and scene changes in *Der Lohndrücker* is an epic means of encouraging input from an audience.[47] Yet the productivity of the dialogue's simplicity tends to go unremarked. Müller's technique of stripping language down to its simplest parts is not only

---

[45] Cited in *Spuren: Texte, Bilder, Dokumente zu 'Der Lohndrücker' von Heiner Müller. Dokumentation 1*, ed. by Alexander Weigel and Grischa Meyer (East Berlin: Deutsches Theater, 1988), p. 14.

[46] Fulbrook, *A History of Germany 1918-2008*, p. 164.

[47] See e.g. Fuhrmann, *Warten auf 'Geschichte'*, p. 72; and Hans-Thies Lehmann, 'Ästhetik des Textes — Ästhetik des Theaters: Heiner Müllers *Der Lohndrücker* in Ostberlin', in *Spiele und Spiegelungen von Schrecken und Tod*, ed. by Klussmann and Mohr, pp. 51-62 (pp. 53-56).

mimetic of the situation of the East German working public in the early GDR, and their lacking opportunity to participate in politics, but also a dialectical strategy for engaging the audience. In this sense, it borrows from a Brechtian epic form of theatre which, in Brecht's words, 'macht den Zuschauer zum Betrachter, aber [...] weckt seine Aktivität'.[48] Benjamin describes the productivity of the epic aesthetic in a way that appears fitting for Der Lohndrücker:

> Das epische Theater seinerseits rückt [...] in Stößen vor. Seine Grundform ist die des Chocks, mit dem die einzelnen wohlabgehobenen Situationen des Stücks aufeinandertreffen. Die Songs, die Beschriftungen im Bühnenbilde, die gestischen Konventionen der Spielenden heben die eine Situation von der andern ab. So entstehen überall Intervalle, die die Illusion des Publikums eher beeinträchtigen. Diese Intervalle sind seiner kritischen Stellungnahme, seinem Nachdenken reserviert.[49]

Benjamin's concern here is with examples of epic theatre that make use of placards announcing stage directions and include songs, which are not to be found in the text of Der Lohndrücker. None the less, what he says of the creation of intervals that are reserved for the audience's reflection holds true of Müller's text. Rather than creating a stage of illusion, Müller's language constantly disturbs any sense of illusion in order to invite the audience to enter into the play and supply their own thoughts to fill the discursive silence left by the workers regarding the reality their language cannot address.

We can see from the initial reception of Der Lohndrücker in performance that the precision of Müller's language was indeed praised for its productive capabilities. Notwithstanding the different performance techniques adopted at its premiere in Leipzig at the Städtisches Theater, directed by Günter Schwarzlose, and its first Berlin production at the Maxim Gorki Theater, directed by Hans-Dieter Mäde, both in 1958, reviewers tended to emphasize the role of the language in their experience of the play. W. Stie, writing for the East German National-Zeitung, found that the greatest strength of the Leipzig production lay in the 'schonungslose Offenheit, mit der die Widersprüche innerhalb des Betriebes wie in den handelnden Personen bloßgelegt werden'.[50] Crucial to this insight is that Stie is writing about the strengths of the text itself and then adds that Schwarzlose succeeded in transposing the text to the stage: the simplicity of the language is a major contributing factor in the text's ability to lay the contradictions within it bare. Reviewers of Mäde's production tended to agree that the precision of the language engaged spectators in a great degree of intellectual participation. Peter Edel found it

---

[48] Bertolt Brecht, 'Anmerkungen zur Oper Aufstieg und Fall der Stadt Mahagonny', in Werke: Große kommentierte Berliner und Frankfurter Ausgabe, ed. by Werner Hecht and others, 30 vols (Berlin and Weimar: Aufbau; Frankfurt a.M.: Suhrkamp, 1988-98), XXIV: Schriften 4 (1991), pp. 74-84 (p. 78).

[49] Benjamin, 'Das Land, in dem das Proletariat nicht genannt werden darf', pp. 515-16.

[50] W. Stie, 'Eine Woche der Uraufführungen', National-Zeitung (East Berlin), 30 March 1958.

to be 'ein Genuß für den Mitdenkenden, die Dialektik solcher pointierten Dispute zu verfolgen, die mitunter in ein paar Zeilen den Gehalt einer ganzen Lektion konzentrieren';[51] while for Helmut Ullrich, the concentration of the language of the play 'ermöglicht es viele Fragen zu stellen, weil immer auch eine Antwort gefunden wird'.[52] Notably, Ullrich found the answers to be already within the play, rather than left open to the audience; yet he also found that too many questions were asked without answers being provided. Despite this, the latter quotation demonstrates that the brevity and condensation of the language in Müller's text played an integral part in creating a work which held more doors open than it closed. In doing so, the textual means for inviting audience participation, largely borne out in the language, appear to have created the potential for multiple responses to the production.

'Das neue Publikum'

As Müller's preface to the piece states, *Der Lohndrücker* has nothing to teach and instead leaves the audience to generate a lesson or a meaning. Furthermore, as the above discussion of the workers' language illustrates, the text's openness and potential productivity lie chiefly in the simplicity and directness of this language. Müller's text lays the contradictions of the new Socialist society bare to an audience and, rather than reaching sure conclusions in the dialogue, or, for that matter, in the plot, invites the audience to consider what they have been shown and relate it to their reality. In turn, Müller points to the possibility for discussion about this reality, through which it may be changed. The public depicted in *Der Lohndrücker* cannot change their social reality because they have no voice with which to do so: their vocabulary neither fits the reality nor suffices to describe it; and they are prevented from participating in politics by a system of representation that further serves to remove their voices.

The 'neue[s] Publikum' (p. 116) that Müller addresses is simultaneously the same public as that depicted on stage and formally very different. Through presenting an audience with a text laden with contradictions and numerous different ways of responding to these, *Der Lohndrücker* offers that audience the possibility of becoming a participatory public, unlike the purely represented public that attempted to speak in 1956: the public in the theatre can question their reality, but there is no single way of doing so. In finding their own individual voices, audience members participate in politics by discuss-

---

[51] Peter Edel, '"Der Lohndrücker" und "Die Korrektur"', *BZ am Abend* (East Berlin), 8 September 1958.
[52] H[elmut] U[llrich], 'Der Arbeiter der Gegenwart auf dem Theater', *Neue Zeit* (East Berlin), 24 September 1958.

ing their reality with their contemporaries, and changing the shape of GDR politics.

Indeed, according to two individual spectators of Mäde's production, writing on the same day in November 1958, the play opened a very real space for dialogue, in which audience members grasped every available opportunity to discuss what they had seen on stage. One audience member notes that the audience was captivated right until the end of the performance.[53] This impression is confirmed by another spectator, who commented that, while the audience was silent during the scenes themselves, between scenes there was a great deal of discussion within the entire audience. The author of this letter also emphasized that the journey home after the performance was filled with lively discussion.[54] While these sources illustrate the degree to which Mäde's production encouraged dialogue within the audience, they are very limited in terms of what they can tell us about the form and content of the discussions generated among spectators, or about the extent to which the audience was reacting to the specific questions asked by the silence of the text. Nevertheless, the fact that dialogue stands in the foreground of these responses is important.

In this sense, we may be able to read Müller as partaking in the so-called 'Literatur der Selbstverständigung', albeit ahead of his time: according to the East German literary theorist Dieter Schlenstedt, this way of understanding the role of a particular form of literature emphasizes the act of communication with and between members of the public. The importance of discussion in the process of a public's 'Selbstverständigung' appears, for Schlenstedt, to have emerged with the Seventh Writers' Congress of the GDR in 1973,[55] and, furthermore, is situated within a 1970s discourse of democracy in the GDR: as he writes in 1979, '[e]s handelt sich um den Entwurf eines demokratischen Wirkungskreises sozialistischer Literatur'.[56] This discourse of democracy and literature is one in which discussion stands at the very centre, and it demonstrates the aspiration, in the words of Schlenstedt,

daß in [der Literatur der Selbstverständigung] eine Möglichkeit liegt, durch den Austausch verschiedener Erfahrungen zu mehr Gemeinsamkeit zu kommen, daß sie als ein kollektiver Vorgang zu sehen ist, [. . .] ein Prozeß, der die ganze Gesellschaft betrifft und in dem sich unsere gemeinsame Wahrheit bildet.[57]

[53] Letter from K.L. to the Artistic Directorship of the Maxim Gorki Theater, 30 November 1958, Maxim Gorki Theater Archiv, Lfd Nr. 38/39, unpaginated.
[54] Letter from F.C.S. to the Artistic Directorship of the Maxim Gorki Theater, 30 November 1958, ibid.
[55] Dieter Schlenstedt, *Die neuere DDR-Literatur und ihr Leser: Wirkungsästhetische Analysen* (Munich: Damnitz, 1980), p. 37. This work was initially published in the GDR in 1979 as Dieter Schlenstedt, *Wirkungsästhetische Analysen: Poetologie und Prosa in der neueren DDR-Literatur* (East Berlin: Akademie, 1979). See also Dieter Schlenstedt, 'Prozeß der Selbstverständigung: Aspekte der Funktionsbestimmung in unserer neueren Literatur', *Weimarer Beiträge*, 22.12 (1976), 5–37.
[56] Schlenstedt, *Die neuere DDR-Literatur und ihr Leser*, p. 41.
[57] Ibid., p. 37.

In recognizing literature as a collective activity and one which encourages dialogue, the 'Literatur der Selbstverständigung' therefore plays an invaluable role in the formation of a social reality in which everyone can participate; although Schlenstedt's concern is with East German prose in the 1970s, this comes close to characterizing Müller's position as a dramatist in the late 1950s. None the less, while Schlenstedt prizes the building of consensus through being given information by a responsible author,[58] and therefore posits a potential end of dialogue in commonality, the case of *Der Lohndrücker* is somewhat different: Müller purposefully revokes any such authorial responsibility, and 'Gemeinschaft' is far from the intended outcome of the play.

In an interview from 1985 Müller states: '[e]in geschriebener Text ist irgendwann oder wird als beendet verabschiedet. Aber ein Gespräch kann man erst beenden, wenn man nicht mehr sprechen kann, also wenn man tot ist.'[59] Although here Müller is discussing the relative merits of the interview format with his interlocutor, it can help us to grasp the potential efficacy of the aesthetic of *Der Lohndrücker*. Even though it is a text which appears to be finished, it is written for an audience, and primarily for the instigation of dialogue with and within an audience. Furthermore, it is not closed, but open to the active participation of individual audience members. To this extent, the dialogue activated by *Der Lohndrücker* is never-ending; and in this light, it is not surprising that Müller decided to direct his own production of it at the Deutsches Theater thirty years after its initial composition. Just as the late 1950s were a time when demands were being made in the Eastern bloc for democratic reform, so too was the latter half of the 1980s, when Mikhail Gorbachev's reform programmes of *glasnost* and *perestroika* in the Soviet Union sowed the seeds of hope for democracy and freedom of speech in Eastern European states, including the GDR. The language of a people in a land in which they could only be talked about once again became a means of getting them to try to do the talking themselves and actively participate in a democratic public sphere.[60]

UNIVERSITY OF EDINBURGH   MICHAEL WOOD

[58] Ibid., p. 67; and Schlenstedt, 'Prozeß der Selbstverständigung', p. 9.

[59] Heiner Müller, '[Erst mal: das Gespräch damals — aus einem Jahr Abstand...]', in *W*, x, 769–89 (p. 769).

[60] For some documentation of this 1988 production see *Der Lohndrücker: Dokumentation 2*, ed. by Akademie der Künste (East Berlin: Deutsches Theater, 1988).

'LONG LIVE POLAND!': REPRESENTING THE PAST IN POLISH COMIC BOOKS

Traditionally comic books have been products of mass culture, as well as being hybrid forms merging text and image, and having a global reach, facilitated by popular translations and film adaptations.[1] Often relegated to the category of 'low' literature, comics have long fought for recognition as a legitimate literary and artistic form, while their fans have been frequently denigrated and seen as second-class readers.[2] With the emergence of the term 'graphic novel', which is gradually becoming an umbrella term for the entire genre, 'funnies' gained importance, slowly turning into a sanctioned form of 'high' literature.[3] According to some scholars, this new nomenclature has the potential to 'rescue comics from their critical neglect, as well as to recognize the emergence of specifically adult comics and book length works'.[4] None the less, to some extent comic books continue to be viewed as a form of light entertainment, associated mostly with a young and inexperienced reader, while paradoxically becoming an important educational resource used in classrooms across the world. Some primary-school teachers contend that 'graphic novels have the potential to scaffold struggling students into fluent readers and enhance the literacy experiences of more proficient readers'.[5] Others suggest that this particular genre is more appealing to adolescents than traditional literary texts, and that this in turn increases literacy levels in the modern classroom.[6] Moreover, teachers and lecturers at secondary and third level respectively consider the comic book as an invaluable resource in history teaching, with

---

[1] Catherine Labio, 'What's in a Name? The Academic Study of Comics and the "Graphic Novel"', *Cinema Journal*, 50.3 (2011), 123–26 (p. 124).

[2] Sarah Ziolkowska and Vivian Howard, '"Forty-one-year-old female academics aren't supposed to like comics!": The Value of Comic Books to Adult Readers', in *Graphic Novels and Comics in Libraries and Archives: Essays on Readers, Research, History and Cataloging*, ed. by Robert G. Weiner (Jefferson, NC: McFarland, 2010), pp. 154–66 (p. 163).

[3] Despite having been readily embraced by publishers and readers alike, the use of 'graphic novel' to describe the whole genre is still widely contested in scholarly circles. For example, Catherine Labio argues that the new term 'sanitizes comics; strengthens the distinction between high and low, major and minor; and reinforces the ongoing ghettoization of works deemed unworthy of critical attention, either because of their inherent nature (as in the case of works of humor) or because of their intended audience (lower, less-literate classes; children; and so on)' (Labio, 'What's in a Name?', p. 126). Despite recognizing the need for clearer distinctions in the existing nomenclature, this article will chiefly use the two broad terms 'graphic novel' and 'comic books'. They will be understood here as fiction and non-fiction works of varying length that use sequential art and are published in book format, as opposed to magazines.

[4] Hugo Frey and Benjamin Noys, 'Editorial: History in the Graphic Novel', *Rethinking History*, 6 (2002), 255–60 (p. 255).

[5] Diane Lapp and others, 'Graphic Novels: What Elementary Teachers Think about their Instructional Value', *Journal of Education*, 192.1 (2011–12), 25–35 (p. 24).

[6] Gretchen E. Schwarz, 'Graphic Novels for Multiple Literacies', *Journal of Adolescent and Adult Literacy*, 46 (2002), 262–65 (p. 262).

Art Spiegelman's *Maus* being the most commonly read one, especially in courses on Holocaust, the Second World War, and genocide.⁷

Indeed, *Maus* has simultaneously transformed history writing and the history of comics, asking important questions about limits of representation, the workings of memory, the ethical dilemma stemming from retelling a painful past, and, more broadly, the relationship between aesthetics and history.⁸ Other graphic narratives portraying experiences of war, conflict, and genocide continue mapping sensitive areas of family, national, and world histories, particularly Marjane Satrapi's story of growing up in revolutionary Iran told in *Persepolis*, Joe Sacco's travels to some of the world's hot spots presented in *Palestine* and *Safe Area Goražde*, and Jean-Phillipe Stassen's *Deogratias*, offering a harrowing depiction of the Rwandan genocide.⁹ The success of these narratives suggests that, like any other artistic and literary form, the comic book provides an ideal platform for exploring complex historical themes, while its hybridity might offer a testing ground to probe the limits of historiography, along with constituting a site where *representations* of war and genocide are questioned, challenged, and undermined.¹⁰

It is precisely this act of representing, reinventing, and interrogating a national past in comics that is the focus of this article. Using Poland as a case study, it will examine different ways of writing history in the graphic novel. While doing so, this article will also seek to investigate the dominating patterns of production and distribution of comic books in contemporary Poland. A brief history of Polish comics, with a particular emphasis on works dealing with historical events, will be presented below, followed by a discussion of dominant narratives of the past in public discourse in Poland. Analysis of specific primary sources published predominantly in the last decade will constitute the main part of the discussion.

The History of Polish Comics

Comics appeared in Poland shortly after independence in 1918, functioning initially in the form of panel cartoons published in magazines and newspapers, and having a humorous and satirical content. It was, however, the 1930s creation of Kornel Makuszyński and Marian Walentynowicz called *Koziołek Matołek* (*The Silly Little Goat*) that marked the real beginning of the genre in

---

⁷ See e.g. Alicia C. Decker and Mauricio Castro, 'Teaching History with Comic Books: A Case Study of Violence, War, and the Graphic Novel', *History Teacher*, 45 (2012), 169–88 (p. 169).

⁸ See Hillary Chute, '"The Shadow of a Past Time": History and Graphic Representation in *Maus*', *Twentieth-Century Literature*, 52 (2006), 199–230 (p. 201).

⁹ Marjane Satrapi, *Persepolis: The Story of a Childhood and the Story of a Return* (London: Cape, 2006); Joe Sacco, *Palestine* (London: Cape, 2001); id., *Safe Area Goražde: The War in Eastern Bosnia, 1992–95* (London: Cape, 2007); Jean-Phillipe Stassen, *Deogratias: A Tale of Rwanda* (New York and London: First Second, 2006).

¹⁰ Frey and Noys, 'Editorial', pp. 258–59.

Poland. Aimed at children and recalling adventures of a clumsy goat, the story quickly became a favourite of the nation, making it one of the most popular children's books of all time.[11]

In the immediate aftermath of the Second World War, particularly after 1948, comics rapidly became a potent tool of Stalinist indoctrination. Newspapers and youth magazines published comic strips that praised Socialist heroes, such as shock workers and peasants, and demonized actual or imagined enemies of the system, including imperialist spies working to damage Polish interests. All of these stories fashioned one-dimensional realities based on binary opposites of good/evil and Socialist/imperialist respectively.[12] Jerzy Szyłak argues that, while constituting examples of blatant Communist propaganda that were ineptly drawn and scripted, these works appealed mostly to young and uncritical readers.[13] In the early 1950s, following a period of heightened anti-American propaganda, both the term *komiks* and the genre itself began to be associated with Western culture and frowned upon by Communist authorities. It was only after the Polish October of 1956, when the regime loosened its grip on cultural production, that comics were restored to their status of legitimate entertainment, free from overt state propaganda.[14]

The rapid expansion of television in the late 1960s brought important changes also for other forms of popular culture in Communist Poland, including comics. Their dissemination and visibility increased, shifting to an independent format of magazine-like books, described as *zeszyty komiksowe* or 'comic notebooks'. This new format reinvigorated the interest of the ruling authorities in the genre and, especially in the early 1970s, numerous comic series adhering to the state-controlled vision of Poland's past were published, such as *Kapitan Kloss* (*Captain Kloss*) and *Podziemny front* (*The Underground Front*). Often based on popular television programmes, the series emphasized the enduring struggle against Nazi oppressors and the involvement of Red Army and aligned Polish troops in fighting the enemy during the Second World War. Inconvenient topics such as the role of the Home Army or the border shifts following the war were either omitted or distorted to match Communist historiography.[15] Michał Słomka shows that comic books at the time used uncomplicated plots, while their aesthetics tended to remain a matter of secondary concern as long as the publications served their main purpose, namely the legitimization of power. He also asserts that propagandistic and educational principles formed the basis on which 'historical' comics

---

[11] Adam Rusek, 'Krótka historia opowieści obrazkowych w Polsce Ludowej', in *45–89: Comics behind the Iron Curtain*, ed. by Michał Słomka (Poznań: CENTRALA Central Europe Comics Art, 2009), pp. 31–41 (p. 31).
[12] Ibid., p. 33.
[13] Jerzy Szyłak, *Komiks: świat przerysowany* (Gdańsk: słowo/obraz terytoria, 1998), pp. 133–34.
[14] Rusek, 'Krótka historia opowieści obrazkowych w Polsce Ludowej', p. 35.
[15] Ibid., p. 38.

in Poland developed; this was a factor which greatly affected the standing of the genre after the fall of Communism.[16]

Following the workers' protests in 1970, and the subsequent takeover of the leadership by Edward Gierek, the country experienced a short period of economic and cultural revival, particularly in the first half of the decade. Poland opened up to Western influences which rapidly began to change the range of comics on the market. Reprints of French- and English-language strips such as *Astérix* and *Tarzan* were appearing in satirical periodicals, including the popular weekly *Szpilki*. In 1975 the first issue of a home-grown comic magazine *Relax* came out, and although it was modelled on the Franco-Belgian magazines *Tintin* and *Spirou*, it published and promoted works by Polish artists alone.[17] Szyłak maintains that the overall quality of the monthly was uneven, ranging from high-calibre strips by some of the most accomplished illustrators such as Grzegorz Rosiński and Janusz Christa to poorly drawn pieces of Communist propaganda that eulogized certain aspects of Poland's past. According to him, however, the latter was a small price to pay given the contribution made by *Relax* to popularizing the genre, demonstrating its potential to readers and energizing the comics community as a whole.[18]

In the 1980s two important comics, which alluded to the contemporary political situation in Poland, came to the fore. Despite representing two distinct types of the genre, science fiction and horror respectively, *Funky Koval* and *Wampirus Wars* were addressed to an adult reader well versed in the complexities of double speech. Both series gained a significant following at the time but were largely forgotten in the period immediately after the fall of Communism, when comics had become chiefly associated with banal propagandistic pieces of mediocre quality from a bygone era.[19]

Although the position of the genre in Poland is gradually improving thanks to initiatives such as the annual International Festival of Comics and Games organized in Łódź since 1991 and accompanied by scholarly conferences on comics studies, there is still a tendency to view the genre as a convenient medium through which various didactic and political goals can be achieved. In the last few years, state money has been pumped into projects aimed at promoting Polish history among schoolchildren, often reducing comics to a

---

[16] Michał Słomka, 'Polacy lubią brąz: czyli o heroizacji polskiej historii w komiksie. Zarys zagadnienia', in *Komiks a problem kiczu: 9 Sympozjum Komiksologiczne. Antologia Referatów*, ed. by Krzysztof Skrzypczyk (Łódź: Stowarzyszenie Twórców 'Contur', 2009), pp. 80–81 (p. 80).

[17] Szyłak, *Komiks*, p. 137.

[18] Ibid.

[19] For a longer discussion of the situation of comic books in the early 1990s see Jerzy Szyłak, *Komiks* (Kraków: Znak, 2000), pp. 170–73; and id., *Komiks w kulturze ikonicznej XX wieku: wstęp do poetyki komiksu* (Gdańsk: słowo/obraz terytoria, 1999), pp. 72–73.

mere packaging that holds and transmits interpretations of the national past encouraged by the political establishment.

Comics and the Politics of Memory

In contemporary Poland public debates concerning history are as multifarious as they are vehement, with diverse memories and interpretations of the past competing for recognition and ascendancy. On the official level, and especially in conservative circles associated with the Law and Justice Party, two dominant narratives of the national past can be identified. First is the narrative of martyrdom and victimhood, associated with Poland's forced submission to its powerful neighbours and the ensuing tragic events: the Katyń massacre of 1940, where an estimated 22,000 Polish officers and civilians were killed by the NKVD, the anti-German Warsaw Uprising of 1944, in which many young people perished, and the post-war period of subjugation to the Soviet Union. Although significantly weaker, closely intertwined is the narrative of Polish heroism and resistance in the face of foreign oppression.[20] Memories that contradict these visions of Polishness are often viewed as unpatriotic and, consequently, refused legitimacy. For example, debates on Polish anti-Semitism and pogroms during and after the war, initiated by Jan T. Gross's *Neighbours*, caused uproar in Poland and led to a renewed wave of anti-Semitism, particularly in the media empire of Father Rydzyk.[21] Equally, discussions of expulsions of Germans from western territories after 1945 suggest that accounts of the wartime suffering of other nations, especially those whose stereotypical role was that of perpetrator, tend to be seen in Poland as an attempt to falsify history and undermine the extent of Polish suffering.[22]

It is this very model of collective memory that has had the biggest effect on Polish comic books in the last decade. Examples of individual projects offering alternative representations of history are few and far between. Not only does this status quo hamper the development of independent comics in Poland but it also discourages open debate about the past, further marginalizing and silencing contentious aspects of Polish history. The sections that follow analyse these graphic narratives by concentrating on several albums published in Poland since 2004. In an attempt to unravel complexities and identify the main trends in the portrayal of twentieth-century Polish history, this article will be structured according to ways in which the selected stories

---

[20] See e.g. Gregory Slysz, 'Poland: History as Crucible', *Transitions Online*, 22 September 2009, pp. 1–4 (pp. 1–2).

[21] Paweł Słupski, 'Stowarzyszenie im. Jana Karskiego żąda ukarania felietonisty Radia Maryja', *Gazeta Wyborcza*, 14 April 2006.

[22] Pawel Lutomski, 'The Debate about a Center against Expulsions: An Unexpected Crisis in German–Polish Relations?', *German Studies Review*, 27 (2004), 449–68 (p. 452).

are produced, funded, and disseminated, while simultaneously offering an analysis of their content.

Popularizing History through Comics: The Zin Zin Press Phenomenon

Zin Zin Press has been present in the Polish market since 1997 and is now one of the most prosperous comic publishers in Poland. Created by Witold Tkaczyk as a publishing business responsible for the production of the comic magazine *AQQ*, after several years the enterprise took on a life of its own, becoming the chief publisher of 'historical' comic books in Poland. To date Zin Zin Press has produced nearly twenty albums on various topics dealing solely with twentieth-century Polish history. Works on the Second World War published since 2004 have focused on a wide variety of issues and events, including the Battle of Westerplatte and the Defence of the Polish Post Office in Danzig in September 1939, the Katyń massacre, and the Holocaust. Equally well represented have been the albums on Communism, some of them commemorating important anniversaries, for example the twenty-fifth anniversary of Solidarity and of the 1981 massacre at the Wujek coalmine, and the fiftieth anniversary of the 1956 workers' revolt in Poznań. Alongside these examples, two narratives emphasizing the role of the Catholic Church in the dissident movement and in sustaining the national spirit under Communism deserve to be mentioned, one of them recalling the first Polish pilgrimage of Pope John Paul II in 1979, another telling the story of the murder of Jerzy Popiełuszko, the Catholic priest killed by Security Service officers in 1984.

While tackling themes that were either forbidden or distorted prior to the fall of Communism, these graphic narratives are aimed predominantly at educating young people; more specifically, they are addressed to readers 'who were lucky enough to be born in free Poland'.[23] The susceptibility of comics to didacticism is emphasized in either the forewords or blurbs found in most of the albums. For instance, *1956: Poznański Czerwiec* (*Poznań: June 1956*) praises the accessibility of comics, while *Pierwsi w boju* (*First in Battle*) explicitly states that '*as befits* the medium used, the book is aimed primarily at the young reader'.[24] To some extent, these remarks reiterate the stereotypical perception of the genre as appealing *only* to children and adolescents, along with the suggestion that the comic is a convenient medium which makes it possible to get across complex messages in a clear and comprehensible manner. The educational function of the publications is underpinned by solid historical research. Lengthy bibliographical references are often listed, includ-

---

[23] Lech Wałęsa, 'Wstęp', in *Solidarność: 25 lat. Nadzieja zwykłych ludzi*, ed. by Maciej Jasiński and others (Poznań: Zin Zin Press, 2005), p. 3. All translations from Polish are mine.

[24] Maciej Jasiński and others, *1956: Poznański Czerwiec* (Poznań: Zin Zin Press, 2006), front cover flap; Mariusz Wójtowicz-Podhorski and Jacek Przybylski, *Pierwsi w boju: obrona Poczty Polskiej w Gdańsku* (Poznań: Zin Zin Press, 2010), p. 3 (emphasis added).

ing accounts by eyewitnesses such as diaries and life stories.[25] In some cases, almost entire scripts are built on personal narratives, for example *1940 Katyń: zbrodnia na nieludzkiej ziemi* (*Katyń 1940: Crime in an Inhuman Land*), which draws on memoirs of Starobilsk camp survivor Józef Czapski.[26] The scripts' strict adherence to scholarly sources and eyewitness testimonies is meant to create an appearance of 'objective' historical knowledge that is free from constraints imposed by political influences. As such, the books are presented as trustworthy educational material. Further, most albums are supplemented with articles or epilogues providing additional background information on the events they represent. Some of these sources contain archival photographs and images of weapons used by Polish soldiers, as in *Pierwsi w boju*; annotations and a timeline of events, as exemplified by *1956: Poznański Czerwiec*; and drawings of military uniforms, for example in *1940: Katyń*.

Not surprisingly, given their function, the majority of Zin Zin Press albums have been financed by the state.[27] One of the subsidies came from the programme 'Patriotism of Tomorrow', overseen by the Polish History Museum, which intends to support 'those educational and art initiatives that promote patriotic attitudes and active citizenship through history-learning'.[28] This is how the then Minister of Culture, Kazimierz Ujazdowski, defined its aims in a foreword to the comic on the 1956 workers' protest in Poznań:

It is a new programme supporting initiatives that promote history in modern and communicative ways. Historical comics are one of them. As the Minister of Culture and a father of two school-age boys, I am in favour of such projects. Together we should look for fresh and light formats that will restore the positive and happy character of [Polish] patriotism.[29]

Besides replicating the formulaic definition of comics as a light genre written for schoolchildren, Ujazdowski's statement projects a far more optimistic vision of Polish patriotism than the graphic narrative it introduces. In fact, both this and most of the other historical albums produced by Zin Zin Press seem to fit into a quite different national discourse, one that is firmly grounded in the idea of Poland as the 'Christ of Nations', torn by powerful enemies and sacrificing itself for other countries.[30] According to Dieter De

[25] See e.g. Wójtowicz-Podhorski and Przybyski, *Pierwsi w boju*, p. 4.
[26] Tomasz Nowak and others, *1940 Katyń: zbrodnia na nieludzkiej ziemi* (Poznań: Zin Zin Press, 2010).
[27] An interesting case in point is the album *Pierwsi w boju: obrona Poczty Polskiej w Gdańsku*, on the defence of the Polish Post Office in Danzig on 1 September 1939, funded entirely by the state-owned Poczta Polska, the Polish postal service.
[28] 'Patriotism of Tomorrow' <http://www.en.muzhp.pl/programs/ongoing/217/patriotism-of-tomorrow.html> [accessed 2 January 2013].
[29] Kazimierz M. Ujazdowski, 'Wstęp', in Jasiński and others, *1956: Poznański Czerwiec*, p. 3.
[30] The idea of Poland as the 'Christ of Nations' or the rampart of Christian Europe is a fifteenth-century invention that was revived in the nineteenth century and often linked with the

Bruyn, who analysed comics on the Warsaw Uprising, 'this new tendency in comic art [...] threatens to reinvigorate the "typically" Polish martyrological-messianistic mythology of suffering', and as the traumatic historical 'events are increasingly claimed as the sacrosanct landmarks of the newly forged Polish identity, they may themselves start to take on an ideological and even propagandistic guise'.³¹

This opinion is reiterated, to some extent, by Michał Słomka, who claims that the state-controlled popularization of history through comics has led to the deterioration of the genre, resulting in very few original graphic narratives being created in Poland in recent years. He notes, for example, that contemporary comic books bring back to life some of the strategies used in the Communist-era publications, including one-dimensional characters, conventional representation, arbitrary choice of themes, and unnatural dialogues. However, he considers *Achtung Zelig! Druga Wojna* (*Achtung Zelig! The Second World War*) to be an exception to the rule and the only noteworthy comic ever produced by Zin Zin Press.³² The album was published in 2004, in co-operation with the Warsaw-based Kultura Gniewu, over a decade after its first pages appeared in the magazine *AQQ*. This album, the creation of Krzysztof Gawronkiewicz (artwork) and Krystian Rosenberg (script), has been nominated for and awarded several prizes in both Poland and Belgium.³³ On the surface, it is a Holocaust story recalling the escape of a father and son from what is possibly a death-camp train, their encounter with and capture by an SS unit, and subsequent release by the Communist People's Army. The narrative is told from the perspective of Zelig, the son, who is now an old man. It develops in a dreamlike fashion, pointing to the unreliability and volatility of memory. On the graphic level, the comic can be considered as a Polish response to *Maus* since, like Spiegelman, Gawronkiewicz uses allegory to draw his characters. The portrayal of father and son proves to be particularly compelling; their deformed, amorphous faces are meant to convey their otherness, along with suggesting the impossibility of employing realistic representation in the aftermath of the Holocaust (Figure 1).³⁴ The artist also seems to engage in polemic with Spiegelman in his rendering of the Polish

---

Polish opposition movement under Communism. See Gerhard Wagner, 'Nationalism and Cultural Memory in Poland: The European Union Turns East', *International Journal of Politics, Culture, and Society*, 17 (2003), 191–212 (pp. 202–05).

³¹ Dieter De Bruyn, 'Patriotism of Tomorrow? The Commemoration and Popularization of the Warsaw Rising through Comics', *Slovo*, 22 (2010), 46–65 (pp. 50–51).

³² Słomka, 'Polacy lubią brąz', pp. 80–81.

³³ These have included Prix Millepages BD (2005) and Prix Festival BD Vaison la Romaine (2006).

³⁴ The illustrations may be viewed in greater detail (Figure 2 in colour) in the online version of this article, available at www.jstor.org.

FIG. 1. Krzysztof Gawronkiewicz and Krystian Rosenberg, *Achtung Zelig! Druga Wojna* (Warsaw and Poznań: Kultura Gniewu and Zin Zin Press, 2004), p. 8. Courtesy of Witold Tkaczyk/Zin Zin Press

characters, who, in contrast to *Maus*, are presented here as cats, not pigs.[35] Interestingly, the People's Army partisans, who save the two men, only wear cat costumes: they are not *real* cats.[36] While the oneiric quality of this story lends itself to various interpretations, it is clear that this metaphor is meant to present the Soviet-backed partisans as unpatriotic and not 'genuinely' Polish, while alluding to Communist-era comics which praised them as true heroes.

This accumulation of messages and cultural references, including Woody Allen's *Zelig*, detracts at times from the Holocaust story, making it a mere backdrop against which other historical issues are explored. As the Zin Zin Press editor-in-chief, Witold Tkaczyk, observes:

Achtung Zelig! is not a historical comic. It is a comic about the understanding of history by the generation who grew up under Communism, being fed with the distorted image of the past, and drawing its knowledge, including knowledge of the Second World War, from popular TV series (*Stawka* [*większa niż życie*], *Podziemny front* [. . .]), comics and books that omitted the involvement of the Home Army and claimed it was the Polish Workers' Party, People's Guard, and People's Army who won the war.[37]

In the light of Tkaczyk's remarks, it seems legitimate to say that the graphic novella uses the Shoah as a justification to revisit the past that is temporally closer to the authors and of which they have a personal memory. The dreamlike atmosphere of the album, best represented by the character of Austrian-born SS officer Emil, a dwarf, is also a legacy of the times, particularly the 1970s and 1980s, when fantasy became a popular comic genre.[38] The undefined faces of the Jewish characters might then be read as a reference to the silencing and falsifying of Holocaust memory under Communism. The Polish national past proves to be as important here, with the memory of Communism and the regime's distorted interpretations of history taking centre stage in the comic.

Despite avoiding the hyper-realistic convention of other Zin Zin Press albums, this narrative could be seen to correspond closely with the publisher's didactic goals in that it uses the comic genre as a means of popularizing the dominant interpretations of the Communist past and replicates, even if implicitly, the potent myth of Polish victimization. So far this strategy has been successful with the government and a portion of Polish comic-book readers. The enterprise has been thriving, and in 2010 Witold Tkaczyk was awarded a state honour for his contribution to promoting the genre in Poland.

---

[35] It is worth mentioning that in *Maus* it is the Nazis who are represented by cats.
[36] For examples of these representations see Krzysztof Gawronkiewicz and Krystian Rosenberg, *Achtung Zelig! Druga Wojna* (Warsaw and Poznań: Kultura Gniewu and Zin Zin Press, 2004), pp. 20–21, 31–33.
[37] Witold Tkaczyk, 'Komentarze do notki' <http://jan.bodakowski.salon24.pl/428960,klasyka-komiksu-achtung-zelig-druga-wojna> [accessed 4 January 2013].
[38] Ibid.

Although it is the most popular publisher of historical comic albums at the moment, Zin Zin Press is not by any means the only one. Since 2005 the Polish publishing market has witnessed a proliferation of this kind of narrative, created by and large under the patronage of state institutions. Some of these institutions view comics as part of their broader educational agenda, as is the case with the Warsaw Rising Museum, opened in 2004. According to Dieter De Bruyn:

> One of the main goals of the museum seems to be the historical and patriotic education of those who have grown up in post-Communist Poland, in a period in which national history was considered to be threatened by the effects of unbridled capitalism and rapid globalization. One of the most effective ways to tighten the intergenerational bonds between grandparents and their grandchildren has been the use of and support for all kinds of pop-cultural representations of the events. Of particular interest here is a yearly comic competition.[39]

Discussing the development of the annual competition from 2005 onwards, De Bruyn goes on to show how despite stimulating interest in the events of 1944, the initiative has not managed to engender high-quality works that would abandon the master narrative on the inevitability and necessity of the Uprising.[40] He also argues that although the majority of comics selected for publication show a tendency to favour realistic and fact-based representations that foster the narrative of Polish heroism and martyrdom, 'the museum still seems to offer certain opportunities for alternative narratives to come to the surface', most notably the highly accomplished works of Jacek Frąś, which often run counter to popular interpretations of history.[41] Notwithstanding its small scale, the above-mentioned instance of pluralization of memory is a hopeful one. Other publishing initiatives of this kind are not as promising. Representative examples include historical albums, primarily on the Second World War, published by the Institute of National Remembrance, and a series of comics on Auschwitz produced by K&L Press since 2009. Unlike Zin Zin Press, these outlets opt for lesser-known stories but equally strive to create narratives with a high level of factual content and realism that would be accessible and appealing to adolescents. K&L Press, for example, advertises its books as attractive educational material, conceived in co-operation with historians of the Second World War, specializing in the history of the death camps, while its website encourages teachers to incorporate additional resources available free of charge online into their lesson plans.[42]

Despite selecting unconventional plotlines, with the first album recalling

---

[39] De Bruyn, 'Patriotism of Tomorrow?', p. 52.
[40] Ibid., pp. 53–54.
[41] Ibid., pp. 55 and 64.
[42] See 'Comic Book as Educational Material' <http://www.episodesfromauschwitz.pl/en/?id=3> [accessed 3 January 2013].

the true story of an Auschwitz love affair between a Jewish woman and a Polish man, the narratives disappoint because of the poor quality of the artwork. Equally, the scriptwriters are fastidious about 'faithfulness' of representation to the point of literality.[43] Issues that might be unclear or considered problematic by the reader are explained in both the introduction and the afterword, as is the case with the third album in the series, recalling the story of the 'saint of Auschwitz', Father Maksymilian Kolbe, who sacrificed himself for another prisoner selected to die of starvation. As the editors rightly point out, Kolbe's pre-war 'journalism is criticized at times as anti-Semitic'.[44] They argue, however, that his criticism of Jews should not be viewed as racially motivated but as an outcome of the socio-economic climate of his time.[45] The comic itself presupposes, none the less, that the Franciscan's views originated in his reading of *The Protocols of the Elders of Zion*, a fraudulent description of alleged Jewish plans to dominate the world, which lies at the basis of twentieth-century anti-Semitism.[46] To balance this representation, the album gives examples of the monk's compassion towards his Jewish fellow prisoners at Auschwitz.[47] While it is clear that the scriptwriter attempts to present a judicious portrayal of this sensitive issue, the brevity, simplicity, and educational function of the comic render it impossible to provide a convincing argument. What makes it even more difficult is that, after all, *The Protocols of the Elders of Zion* provided a source of unceasing inspiration for Hitler and as such constituted a prime rationale for the Holocaust.[48] In this respect, Will Eisner's graphic novel *The Plot: The Secret Story of 'The Protocols of the Elders of Zion'*, which provides a full-length critique of this hoax text, would be an excellent context for the K&L Press comic, if not an educational resource in its own right.[49]

As the discussion of the popularization of history through comics suggests, in Poland state-sponsored initiatives rarely yield satisfactory results. Despite increasing the visibility of graphic narratives in the public sphere, the recent politicization of comics, particularly in the period following the upsurge of support for the conservative Law and Justice Party, has led to the decline of the genre and revival of the propagandistic trend whereby unitary narratives of the past are encouraged and funded. Subservient to a rigid national

[43] Michał Gałek and Marcin Nowakowski, 'Posłowie', in *Epizody z Auschwitz: miłość w cieniu zagłady* (Oświęcim and Babice: K&L Press, 2009), p. 39.
[44] Michał Gałek and Michał Poller, 'Posłowie', in *Epizody z Auschwitz: ofiara* (Oświęcim and Babice: K&L Press, 2009), p. 39.
[45] Ibid.
[46] Gałek and Poller, *Epizody z Auschwitz: ofiara*, p. 11.
[47] Ibid., p. 26
[48] See Henry Gonshak, 'Beyond Maus: Other Holocaust Graphic Novels', *Shofar: An Interdisciplinary Journal of Jewish Studies*, 28.1 (2009), 55–79 (p. 64).
[49] Will Eisner, *The Plot: The Secret Story of 'The Protocols of the Elders of Zion'* (New York and London: Norton, 2005).

curriculum and restricted to a set number of themes, these publications inevitably lead to the marginalization of projects that do not fit the narrowly defined educational agenda. Although recent cultural initiatives, supported by the conservative-liberal government of the Civic Platform Party, seem to be heralding changes, most remarkably with the highly controversial film inspired by the Jedwabne story, *Pokłosie*, being part-funded by the state, it remains to be seen whether and how this is reflected in the production and dissemination of historical comics in future.[50] Meanwhile, it is worth looking at more alternative ventures by Polish artists and scriptwriters that stand out for the different take on history that they propose.

The Memory of Communism in Graphic Memoirs

Recently the graphic memoir has become one of the most popular and best-selling comic genres in the world. Marjane Satrapi's highly acclaimed *Persepolis: The Story of a Childhood* (2000) sold more than 400,000 copies in France and over a million worldwide, winning several prizes and being made into a film in 2007. Praised for its accessible representation of Iranian culture and history told from the perspective of a child, the memoir is also a story of exile and a salient commentary on the Arab world.[51] Together with other graphic autobiographies, such as Craig Thomson's *Blankets* (2003) and Alison Bechdel's *Fun Home* (2006), *Persepolis* paved the way for new narratives of childhood and adolescence.[52] In the Polish context *Marzi*, scripted by Marzena Sowa and illustrated by Sylvain Savoia, is unquestionably the best example of the graphic memoir.[53] Originally written in French and published in six volumes by the Belgian publisher Dupuis between 2005 and 2011, the story constitutes a chronicle of growing up in Stalowa Wola, a small town located in south-eastern Poland.

Just like *Persepolis*, the memoir was written in exile, albeit self-imposed, in France and Belgium, and in a similar manner to Satrapi, Sowa creates her literary alter ego, Marzi, in an attempt to revisit her childhood, lived against the backdrop of momentous historical changes. Born in 1979, she is an only child in a working-class family witnessing her country in the process of extricating itself from Communism. Like any other little girl of her time, she

---

[50] *Pokłosie*, dir. by Władysław Pasikowski (Monolith Films, 2012).

[51] Manuela Constantino, 'Marji: Popular Commix Heroine Breathing Life into the Writing of History', *Canadian Review of American Studies/Revue canadienne d'études américaines*, 38 (2008), 429–77 (p. 432).

[52] Although Thompson's and Bechdel's works do not deal with national histories, focusing predominantly on private and family histories, they are undoubtedly the classics of the graphic memoir genre.

[53] In Poland it was published in a series of three books: *Dzieci i ryby głosu nie mają* (2007), *Hałasy dużych miast* (2008), and *Nie ma wolności bez solidarności* (2011). This article will use the English edition published as one album in 2011.

is preoccupied with small matters, longing to own a Barbie doll and eat lots of chocolate, while admitting plainly many years later: 'I didn't want to carry the weight of my nation, nor search for our identity. In truth, I didn't care. I had no desire to settle History's accounts, to try to figure out who was good and who was bad. I wanted to get away from all that.'[54] Despite her attempts to detach herself from the vicissitudes of history, her script shows an acute awareness of the complex intertwining of her family life and the life of her nation under Communism, on the brink of independence, and post-1989. As such, alongside telling her deeply personal story, Sowa represents Polish realities of the 1980s and early 1990s.

We meet Marzi one winter as she watches a carp swim in the bathtub before it is butchered by her father and eaten for Christmas Eve dinner, a ritual performed by countless families in Poland. Gradually we learn more about Marzi's life in a high-rise apartment block, a symbol of the country's rampant urbanization and standardization of life under Communism, where everyone lives in flats of identical layout (albeit available in two variants), has the same brand of Soviet-produced refrigerator, very little space, and even less privacy.[55] Although her everyday life is seldom rosy, with long queues in shops, food rationing, and mean shopkeepers, she seems to have a happy childhood, where rationing is being overcome by growing fruit and vegetables on a piece of ancestral land in the country, gifts from abroad, mostly from Czechoslovakia and the United States, and occasional deliveries of scarce products, such as oranges.[56] Her free time is spent playing with friends on the staircase or going to the countryside, while her leisure activities are visibly influenced by her Roman Catholic upbringing. For example, we see Marzi re-enact the Pope's 1979 Polish pilgrimage from documentary slides she was given by her mother, take her first communion, and attend mass in a country church at Easter.[57] She also imagines what talking to God would be like, with one of the panels bearing a resemblance to Satrapi's fantasy of being 'the last prophet'.[58]

Even though for most of the time Marzi is only an unsuspecting observer, she becomes more aware of politics when important events unfurl before her eyes and begin to affect the life of her family. In the spring and summer of 1988 her father, a worker at the local steel mill, takes part in a series of strikes in which workers demand the relegalization of Solidarity. The strike lasts as long as eleven days and is one of the most important acts of workers' resistance

[54] 'Introduction by Marzena Sowa', in Sylvain Savoia and Marzena Sowa, *Marzi: A Memoir*, trans. by Anjali Singh (London: Vertigo, 2011), pp. i–ii (p. ii).
[55] See e.g. Savoia and Sowa, *Marzi*, pp. 6–7, 40, 104.
[56] Ibid., pp. 14, 17–18, 28, 70.
[57] Ibid., pp. 34–35, 42–44, 55.
[58] Ibid., p. 68; cf. Satrapi, *Persepolis*, p. 14.

in the late 1980s. This is when the little protagonist experiences history in the making and loses some of her innocence as she attempts to understand both her father's and her fatherland's plight:

> We're all in the same boat, say the adults, and we're beginning to feel seriously seasick. We need more arms to speed up our progress, to reach land. And not just any land, but the one that'll suit all of us. One that's the way we want it to be. Open and free, a real home![59]

She learns quickly that national history is intricately bound up with private history, most notably when she experiences the exhilaration of seeing her father leave the factory after a strike lasting eleven days, while the workers celebrate the successful outcome of negotiations, having secured a promise that their demands will be met. The round-table talks ensue in February along with the first parliamentary elections in June 1989, and Marzi's narrative shifts to include insights on freedom, showing at times Sowa's adult perspective when, for example, she tries to explain the battle her nation has just finished fighting, and to define its future trajectory: 'They repeated the news on the radio, on TV. Everyone was talking about it. We were trapped in a nightmare but it's over now and we have to learn to talk about it as the past.'[60] Here the memoir presents a modern, forward-looking vision of the nation which is not afraid to stand on its own two feet, take responsibility for itself, and make the most of its newly gained freedom without looking back.

Sowa's representation of Poland's past is a deeply personal and personalized one. Lending a voice to her younger autobiographical self, she manages to achieve a good balance between presenting the complexities of Polish history and not letting the perspective of a child restrict her thematic choices. Despite depicting iconic events of the 1980s, she avoids providing an over-historicized chronicle of the times by always keeping the story of her growing up at the centre of the narrative. Therefore, national history tends to be treated here as the background to a personal narrative, rather than the main focus of the story, as was the case with the state-sponsored albums discussed above. Sowa's memoir steers clear of the mainstream narratives of the past fostered by the political elites in present-day Poland, and, focusing on the perplexities of childhood in general, it has a more universal appeal. Perhaps this is one of the reasons why *Marzi* has been so popular with its original French-speaking audiences.

Sylvain Savoia's colour illustrations make this memoir a happy one, breaking the stereotypes of greyness and dreariness of Polish life under Communism and captivating the imagination of the reader. Panels of the same size are used consistently throughout the story, bearing a resemblance to photo-

---

[59] Savoia and Sowa, *Marzi*, p. 187.
[60] Ibid., p. 204.

graphs neatly stacked in the family album. According to Dana Mihailescu, this technique is meant to indicate the gradual development of both the life of the Sowa family and Polish society under Communism.[61] The extensive captions can be compared to those found in family albums, making *Marzi* an important artefact documenting personal history, the role of family in one's upbringing, and the impact of politics on the life of a child.

As a graphic novel bringing Polish realities of the 1980s closer to the Western reader, *Marzi* offers a positive, life-affirming representation of a childhood behind the Iron Curtain, where people's values, including family and friendship, turn out to be similar to those of their Western counterparts. Since finishing her work on the series, Sowa has published another graphic novel, this time in co-operation with Sandrine Revel, telling an endearing fictionalized story of growing up in Stalinist Poland.[62] As the following section will show, it is precisely the non-autobiographical works that constitute the most remarkable examples of Polish comic art to come to the fore in recent years.

Fictional Stories about Communism

Although *Marzi* is certainly the most popular graphic account representing the Communist past, it is not the only one. In recent years, as a result of the eruption of the historical trend in Polish comics, some interesting fictional accounts have also appeared. One of them is Jacek Frąś's mini-graphic novel *Stan* (2006), which looks at how the life of a little boy changes on one earth-shattering day under martial law. The author does not give away much, but it is possible to infer that the plot is set on the night between 1 and 2 September 1982 in the small copper-mining town of Lubin in Lower Silesia. We are told that the boy's name is Andrzej and that his father, Tomasz, had apparently sustained a head injury while at work in the local mine. The novel recalls Andrzej's dash to get to the hospital where his father had supposedly been taken. It is after curfew, and on the way he meets several militia officers patrolling the streets. One of them tells him that during a demonstration in town Tomasz has been killed by a shot to the head by a mad officer named Bikerski. When the boy reaches the hospital, he finds his father alive, resting with his head bandaged. They embrace, happy to see each other. Meanwhile, Andrzej's mother reports him missing.

Up to this point, the story of Andrzej's night-time dash is interspersed with documentary-like, six-panel pages presenting his father's friends and

---

[61] Dana Mihailescu, 'The Legacy of Communism through a Child's Lens: The Thrusts of Emotional Knowledge out of Marzi's Poland', in *Literary and Visual Dimensions of Contemporary Graphic Narratives*, ed. by Mária Kiššová and Simona Hevešiová (Nitra: Constantine the Philosopher University Press, 2012), pp. 45–75 (p. 54).

[62] Marzena Sowa and Sandrine Revel, *Dzieci i ludzie* (Poznań: CENTRALA Central Europe Comics Art, 2012).

colleagues sharing their memories of him. It is clear from these reminiscences that years have passed by, the boy has grown up, and his father is now dead. Not only do these accounts supplement the story of Andrzej's childhood distress, they also provide a commentary on the narrative strategies used in the graphic novel. Throughout the main body of the comic the boy's identity is performed visually in the third person since the lack of captions makes it difficult to identify him as the narrator. It is only through the documentary-like memories of other people who address him as they speak that we learn that he is also the person collecting their accounts, and as such controls the overall narrative. The information he provides is intentionally sparse, and it is only the penultimate page of the comic that provides the climax for his narrative. It is a splash page, one out of two in the entire comic, which presents the boy hiding in his neighbour's wardrobe and holding on to his father's photograph. At the bottom of the page we can see a small speech bubble conveying the neighbour's words: 'He was in my wardrobe all this time' (Figure 2).[63] The splash's combination of minimalistic script and artwork, together with the compelling message, can be aptly described with Scott McCloud's term 'amplification through simplification', which he considers to be one of the most powerful tools of comic art.[64] After all, it is this particular page that renders most of the earlier narrative a product of Andrzej's imagination and an expression of bereavement following his father's tragic death. Its simplicity and paucity magnify the sense of loss experienced by the little boy, and provide a powerful closure to the story. The final page, also a splash, constitutes a form of graphic postscript, showing Andrzej with his father and sister, standing with their backs to the reader. Here the narrator uses captions for the first time in the comic and admits that he had known of his father's death from the very beginning but will never accept it, continuing his quest to find him.

Although Frąś's graphic novel can be read as a universal story of loss and anguish following the sudden death of a parent, the historical context is crucial here, providing a trigger which sets the events in motion. Indeed, his narrative alludes to the events of 31 August 1982, when inhabitants of the small town of Lubin came out onto the streets to commemorate the second anniversary of Solidarity, which had been suspended with the imposition of martial law in December 1981. During the peaceful demonstration, three young men were killed, two of them married with children. Despite being based on these true events, *Stan* avoids literality. Frąś understands that there is no one 'correct' version of history, but instead a collection of memories that different people have of a particular event, its victims, and their deaths. By intertwining Andrzej's story with recollections of his father's friends, the

[63] Jacek Frąś, *Stan*, in *Przekrój* (suppl.), 6 December 2006, pp. 1–20 (p. 19).
[64] Scott McCloud, *Understanding Comics: The Invisible Art* (New York: Harper Perennial, 1994), p. 30.

FIG. 2. Jacek Frąś, *Stan*, in *Przekrój* (suppl.), 6 December 2006, p. 19. Courtesy of Jacek Frąś

comic emphasizes the impossibility of creating a unitary narrative of the past. Needless to say, Tomasz himself is an artistic and literary creation, perhaps a synecdochic representation of the three men or a metaphor for all victims of the period of martial law. This subjectivity and plurality of cultural memory are well expressed in the choice of general theme for the novel. The album steers clear of big history and instead presents events that normally remain on the margins of mainstream narratives of the period of martial law. It looks at local histories while avoiding their potentially politicized interpretations. Frąś speculates, for example, on the possible causes of the tragedy as if accounting for the fact that those who shot at demonstrators were never identified. This is how he invents Private Bikerski, a lightweight simpleton and laughing-stock responsible for Tomasz's death, whose motivations are anything but political. While refraining from judging the events at Lubin directly or providing one-dimensional answers to the tragedy, the artist uses his narrative to suggest that not necessarily all incidents of Communist-era violence were based on ideological grounds. Consequently, he demythologizes one of the most powerful narratives in the Polish national discourse, stripping away its martyrological veneer.

The multiplicity of perspectives and openness to various interpretations of history are shown skilfully in the artwork used. For example, Andrzej's childhood story is told in colour using predominantly dark shades, and it employs panels of different shapes and sizes, depending on the situation. The narrative of the militia officer who informs the boy about his father's death is presented in red, chiefly with the use of caricatural, childlike drawings and irregular panel frames. This helps to express the accidental and reckless nature of the shooting, represented on the textual level by the figure of Bikerski. Finally, the reminiscences of Tomasz's friends are presented on pages consisting of six panels of uniform size which use different shades of grey. As such, they express the purported documentary nature of those accounts, while the regularity of the panel frames signals the protagonists' emotional detachment that comes with the passing of time (Figure 3).

Stan is perhaps the greatest achievement of contemporary Polish comic art that deals with the theme of Communism. This comes as no surprise, given that one of Frąś's earlier stories, *Kaczka* (*The Duck*, 2001) was praised for its unconventional take on the Warsaw Uprising and awarded the Prize for Young Talent at the Angoulême International Comics Festival.[65] Despite the emergence of other fictional graphic narratives exploring the Communist period from the perspective of a child, most notably Michał Śledziński's *Na szybko spisane 1980–1990* and Marzena Sowa's new graphic novel *Dzieci i ludzie* mentioned above, to date there have been no works to match Frąś's

[65] For a longer discussion of *Kaczka* see De Bruyn, 'Patriotism of Tomorrow?', pp. 57–58.

Fig. 3. Jacek Frąś, *Stan*, in *Przekrój* (suppl.), 6 December 2006, p. 13. Courtesy of Jacek Frąś

achievement. None the less, his stories have not yet succeeded in attracting a wider readership, and they remain, to some extent, part of the alternative comic scene known to a narrow group of comic specialists and enthusiasts. This leads to broader questions on the efficacy of the historical trend in Polish comics and the future development of the genre.

Conclusion

In post-Communist Poland creators of historical comic books have faced the difficult task of changing the cultural status and common perception of this hybrid genre. As a medium traditionally reserved for fun, propaganda, or fantasy, comics have had to reinvent themselves as a valid form of literary and artistic expression that was 'serious' enough to tackle national history. However, we have seen that this process has been inextricably bound up with the redefinition of national identity and the shifting of the cultural economy following the collapse of Communism. Consequently, the production of historical comic albums has become largely subservient to mirroring dominant narratives of Poland's traumatic past. Graphic accounts adhering to such a vision of history have been mushrooming in Poland, especially between 2005 and 2010, as a result of generous state funding, an annual comic competition organized by the Warsaw Uprising Museum, and the growing importance of certain publishing outlets such as Zin Zin Press. Though in existence, alternative projects exploring fictionalized stories of the past have been less fortunate in attracting government subsidies and not as vital in shaping the popular view of the past. This deliberate politicization of comics made them once more powerful tools of ideological struggle, enforcing fact-based plotlines that were meant to run counter to the propagandistic and 'distorted' stories of the Communist era. Paradoxically, however, it is the fictional graphic narratives, such as Frąś's *Kaczka* or *Stan*, that are beginning to change the face of contemporary comic art in Poland, offering readers the possibility of critical engagement with well-known historical events, nurturing their visual imaginations, and depicting a painful past without trivializing it. With any luck, these stories could be the harbinger of a wider revolution in Polish comic art and mark the beginning of a more open cultural debate about the past.

TRINITY COLLEGE DUBLIN   EWA STAŃCZYK

LOOKING FOR THE CREATOR: PELEVIN AND THE IMPOTENT WRITER IN *T* (2009) AND *ANANASNAIA VODA DLIA PREKRASNOI DAMY* (2011)

> The author was an invisible point from which the books came, a void travelled by ghosts.
> (ITALO CALVINO)[1]

> When characters are alive, truly alive before their author, he has only to follow them in their words and actions, which they precisely suggest to him... And he's in for trouble if he doesn't!
> (LUIGI PIRANDELLO)[2]

> 'What, God enjoys the play? Reads the book of life?'
> 'God does not read the book of life [...] he burns it. And then eats the ash.'
> (VIKTOR PELEVIN)[3]

Viktor Pelevin is known for his iconoclasm; unsurprisingly, therefore, in his 2009 novel, *T*, Pelevin takes the nineteenth-century writer Lev Tolstoi and remakes him mercilessly as a form of action hero. Most obviously, he does so in order to make a point familiar to his readers about the post-glasnost commoditization of high culture, for this version of one of the grand old men of literature is partly a creation of Russian marketeers hoping that a novel about Tolstoi, in his centenary year of 2010, might be profitable. Thus the proponent of non-resistance is transformed into a fighter, T, hero of a pastiche thriller with 'adventures, shooting', and 'erotic scenes', but also with moments of historical retrospective and 'intellectual conversations' (p. 100). T battles free from the gun-toting Knopf to find himself on a boat discussing theology with one Princess Tarakanova, and we meet notables of Russian history and culture, such as the Red Army Commander Vasilii Chapaev, and the philosopher Vladimir Solov'ev. T is also joined by Dostoevskii, now a warlike figure battling 'dead souls', required to act rather like a 'gladiator in a circus' (p. 206) and introduced in a bid to boost potential sales, as Oprah might be recommending a Dostoevskii novel to her viewers (p. 143). In this alternative history, the excommunicated T makes his peace with the Church

---

[1] Italo Calvino, *If on a Winter's Night a Traveller* (1979) (London: Minerva, 1992), pp. 101–02.
[2] Luigi Pirandello, *Six Characters in Search of an Author* (1921), in '*Six Characters in Search of an Author' and Other Plays*, trans. and ed. by Mark Musa (London: Penguin, 1995), p. 56.
[3] Viktor Pelevin, *T* (Moscow: Eksmo, 2009), p. 104. All quotations refer to this edition; translations are mine. Page numbers are given hereafter in parentheses after the quotation.

to facilitate 'product placement' for the latter; spirituality, like literature, has become a commodity to be marketed.[4]

The writer now, Pelevin suggests, operates rather like a computer (a 'Turing machine'), producing texts according to generic formulae. Rather than in the past, when the writer 'absorbed into himself, figuratively speaking, the tears of the world, and then created a text that cut the human soul', now the writer 'must transform his impressions of life into a text that will bring maximum profit' (p. 88). The writer has been replaced by a team of specialists, each responsible for churning out one aspect of the narrative (p. 90).

Here we come to the central concern of the novel: Pelevin asks, 'What *is* authorship, in a (post)modern world?' It is not only that the author now is less creator than 'commodifier', churning out potboilers to make sales. Pelevin also asks whether any remaining vestiges of the author's creative power may have been delegated to the reader or even to the characters. Pelevin's powerful 'action-man' T is a means of introducing the theme of authorial impotence.

Pelevin depicts the relationship between reader, author, and character as collaborative, entering into the list of writers whose prose shows an experimental interest in what Kingsley Amis termed 'buggering about with the author' (when commenting on Martin Amis's 1984 novel *Money*, in which the character 'Martin Amis' himself appears), or what Patricia Waugh more sedately calls the 'exaggeration of authorial presence',[5] part of the move from mimetic fiction to texts of 'process made visible'.[6] This interest in the notion of authorship, of creativity, can be placed within various literary-historical frameworks. It can be defined as a function of modernist experimentation with the notion of viewpoint, both readerly and writerly, as an aspect of anti-mimesis, or as part of a postmodern questioning of identity formation and philosophies of the subject; or as metafictional self-referentiality.[7]

Although Pelevin has labelled his own literary style as 'turborealism' rather than postmodernism, the latter appellation broadly fits his preoccupation with the 'illusion of reality' within which all his characters live, an interest conveyed through an emphasis on solipsism as well as pastiche.[8] In this discussion of

---

[4] Pelevin has created a character named Tolstoi before—in his story 'Sinii fonar'', in which the name applies to a schoolboy adept at telling horror stories.

[5] Patricia Waugh, *Metafiction: The Theory and Practice of Self-Conscious Fiction* (London: Methuen, 1984), p. 131.

[6] Linda Hutcheon, *Narcissistic Narrative: The Metafictional Paradox* (New York: Methuen, 1984), p. 6. See also Andreas Jäger, 'Self-Referentiality in Twentieth-Century Poetry', in *Self-Referentiality in Twentieth-Century British and American Poetry*, ed. by Detlev Gohrbandt and Bruno von Lutz (Frankfurt a.M.: Peter Lang, 1996), pp. 7–23 (p. 8), and Robert Scholes, *Fabulation and Metafiction* (Urbana: University of Illinois Press, 1980).

[7] Patricia Waugh, 'What is Metafiction and Why Are They Saying Such Awful Things about It?', in *Metafiction*, ed. by Mark Currie (London: Longman, 1995), pp. 39–54 (p. 43).

[8] On solipsism in Pelevin's work see Vladimir Gubailovskii, 'Gegel', Evgenii i graf T', *Novyi mir*, 2010, no. 3, 190–99.

Pelevin's work and of some of the contemporary writers whose interest in the author offer some context to Pelevin's own concern with authorship, the broad term 'postmodernist' will be used, to suggest his general preoccupation with a concern that spans both modernism and postmodernism, namely, the issue of consciousness.[9] How this preoccupation manifests itself in the context of the notion of authorship is the focus of the following discussion.

Arguably all Pelevin's work, broadly speaking, can be defined as centred on the theme of consciousness, from his depiction of manipulated perceptions in *Generation 'P'* (1999), or of fragmented self-awareness in *Chisla (Numbers*, 2004),[10] of ideology and illusion in *Sviashchennaia kniga oborotnia (The Sacred Book of the Werewolf*, 2004), to that of self-referentiality in his 2005 *Shlem uzhasa (The Helmet of Horror)* and of the use of 'glamour' to keep humans ignorant of their true status as cattle ruled by vampires in *Empire 'V'*.[11] Political deception is a strong thematic strand: Pelevin's latest book, *Ananasnaia voda dlia prekrasnoi damy (Pineapple Water for a Beautiful Lady)*, which appeared in 2011, satirically portrays the leaders of the USA and Russia as victims of each other's ideological machinations. The text, a collection of novellas and stories, is labelled by Pelevin 'a War and Peace for this epoch, one without peace or war', as international relations are played out in secret, by each side pretending to offer divine or occult advice to the president.[12] The first part of the book details the story of one Semen Levitan, who is hired by two anti-Semitic misanthropes who implant a transmitter tooth into his jaw so that he can communicate with US President George W. Bush as the 'voice of God' (p. 39).[13] During 'Operation Burning Bush' the so-called 'angels' who work with Semen exploit Bush's faith to get him to invade Iraq and Afghanistan, and to do other 'crazy and harmful things' (p. 90). Later we discover that Russian rulers since Stalin have been receiving instructions

---

[9] Sarah Wilson, 'Victor Pelevin's Feminist Polemic: An Intertextual Exploration of (Post-)Soviet Gender and Sexuality' (unpublished honours thesis, Dartmouth University, 2008). Wilson gives a brief overview of critical views on Pelevin's postmodernism, from Andrei Minkevich's suggestion that the term can only be broadly applied, to Sergei Kornev's belief that Pelevin is the founder of 'Russian classical postreflexive postmodernism', to critics such as S. Kuznetsov, P. Basinskii, A. Arkhangel'skii, N. Aleksandrov, or K. Diakova, who tend to deny any postmodernist aspect to Pelevin's work. See <http://74.125.155.132/search?q=cache:L16cOAIwglQJ:pelevin.nov.ru/stati/s-Sarah.Wilson.doc+pelevin+empire+v&cd=19&hl=en&ct=clnk&gl=au> [accessed 9 December 2011]. On the theme of consciousness see S. Dalton-Brown, 'Illusion—Money—Illusion: Viktor Pelevin and the "Closed Loop" of the Vampire Novel', *Slavonica*, 17 (2011), 30–44.

[10] Boris Noordenbos, 'Breaking into a New Era? A Cultural-Semiotic Reading of Viktor Pelevin', *Russian Literature*, 64 (2008), 85–107, examines *Chisla* and *'P'*.

[11] Keith Livers, 'The Tower or the Labyrinth: Conspiracy, Occult, and Empire-Nostalgia in the Work of Viktor Pelevin and Aleksandr Prokhanov', *Russian Review*, 69 (2010), 477–503.

[12] Viktor Pelevin, *Ananasnaia voda dlia prekrasnoi damy* (Moscow: Eksmo, 2011), inside cover. All quotations refer to this edition; translations are mine. Page numbers are given hereafter in parentheses after the quotation. Pelevin also subtitles the book *War and Peace*, although one should note the spelling—*Voin@ i mir*.

[13] Presumably this is a reference to the Stalin-era radio announcer Iurii Levitan.

from the US embassy, and thus the USSR has fallen into ruin ('nizvergalsia vse nizhe', p. 97).[14] Ironically, the voice in one's head *is* real—if neither divine or literally devilish.

The political strand to *Ananasnaia voda* is interwoven with comments on popular culture (post-Soviet 'Capital's' appropriation of Soviet ideology, now become 'marketing'), for both politics and culture are in Pelevin's view equally 'postmodern' (p. 151) in a country in which 'one can steal and use any form' (p. 152). Pelevin adds a further layer to the familiar postmodern world of disconnected unrealities and signifiers by ensuring that his characters are often aware to some degree of how prevalent ideological manipulation is.

The fear deriving from this sense of constantly being deceived is often palpable even in Pelevin's pun-ridden and comedic texts—for how does one know how far such manipulation goes? The greater existential fear is of course that of not knowing how to find any truth at all. One expression of this terrifying state of unknowing is presented in *Shlem uzhasa*: characters trapped in bland rooms in unknown places are reduced to trying to find where they are via an Internet chat room, but are prohibited from giving any concrete details to the others about themselves and their lives. They are in fact trapped in a labyrinth ruled by a minotaur; the labyrinth and the minotaur's helmet are both offered as symbols of the brain, leading to a familiar suggestion by Pelevin that, as the mind is used to understand the mind, confusion—and even terror, as the word 'horror' suggest—is the inevitable result:

the helmet of horror is the contents of the mind, which attempts to supplant the mind by proving that they—the contents—exist, and the mind in which they arise doesn't. Or that the mind is no more than its function.[15]

The above statement suggests a consciousness at war with itself in terms of content and function. In *T*, Pelevin suggests that we read and write (think) ourselves into being; and thus it is impossible to tell where our consciousness begins. We created it, or did it create us? Or perhaps we only *think* we created ourselves. This is our own private labyrinth or endless, questioning loop. It is no wonder that Pelevin once formulated his major concern as that of 'the source of awareness'.[16] The problem of consciousness, of how we can be aware of awareness, the problem of the 'closed loop' of consciousness, of solipsism, is arguably the most enduring motif of Pelevin's work. In *T* this dilemma is examined in terms of authorship, or creative awareness, the *fons et origo* of life-as-text.

[14] As per Andreev's 'Rose of the World', the story goes that Stalin ordered a special room to be prepared in the Kremlin, windowless and faced in red granite, with a throne of Gagtungra, on which he might receive messages from Satan—an opportunity exploited by the United States.

[15] V. Pelevin, *Shlem uzhasa* <http://pelevin.nov.ru/romans/pe-shlem/index.html> [accessed 9 December 2011].

[16] Roger Clarke, 'A Shot of New Russian Spirit', *The Independent on Saturday*, 29 April 2000.

The author's sovereignty has declined ever since Barthes proclaimed his ending in 'The Death of the Author' (1967), and Foucault relegated him to a 'certain functional principle', merely part of the text's structure, in 'What Is an Author?' (1969).[17] As Barthes argues, the author should no longer be regarded as author/authority but as author/scriptor, merely as creator of language. Foucault's formulation of the author function as an interpretative construct implies the author figure both as 'cause and as effect, as arising from the text and as imposed upon it'.[18] For Barthes, the writing subject is born with his text; so is the reader, whose role, with the author's 'death', becomes more important; no longer is the author omniscient or omnipotent, for he has no more power than the reader, or the characters.[19]

Pelevin's novel covers most of the aspects of authorial impotence familiar to readers of Western literature, and which can be expressed as a series of questions: Is the author trapped inside his own mind, and what are the consequences of that entrapment? Is the author able to offer only personal 'truths', if a mimetic depiction of external reality is fatally flawed? Thus, who or what exactly is the 'author'? Who creates textual 'reality', if not a central and knowledgeable author—the reader and/or character? Or is there some other 'creator?'

The following discussion will, with brief reference to Western fiction that looks at the issue of authorship, indicate how Pelevin's *T* and *Ananasnaia voda* show the attempt to find the greater Writer or Creator—or God. In the view of critics such as Konstantin Frumkin, Pelevin's work is a form of religious quest that looks now beyond the Buddhism in which he has demonstrated interest in earlier texts such as *Chapaev i Pustota* (1996—translated both as *Buddha's Little Finger* and as *The Clay Machine Gun*). Thus in Pelevin's latest work, *Ananasnaia voda*, we find:

on the one hand, union with God. On the other, sorting out the Americans. [. . .] how can one fight against money and American imperialism, and at the same time consider the world an illusion? [. . .] [Because] man must fight the seductions of the external world... despite everything being illusory, there is a spiritual reality that one might call God or Mind.[20]

But firstly, before one looks for the creator, the question to be answered is

[17] Michel Foucault, 'What Is an Author?', in *The Foucault Reader* (New York: Pantheon, 1984), pp. 101–20 (pp. 118–19).
[18] Adrian Wilson, 'Foucault on the "Question of the Author": A Critical Exegesis', *Modern Language Review*, 99 (2004), 339–63 (p. 359).
[19] Roland Barthes, *Image, Music, Text*, trans. and ed. by Stephen Heath (London: Fontana, 1977), p. 145. 'The author is no longer in a position of absolute authority over his or her creation' (Wenche Ommundsen, *Metafictions? Reflexivity in Contemporary Texts* (Melbourne: Melbourne University Press, 1993), p. 68).
[20] Konstantin Frumkin, 'Lozhka skrebet po dnu', *Znamia*, 6 (2011) <http://magazines.russ.ru/znamia/2011/6/fr18-pr.html> [accessed 4 May 2013] (page 4 of 4).

whether the writer can actually say anything that is 'real'. Can he mimic reality or is he destined in the (post)modern age merely to create his own very personal version of it—that is, is he 'God'? As Scarlett Thomas suggests in *The End of Mr Y* (2006), a novel that uses particle physics and a narrator called Ariel Manto (an anagram of 'I am not real') to discuss Baudrillard's view of reality as simulacrum, matter can be *thought* into existence.[21] The world is 'made of language' (p. 337) and 'if thought is matter, then everything is real' (p. 394)—and presumably any thinking person can create 'reality'.

Yet the solipsistic writer faces other challenges, discussed most poignantly perhaps by J. M. Coetzee in his 'autobiographical' trilogy *Boyhood: Scenes from Provincial Life* (1997), *Youth* (2002), and *Summertime* (2009)—three texts that are failed confessions[22] in which the author/narrator promises an intimacy—just as he does to the women with whom he has relationships in these texts—that can never be realized.[23] *Boyhood*'s focus on hiding the 'real' self sets the foundation for becoming a 'liar to the world in general'.[24] In *Summertime* there is no truth, merely a set of narratives created by fictioneers, or the novel's six 'authors'.[25] Apart from Coetzee himself, there are four women who describe their relationship with Coetzee, each of whom may be biased; the sixth 'author', the interviewer collecting their stories for his biography of Coetzee, realizes that his work may just be 'women's gossip' (p. 218). But Coetzee's letters and diaries may be even less trustworthy than such biased accounts (pp. 225-26). Coetzee offers a 'conflict of discourses' that 'generate contestation', every thought refracted through others' discourse, and that subverts the notion of autobiography completely. No wonder the novel ends with a laryngectomy—an apt image of the devoicing that Coetzee has taken pains to assume through his deliberately self-neutering narrative form. The author is silenced in his own autobiography, an image of utter impotence.[26]

In Philip Roth's *Operation Shylock: A Confession* (1993) we find an 'other

---

[21] Scarlett Thomas, *The End of Mr Y* (Melbourne: Text, 2006), p. 258.

[22] Coetzee suggested that confession is an ontological mode that focuses on the issue of the author confronting or evading 'the problem of how to know the truth about the self without being self-deceived, and of how to bring the confession to an end in the spirit of [. . .] absolution' (J. M. Coetzee, 'Confession and Double Thoughts: Tolstoy, Rousseau, Dostoevsky', *Comparative Literature*, 37 (1985), 193–232 (p. 194)).

[23] Coetzee 'avoids traditional autobiographical narrative technique by referring to himself in the third person [. . .] thus creating an artificial distance between "author" and "narrator"' (David Coad, 'J. M. Coetzee: *Boyhood: Scenes from Provincial Life*', *World Literature Today*, 72.2 (Spring1998), 442–3 (p. 442)).

[24] J. M. Coetzee, *Boyhood* (London: Vintage, 1998), pp. 18, 29.

[25] J. M. Coetzee, *Summertime* (Sydney: Knopf, 2009), p. 226. Further quotations are taken from this edition.

[26] 'Breyten Breytenbach and the Censor', in *De-Scribing Empire: Post-Colonialism and Textuality*, ed. by Chris Tiffin and Alan Lawson (London: Routledge, 1994), pp. 86–97 (p. 91). See Benita Parry, 'Speech and Silence in the Fictions of J. M. Coetzee', in *Critical Perspectives on J. M. Coetzee*, ed. by G. Huggand and S. Watson (London: Macmillan, 1996), pp. 37–65.

Philip Roth'[27]—an authorial alter ego who travels the world pretending to be the author Philip Roth.[28] Perhaps the impostor is a con artist (p. 111), or someone attempting to exploit Roth's reputation to further the cause of diasporism, or a co-personality, or a 'contending subself' (p. 152). More significantly, he represents an expression of the authorial sense of his own precarious 'existence'—perhaps the author is a 'vacuum into which is drawn your own gift for deceit', as a friend tells Roth (p. 107), or an antidote to the temptation of desubjectification or self-annihilation (p. 114).[29] It seems that he is a form of stylistic analogue, 'what in poetry would be a near rhyme' (p. 187), an authorial clone reflecting the narcissistic condition of 'me-itis... drowning in the tiny tub of yourself' (p. 55) that is, Roth suggests, the condition of authorship.

However, both Roth and Coetzee, despite their visions of silent, or narcissistic, impotence, suggest one way towards authorial 'power', namely the ability to create something 'real', for perhaps the created character is not merely Roth's clone or Coetzee's biased narrator, but something that may acquire 'reality'. In his *New York Trilogy* (1985–86), specifically the first novel *City of Glass*, Paul Auster offers a novel about detection, one strand of which relates to the question of who the author of *Don Quixote* really was. (One notes that also in Auster's novel, Quinn, a writer, states that he 'did not consider himself to be the author of what he wrote'.[30]) On the suggestion that Cervantes attempts to 'convince the reader he is not the author' (p. 67), the case is built that the text was actually written in Arabic by one Benengeli. But Benengeli is actually a composite of four of the novel's characters: Sancho Panza, the barber, the priest, and the bachelor from Salamanca (p. 88). Sabotaging the notion of 'character' itself (p. 230) in order to rework it,[31] Auster offers the idea that the characters themselves have colluded in their own text and have achieved the status of becoming the 'real' writer Benengeli (whom Cervantes would like to be).

Playing with the hierarchy of conventional author–character relationship—

[27] Philip Roth, *Operation Shylock: A Confession* (London: Cape, 1993), p. 17. Further quotations refer to this edition.
[28] Apparently an impostor actually did turn up in Jerusalem, in real life; see Elaine B. Safer, 'The Double, Comic Irony, and Postmodernism in Philip Roth's *Operation Shylock*', *MELUS*, 21.4 (Winter 1996), 157–72 (p. 161).
[29] Elaine M. Kauvar, 'This Doubly Reflected Communication: Philip Roth's "Autobiographies"', *Contemporary Literature*, 36 (1995), 412–46 (p. 413). See also Harold Bloom's 'Operation Roth', *New York Review of Books*, 22 April 1993, pp. 45–48, in which Bloom notes 'the author's experimentation in shifting the boundaries between his life and his work' (p. 45).
[30] Paul Auster, *Collected Novels* (London: Faber & Faber, 2004), p. 6. Further quotations refer to this edition.
[31] William Lavender, 'The Novel of Critical Engagement: Paul Auster's *City of Glass*', *Contemporary Literature*, 34 (1993), 219–39. See also William G. Little, 'Nothing to Go on: Paul Auster's *City of Glass*', ibid., 38 (1997), 133–63.

suggesting characters as authors—is of course not new. Stephen King's *Dark Tower* series, for example, contains characters who meet Stephen King and alter events in the latter's 'real' world, outside of the books. Jasper Fforde reminds us that characters may be autonomous to a degree in his series of novels in which his literary detective Thursday Next is able to enter 'book-worlds', topoi of 'real' action—in *The Eyre Affair* (2001) Thursday defeats nemesis Acheron Hades in the world of *Jane Eyre*—while Fforde's characters (like those in Flann O'Brien's *At Swim-Two-Birds*, 1939) are able to carry on their own private lives when not on story duty.

In Pirandello's *Sei personaggi in cerca d'autore* (*Six Characters in Search of an Author*, 1921) his six characters grapple with the question of how they can really 'live'.[32] They enact a Platonic debate about how representational form (or shadow) links to true or 'real' Form, searching for an author to provide the missing link between that Form and their form within the world of drama. Moving from life into Form, they achieve a more 'real' form of life through the fictional process, for the '"self" does not exist a priori but must be continuously created'.[33] However, the author himself at times 'must follow his characters' when they appear 'alive' before him.[34] One amusing example of such 'following' appears in Tom Robbins's partly picaresque *Even Cowgirls Get the Blues* (1976), in which the reader encounters a therapist named Dr Robbins, who is asked to counsel the protagonist, hitch-hiker Cissy Henshaw. Rather than treating Cissy, Dr Robbins is impressed by her to the point where he calls her the 'yeast and butter of the loaf of his being'.[35] Robbins, the therapist/writer, theoretically in charge of his character Sissy's mental health/destiny, is envious of her freedom. Sissy is a nomad, a hitch-hiker, and in her constant hitch-hiking, can perhaps 'conquer time' (presumably through conquering space) and so become more 'authentic' than certainly Robbins the therapist feels he is (pp. 220–21) The author Robbins, unhappy at being bound by time and by his own *fabula*, 'hitches a ride' perhaps on his free-spirited character.

The character might be able to embody some form of potency unattainable to the author, to 'live beyond the text' in which the author himself is trapped. The problem, however, is that the character might in fact wish to *destroy* his or her author, indeed, perhaps must do so in order to attain power. As Brian McHale has suggested, characters can serve as agents of *metalepsis*, or

---

[32] James V. Biuno, *Moments of Selfhood: Three Plays by Luigi Pirandello* (New York: Peter Lang, 1990), pp. 12, 61.

[33] M. John Stella, *Self and Self-Compromise in the Narratives of Pirandello and Moravia* (New York: Peter Lang, 2000), p. 7.

[34] Ibid., p. 56.

[35] Tom Robbins, *Even Cowgirls Get the Blues* (London: Bantam, 1990), p. 245. See Laurence Gerald, 'Basking Robbins: An Interview with Tom Robbins' <http://www.sirbacon.org/4membersonly/robbins.htm> [accessed 17 June 2011] (question 4).

violation of narrative levels, due to their awareness of the recursive structures in which they find themselves. Some demonstrate not only such awareness strongly, but can even mock their creator—as in *Money*, in which Martin Amis's protagonist calls Martin Amis a 'little smirkbag'.[36] McHale refers to Muriel Sparks's *The Comforters* (1957), in which the heroine resists the progress of the novel, trying to spoil it.[37] There are other examples: in Jonathan Safran Foer's *Everything Is Illuminated* (2002) the narrator Alex refuses to follow the advice on how to write of the writer character who has created him.[38] In Flann O'Brien's *At Swim-Two-Birds* the writer Trellis is drugged and tortured by his own characters. And in Bret Easton Ellis's *Lunar Park* (2005) the protagonist, Bret Easton Ellis (BEE), is tormented by a Patrick Bateman lookalike who is committing the same series of crimes of which Ellis wrote in his own novel *American Psycho*. In Chapter 11, when BEE is confronted by a detective with news of the crimes, and begins to panic at the thought of his own potential victimhood, the irony of the detective's statement that he has nothing to fear, for he is 'not a character in the book', sets up the reader's understanding of BEE's terror.[39] Bringing himself into a horror novel suggests an extreme form of authorial impotence, further emphasized by the use of a character with the same name as the actual author. This hints at a creativity/destruction linkage between the author and his/her character—one that Pelevin approaches in his own work.

Destruction is a topic that Pelevin links to the 'dark forces' of marketing and ideology. Firstly, as briefly mentioned, 'Miten′ka's marketing team' (mechanically churning out generic pieces of text) has turned a thinker, would-be ascetic and pacifist into a gun-toting narrative cliché. Miten′ka's group are presumably identifiable as that 'choir of dark essences, chasing terrifying goals' (p. 28) to which Pelevin refers, and work with Ariel′, an angel hoping to rise again (p. 48). Ariel′, suggesting that 'nobody has free will', describes man as ruled by dark, base instincts:

In reality human decisions are worked out in dark corners of the mind to which science cannot penetrate, and are accepted mechanically and unconsciously, as in an industrial robot that measures and punches holes. And that which we call 'human individuality' simply stamps onto these decisions its own stamp, with the words 'I confirm!' (p. 176)

Such instincts, as Pelevin has suggested in other texts, allow the forces of ideology or marketing to manipulate the populace. When T argues that he is no marketing creation, but really exists—'I am not merely some creation ruled by dark forces'—Ariel′ tells him that this sense of being real is merely

---

[36] Martin Amis, *Money: A Suicide Note* (London: Cape, 1984), p. 347.
[37] Brian McHale, *Postmodernist Fiction* (New York and London: Methuen, 1987), pp. 121–22.
[38] Jonathan Safran Foer, *Everything Is Illuminated* (London: Hamilton, 2002), p. 179.
[39] Bret Easton Ellis, *Lunar Park* (London: Picador, 2005), p. 124.

another creation of Ariel''s (pp. 177–78). Stating that 'reality and unreality are defined by my will', Ariel' explains that he is T's chief creator (p. 90).

Yet Ariel' himself feels that he is a 'marionette'—although he does add the proviso that he is a marionette with a 'very complex mechanism' (p. 176).[40] For Ariel', a 'hero, whose role is to be an author' (p. 340), achieving the role of an author is a difficult task. After all, he has been created by Pelevin presumably with a hint towards Shakespeare's sprite from *The Tempest*, servant to Prospero. Prospero eventually sets Ariel free, but for Pelevin, this is not quite so easy to do.

Ariel' has another identity apart from that of 'fallen angel', sprite, or 'marketeer'. One might note at this point that if the character is more 'real' or more powerful than his/her author, this is not to say he has any particular potency in the sense of stability, self-awareness, or ability to contain chaos into narrative form. In postmodernist theory the notion of 'character', as Thomas Docherty notes, is dominated by 'disappearance'; character never *is*, but is always *about-to-be*, endlessly deferred, fragmented, elusive, less an epistemological conundrum than an ontological one in terms of which the fictionality of the characters (and text) can be called into question.[41] Postmodern characters tend to be protean, disparate, decentred, multidimensional, changeable, created within an environment of imposture.[42]

No one has expressed this better than Douglas Coupland (occasionally linked to Pelevin in terms of being equally 'Zeitgeisty'), and whose characters, for example in *JPod* (2006), are still unreal or fictive. (They are, however, despite their fictiveness, able to mock their creator, who places 'himself' into the text as author Douglas Coupland, a 'professional liar'.[43]) Coupland's characters are 'pod people' (a reference to the dehumanized characters of the 1956 film *Invasion of the Body Snatchers*), and products of a particularly commodified existence, in one scene even writing 'product descriptions' of themselves as if about to be marketed on eBay. They live an increasingly virtual life in cyberspace, and each is a type, representing contemporary social issues (diets,

---

[40] Vasilii Kostyrko, 'Dva L'va', *Novyi mir*, 2010, no. 3, 1–5 <htpp://magazines,russ.ru/novyi_mir/2010/3/ko15.html> [accessed 1 December 2011], argues that Brakhman and T are in fact doubles (p. 2) and that the novel may be a dream by Count Leo Tolstoi himself (p. 3). See also M. V. Zagidullina, 'Mutatsiia otsenki: temporal'nyi transfer klassicheskogo teksta (romany V. Pelevina *T* i B. Akunina *F.M.*)', *Russian Literature*, 69 (2011), 157–68.

[41] Thomas Docherty, 'Postmodern Characterization: The Ethics of Alterity', in *Postmodernism and Contemporary Fiction*, ed. by E. Smyth (London: Batsford, 1991), pp. 169–88 (pp. 169, 172).

[42] Walter Anderson, *The Future of the Self: Inventing the Postmodern Person* (New York: Putnam, 1997), p. 34; see also Kenneth Gergen, *The Saturated Self: Dilemmas of Identity in Contemporary Life* (New York: Basic, 1990), p. 69.

[43] Douglas Coupland, *Jpod* (London: Bloomsbury, 2006), p. 325. In the first full-length study of Coupland, Andrew Tate sees such (negative) authorial insertion of self into text as 'a sign of Coupland's willingness to critique his own reputation', but also suggests that it (obviously) raises questions about 'authority, identity and originality' (Andrew Tate, *Douglas Coupland* (Manchester: Manchester University Press, 2007), pp. 164–65).

instant gratification, conformity, etc.). Coupland creates deliberately inauthentic characters, and then places himself into the narrative as a deliberately 'inauthentic' author to suggest that all are equally 'unreal' in a commodified universe in which everything is ultimately a creation of marketing. No wonder that in *The Counterlife*, Philip Roth has his character Zuckerman state that everyone is the invention of everyone else.[44]

Pelevin's characters are usually fragmented, undermined as authentic, or multiplied in some way, such as his Alisa Li, whose name is a pun on the phrase 'is she really a fox?' (*a lisa li?*) and who swaps different identities like 'dresses' in *Sviashchennaia kniga oborotnia*. Thus Ariel' may be various things, including being Ariel' Edmundovich Brakhman, to whom Pelevin refers when discussing a form of afterlife for writers. There is a certain amount of humorous ludism in all this, as characters adopt deceptive or carnival identities,[45] but Pelevin has a more serious message as well, relating to authorial identity as weakly indeterminate. Pelevin suggests that authors become shades in a limbo or hell (presumably the first circle of Dante's inferno, reserved for writers):[46]

> There once lived Count Tolstoi, who by will brought into motion an entire dance of shadows. No doubt he thought he had dreamt them up himself, but in actuality they were souls of scribblers who [. . .] were paying for their sins, for Odysseus, Hamlet, Madame Bovary and Julian Sorel. And after his death Count Tolstoi himself began to play such a role. Now he has become a rider in a blue uniform, travelling to Optina pustyn'. The world, where the Count [. . .] travels to an unclear goal, has been thought up by Ariel' Edmundovich Brakhman, who after his own death awaits such a fate. Thus one cannot say that Ariel' Edmundovich Brakhman in actual fact created Count T, although he appears to be his creator. (p. 68)

The final sentence contradicts Brakhman/Ariel''s assertion that he has created T. Ariel' merely *thinks* he is a creator. Writers are destined apparently to return to the world of fiction after their death, in some form of closed loop—a very familiar image to readers of Pelevin. Thus Ariel' may have been the writer Brakhman, who then became the character Ariel'. The same applies to T, created by Ariel' and others, but who wishes also to become an author.

Pelevin suggests, by introducing the notion of an afterlife, that what the author really seeks might not even be reality, whatever that is, or the power to understand and depict it, but immortality—not only to live, but to live for ever. Yet the closed loop is an endless loop—being trapped inside it is not immortality, but endless repetition.

A further problem other than that of the closed loop (or 'shadow dance')

---

[44] See Timothy Parrish, 'Introduction: Roth at Mid-Career', in *The Cambridge Companion to Philip Roth*, ed. by Parrish (Cambridge: Cambridge University Press, 2007), pp. 1–8.

[45] On the trickster trope in Pelevin see Mark Lipovetsky, *Charms of the Cynical Reason: The Trickster's Transformations in Soviet and Post-Soviet Culture* (Boston: Academic Studies Press, 2011), pp. 233–75.

[46] Or Solzhhenitsyn's *V kruge pervom* (*The First Circle*, 1968).

can now be introduced. We might now ask whether it is actually the reader who has the power to 'create', if the character and author are caught in some form of impotent loop. Ariel', as well as being a sprite or angel, is also described as a child of the Stalinist times, and as the grandson of a cabbalist. As the latter, he offers an opportunity for Pelevin to discuss the notion of 'divine language':

> Grandfather explained that since ancient times Jewish mystics have believed that our entire world was created by the thought of God. The Greeks knew the same [. . .] Xenophon stated, 'without force, by the strength of mind he shakes the world' [. . .] Man, grandfather said, is a history told in a divine language, of which the languages of earth are but pale shadows [. . .] The writer, describing a world that doesn't exist with the help of the alphabet, does practically the same as the creators of the universe [. . .] [thus] the false hero of some women's romance or other is no less real from the divine point of view than passengers in the Metro who read that romance. Moreover, a fictional person is possibly even more real than an ordinary person. For man is a book that God reads only once. But the hero of a novel appears as many times as the novel is read by different people. (pp. 63–65)

Pelevin, typically, renders this notion of the reader as creator more complicated. T appropriates the idea, allegedly of the philosopher Vladimir Solov'ev, that 'a man busy with mystical matters should as it were divide himself into a book and its readers' (p. 210), thus finding, as well as one's own narrative, 'the reader in oneself' (p. 213). At a meeting of the followers of Solov'ev, T hears of the attempt to 'sense the reader in ourselves—that secret force, creating us at the very same moment as we read' (pp. 297–98). Although Pelevin's marketeers believe 'that any attempt to weave the reader into the fabric of the narrative would not be interesting to the broad mass' (p. 256), Solov'ev urges T to believe that he is:

> not a line in the Book of Life, but its reader. That light that renders the page visible. And the essence of all earthly tales lies in the fact that eternal light trudges behind the daubings of paltry authors [. . .] only the light can know, in which the fate of the lights lies. (p. 296)

Pelevin makes a philosophical point that the purpose behind literature—the 'light'—is the familiar and indeed old-fashioned one of illuminating our life, to allow us to come closer to an understanding of why we were created. This renders reader and character alike in quest.

The notion of light suggest Pelevin's interest in religious philosophy, particularly Eastern philosophy, running alongside his concern with those forces of capitalism and politics that perpetuate man's ignorance, keeping him from seeing the 'light'.[47] Solov'ev is linked to the concept of the man-god—man both revolts against God and yet is the equal of God; he is a fallen being in a

---

[47] Jasper Fforde has suggested in *First among Sequels* (London: Hodder & Stoughton, 2007) that

finite universe, yet carries that seed of the absolute that will allow him to save the fallen world and return to the divine. The man-god is both created, and yet potentially a creator.

T (apart from saying that he can 'create Ariel''s world' just as 'Ariel' created his') offers a Solov'evian statement of sorts on the divinity in man: 'There is only one ray of light, running through all that exists. Through him who writes the Book of Life, and him who reads it, and him about whom the Book narrates. And this ray of light is I myself' (p. 374).

Yet Pelevin creates Solov'ev as a character who states that reality is a mixture of truth and lies, for 'truth always depends on the beholder' (p. 337); after all, 'all practical substantiations of this reality were a part of that very reality that they substantiated' (p. 339). How do we even create a self that might seek the divine? Pelevin offers a brief revision of the famous Cartesian *cogito ergo sum*:

> Descartes was right in the sense that this 'I' exists only to that point when he thinks about it. He should have said not 'I think', but 'Think I'. But this very 'I' cannot think or exist, because it ceases as soon as Descartes stops thinking about it, having decided to drink some red wine. (p. 159)

To illustrate this point, that the self-created person has to think about his/her self in order to have a self that might create the self to seek the Creator, Pelevin's character T winks out of existence, but then manages to again appear out of nowhere, through frantically thinking about tangible details, making his memories more real until he gains 'reality'. T manages to think up pen, desk, paper, and a room for himself (pp. 161–62), writing himself into being. Punning on the notion of a 'self-made man', Pelevin suggests that the paradox of existence is based on circularity:

> a new entity arises simultaneously with that action through which it manifests itself [. . .] This action has neither basis, nor conditionality. It proceeds of its own will, completely spontaneously, outside of the laws of cause and effect—and becomes its own support. It is like the birth of the universe out of nothing. After this we can say that we create ourselves. (p. 222)

Thus 'life really is like a text that we create as we breathe' (p. 160). The problem for Pelevin is that of entrapment within this circular process, for 'one mirror reflects another... [. . .]having understood this, you will immediately see how the trap of this world is made. [. . .] It means that consciousness looks at consciousness, pretending to be something else. One mirror reflects another' (p. 270). Looking for a creative Origin seems a futile task, therefore.

if 'reading is believing' (p. 54) then fiction is almost a religious activity, a quest to see if 'we are just part of a bigger story that we can't see'; were we 'created by the Grand Panjandrum', or are we 'merely in the mind of the grand Panjandrum' (p. 260)? Like Borges's characters in 'The Library of Babel' (1941), in which the universe is a library containing all possible texts, we are driven to seek a coherent narrative, seeking our creation myth.

Yet Pelevin still seeks. His interest in spiritual matters, evident from texts in which he refers to Buddhism and Babylonian religions, for example, as well as to folk beliefs, is apparent also in both his recent works *Ananasnaia voda* and *T*. In the former, Pelevin appears interested in the circularity of religious belief—man believes in what he has himself created through his own belief—and also in the hallucinatory quality of divine visions.[48] His protagonist in the first part of the book (through liberal drug usage) comes to see that 'God is the only soul in the world, and all other consciousnesses are only mechanisms dancing within that soul, and He personally fills each of these mechanisms with Himself, and He fills each entirely' (p. 56). Realizing that God is a higher form of love, he suggests a familiar Pelevinian circularity:

One cannot say about this love, who is its subject or its object, because if you try and trace its end and its beginning you understand that there is nothing apart from it, and you yourself are the same as it... for you and He—are one. (p. 57)

This is a little different from the morose statement in *T* that 'we create the gods just as much as they us', and that man is just a 'theatrical suit' worn in turn by men and gods, who seem no more than actors (p. 28). T is told, 'Man thinks himself God, and he's right, because God is within him. He thinks himself a pig—and he's right again, because there's a pig also in him. But man makes a real mistake when he takes his inner pig to be God' (p. 358). Between the notions of man as pig and man as part of divine love there is clearly some distance.

The question of who is the author, and of his impotence, can now be rephrased along the lines of whether Pelevin really does believe in any loving Creator, greater than the man he depicts in his texts as ignorant, animalistic, and criminal; of whether man can be saved from his state of unknowing, and from his closed loop of consciousness, by a Creator. Pelevin expressed something partly similar to this notion in an interview in 2002:

Well, Buddhism seemed to me to be the only religion that didn't resemble the projection of the Soviet power onto the domain of spirit. It was only much later that I understood that it was exactly the other way around—the Soviet power was an attempt to project the alleged heavenly order onto Earth. Well, Buddhism was totally out of this vicious circle and there was something so strangely compelling and soothing about it.[49]

---

[48] See Aleksandr Kuz'menkov, 'Plastilinovoe evangelie', *Ural*, 5 (2011) <http:/magazines.russ.ru/ural/2011/5/ku21.html> [accessed 5 December 2011]. S. Kostyrko, in his review of the novel, sees it as a text about external politics, IT as a weapon, the mutation of the contemporary intellectual-patriot, and 'the transformation of the very idea of God in contemporary society' with Pelevin's talent being for 'artistic examination of the metaphysics of a technologically organized social, political, and economic life' (*Novyi mir*, 2011, no. 3 <http://magazines.russ.ru/novyi_mir/2011/3/kn21-pr.html> [accessed 9 December 2011]).

[49] Leo Kropywiansky, 'Interview with Victor Pelevin', *BOMB*, 79 (Spring 2002) <http://bombsite.com/issues/79/articles/2481> [accessed 9 December 2011].

In *T*, we are told that T was created 'to come to salvation through all this. To be saved from that place where there is no hope, where there is not and cannot be any salvation' (p. 346). The creation of a quest narrative, with T attempting to reach Optina pustyn' while chased by the deadly agent Knopf, is ironic in this context (as is Ariel''s likening of T to Raskol'nikov, for there is no religious epiphany offered to the former, as there is for the latter).

In *T*, Pelevin suggests that if we have created the gods, we have created ourselves to be destroyed, not saved. When 'Dostoevskii' asks T whether 'we exist as gladiators in a circus [. . .] run by cruel and capricious gods', T responds that it is 'worse, for we live to feed the gods. Like rabbits' (p. 206), a telling image of hopelessness and of being hunted—for after all, 'God is the eater of people' (p. 335). One of Pelevin's most chilling images occurs when in response to the question 'What, God enjoys the play? Reads the book of life?' Ariel' replies, 'God does not read the book of life [. . .] he burns it. And then eats the ash' (p. 104). Thus 'man is a temporary distortion of emptiness, and as 'the consciousness that man considers his own is actually God's', God is, therefore, emptiness, and so 'the most ineffable quality of God lies in the fact that there is no God' (pp. 299–300).

This does not bode well for Pelevin's search for any Origin, as it would appear that man remains trapped within the creator/destroyer endless cycle of life and narrative, locked within a self-destructive loop, one empty of any 'reality'. No wonder that in *Ananasnaia voda dlia prekrasnoi damy* Pelevin turns to an image of the creator/destroyer, the Hindu god Kali.

And yet: the notion of emptiness, central to Buddhist thought, is essential for liberation from the confines of the self and the attainment of enlightenment. Thus Pelevin suggests greater focus on that sense of being that comes often through Eastern meditation, where the I ceases to be important. At the end of *T*, T himself realizes that 'While I think "I am T", I am working as an accomplice in Ariel''s office. But as soon as I shorten the thought to "I am", I immediately see the real author, and the final reader' (p. 368). The idea is not to create a self, but simply to accept one's existence without claiming any individual understanding. This bypasses the notion of the mirrored consciousness that examines itself; there is simply a sense of being, rather than a self that sees that it exists.

Yet the ending to *T* offers us a final, ambiguous, and only potential epiphany. Travelling in a peasant cart across the steppe, T wonders if he sees God, that 'which is neither light nor dark' (p. 381). The horse tells him that as 'author, you must decide where the last full stop will be' (p. 382). These two contradictory statements, that T looks for a creator, yet is the one who will create ending in the book of the text/life, introduce the final paragraph, a brief meditation on an insect (a *bukashka*) which looks like a small green man praying to the sun:

> Most likely, there was no meaning in these movements. But perhaps the insect wanted to say that it is quite insignificant in comparison with the raspberry sphere of the sun and of course there could be no comparison between them, But the strange thing is that this huge sun together with everything else in the world in some strange way arises and disappears in a meek creature sitting in a ray of sunlight. And this means it is impossible to say what the insect, and the sun, and this bearded man in a cart (that has almost vanished in the distance), really are—because any words would be a stupidity, a dream, and a mistake. And all this was clear from the movements of four insect legs, from the quiet rustle of the wind in the grass, and even from the quiet that arose when the wind died down. (p. 383)

The solipsistic nature of the insect being able to create the 'huge sun together with everything else in the world' is placed with a final statement of authorial impotence. The writer, Pelevin suggests, might find his salvation in silence. Given that he has taken 383 pages to come to this conclusion, the reader can only take comfort in a certain sense of irony.

Yet Pelevin is not done with this problem, returning to it in *Ananasnaia voda dlia prekrasnoi damy*—a title that at first makes one think of Symbolist mysticism, or the yearning for that female embodiment perhaps of Sophia or wisdom that we find in the poetry of Aleksandr Blok about his 'beautiful lady' (*prekrasnaia dama*). Here Pelevin offers further comment on salvation from the closed loop of consciousness.

Whereas critics Gennadii Barkhudaev and Evgenii Kriuchko see Pelevin as a game-master, his text dealing with the 'instructions' for (and mechanisms of) the game of life, Frumkin argues for the text as an expression of Pelevin's 'disappointment' in Buddhism, based on the problem already identified in *T*, of the self: Buddhism 'denies the reality of the human I, seeing the person as also as illusion… so who must escape illusion, if there is no "who"?'[50] In *Ananasnaia voda* Pelevin turns to Hinduism and to Greek philosophy, in search of spiritual enlightenment, namely a state that predicates 'no-self'.

This collection of novellas and stories depicts in microcosm Pelevin's authorial preoccupations, as it takes the reader through depictions of the dark forces of politics and capitalism, to philosophical musings on the nature of the self and of creation. Thus we have a few comments on the 'new dark age' that awaits, one in which:

---

[50] Frumkin, 'Lozhka skrebet po dnu', page 3 of 4; G. Barkhudaev and E. Kriuchko, 'Fiktivnyi realizm', *Znamia*, 7 (2011) <http://magazines.russ.ru/znamia/2011/7/ba18.html> [accessed 9 December 2011] (page 8 of 15). See also Aleksandr Chantsev, 'Strasti po Danilu', *Novyi mir*, 2011, no. 8 <http:/magazines.russ.ru/novyi_mir/2011/8/ch15-pr.html> [accessed 9 December 2011] (page 2 of 9), and Aleksei Kolobrodov, 'Charodei I ucheniki', *Volga*, 1–2 (2011) <http://magazines.russ.ru/volga/2011/1/ko17.html> [accessed 18 December 2012].

there will be no ambiguous Christian God—but only transnational arks, hidden in dark waters [. . .] [which] will take mankind to such a degree of filth that divine empathy towards man will become technically impossible—and the earth will have to burn again in fire. (p. 231)

Against this fatalism, Pelevin suggests that imagination is stronger than nature and death (p. 193). Thus even if there is no God, man still has his own powers of creation.

Pelevin focuses at first in *Ananasnaia voda* on political ideology, the first section of the collection dealing with 'Operation Burning Bush' and the exploitation of President Bush's faith to get him to invade Iraq and Afghanistan—the irony being that Russian rulers since Stalin have been receiving instructions from the US. The notion of psychological warfare is developed in the second piece in *Ananasnaia voda*, 'Freedom Liberator', about a Pentagon military computer system developed for military jet fighters that mimics the human brain (to which American talk shows have been uploaded in order to give it 'human experience', p. 170). When emotion is evoked in the neural net (p. 190), the machine possibly wakes to full consciousness, leading to a discussion of the question 'What is man?': is he a creator who can endow his creations, such as machines, with a soul? Does that mean that he himself has a soul, and does he therefore also have a creator? Or is he just the creation of political and cultural manipulation?

Pelevin suggests that 'man has no constant essence' ('nikakoi postoiannoi sushchnosti u cheloveka net'), nor a soul, but argues that in order to see that one does *not* have a soul, man in fact needs to possess one (p. 194). We find ourselves back at that insoluble knot at which Pelevin worries in every text.

Pelevin also returns to the notion of the 'shadow dance' mentioned in *T*, now given a fuller expression via references to Plato in the fourth text in the *Ananasnaia* collection, the story 'The Shadow Watcher' (Sozertsatel' teni'). Tour guide Oleg, in India with a group of Muscovites, hears about the legend of the 'shadow speaker'—'if one concentrates long enough on the shadow, it will answer and show truth' ('dolgo kontsentrirovat'sia na teni, ona otvetit na voprosy i pokazhet istinu', p. 242). Oleg does in fact begin to talk with a shadow, who explains that Oleg is also a 'shadow that he has taken to be self' (p. 266) and who introduces the well-known Platonic image of humanity chained in a cave, able to see only the shadows that a fire casts on the wall before them, and so accepting shadows for reality.

This may be all there is for man: namely, a shadow dance or a cave of shadows, for he is unfit for more. The second section of the collection opens with a quotation from Plato's Doctrine of Truth: 'If you force him to stare into the light itself, will his eyes not hurt, and will he not run back to that which he is able to see, considering that this is more authentic than those things which he has now been shown?' (p. 237). Pelevin is in a familiar solipsistic vein when he tells us that reality is created by us, and is therefore fragile and ephemeral:

> the world thought up by him [Oleg] would vanish as simply and naturally as a shadow when you turned off the light. The world in which Oleg had spent his entire life really was a shadow... and nothing was known of anything beyond it.... The light became invisible when the world it illuminated went away, and any questions on the subject would then disappear too, as there was nobody to ask or answer about it. (pp. 284–85)[51]

Pelevin suggests that man should perhaps accept that life is a shadow. This is in broad terms similar to the Hindu notion of *maya*, or illusion, which shrouds reality from our sight (p. 278)—*maya* equating to Platonic 'appearance', in other words.[52] The dualistic metaphysics of the Vedas and Upanishads, as well as other sacred Hindu texts, parallels the Platonic idea of man's limitation to a material world while aware of the greater spiritual reality he can only partially glimpse or comprehend.

Yet Hinduism suggests that one's self (*atman*) might merge with a transcendent self (*paramatman*); Buddhism suggests that once attachment to the self is removed, one may approach the unbounded eternal. Both offer a mystical path of 'no-self' in the journey to enlightenment, to a vision of the divine.[53] Pelevin's 'disappointment' with Buddhism may be only superficial, in that he still espouses a similar, Eastern methodology in the pursuit of wisdom. Pelevin's Zen Buddhism has a strong emphasis on praxis, i.e. on meditation and mental exercises (*koan*s, or riddles);[54] and his stay at a Buddhist monastery in South Korea, for example, is one he discussed in terms of meditation practices rather than doctrine.[55] Pelevin sums up what Buddhism means to him when he argues for such praxis:

> I can't really say I study Buddhism. I'm not a Buddhologist. I can't even say I'm a Buddhist in the sense of rigidly belonging to a confession or a sect, following rituals, et cetera. I only study and practice my mind for which the Dharma of Buddha is the best tool I know: and it is exactly what the word Buddhism means to me. And I also

---

[51] In addition, Oleg suggests, the world is designed in such a way that 'as soon as someone seriously gets interested in the question of the meaning of creation, then he disappears unnoticed, and creation continues' (p. 290).

[52] A. N. Marlow, 'Hinduism and Buddhism in Greek Philosophy', *Philosophy East and West*, 4 (1954), 35–45 <http://ccbs.ntu.edu.tw/FULLTEXT/JR-PHIL/marlow.htm> [accessed 11 December 2011].

[53] Frumkin argues that Pelevin has moved from Tibet to India, and has changed his stance a little on what might be 'real': 'Yes, reality is illusory, yes, the individual is illusory, so there only exists the original spiritual reality which one might call God or Mind, and everything else is a dream' ('Lozhka skrebet po dnu', page 3 of 4).

[54] Joseph Mozur, 'Viktor Pelevin: Post-Sovism, Buddhism, and Pulp Fiction', *World Literature Today*, 76.2 (Spring 2002), 58–67 (p. 63).

[55] Jason Cowley, 'Victor Pelevin', *New York Times*, 50 (March 2000) <http://www.jasoncowley.net/interviews/I200003_P.html> [accessed 11 December 2012], states that Pelevin referred to the importance of the 'practice' of Buddhism—while also stating that he accepts the 'morality' of Buddhism.

totally accept the moral teaching of Buddhism because it is the necessary condition of being able to practice your mind. But it is not too different from the moral teachings of other traditions.[56]

Perhaps what Pelevin really appears to be seeking is a 'practice of the mind' that leads to the overcoming of mind, or self within a moment of *nirvana*, or spiritual enlightenment (a term that belongs to both Hinduism and Buddhism). In the final piece of the *Ananasnaia voda* collection, 'The Hotel of Good Incarnations' ('Otel' khoroshikh voploshchenii'), Pelevin describes reality as 'only the discharge between [an angel's] horns' (p. 347).[57] The reference to the angel suggests a writer still grappling with the notion of man as a divine creation, and offering as partial solution the idea of 'thinking beyond self'. Having suggested that the beautiful lady of the novel's title is no incarnation of wisdom, as she will never really know anything (not even the taste of pineapple water) because she is 'less' than her creator, the angel describes the lady as the 'house of my dreams, a live space, where I might think selflessly ('zhiznennoe prostranstvo, gde ia mogu samozabvenno dumat", p. 347). The entire novel is presumably a creation of a textual space within which the author attempts self-forgetfulness, a 'live space' in order to think in a way that is not entirely consumed by Roth's 'me-itis'.

Imagination may offer a glimpse of divine creativity, and allow one to transcend to a very limited degree one's own cave of shadows, and approach some sort of mystical awareness. The final lines of this story, and of the collection, may support this. Pelevin concludes with 'and all again became That, which was and always would be' ('stalo Tem, chto bylo i budet vsegda', p. 349), an almost Chekhovian line that hints at an endless and repeated cycle that cannot be combated, yet with an overtone of divine awareness in the capitalization of 'Tem'. The author, much as the Romantics did, seems now merely to be trying to glimpse that absolute or perfect beauty, some form of that Sublime that contains the divine spark from which their own creativity, like Creation, is derived.

Pelevin comes no closer to 'unlooping' his endless and solipsistic loop, but reminds his readers that the writer writes because he eternally strives to do so, practising the state of 'no-mind'. He may therefore be, himself, impotent, but in his creativity he may yet occasionally glimpse eternal Creativity—whatever that is. Pelevin suggests an Eastern mysticism that aims at self-forgetfulness.

This path is, however, not easy. His character Oleg still seeks the light, being particularly interested in the Platonic section dealing with man being freed

---

[56] Leo Kropywiansky, 'Interview with Victor Pelevin', p. 78.

[57] Pelevin likes this image—Oleg views his thoughts as created between the two tips of a moon (p. 288), an image similar to that in *T*, in which consciousness is described as like the 'tension between magnetic poles' (p. 158).

to look into the sun itself.[58] Believing that he, Oleg, is the Creator (p. 287), he 'wakes' the light within him, for 'God is light, flickering from one sacred book to another. And people were also light—but the light slept and dreamt of the dark' (p. 287). The task of waking the 'light' offers the difficulty that it is unclear to Oleg whether he is in fact asleep and dreaming—the light may not be 'real'.

Oleg turns to Hinduism, to the god Shiva, simultaneous creator and destroyer, who possessed both the flame that enlivens and destroys the material world, and also the veil of *maya*. This may be a hint that one can only choose to worship both the cycle of creation/destruction itself and the ignorance or illusion it creates—in other words, one accepts the mystical, the blindness of such belief.

As Flaubert stated in *Madame Bovary*, the author's task—indeed, the task of anyone attempting to make sense of this life—is a lesson in frustration and impotence, for 'human speech is like a cracked kettle on which we tap crude rhythms for bears to dance to, while we long to make music that will melt the stars'.[59] Like his fellow authors who also struggle with authorial impotence, Pelevin has no particular answer to this postmodern problem, but unlike his Western counterparts, he hints at his literary context in continuing that familiar (and very nineteenth-century Russian) spiritual search for answers to the 'eternal questions' of who we are, and what life is really all about. A state of 'not knowing' is to be embraced, for it brings us closer to the divine mystery of life. Perhaps we can only know that we do not know, but maintain hope that truth might be out there. Somewhere.

TRINITY COLLEGE, THE UNIVERSITY OF MELBOURNE

SALLY DALTON-BROWN

[58] This is slightly reminiscent of the ending to *Empire 'V'*, in which the protagonist Rama tells of an immensely bright light that tears into the 'quiet house' of our lives.

[59] Gustave Flaubert, *Madame Bovary*, e-text, University of Virginia Library <http://etext.virginia.edu/etcbin/toccer-new2?id=FlaBova.xml&images=images/modeng&data=/texts/english/modeng/parsed&tag=public&part=21&division=div2> [accessed 10 December 2011] (p. 209).

REVIEWS

Author, Reader, Book: Medieval Authorship in Theory and Practice. Ed. by STEPHEN PARTRIDGE and ERIK KWAKKEL. Toronto: University of Toronto Press. 2012. x+306 pp. $75. ISBN 978-0-8020-9934-1.

The overall impression of this book, conceived as a response to Alistair J. Minnis's seminal *Medieval Theory of Authorship*, 2nd edn (Aldershot: Scolar Press, 1988), is of one with aspirations to contribute to important debates but which, despite its title, does not always put theory into practice. The introduction highlights the importance of expanding 'the chronological scope of debate about medieval authorship' and of considering Latin texts 'together with those of the vernacular' (p. 4), but these worthy theoretical ideals are not upheld in the individual essays. For example, while several chapters do indeed engage with Latin as well as vernacular texts, only one makes such linguistically comparative research its central focus (Anita Obermeier). This means that, despite its laudable aims, the collection is less coherent in its theme than the title suggests. However, Stephen Partridge and Erik Kwakkel have undoubtedly brought together several useful contributions in a thoughtful manner.

The essays, ordered chronologically, range from the later twelfth to the early sixteenth centuries. The collection begins with Alastair Minnis's lucid analysis of the problems inherent in theological and 'secular' poetics in the high and later Middle Ages. Minnis ends by posing the question of 'what sort of pedagogy the great medieval schoolmen believed to be appropriate to Christianity' (p. 34), which is to a certain extent taken up by some of the later essays. Sebastian Coxon's short essay on Walter Map's 'author-mythology' in *De nugis curialium*, which follows, is underwhelming. Despite some good observations about Map's different compositional techniques, it is spoiled by a failure to engage with the complex textual situation of the work; in a piece that assumes Map's authorship it is not adequate to leave until the final paragraph the fact that one of the crucial textual examples may not have been originally composed by Map (p. 47). There follows Erik Kwakkel's extremely useful and very readable account of various types of manuscripts containing texts by a single author, with reference to Middle Dutch, the first of three essays in the collection that focus on manuscript issues (those of Partridge and Mark Vessey are the others). Two essays on Chaucerian issues follow, first Obermeier's ambitious interpretation of the Manciple's Tale with reference to its Ovidian context, and then Partridge's analysis of the rubrics of the *Retraction*. Obermeier's chapter reads Phebus in the Manciple's Tale as 'a mirror of Richard II, a *Fürstenspiegel* on how not to act' (p. 91), and as a warning to his outspoken fellow poet John Gower; it is a thought-provoking piece with a lot of important material. Partridge's essay, the longest, concludes that the *Retraction* and its rubrics work together to promote the idea of Chaucer as author, both 'maker' and 'book maker'; it is perhaps overly detailed in relation to the points it makes, and the decision to list the many manuscripts in abbreviated forms alone in both text and notes makes it hard to follow for a non-Chaucerian. Deborah McGrady's work reads Christine de Pizan as an author concerned to shape her identity via her reading techniques, drawing on both 'clerkly' and 'lay' reading strategies to do so. Kirsty Campbell, in the only essay to focus wholly on devotional and instructional rather than 'secular' literature, gives an interesting portrait of Reginald Pecock as an author negotiating the Arundel *Constitutions*. Ian Macleod Higgins goes on to discuss Henryson's use of Aesop as narrator in his *Moral Fabills*, and the collection finishes with Mark Vessey looking at Erasmus's early publication history.

As this overview of the topics shows, the approach of the book is in fact the traditional author-centric model for the most part, focusing on such canonical giants as the inevitable Chaucer, Christine de Pizan, Henryson, and Erasmus. Partridge and Kwakkel's determined efforts to counter this model highlight how persistent it still is, which itself is a useful insight. Given the model's dominance, my suspicion is that the book will be read for its interesting individual components rather than its holistic approach, a mode of reading that will sadly undermine to some extent the purpose, stated on the cover of the volume, of examining 'the persistence of literary concerns that remain consistent through different periods, languages, and cultural contexts'.

UNIVERSITY OF YORK   VENETIA BRIDGES

Torture and Brutality in Medieval Literature: Negotiations of National Identity. By LARISSA TRACY. Cambridge: Brewer. 2012. x+326 pp. £55. ISBN 978-1-84384-288-0.

In recent times, such scholars as Robert Mills and Jody Enders, building on earlier work by Mitchell Merback, have created a lively set of writings on torture and brutality in the Middle Ages, in both literary and iconographic representations. Larissa Tracy's substantial book builds on this work, paying particular attention to literary representations. Rightly, she dismisses the usual modern synecdoche linking torture and the Middle Ages, arguing instead that medieval representations are rarely mimetic and that the image of an era of extreme brutality is an exaggerated one. To this, she adds a concern with national self-definition, suggesting that certain literary presentations of violence are constructed in such a way as to distance nascent nations from practices elsewhere. Most obviously—she argues—this can be seen in English texts which exhibit resistance to the inquisitorial torture that was legal on the Continent.

In six chapters plus a substantial introduction, Tracy examines saints' Lives; the *Chanson de Roland*; Icelandic sagas; *Havelok the Dane*, the Anglo-Latin *Arthur and Gorlagon*, and the Prioress's Tale; comic representations, in Old French fabliaux and the Miller's Tale; and, in a final chapter on the early modern period, Foxe's *Actes and Monuments* and works by Shakespeare, Marlowe, and Nashe. This is, then, a substantial and broadly based approach to the topic, one in which scholars from many different fields of medieval literature will find material of interest. There is a wealth of close reading here, expanding our sense of the uses of violence in medieval literary culture.

Inevitably, the range of material weakens the argumentative focus. As Tracy is well aware, torture, strictly speaking, refers to the application of pain to get at truth. It is closely related to, but not the same as, judicial punishment. But torture is also often used in a loose sense to refer simply to the giving of pain. Tracy takes advantage of this, letting the word's applications expand and contract at need. Relatively little of the material discussed here is about torture in the true sense. Even the richly painful saints' Lives are rarely about 'the question'.

The book's argument against the mimetic character of the texts is certainly put strongly. But in trying to defend the Middle Ages from the charge of brutality, it frequently goes too far. Tracy comes up with an intriguing reading, for example, of why the closing executions in the romance of *Havelok the Dane* are interestingly different from one another. She argues for Havelok's form of justice as un-English, and Goldeborw's milder form as the more English type of vengeance. It is a plausible way of explaining the additions to the poem's sources. But the romance as a whole does not support the reading. The poet of *Havelok* makes it completely clear at the outset that judicial violence is the hallmark of the reign of the English king Aethelwold: rapists, for example, could expect to lose their limbs, the poet says with unmistakable approval, also stating that the people loved their (violent) king.

Havelok, in other words, could be read as evidence that sectors of the medieval English audience were entirely in favour of torture and brutality. The early fourteenth-century poem in MS Harley 2253 on the historical executions of Simon Fraser and William Wallace similarly dwells lovingly on the detail of the execution ritual, but is nowhere mentioned by Tracy. It is not that this is the only kind of evidence about attitudes to punishment; but the picture is skewed without it.

Torture and Brutality in Medieval Literature takes, nevertheless, a usefully compendious approach to this area of increasing interest to medievalists. Future work will be able to build on it.

UNIVERSITY OF MANCHESTER   DAVID MATTHEWS

Desire in Dante and the Middle Ages. Ed. by MANUELE GRAGNOLATI, TRISTAN KAY, ELENA LOMBARDI, and FRANCESCA SOUTHERDEN. London: Legenda. 2012. xvi+260 pp. £45. ISBN 978-1-907747-96-0.

Desire in Dante and the Middle Ages brings together works initially presented at an international conference held in Oxford in 2010. The volume's ambitious scope is to 'explore and contextualise notions of desire from the Middle Ages to the present through the study of complementary fields and discourses, encompassing language, sexuality, corporeality, subjectivity, perception and knowledge' (p. 2). What emerges, therefore, is not abstracted theoretical studies of desire *per se*, but a collection of essays that demonstrate a rich network of interlocking ideas. It is characterized by both adherence to close textual analysis and advanced theorization of the issues under discussion.

The fourteen essays have been grouped into three overarching categories. 'Transformations' considers 'the role desire plays in a series of metamorphoses of language

[. . .] of selfhood' (p. 2) in studies of both Dante's works and those of other medieval authors. 'Senses and Intellect' focuses on the role of these two elements in the experience and communication of desire, and contains the essays which perhaps most overtly theorize Dante's ideas on desire in relation to classical and Christian precedents. Augustine is a consistent intertext in essays by Peter Dent and Robert S. Sturges that explore the recurring issue of sight, and in Paola Ureni's study of intellect and memory. The final section, 'Textuality and *Translatio*', focuses on issues of intertextuality and writing. Essays consider writers apart from Dante (those by Almut Suerbaum and Monika Otter) or textual relationships between Dante and other writers (Tristan Kay and Francesca Southerden).

While these three categories are useful, the quantity and range of these essays mean that they are both more disparate and more universally and intimately connected than the categories can suggest. The essays not only present a rich view of contemporary thinking on medieval notions and expressions of desire but address some of the most compelling issues of modern Dante and medieval scholarship. In the interests of brevity I will here suggest three issues of particular significance. The first is how we might effectively use contemporary theoretical or psychological ideas to produce new readings of medieval texts without excessive or inconsistent imposition of modern expectations. Essays in this volume use psychoanalysis (Bill Burgwinkle, Sturges, Fabio Camilletti), gender theory (Marguerite Waller), and queer theory (Jonathan Morton) to provide contemporary lenses through which to look again at medieval texts. These exciting readings draw sufficiently from the texts themselves to avoid forced interpretations. The second issue, closely connected to the first, is that of intertextuality. What is the scholarly aim of reading one text in the light of another? What is the aim of poets who engage with others' texts in their own creative work? Many of this volume's essays explore these questions in relation to particular case studies. Particularly considered are the works of Augustine (Dent, Sturges), the troubadours (Burgwinkle, Kay), German mystic writers (Annette Volfing, Suerbaum), and poets and thinkers of the Arabic world (Daniela Boccassini). The third issue is the ever-present question of language. Language emerges in theoretical, linguistic, lyrical, rhetorical, and theological guises; it is the literal, physical expression of desire, the means by which poets distance themselves from or align themselves with others (including their former selves), the manifestation of human creativity and sexuality. In particular, the essays by Kay, Southerden, and Morton consider these questions. Those by Giuseppe Ledda, Suerbaum, and Volfing consider more classical, rhetorical issues, in particular the significance of metaphor and its relation to desire.

A large part of this volume's merit stems from the fact that it does not just consider desire as a theme in medieval works. Instead desire in the medieval context emerges as an issue to be expressed through the unique capabilities of poetry, an experience to be physically, spiritually, and emotionally undergone, and, ultimately, a state to be manifested in the very act of writing.

UNIVERSITY OF LEEDS   RUTH CHESTER

Vital Matters: Eighteenth-Century Views of Conception, Life, and Death. Ed. by HELEN DEUTSCH and MARY TERRALL. Toronto: University of Toronto Press. 2012. x+334 pp. $70. ISBN 978-1-4426-4258-4.

Arising from a series of conferences held at UCLA in 2005–06, which themselves were inspired by the reflection that matter has a history, *Vital Matters* is a book marked by ambition. The guiding concern of the gatherings that gave rise to this collection was to explore a range of perspectives on no less a topic than 'eighteenth-century attempts to portray, analyse, and speculate about life, living bodies, and organic matter' (p. 3). The result is a collection that is breathtaking in its range: an essay on seventeenth-century English translations of Lucretius rubs shoulders with others on French doctors' views of digestion or Augustan verse epistles. The sheer scope of these essays renders this volume a vital contribution to eighteenth-century studies.

The book is somewhat broader in its range of topics than its interdisciplinary scope: apart from a single contribution from the history of art, the essays are divided between literary and historical approaches. The absence of a philosophical or theological contribution (notwithstanding Jonathan Kramnick's essay, which comes closest) is surprising, given the emphasis in the volume on materialism, an idea productive of intense philosophical and religious debate during the period in question. Nevertheless, given the breadth with which they had to contend, the editors do well to identify key themes that unite the essays. Among the strongest and most recurrent of these are the reflection that 'life' and 'death' are not simple opposites, but exist 'in intimate and immanent relation' with one another (p. 7), and an exploration of Enlightenment concepts concerning the origins of life. Most of the contributions to the collection relate to either the first (Kramnick, Helen Deutsch, Kevin Chua, Elizabeth A. Williams, Simon Chaplin, Anita Guerrini, Lorna Clymer) or second (Raymond Stephanson, Mary Terrall, Corrinne Harol) of these themes.

While each of these essays is excellent, several stand out. Kramnick's study of translations of Lucretius sets out the terms of the materialism debate, and the stakes of subsequent contributions to the collection, in his statement that 'free will and determinism are conclusions made from rival conceptions of matter, not qualities inherent in people' (p. 32). The interplay of life and death is highlighted in several contributions. Chua's study of Anne-Louis Girodet's *Sleep of Endymion* (1793) argues that the painting represents a vision of the afterlife that is the result of an open-ended cycle of life and death. Williams's essay unpacks debates about digestion among French medics, particularly whether food is a dead mass of matter or inherently life-giving (or both); hers is a powerful contribution to the body of scholarship dedicated to showing that scientific 'advances' in the eighteenth century were as much (if not more) the result of philosophical commitments as they were of any genuine progress of knowledge. Chaplin and Guerrini respectively examine the two brothers John and William Hunter, and the parts that they (and their collections of body parts) played in simultaneously constituting medical authority and qualifying its 'gentlemanly' credentials. The origins of life are the subject of Terrall's impressive essay on the shift from the (mechanical) power of the mother's imagination to the (vital) capacity of bodily matter to shape offspring. One contribution outwith these themes, but none the less worthy of note, is Minsoo Kang's study of mechanical metaphors: moving from man-machine to automaton-man, this valuable analysis builds upon recent work by Julia Douthwaite, among others.

Less successful than these contributions are two chapters that extend the guiding themes of the collection into more metaphorical realms. Deutsch's essay examines verse epistles and their power to animate writer and reader through mutual recognition. Deutsch deftly weaves Lucretius and the themes of Epicureanism into an analysis of verse epistles by Alexander Pope and Mary Leapor, but it is only with difficulty that her argument can be ascertained. Helen Thompson's contribution claims that Sarah Fielding used empirical philosophy to postulate a feminine 'essence', thereby reconciling a wife's mental autonomy and her husband's marital prerogatives. This is an intriguing argument, but it is difficult to tell how it fits into the collection at all. Deutsch and Terrall do their best in their introduction, relying on a comment in Thompson's piece that takes up all of nine words, but one is left wondering how this essay—which is confusingly written in parts—fits into the overall collection.

But the last words on this ambitious, stimulating collection should be ones of praise. Deutsch and Terrall have compiled an admirably broad range of contributions on a topic of crucial importance for eighteenth-century studies, and this is a book that deserves to be read by students of its themes and period. In the final analysis, *Vital Matters* matters.

UNIVERSITY OF EDINBURGH   ANDREW WELLS

Tropen und Metaphern im Gelehrtendiskurs des 18. Jahrhunderts. Ed. by ELENA AGAZZI. (Archiv für Begriffsgeschichte, 10) Hamburg: Meiner. 2011. 235 pp. €98. ISBN 978-3-78731972-5.

This stimulating, wide-ranging volume makes available seventeen papers presented at the Trilateral Congress of the Italian, German, and French Eighteenth-Century Societies at the University of Bergamo, 2009. It is both daunting and rewarding given its intellectual breadth and the linguistic demands it makes upon readers. As stated in Elena Agazzi's informative introduction, the volume focuses on the use of metaphors in eighteenth-century scholarly discourse from a variety of theoretical angles.

Within this broad category, the essays probe metaphors in three distinct areas. The first group investigates eighteenth-century discourse on metaphor. Katrin Kohl directs attention to its cognitive aspect, arguing that the cognitive function of metaphor is not only exploited in the scholarly and scientific discourse at the time, but finds theoretical reflection in such authors as Gottsched, Dumarsais, and Sulzer. Christine Künzel focuses on the use of metaphor in rhetoric itself, and documents the consistent female gendering of the trope in rhetoric from Gottsched to Herder. Charlotte Kurbjuhn argues that *Umriss*, a self-reflective metaphor in and for aesthetics at its inception (Winckelmann, Herder), delimits the territory of aesthetics on the academic map. Laura Benzi investigates Klopstock's revision of traditional rhetorical tropes, including metaphor, assigning it a central role within Klopstock's 'energetic' concept of poetry.

The importance of metaphor in conceptual history as diagnosed and implied by these contributions is the focus of the second group of essays. Andreas Blödorn traces the trajectory of 'Entwickelung' as a creative metaphor in the early eighteenth century, noting its conceptual solidification and its prominent role in the naturalization of social phenomena, as evident in the work of Herder. Ulrike Zeuch argues that the dynamization of *scala naturae* occurs in successive stages in the eighteenth century and introduces a paradigm shift. Julia Weber unfolds the role of the camera obscura as an absolute metaphor in the Blumenbergian sense in the philosophical writings of Descartes, Locke, Hume, Rosseau, and Kant, concluding that this metaphor shifts from being a mere *tertium comparationis* for the human eye (Descartes), to becoming a spatial metaphor of the human soul, whose medial and mechanical aspect is explored by Hoffmann and Jean Paul. Federica La Manna discusses anatomy as a metaphor from Zedler's encyclopedia entry onwards, arguing that human anatomy functions as the symbol of investigation and discovery of the human body as well as the soul. Claudia Stancati explores the role of metaphor at the birth of the 'sciences of language', seeing their role as a step towards reflection on taxonomy and classification.

The third group of essays explores novel and ironic uses of classic metaphors by single authors. Marita Gilli's essay analyses Georg Forster's creative scientific metaphors and allegories in his *Parisische Umrisse*, which in her view reinforce and complement reasoned argument to steer the reader towards acknowledging the French Revolution as a moral process parallel to natural processes. Rosamaria Loretelli draws attention to the connection between the practice of silent reading and the maturation of the metaphor of the camera obscura in the writings of Joseph Addison. Klaus Semsch argues that Diderot develops a writing method based on *rapports*, generating a system of comparative knowledge of experimental valence. The dynamic comparative and explorative, however, often lapses into allegory, as Semsch convincingly argues on the basis of Diderot's *Paradoxe sur le comédien*. Elena Agazzi diagnoses in Lichtenberg's aphorisms a recognition that the metaphoric inventory of cultural memory has a tendency to become obsolete, arguing that Lichtenberg counteracts this tendency both by using aphorisms (through the lightning-fast/immediate connection of disparate areas of knowledge) and by coining novel metaphors involving neologisms and terms associated with electricity to open up the field. Daniela Mangione investigates light as metaphor in Franceso Algarotti's *Newtoniasmo per le dame*, arguing that the metaphor of light is used as a political weapon against censorship. The volume closes with Carsten Zelle's essay on the virtuoso use of metaphors in the popular scientific writings of the 'vernünftige Ärzte' in Halle, focusing in his title on the 'Bratenwender' as an ironically critical response to the classic mechanical metaphor of clockwork.

For example, Johann Gottlieb Krüger's 65th 'dream' presents contentious natural scientific matters (such as the relationship between body and soul) in an accessible and entertaining way, and is read in this essay on the literary level as systematic interference with the underlying philosophical ideas.

Each of the essays fully engages with the relevant established literature, and together they draw on a wide range of theoretical angles, including 'metaphorology' in the Blumenbergian vein, cognitive literary theory, and poetology of knowledge. Given the specialist nature of the topics discussed, this can hardly be considered an introductory volume, but experts in eighteenth-century discourse interested in the intersections of literature and science as well as conceptual history will find much in it to enjoy. A minor practical drawback is the absence of an index; the abstracts included at the end represent a welcome addition for those not fluent in French, German, or Italian.

NEW COLLEGE, OXFORD   ORSOLYA KISS

George Frederick Nott (1768–1841): un ecclesiastico anglicano tra teologia, letteratura, arte, archeologia, bibliofilia e collezionismo. By STEFANO VILLANI. (Atti della Accademia Nazionale dei Lincei, 408 (2011), Classe di Scienze Morali, Storiche e Filologiche, Memorie, 9th ser., 27.3) Rome: Edizioni di Scienze e Lettere. 2012. 139 pp. €30. ISBN 978–88–218–1046–6.

Stefano Villani's contribution on the English clergyman and scholar George Frederick Nott aims to fill a gap in existing scholarship. It reconstructs the life and work of a relatively neglected personality of the late eighteenth and early nineteenth centuries, giving at the same time a broad and stimulating overview of his individual and cultural parabola in the crucial years between the French Revolution, the Napoleonic Wars, the Bourbon Restoration, and the first decades, in England, of the Victorian age. The careful overview of Nott's life between England and Italy, where he came into contact with the most important intellectual personalities of that time, is accompanied by a scrupulous critical apparatus, always setting biographical information within the broader Italian and European cultural contexts. The book is enriched by a bibliography of primary and secondary sources, as well as a complete survey of available manuscripts and archival documents in the UK, Italy, the Vatican City, and the United States, which will surely be a solid starting-point for scholars working on the same intellectual environments in the future.

Within the history of Anglo-Italian cultural exchanges between the eighteenth and nineteenth centuries, Nott seems to be a central figure, both because of his intellectual connections between England and Italy and because of his own cultural production—including an Italian translation of *The Book of Common Prayer*, plausibly intended to justify to his Anglican superiors his prolonged absence from his pastoral duties, and other editorial projects, influenced by the early nineteenth-century rediscovery of Dante and by the recovery of fourteenth-century writers within the milieu of the 'questione della lingua'.

Nott (1768–1841) literally lives between two centuries. On the one hand, his profile seems that of a typical eighteenth-century character: his first journey to Italy, as a tutor of the Irish nobleman Thomas Pakenham, takes place in 1793, when the Grand Tour is increasingly popular as a step in the typical *cursus honorum* of the British gentleman. At the same time, his eclecticism, moving between theology, literature, antiquarian philology, archaeology, history of art, bibliophilia, and collecting, testifies to a plurality of interests that Nott shares with many other intellectuals on both sides of the Channel. On the other hand, his life spans years that are especially crucial for European history and, more specifically, for the relationship between England and Italy. The overview of his intellectual contacts is, from this angle, particularly telling, marking a fluid and unstable point between a pre- and a post-Revolutionary world, as well as between Neoclassicism, pre-Romanticism, and Romanticism. Nott meets such protagonists of Italian Classicism as Vincenzo Monti and Giovan Battista Niccolini; he corresponds with Giacomo Leopardi from 1823, meeting him, years later, in Rome; he is in touch with the family of Jane Austen, with Byron and the Shelleys, and with the 'spiritual father' of the German–Roman artistic movement of the 'Nazarenes', Joseph Anton Koch; he is part of the antiquarian-philological scene between Italy and central Europe, as testified by his contacts with Christian Karl Josias von Bunsen and by his participation in the excavations of the Etruscan necropolis of Vulci promoted by Napoleon's brother Luciano Bonaparte. As a consequence, the analysis of Nott's life helps to erase the borders between disciplinary domains, such as eighteenth- and ninteenth-century studies, or English and Italian studies, as well as between historical and critical distinctions, such as those between Neoclassicism, pre-Romanticism, and Romanticism in the Italian literary scene, or between Romanticism and Victorian culture in the English one. His own cultural parabola (from the late eighteenth-century vogue of the Grand Tour to the edition of a fourteenth-century 'testo di lingua' in 1832, and to the long-pursued project of a translation of Dante's *Comedy* throughout the 1830s) epitomizes a shift in sensibility that belongs to the entire Continent, from Classicism to the neo-medievalist fashion, and to the recovery of Dante as a canonical author for Italian and European identities.

Alongside the undoubted historical value of Villani's erudite work, this book is of value for the wider audience of scholars in early nineteenth-century and Romantic studies. Reconstructing Nott's travels and his European network of contacts means not only shedding light on the life of a minor protagonist of the age of revolutions: it can also be an inspiration for rethinking those established critical distinctions and forms of periodization that sometimes run the risk of underestimating the great intellectual mobility that takes place in Europe at the turn of the nineteenth century, giving birth to the copresence of multiple positions and orientations that criticism tends often to conceive as reciprocally incompatible.

UNIVERSITY OF WARWICK   FABIO CAMILLETTI

Realism and Space in the Novel, 1795–1869: Imagined Geographies. By ROSA MUCIGNAT. Farnham: Ashgate. 2013. viii+182 pp. £55. ISBN 978-1-4094-5055-9.

Rosa Mucignat aims with this book to fill the gap in current scholarship on the Realist novel that gives short shrift to the role that space plays in literary representation. Space, which until now, Mucignat suggests, has been considered a mere 'background to the plot' (p. 159), is worthy of consideration because it 'works alongside plot incidents, time, character and style to construct an increasingly complex and lifelike image of the world' (p. 1). In her own smart and theoretically sophisticated study, Mucignat builds on foundational work in 'literary geography' by scholars such as Franco Moretti and shows how, and to what ends, a select group of nineteenth-century European novelists—Goethe, Austen, Stendhal, Manzoni, Dickens, and Flaubert—became progressively more interested in the potential for space to convey a convincing sense of our everyday experience.

In Chapter 1 Mucignat delineates three qualities of narrative space—visibility, depth, movement—that 'constitute the great breakthrough of nineteenth-century novels' (p. 71) and thus form a useful scaffolding upon which to build a series of more focused analyses of individual texts in later chapters. Mucignat clearly defines what she means by these terms and develops the critical discourses that subtend her understanding of each. Taking her cue from Bakhtin's theorization of the chronotope, Mucignat proposes that Realist novels in the nineteenth century can be characterized by a an 'intense engagement with everyday experience' that 'gives a more solid, visible appearance to the fictional world' (p. 11). As such, the Realist chronotope makes space visible in a decidedly more concrete way than earlier modes. The focus on materiality and the everyday also allows Realist novels to realize the potential for various layers of energy fomenting under the surface of things to affect narrative progression. The Realist conceptualization of depth, informed by a variety of developments in fields such as biology, geology, archaeology, and history, which witnessed 'an increased interest in causes and historical developments in nineteenth-century culture' (p. 17), models Foucault's characterization of the nineteenth-century *epistēmē* as 'vertical' (p. 18). As Mucignat elegantly proposes, it is also palimpsestic: 'there is a hidden profundity in the space of everyday life, where relics of another time rest, and past and future revolutions "slumber"' (p. 22). Finally, Realist novels consistently associate space with movement. Each writer's own distinct 'geography' is made up of multiple, heterogeneous stations, real and imaginary, through which characters travel. The Realist novel, Mucignat argues, distinguishes itself in the way it problematizes its young heroes' peregrinations, both geographical and social: movement is so crucial because it becomes 'the very expression of will, choice, and personal disposition, or the result of desire' (p. 25).

Chapter 2, 'Our Daily Adventure', focuses primarily on how Realist novels experiment with style to establish a middle ground between the 'adventurous and unexpected' and 'plain everyday life' (p. 37). The nineteenth-century novel imbues even the most routine moments of the quotidian with potentially significant meaning, all the while humanizing the most extraordinary, historic, and dramatic events. As such, they provide a space for their primarily middle-class characters to evolve across an 'unprecedented' variety of environments: 'They have the special gift of being unmarked, undetermined, and thus free to move and explore the territory' (p. 35).

The second half of the book proposes six case studies that collectively sketch the Realist novel's development of a spatial poetics over the course of the century. Each chapter pairs two texts linked chronologically and illustrative of a particular mode of spatial representation. Goethe's *Wilhelm Meisters Lehrjahre* (1795) and Austen's *Mansfield Park* (1813), the two earliest novels under consideration here, are representative of the most abstract depiction of novelistic space, what Mucignat calls the symbolic, which privileges 'the general, universal meaning behind individual representations over their specific and tangible existence' (p. 50). In the next chapter, the map serves as the primary metaphor underpinning the organization of space in Mazoni's *I promessi sposi* (first edition 1827) and Stendhal's *Le Rouge et le Noir* (1830). Here Mucignat argues that, as we move through the century, novelists construct more recognizable and meaningful, but also more complex, literary itineraries in which the relation between places, what Moretti refers to as a 'matrix of relations' (p. 83), is responsible for the necessary tension that drives narrative forward. Finally, Mucignat effectively mobilizes Pierre Bourdieu's theorization of the cultural 'field' to unpack the role of setting in Dickens's *Great Expectations* (1860) and Flaubert's *L'Éducation sentimentale* (1869). In the book's final pair of close readings, Mucignat proposes that both texts 'make space work like a field of forces that orients and even coerces movement' (p. 123). Unlike novels characterized by a more cartographic form of spatiality, 'field novels' such as *Great Expectations* and *L'Éducation sentimentale* 'assign a specific value to space that goes beyond its structural function', thereby transforming 'characters into highly responsive and susceptible vectors' (p. 123).

Throughout, Mucignat's readings are informative and well researched. At times, however, the author's interpretative framework seems schematic, relying perhaps too heavily on 'the usual rubrics of visibility, depth, and movement' (p. 140). Additionally, the book would have benefited from a more sustained consideration of the essential distinctions between space and place, two terms that are used interchangeably here, yet which have been at the centre of debates about spatiality in recent decades. That said, scholars of nineteenth-century fiction, especially those working on texts in the corpus, will find much of interest here.

University of Virginia   Ari J. Blatt

The Deliverance of Others: Reading Literature in a Global Age. By David Palumbo-Liu. Durham, NC: Duke University Press. 2012. xiv+226 pp. £15.99. ISBN 978-0-8223-5269-3.

David Palumbo-Liu is concerned with how literature establishes readers' sense of responsibility towards others—'how much otherness is required for literature

to have any traction at all, and how much pushes it over the edge' (p. 22)—
and how reading contemporary texts contributes to ethics. Literature, he argues,
should 'deliver difference, otherness' (p. 12). He explores how radical otherness
in different contemporary historical contexts affects 'delivery systems', and the
problems literary aesthetics faces in the globalized world, through close readings
of works by J. M. Coetzee, Nadine Gordimer, Kazuo Ishiguro, and Ruth Ozeki.
The Deliverance of Others asks whether otherness changes readers' assumptions
about what is realistic, and whether it challenges realism's power of representation
in Coetzee's novels. Palumbo-Liu argues that there are traces of Levinas's 'call to
radically reconceive our ontological presumptions and see the emergence of self
as always preceded by an irreducible other' (p. 59) in *Elizabeth Costello*. There
is too much otherness delivered in this novel, whereas the ending of *Disgrace*
shows that a potential 'common ground' may be achieved by a '"delivery system"
that now incorporates blacks and whites' (p. 65), which used to be unthinkable
because previously they were absolutely separate. A 'radical commonality' is shown
in both novels: human and 'nonhuman animal' are no longer separated (ibid.). In
Gordimer's *My Son's Story* art and politics are blended, and self and the other
are bridged (p. 95). The story of one person is imbricated with that of others.
By comparing Jean-Luc Nancy's organ-transplant experience and his philosophical
writings, Palumbo-Liu explores how technological advancements of bioeconomy
change the notions of community, identity and otherness, life and death. He engages with Nancy's conception of 'singularity plural existence' (p. 102), or the
'ontology of being-with-one-another' (p. 103), arguing that humans must never
isolate death from life, and that any essence 'becomes replaced by a global notion
of commonplacedness' (p. 112). But 'immortality' can be enjoyed only by the privileged, whereas others sacrifice their lives. This tension is shown in *Never Let Me
Go*, whose author, Ishiguro, claims that it is about 'growing up' (p. 114), perhaps
an attempt to dismiss any ethical reading. Palumbo-Liu disagrees, arguing that
Ishiguro's allegorical reading 'erases [. . .] the difference history makes', and suffers
from having an 'anachronistic liberal sentimentality' (p. 117). Palumbo-Liu asks
for a critical literary practice that 'addresses art and history, culture and race, in
all their contingency' (p. 132). Discussions concerning affect informed by Freud's
concept of 'oceanic feeling' and Spinoza's moral philosophy follow. Palumbo-Liu
asserts that 'literature brings us into imaginative contact with others' (p. 178).
Reading, for him, 'will be a self-reflective act that puts the question of ethics before
that of epistemology' (p. 196).

The Deliverance of Others refers only to Levinas's 'Enigma and Phenomenon'
(1965), omitting his other major works. Levinas calls the condition of insomnia,
which lasts the night, the *il y a*: 'This impersonal, anonymous, yet inextinguishable "consummation" of being [. . .] murmurs in the depths of nothingness itself'
('There Is: Existence without Existents', in *The Levinas Reader*, ed. by Seán Hand
(Oxford: Blackwell, 1989), pp. 29–36 (p. 30)). The *there is* is the existence that
the 'self-identical existent' discovers: 'to be conscious is to be torn away from the
there is, since the existence of a consciousness constitutes a subjectivity, a subject

of existence' (ibid., p. 32). The *there is* destabilizes the subject that it holds: 'the other's entire being is constituted by its exteriority, or rather its alterity' ('Time and the Other', in *The Levinas Reader*, ed. by Hand, pp. 37–58 (p. 43)). *The Deliverance of Others* does not engage enough with Levinas, assuming the self/other distinction as fixed. Although Palumbo-Liu refers to Freud, his psychoanalytic understanding of subjectivity is inadequate. He ignores Freud's thesis that the source of 'oceanic feeling' is actually the 'restoration of limitless narcissism' ('Civilization and its Discontents', in *Penguin Freud 12* (Harmondsworth: Penguin, 1991), pp. 243–340 (p. 260)), but rather extracts conveniently the description of the 'oceanic feeling' as 'a sensation of "eternity", a feeling as of something limitless, unbounded' (ibid., p. 251). There is no discussion of Lacan's claim that 'man's desire is the Other's desire' ('The Subversion of the Subject and the Dialectic of Desire' (1960), in his *Écrits*, trans. by Bruce Fink (New York: Norton, 2006), pp. 671–702 (p. 693)). In 'Aggressiveness in Psychoanalysis', by applying Hegel's Master-and-Slave dialectics, Lacan maintains that 'the satisfaction of human desire is possible only when mediated by the other's desire and labor' (ibid., pp. 82–101 (p. 89)). Self is constituted by the other's desire. Another neglected critic of literature and otherness is Bakhtin, who argues that the novel is the site of 'heteroglossia' ('Discourse in the Novel', in *The Dialogic Imagination*, trans. by Caryl Emerson and Michael Holquist (Austin: University of Texas Press, 1981), pp. 259–422 (p. 301)): different voices speak with no controlling stance, because before 'one's own' word is appropriated, 'it exists in other people's mouths, [. . .] serving other people's intensions: it is from there that one must take the word' (p. 294).

These three critics' ideas subvert the assumption that otherness is outside the subject, which leads only to Palumbo-Liu's question: how much otherness is enough, and how to 'maintain equilibrium or growth without danger' (p. 181)? But otherness cannot be quantified. Although George Eliot's 'The National History of German Life' on art and sympathies is discussed, more should be said on *Daniel Deronda*, which includes otherness by not merely describing Jewish culture, but representing the protagonist as the embodiment of both English and Jewish. Otherness is not 'delivered', but embedded in the texture of Western culture. Literature *is* otherness, and reading is to encounter the other, the heterogeneous, or evil, as Bataille affirms in *La Littérature et le mal* (Paris: Gallimard, 1957).

NATIONAL TAIPEI UNIVERSITY OF TECHNOLOGY   LOUIS LO

Atmosphere, Mood, Stimmung: On a Hidden Potential of Literature. By HANS ULRICH GUMBRECHT. Trans. by ERIK BUTLER. Stanford: Stanford University Press. 2012. viii+140 pp. $18.95. ISBN 978-0-8047-8122-0.

With this book, Hans Ulrich Gumbrecht offers his personal critical perspective on the mainly German hermeneutical and theoretical discussion of the concept of *Stimmung*, a term that is somehow untranslatable into any other European language, and which is normally rendered, as in the case of this English translation by Erik Butler, as 'atmosphere' or 'mood'. Because of its semantic root—*Stimme*, 'voice'—it can also be employed in the sense of 'harmonic intonation' or 'consonance'. In reference to Karlheinz Stockhausen's *Stimmung* (1968), for instance, Paul Hillier explains that the title implies both 'the outward tuning of voices or instruments' and 'the inward tuning of one's soul' (p. 4). In some way the concept points to the struggle for a 'consonance' between subject and object, individual and natural or social environment, a 'fusional' overcoming of the modern separation of objectual reality and reflective consciousness. For this reason *Stimmung* cannot be taken or approached in purely linguistic or metaphorical terms, as Tonino Griffero has recently stated in *Atmosferologia: estetica degli spazi emozionali* (Rome: Laterza, 2010), as it coincides with its 'phenomenal character' (p. 127).

Gumbrecht is thus seeking to 'retune' the concept of *Stimmung* in order to make it newly available for literary criticism. His aim is also to move beyond the epochal impasse experienced by contemporary literary studies, stranded between the Scylla of deconstruction, with its loss of faith in any possibility of grasping an external reference, and the Charybdis of cultural studies, with its increasing interest in quantitative approaches to artistic production. 'Reading for *Stimmung*', Gumbrecht argues, is a third option that can reconnect the reader with an 'authentic' aesthetic experience which goes beyond a purely interpretative approach. It 'means to pay attention to the textual dimension of the forms that envelop us and our bodies as a physical reality' (p. 3). Although Gumbrecht claims that 'a special affinity exists between performance and *Stimmung*' (p. 5), more than the idea of performance, the concept could be linked to the notions of 'immersion' and 'embodiment' which pertain to a variety of aesthetic experiences, with particular reference to those which imply the technological recording of a specific performance or event—a case in point is the chapter devoted to Janis Joplin's 'Me and Bobby McGee'—but could also be extended to literature seen as a form which encapsulates and preserves the particular *Stimmung* of a given historical period. The 'nostalgic principle' that Alois Riegl sees as an essential development of *Stimmung* in the twentieth century has in fact been magnified by the vast array of technological capabilities of reproduction, which allow the modern spectator/reader/listener to move in and out of syncretic temporalities.

In general, *Atmosphere, Mood, Stimmung* should be inserted into the theoretical genealogy of the non-hermeneutic project that Gumbrecht put forward with more ambitious books such as *In 1926: Living at the Edge of Time* (Cambridge, MA: Harvard University Press, 1997) and *Production of Presence: What Meaning Cannot Convey* (Stanford: Stanford University Press, 2004), which focus their attention on all those social and cultural products and artefacts that emphasize effects of presence vis-à-vis effects of meaning. However, this volume is not a systematic critical exercise like *In 1926*, nor a theoretical book like *Production of Presence*, but an 'experiment', as Gumbrecht suggests in the introduction, a series of snapshots, short critical essays, suggestive readings, that he published in the 'Geisteswissenschaften' section of the *Frankfurter Allgemeine Zeitung* in the past years and that were then collected into a book in 2011 for Carl Hanser with the title *Stimmungen lesen*.

In the first part of the book, entitled 'Moments', in a truly comparative tour de force, Gumbrecht moves insightfully and suggestively from *Lazarillo de Tormes* to Shakespeare's sonnets, from Diderot's *Le Neveu de Rameau* to Caspar David Friedrich's paintings, from Thomas Mann's Venice to Machado de Assis's *Memorial de Aries*, making these works apt condensations of particular 'forms of "life"' (p. 20) in different historical periods. In the second section, 'Situations', Gumbrecht then wrestles, in more theoretical terms, with *Stimmung*'s shifting sense, touching upon remarks, comments, and suggestions made by Walter Benjamin, Martin Heidegger, and Jacques Derrida, among others.

In spite of Gumbrecht's desire to keep himself at arm's length from a generation 'who have invested Benjamin with the robes of a "seer"' (p. 104), and his tendency to dwell more on Heidegger's philosophy and its conceptualization of *Stimmung* 'as part of the existential condition of "thrownness"' (p. 9), it is indeed Benjamin who provides one of the best definitions of literary *Stimmung* in his essay 'Surrealism: The Last Snapshot of the European Intelligentsia' (1929), when he comments that 'Breton and Nadja are the lovers who convert everything we have experienced on mournful railway journeys [. . .], on godforsaken Sunday afternoons in the proletarian quarters of great cities, in the first glance through the rain-blurred window of a new apartment, into revolutionary experience, if not action. They bring the immense forces of "atmosphere" concealed in these things to the point of explosion' (quoted in pp. 111–12). Gumbrecht explicitly underplays the political and ideological charge of Benjamin's words. Because of the former's project to propose, shape, and instantiate a post-hermeneutic phase in literary studies, where representational techniques are at the service, not of referential concerns but of a purely aesthetic and emotional enjoyment and fulfilment, Gumbrecht tries to suppress any distinction between aesthetic and historical experiences. *Stimmung* in fact would allow seeing or experiencing history aesthetically, as it were. However, one may wonder if the political can at all be subtracted from the 'mood' of a specific historical moment; if the emotional density that constitutes a particular *Stimmung* could be depurated of the ideological kernel that shapes the collective spirit of many epochs and which infiltrates literary and artistic works. The link between ideology, politics, and emotional states cannot be understated. As a matter of fact, in the chapter entitled 'Tragic Sense of Life', Gumbrecht shows how the condensation of the particular material, cultural, and social experience of modernity in the 1920s resulted in a search for immediate fulfilment, in an aesthetic apprehension of politics, that helped to shape the conservative revolution of Fascism. 'Reading for *Stimmung*' might also imply an exercise of *dissonance* (indeed an emerging trend in twentieth-century European music), of the evocation of negative feelings, of being touched physically by the discomfort we may experience in reading some pages of Céline or Heidegger's obstructive rhetoric produced in the *Zeitgeist* of Nazism.

ST JOHN'S COLLEGE, CAMBRIDGE   PIERPAOLO ANTONELLO

Reading Medieval Anchoritism: Ideology and Spiritual Practices. By MARI HUGHES-EDWARDS. Cardiff: University of Wales Press. 2012. xiv+190 pp. £29.99. ISBN 978-0-7083-2505-6.

This important and stimulating book is the first detailed study of normative English anchoritic ideology from *c.* 1080 to *c.* 1450. Its coverage is impressive: eight anchoritic guidance texts, including every extant guide written for female English recluses, are explored in careful detail. Mari Hughes-Edwards sets well-known guides such as *Ancrene Wisse* alongside texts and redactions which have received less scholarly attention in order to elucidate the richness and complexity of anchoritic culture and its evolution through five centuries. She successfully navigates the extensive and often contrasting range of opinion in this field, providing a useful summary of seminal scholarly works alongside her own original interventions.

The book comprises five chapters subdivided into two sections. The first part seeks to establish the ideological framework of insular anchoritism—by introducing each of the guides in turn, including their manuscript traditions and what is known of their authors in Chapter 1, and then by focusing in the following two chapters on the ideals of enclosure and solitude and what this implies about anchoritic sociability. Part II contextualizes the insular guides in relation to texts and practices from Continental Europe with an emphasis on asceticism in Chapter 4 and contemplative experience in Chapter 5.

Hughes-Edwards predicates her analysis upon four anchoritic ideals (enclosure, solitude, chastity, and orthodoxy) which she discusses in the context of two central spiritual practices (asceticism and contemplative experience). Although the primacy of these categories at the expense of other aspects of the anchoritic experience might be challenged by some, reading the guides through specific themes allows for sustained and detailed comparisons throughout. In particular, the range and depth of analysis allow the author to scrutinize, and in some cases refute, a number of scholarly assumptions concerning the ideology of the anchorhold, in particular the rhetoric of living death often ascribed to it.

The strongest feature of this book is the manner in which the author exploits the broad chronological range of the texts to highlight changes and continuities which previous studies with a more limited focus have been unable to discern. Hughes-Edwards demonstrates the way in which later medieval anchoritic ideology developed from the earlier Middle Ages and characterizes a tradition which is 'mutable and shifting' rather than 'a single perspective set in stone' (p. 108). Her careful reading undermines the notion of a straightforward teleological development and elucidates instead the complex cultural and intertextual indebtedness of each author.

Another stimulating aspect of the book is the author's engagement throughout with the terminology associated with anchoritism. In Chapter 5, for example, she explores 'the vocabulary of contemplation' used by the medieval guidance writers to describe a range of practices and experiences, and notes that the prolific terms of modern critical terminology, including 'mystic', 'mysticism', 'visionary', 'contemplative', and even 'clairvoyant', are interchangeably deployed and too readily synonymized (p. 82). Hughes-Edwards's own close reading enables her to problematize the often anachronistic application of vocabulary not used by the medieval writers and to propose instead a far more nuanced linguistic framework in which the subtlety and complexity of the original texts can be more fully appreciated.

An aspect of the formatting of the book which was presumably beyond the author's control, but which none the less impacts upon its usability, is the relegation of modern English translations of Latin and Middle English quotations to the notes at the end of the volume.

The author's exclusive focus on the ideology and spiritual practices of anchoritism sometimes results in other aspects of the lives of the enclosed being alluded to in passing with little development, although the depth and detail of the study as a whole mostly justify this. In places, however, it feels as though additional explanatory material has been edited out where in fact a little further context or discussion would be welcome. This book is therefore important reading for those already familiar with the practicalities of enclosure who wish to further their understanding of the genre of guidance writing and is a significant and welcome contribution to scholarship in this area.

UNIVERSITY OF EAST ANGLIA   REBECCA PINNER

The Collected Works of John Ford, vol. I. Ed. by GILLES MONSARRAT, BRIAN VICKERS, and R. J. C. WATT. Oxford: Oxford University Press. 2012. xxiv+696 pp. £152. ISBN 978-0-19-959290-6.

This volume contains Ford's lesser-known works, written before he turned his hand to writing plays; it includes two long poems, *Fames Memoriall* and *Christes Bloodie Sweat*; two Neostoical prose tracts, *The Golden Meane* and *A Line of Life*; and a number of shorter poems, including 'A Funerall Elegye for William Peter', only recently attributed to Ford. All of the texts have been newly edited from the original quartos, with the exception of *Fames Memoriall* (where the presentation manuscript has been edited) and *A Line of Life* (where the presentation manuscript and quarto are both edited and printed side by side). The lucid and engaging introductions offer new readings, situate the texts in their intellectual, theological, and literary contexts, and evaluate each work's artistic merits. As a result, the reader gains a clear sense of Ford's wider historical background as well as his development as a writer. The notes provide helpful glosses, additional contextual material, remarks on Ford's characteristic words and stylistic features, and observations as to how these works anticipate the later plays.

Some of the literary interpretations seek to challenge (sometimes sharply) recent work on Ford or to reshape the canon as we know it. For example, Monsarrat refutes Lisa Hopkins's claim that Ford may have been part of a Catholic coterie, suggesting instead that 'Only a convinced Protestant could write *Christes Bloodie Sweat*' (p. 33). Reading the poem alongside other works on Christ's Passion, Monsarrat argues that Ford's interpretation of Christ's suffering and sacrifice demonstrates his 'first-hand knowledge of Reformation theology' (p. 314). With regard to 'A Funerall Elegye' (a poem previously attributed to Shakespeare, among other writers), Vickers draws on a wealth of biographical evidence and verbal and stylistic features to argue that the poem is by Ford. Much of Donald Foster's research, which details biographical connections between the Fords and the Peters, contributes to his case (despite the fact that Foster argues for Shakespeare's authorship). Vickers also demonstrates that there is 'a considerable degree of verbal overlap' between 'A Funerall Elegye' and Ford's other works, and points out that the poem manifests Ford's characteristic blending of Christian and Stoical traditions (p. 262). It all makes for a very convincing case.

Although these early works might seem like odd curiosities to some, they offer a chance to see in embryo some of the enduring poetic and philosophical preoccupations that helped to shape Ford as a playwright. For example, we can marvel at the way in which the somewhat clumsy marriage of humoral theory and Neoplatonic philosophy in *Honor Triumphant* is transformed into something psychologically compelling and complex in *'Tis Pity She's a Whore*; here Giovanni's perversion of Platonic philosophy is blended with his humoral condition (his lovesickess) in a manner which ultimately questions the basis of both. And in the prose tracts, written in the vein of Christian Stoicism, scholars will find the ideas and language that most anticipate Ford's later works. It is here, as Monsarrat points out, that Ford's celebration of courage in adversity sometimes achieves a dramatic energy and simplicity of style characteristic of his great plays. These early works are thus interesting both in themselves and in relation to what is to come; as Vickers argues, they lay the groundwork for Ford the playwright 'both in the conception of moral laws and their transgression, and in the development of a poetic language able to express the widest range of human feelings' (p. 11). Gilles Monsarrat, Brian Vickers, and R. J. C. Watt's authoritative first volume of *The Collected Works of John Ford* will be the standard edition in which Ford's early works are read for many years to come.

BRISTOL UNIVERSITY   LESEL DAWSON

Literary Community-Making: The Dialogicality of English Texts from the Seventeenth Century to the Present. Ed. by ROGER D. SELL. Amsterdam: Benjamins. 2012. x+263 pp. €95. ISBN 978-90-272-1031-9.

This volume proposes a series of engrossing examinations into the dynamics of literary communication through the critical approach developed within Åbo Akademi University's Literary Communication Project. The twelve chapters, by Roger D. Sell (who is director of the project), Helen Wilcox, Anthony W. Johnson, Adam Borch, Juha-Pekka Alarauhio, Inna Lindgren, Jason Finch, Leona Toker, Gunilla Bexar, Janne Korkka, and Elina Siltanen, confront key issues relating to the dynamics of literary texts and the multiple ways in which authors interrelate with their reading communities. The various canonical and non-canonical writers taken into consideration (on the one hand Pope, Coleridge, Arnold, Kipling, Auden; on the other Amelia Lanyer, Thomas Coryate, John Boys, William

Plomer, Walter Macken, Robert Kroetsch, Rudy Wiebe, and Lyn Hejinian), appear a random selection (as Sell himself admits in his introductory chapter). In reality, the adoption of this impressionistic organizational procedure is suggestive of the potentiality of the communicational approach, since each contribution corroborates its applicability to the various levels of literary dialogicality from the point of view of different spatial and temporal perspectives. Consequently, according to their different socio-cultural situations or subjective experiences, the authors are shown to address their communities from a variety of different attitudes: through manipulation or self-affirmation (Lanyer, Coryate, Boys, Johnson, Arnold, Kipling), self-conflict or ideological tension (Plomer, Auden), communicational ethics (Coleridge, Hejinian), or the strengthening of community identity (Kroetsch, Wiebe). Although most of the chapters in the volume tend to approach the issue of dialogicality in terms of the writer's dependency on his/her community, the question of the nature of the reader's response to a text is presented by more than one contributor in terms of a challenge posed by the writers themselves.

In his introductory chapter Sell underlines the debt literary communication owes to Bakhtin's thought (the influence of New Historicism is also apparent), and, in particular, to his concept of heteroglossia. For Sell, Bakhtin's anticipation of postmodern thinking lay in his ability to see 'dialogue and the dialogic imagination of literary authors, as less a matter of dynamic co-adaptation than of predetermined and unceasing conflict' (p. 13). As Sell himself points out, the communication of literary texts is not so much 'a matter of an A sending a message to a B, but as no less possibly a matter of an A and a B comparing notes about something as viewed from within their different life-worlds' (p. 1). In this sense, a community is created not only through mutual recognition but also through difference. Thus, dialogicality can invoke diversity within the same socio-cultural community, just as it can bring about the co-adaption of different positions.

One may, or may not, share Sell's optimistic belief that globalization poses less of a menace in our world today, but the socio-political implications of dialogicality, in terms of its contribution towards an open-mindedness and tolerance that can help to assuage the fear of hegemony brought about by globalization, are an evident concern of the volume. To this end, all the essays illustrate the various ways in which core features of communicational ethics, such as assent and dissent, play a fundamental role in the reception and interpretation of literary texts, especially when one realizes the extent to which the shaping of our own selves depends on our perception of others.

While the volume represents a relatively early stage of the Literary Communication Project, it also promises intriguing future developments (one wonders about the idea of a systematic historical investigation of the phenomenon alluded to by Sell, for example). In the meantime, the temporarily empty gaps in its decidedly thought-provoking chronological presentation make the prospect of including other authors all the more inviting.

G. D'Annunzio University   Renzo D'Agnillo

Fanny Hill in Bombay: The Making & Unmaking of John Cleland. By HAL GLAD-
FELDER. Baltimore: Johns Hopkins University Press. 2012. xiv+311 pp.
£28.50. ISBN 978-1-4214-0490-5.

John Cleland (1709–1789) offers fascinating challenges to literary biography. Until now, the best attempt has been William H. Epstein's *John Cleland: Images of a Life* (New York: Columbia University Press, 1974), whose title warns the reader not to expect a continuous narrative connected by known causes and effects. In many ways, Hal Gladfelder's book is its logical successor: incorporating important discoveries about Cleland's life and work, a significant proportion of which have been made by the author, it sheds much new light on an enigmatic figure whose first novels threatened to make him an outcast, and who unpatriotically suggested the formation of a Portuguese East India Company, but who fearlessly defended victims of injustice, and probably owed his reputation as a sodomite as much to his antimonarchist statements as to evidence about his sexuality. Yet, crucial biographical details are still missing and the attribution of many possible publications, especially letters and reviews in magazines, remains uncertain. Gladfelder, inspired by Roland Barthes and more recent 'theorists of "the author"' (p. 4), acknowledges that he is driven by 'biographical desire' for a figure 'far more a phantom than his fictional persona Fanny Hill' (p. 5). Rather than replacing Epstein, he has sought to 'construct a history or case study of the writer writing', in the knowledge that 'biography should if anything make literary texts *less* stable' (p. 5). The result is an imaginative and compelling study, whose elegance is unencumbered by the formidable weight of the underlying scholarship.

Gladfelder's focus on authorship engenders persuasive interpretations of *Memoirs of a Woman of Pleasure* (1748–49) and *Memoirs of a Coxcomb* (1751), whose own narrators 'have grown into authors who, like Cleland, can both give pleasure and do harm' (p. 138). The idea that reading is 'a sort of voyeurism' (p. 79), and that 'all desire is an effect of imitation, voyeuristically aroused and then acted out' (p. 78), recurs in Cleland's later works, connected with a combination of textual and sexual ambiguity that unmoors the body 'from any single sexual identity, female or male' (p. 11). He undermines assumptions that only one form of desire can be considered natural, making the father of a lesbian transvestite say she is a 'Prodigy of Nature', and that 'Nature must e'en take its Course' (quoted p. 159). He also challenges conventional gender roles, stating that, in the Celtic world which was his political ideal, the rod of justice was often wielded by a Druidess, whom Gladfelder sees as 'a phallic woman' (p. 209).

Gladfelder covers the full range of Cleland's works (original, adapted, and translated), including novels, drama, satirical verse, parody, *The Dictionary of Love* (1753), and travel writing. Intertextuality provides Gladfelder with vital insights: he does not consider Cleland's translations 'marginal or secondary to his "own" or "original" writing' (p. 148), but as examples of the links between all literature. After all, *Memoirs of a Woman of Pleasure* is not considered unoriginal because it began in Bombay in 1730 as an attempt to express in polite language the subject-matter of *L'Escole des Filles* (1655). Links between Cleland's works provide some sense of his life as a patterned progression: for example, his writings on politics, physiology, and philology between 1757 and 1787 comprise a quest for 'the foundations of bodily health, national identity, and the true meanings of words. His assault on the degeneracy of his own times takes the form of a search for lost origins' (p. 217). This varied output was itself a kind of conformity: all professional authors in the middle of the eighteenth century were 'miscellaneous writers' (p. 144). Despite his cosmopolitan tastes and use of French sources, Cleland emerges as that favourite contradiction in terms: a typically English eccentric.

University of Reading   Carolyn D. Williams

A Biocultural Approach to Literary Theory and Interpretation. By Nancy Easterlin. Baltimore: Johns Hopkins University Press. 2012. xiv+324 pp. $65; £34.
   ISBN 978-1-4214-0472-1.

Nancy Easterlin's comprehensive and ambitious monograph aims to explain and—just as importantly—to exemplify in practice an evolutionary and cognitive framework for literary studies. The author is an acknowledged leader in this field, and her book clearly demonstrates her impressive knowledge of evolutionary and cognitive psychologies.

Easterlin's five chapters consist of firstly an apologia for the biocultural approach, and then four successive chapters of explanation and application, focusing respectively on narrative theory, ecocriticism, embodied cognition, and sexual selection. A variety of textual objects are chosen for illustrative readings, including poetry by Wordsworth and Coleridge, Jean Rhys's novel *Wide Sargasso Sea*, and shorter fiction by Raymond Carver and D. H. Lawrence. One cannot fail to be impressed by Easterlin's erudition, which extends from the neurochemistry of love to the nitty-gritty of Romanticist textual scholarship.

At the heart of Easterlin's monograph is her attempt to bring cognitive and evolutionary psychological accounts of aesthetics into a productive dialogue with literary criticism and interpretation. But there are clearly subsidiary objectives as well. Easterlin denounces what she perceives as a covertly political reluctance to make aesthetic value judgements: the more inclusive process of canonization in recent years, she argues, 'creates the illusion that discriminating judgements between works have been avoided, when in fact the criteria for value judgements have merely shifted from the aesthetic to the political' (p. 40). Affective response is also rehabilitated, as when Easterlin asserts, in a reading of Carver's short story 'I Could See the Smallest Things', that readers will find the representations of slugs in the text disgusting because these creatures are 'like things that, according to evolutionary psychology, humans find universally disgusting—rotten meat, decaying flesh, blood, pus, soft tissue' (p. 213).

These are merely simple examples of the way in which, throughout Easterlin's monograph, the psychological components of literary response and interpretation are given greater theoretical significance than is typical in contemporary scholarship. In readings of far greater complexity and nuance, Easterlin invokes attachment theory, accounts of extended mind, and many other theories besides, all of which serve in her view to oppose 'poststructuralist constructionism', which she numbers among 'repressive ideologies' (p. 218).

There is much to admire in Easterlin's extraordinary synthesis of biocultural literary approaches; anyone working in the field as student or researcher will get a great deal of intellectual stimulation from her text. There are caveats. Some degree of parochialism is apparent in Easterlin's rhetoric of tension between biocultural and constructionist approaches. This local intradisciplinary dispute (with its political connotations) tends to suppress investigation of a potential cognitive and evolutionary account of constructionist mechanisms. Furthermore, Easterlin allows contentious psychological subdisciplines to speak with an *ex cathedra* authority in her text. There is little evidence of humanities-informed critique of the cognitive-evolutionary expertise employed in her readings. Her monograph accordingly lacks the ambition of the 'critical neuroscience' movement, which reflects from multiple humanities and social science disciplines on the dangers of contemporary 'neuroideology'. Perhaps future work in the biocultural mode will include more of a reciprocal dialogue between the behavioural and the human sciences.

UNIVERSITY OF GLASGOW   GAVIN MILLER

Hemingway in Africa. Ed. by MIRIAM MANDEL. (Studies in American Literature and Culture) Rochester, NY: Camden House. 2011. xxvii+398 pp. £45. ISBN 978-1-57113-483-7.

The main intention of this comprehensive study of Ernest Hemingway's African writings is exceeded by the content of the volume, which includes not only an informative and challenging introduction as well as nine critical essays, but also two bibliographies: one covering the books that Hemingway owned about Africa, natural history, hunting, fishing, and exploration; the other an annotated bibliography of criticism since 1989 on the author's African-based work. In addition, there is an accurate chronology of Hemingway's two trips to Africa, in 1933–34 and 1953–54, both dedicated to safari in present-day Kenya and Tanzania. Miriam Mandel argues in her introduction that the transient and unsettled nature of safari paradoxically offered Hemingway's restless soul an ideal sense of home, at an extreme psychological distance from the author's conservative upbringing in Oak Park, Illinois. Home as journey and discovery is then allied to creativity and inspiration in Hemingway's life of travel, and home as constant displacement and liminal space is associated with his African narratives' explorations of sexuality, gender, and spirituality. Several essays in this volume examine how Africa also inspired Hemingway to experiment with new genres, crossing boundaries of fiction and non-fiction as well as mixing travelogue, autobiography, memoir, psychological analysis, ecological debate, and teleological treatise. Mandel's orchestration of the volume's factual information, biographical chartings, bibliographic tools, textual analyses, and theoretical insights is certainly to be commended, even though she proposes only a modest aim: to open new avenues of critical debate and to reconsider the importance of the African writings, especially within Hemingway's often derogated late career.

The key publications under consideration are two well-known short stories and the non-fiction book that were produced following Hemingway's first trip to Africa—'The Snows of Kilimanjaro', 'The Short Happy Life of Francis Macomber', and *Green Hills of Africa* (1935)—and the posthumous works written from his second trip: *True at First Light* (1999) and its longer version, *Under Kilimanjaro* (2005), as well as the intercalated African stories in *The Garden of Eden* (1986) and the full archival manuscript of that text. The editor divides the nine critical essays into three sections. The first, 'Knowing What Hemingway Knew', includes Silvio Calabi's expert guide to African big-game hunting, the arsenal of guns Hemingway used, and the huge cost of the safaris (although with a gross income of $400,000 in today's currency from publications, the author still profited from the 1953–54 trip). The following essay, by Jeremiah M. Kitunga (a speaker of Swahili and the Kamba languages), takes Hemingway to task for his misuse of a limited knowledge about African languages and cultures, concluding that the American followed a Western literary tradition of using Africa 'to illuminate Western social crises and as a place to revitalize oneself and one's family life' (p. 136). In the next two sections, 'Appoaches to Reading' and 'On Love and Death', critics tackle both positive and negative implications of Kitunga's assertion. Notable among the more constructive readings of the primary texts is Suzanne del Gizzo's investigation of a key source for *The Garden of Eden* in Beryl Markham's memoir *West with the Night* (1942), along with a subtle analysis of the role empathy plays in the novel's meditation on the nature of authorship. A dense but diffuse argument is developed in Frank Mehring's ecocritical approach to the ethical questions posed in 'The Snows of Kilimanjaro', while Philip H. Melling contributes a rigorously defended critique of *Under Kilimanjaro* that acknowledges Hemingway's sympathy for aboriginal cultures and their sacred beliefs but condemns his promotion of Western consumerism in Africa and his unwillingness to engage with local political realities.

If, as James Plath suggests in the volume's final critical essay, Hemingway found in Africa 'an inspiration for writing and a way to confront his own impending mortality' (p. 314), then that writing also contains several unresolved issues. As other critics here illustrate, besides largely ignoring African politics, Hemingway's work is ambiguous in its treatment of commercial big-game hunting and animistic spirituality, ecological exploitation and pastoral nostalgia, corporate and national imperialism, and the celebrity that he both exploited and sought to escape. The contributors have difficulty themselves with the entrapments of psycho-biographical criticism, but the overall impression that readers will gain from *Hemingway in Africa* is that fresh territory has been marked out and new fields of enquiry have been established by this important publication. Besides the critical essays, the bibliographies will guide readers for years to come, and the most attentive will be rewarded with such aperçus as the ominous entry from Hemingway's library holdings, *Your Shotgun vs. You* by Elliot W. Russell.

LIVERPOOL HOPE UNIVERSITY   WILLIAM BLAZEK

A Journey through American Literature. By KEVIN J. HAYES. Oxford: Oxford University Press. 2012. xvi+192 pp. £45. ISBN 978-0-19-986207-8.

As Kevin Hayes attests at the beginning of *A Journey through American Literature*, in writing the book the author was assisted by his students and readers of his blog, who were encouraged to 'respond to various questions such as what constitutes literary greatness, what are the best short stories in American literature, and what autobiographies deserve recognition as literature' (p. xv). The nature of these three questions gets to the heart of a key problem with the book as a whole: that of who constitutes the work's key audience. Certainly, there has not been a book of this kind for many years, and this might justify its appearance in some respects. However, in the years since synthetic works such as Marcus Cunliffe's *Sphere History of Literature: American Literature to 1900* (London: Sphere Books, 1986) were commonly used as teaching aids, the discipline has become increasingly fractious and sceptical of attempts to organize US writing into a definable tradition. Hayes is certainly aware of this—organizing the book by genre rather than theme, and qualifying his own opening statement that 'American literature is about identity' with 'It is about much else as well' (p. 3)—but *A Journey through American Literature* still feels oddly regressive. Indeed, what critics at the forefront of new work in the field still worry about what constitutes 'literature' or 'literary greatness'? If the book is aimed at general readers then it will merely confirm prevalent cultural attitudes to American literature, rather than destabilize or reshape them. Most of the time, the book does little to advance an alternative or original thesis for how to read American literature, often falling back on passé conceptualizations such as 'The American Dream'. If there is an advance here it lies in the observation that whatever critical consensus there is about American literature has moved on from seeing it as uniquely and exceptionally concerned with 'freedom' or 'liberty'—the primary interest of the Myth and Symbol critics—to a more pluralistic concern with subjectivity.

In fact, it is the persistent and acknowledged presence of the author that really gives the book its character. If American literature is, in aggregate, 'about identity', then *A Journey through American Literature* certainly exists within that tradition, being, as it is, primarily about the identity of Kevin Hayes. To enjoy it, one must think of it more as a new form of autobiography than as a scholarly exercise. Perhaps uniquely for a textbook, one feels as if one is experiencing a highly individualized account, with all the prejudices and personal pleasures that entails. The reader is assured by Hayes that 'private poets' such as Dickinson, Plath, and Robert Bly 'reverberate [. . .] throughout the history of American poetry' (p. 116), that 'William Faulkner may be the greatest American novelist of the twentieth century' (p. 150), and that *The Simpsons* should be considered literature.

It is to the author's credit that he does not dwell too long on problematic ideas such as 'The American Dream', opting instead to compensate for a lack of critical or conceptual depth by echoing Walt Whitman's desire to 'contain multitudes'. The work is remarkably bookish, if not erudite, comprising readings of works that one would seldom find in a more traditional American canon. While the general reader may be impressed with the expanse of the author's reading, one wonders why the book was transitioned from a blog in the first place. Without the capacity to respond and contribute that is permitted by the Internet, *A Journey through American Literature* is a flawed project. Indeed, Hayes's heart seems to lie in the collection of material through other people's suggestions and guidance: the discussion, not dissection, of American books. No one could deny that the bibliography is impressive. Indeed, to finish the review I must, like Hayes, abandon the literary-critical, third-person perspective in saying that the thing I most enjoyed was seeing works such as *Seinfeld* and *The Rockford Files* discussed in the same way as the plays of Eugene O'Neill. However, because these juxtapositions are undertheorized they would sit more contentedly within the more ludic space of the Internet than in an Oxford University Press critical book. For this reason, *A Journey through American Literature* does not come strongly recommended.

UNIVERSITY OF KENT   MICHAEL J. COLLINS

H.D., *Bid Me to Live: A Madrigal*. Ed. by CAROLINE ZILBOORG. Gainesville: University Press of Florida. 2011. lxiv+145 pp. $74.95; £64.50. ISBN 978-0-8130-3731-8.

Caroline Zilboorg's new edition of *Bid Me to Live*, H.D.'s 1960 *roman à clef* detailing her experience during the First World War in England, is thorough, scholarly, and well researched. Zilboorg has 'been working on H.D. for nearly a quarter of a century' (p. xiv), and has previously edited three volumes of H.D.'s and her husband Richard Aldington's correspondence. This text is part of a surge of recent H.D. scholarship, seen in the publication of a number of editions of H.D.'s works by the University Press of Florida, including *Majic Ring*, *White Rose and the Red*, and *The Mystery*, all published in 2009, as well as the recently published *Cambridge Companion to H.D.*, ed. by Nephie J. Christodoulides and Polina Mackay (Cambridge: Cambridge University Press, 2011). *Bid Me to Live* demonstrates an avant-garde mode of writing about the Great War, depicting the experience of non-combatants. Zilboorg's excellent critical edition will help to introduce this fascinating, much underrated modernist text to a new readership.

Zilboorg's approach is autobiographical, advising her reader that 'it is not naïve to begin a reading of the book with an understanding of the people and places, the personal events and larger history that provide at least its background and at times the "actual" material on which H.D. based her novel' (p. xv). She therefore includes, as well as a lengthy Introduction and concluding Editor's Notes, a 'Key to Characters', which gives brief introductions and contexts for the historical counterparts of the characters and includes eighteen 'contemporary photographs of many of the people and places featured in the text' (p. xii). This autobiographical approach is wholly justified, given that 'the novel is based to a large degree on actual people, events, and places' (p. xi).

Zilboorg's account of her editorial decisions is given in the 'Note on the Text', spelling out her practical and philosophical choices and demonstrating her extensive knowledge of H.D.'s writing style and revision process. Since its original publication in 1960 by Grove Press in New York, two further editions of the text have appeared: a 1983 hardcover edition (Redding, CT: Black Swan Books) and a 1984 paperback edition (London: Virago), offset from the Black Swan text. Zilboorg bases her text on the Grove edition as 'this was the version [. . .] that H.D. saw through the press' (p. vii). However, H.D. was away in Switzerland during the time of production, and left many 'practicalities of publication' to Norman Holmes Pearson, her friend and later literary executor. Zilboorg notes that Pearson 'was less than a rigorous editor', and therefore corrects 'occasional and inevitable typographical mistakes', 'idiosyncratic punctuation', and place names (p. viii). By and large, however, she allows 'all inconsistencies to stand', as 'H.D.'s spelling, lexicon, and syntax reflect her dual identity as both British and American' (p. x). Similarly, Zilboorg does not regularize hyphenation, seeing it as indicative of H.D.'s 'propensity to see experience as a series of linked events, overlapping incidents, superimposed phenomena' (p. ix).

The most obvious editorial choices demonstrate a departure from the Black Swan and Virago editions. These are the inclusion of Robert Herrick's complete poem, 'To Anthea', as an epigraph for the text (previous versions have included only four of the six stanzas); the removal of the blank pages between chapters (which appear in the Grove edition) and of H.D.'s drawing of irises, which both the Black Swan and Virago editions use to fill these blank pages; and the decision to retain *A Madrigal* as part of the title (Zilboorg states that this is unlike the Black Swan and Virago editions, although the subtitle does in fact appear on the title-page of the Black Swan version). There is no manuscript version of the novel available, only two undated typed versions and the galley proofs. Zilboorg notes that there are some 'particularly interesting' excisions as H.D. 'moved from the first typed draft towards the published version' (p. vii), suggesting the possibility of a genetic edition of the text in the future. There are some very minor errors, which may be the result of the text's American publication: Lichfield in Staffordshire is referred to as 'Litchfield in northern England' in the Introduction (p. xxiv), although spelt correctly in the Key to Characters (p. liv), and Newhaven is written 'New Haven' (p. xxvi).

The edition is extensively researched and Zilboorg's editorial decisions are clearly explained and justified. The excellent Introduction, Notes on the Text, and Concluding Notes are very helpful in understanding the text and its contexts more fully, and illumine this neglected but significant novel. It will therefore be of value both to experienced H.D. scholars and new readers alike. A much-needed and very well-executed new edition of this important text.

UNIVERSITY OF CAMBRIDGE   ALICE KELLY

Narrating the Past: Historiography, Memory and the Contemporary Novel. By ALAN ROBINSON. Basingstoke: Palgrave Macmillan. 2011. xiv+226 pp. £50. ISBN 978-0-230-23593-9.

After the waning conceptual appeal of postmodernism for scholars engaged with the philosophy of history or with literary treatments of the past, a space of opportunity has opened up for reconfiguring how we speak about the intersection of narrative and recollection. New subfields including trauma theory and memory studies have in turn enriched that space for alternative conversations about how fiction imaginatively apprehends and bears witness to the aftermath of damaging events. But new critical paradigms have a tendency to assume the kind of prevalence they critique in precisely those models they seek to overtake. Such is the case, arguably, with trauma studies, which has provided a welcome departure from what Alan Robinson, opening this forceful study, denounces as postmodernism's 'modish allegations of the unknowability or sublime unrepresentability of the past' which are themselves 'belied by ordinary experience' (p. xiii). The problem, however, is that trauma, as a focus for critical practice, has also relied on 'allegations' of its own about the way societies and selves collectively or individually work through past experiences. Intervening in this current state of interdisciplinary affairs, Robinson synthesizes different approaches to the narrativization of trauma on various scales—both national and personal—without falling under the spell of its theoretical vogue. In so doing, he lucidly formulates what could be described as a cultural narratology of memory, leading scholarship on contemporary fiction studies alongside life-writing studies into that scene of methodological regeneration occupied by historiography in the wake of postmodernism.

Given the reach of his primary corpus—Robinson ranges widely across late twentieth-century anglophone fiction, from established figures such as Fowles, Rushdie, and Atwood, to less comprehensively studied writers such as Jonathan Coe and Sarah Waters—the current review can offer only snapshots of his intervention and a brief evaluation of the book's structural rationale. Robinson's first section usefully reassesses the narrative 'turn' in historiography before then registering formal developments in the novel's engagement with history. Together these chapters offer a pervasive interrogation of the over-rehearsed and rather tired terms in which many writers were addressed—Graham Swift, Julian Barnes, and Angela Carter, most relentlessly—as practitioners of historiographic metafiction. In departing from this notion of fiction's self-referential scrutiny of historical knowledge, Robinson utilizes narrative theory's recent interest in counterfactuality in order to suggest one key thread for the ensuing chapters: the fictional rendition of *present pasts*. As Robinson explains: 'however much they seek to reconstruct "as it actually was" the *past present* in which historical agents envisaged and planned the *past future*, historiographic emplotments inevitably select matters of perceived relevance to the present, which, in retrospect, can recognise that particular events had or would come to have a significance of which historical agents at the time were usually unaware. Historically fluctuating assessments of this significance are reflected in what at a particular time and place is constructed as a usable *present past*' (p. 46, Robinson's emphases).

This model turns out to be genuinely nimble, as Robinson's case studies in Part II cover an impressive array of topical contexts, from life-writing and epistemology in Atwood and Swift—whose *Waterland* Robinson rescues from the bog of postmodern terminology in which the novel had been mired through much of the 1980s and 1990s—to some bold reinterpretations of what might seem like well-trodden conceptions of the state of the nation in Rushdie and Mistry. The latter benefits from Robinson's sensitive attention to technique, as he notes how 'Narrative focalisation in the characters' *past present* or *past future* arouses pathos in the discrepancy between their optimistic aspirations and the narrator's knowledge and reader's suspicions that these will be crushed' (p. 99). This kind of altertness to mode and to the implications of novelistic perspective is not always sustained as consistently as it might have been, and in some instances (the largely thematic and characterological discussions of Coe, Waters, and Pat Barker, for instance) it becomes apparent that the level of narratological rigour displayed in Part I does not always carry over into some of the ensuing chapters' plot-based commentaries.

However, many readers will appreciate the lightness of touch in this respect. For the density of theoretical reformulation and refinement gives way to highly immersive accounts of the structuration of narrative events in particular novels. And while some of the textual readings seem quite exhaustive—or in need of occasional pauses of a more distanced, metacritical kind—it is with considerable patience that Robinson traces the wider ramifications of novelistic events for what he rightly considers to be our 'current preoccupations with memorialisation and trauma' (p. 192). A timely, thoughtful, and unpretentious contribution to contemporary fiction studies, this maps out a new intellectual terrain for considering the vitality of historical fiction as a genre with the capacity to reanimate the very historiography practised upon it.

QUEEN MARY, UNIVERSITY OF LONDON   DAVID JAMES

The 'Conte du Graal' Cycle: Chrétien de Troyes's 'Perceval', the Continuations and French Arthurian Romance. By THOMAS HINTON. Cambridge: Brewer. 2012. iv+277 pp. £60. ISBN 978-1-84384-285-9.

Thomas Hinton has produced a dense but rewarding study of the Continuations of the *Conte du Graal* in all its versions and redactions. The Continuations are currently enjoying a revival of critical attention, as is shown by a spate of recent monographs, including Matilda Tomaryn Bruckner's *Chrétien Continued: A Study of the 'Conte du Graal' and its Verse Continuations* (Oxford: Oxford University Press, 2009, reviewed in *MLR*, 106 (2011), 256–57), Margherita Lecco's *Caradoc e il serpente* (Alessandria: Edizioni dell'Orso, 2010), and Leah Tether's *The Continuations* of Chrétien's 'Perceval': Content and Construction, Extension and Ending (Rochester, NY: Brewer, 2012, reviewed in *MLR*, 108 (2013), 1279–80). Hinton, however, has plenty of original things to say, and shows very well why the Continuations deserve the attention they have now begun to receive. The Continuations typically follow Chrétien de Troyes's *Conte du Graal* in the medieval manuscript tradition, and as Hinton argues, Chrétien owes a great deal to the Continuators, who made a particular point of mentioning him by name. They responded in diverse ways to the enormous challenges which Chrétien bequeathed to anyone trying to tie up all the loose ends of his unfinished masterpiece. (Our medieval source for the supposition that Chrétien died before he could finish the *Conte du Graal* is again one of the Continuations, the one attributed to Gerbert de Montreuil.) The author of the First Continuation embraced the interlace structure which he found in Chrétien's romance, with its double protagonists and its multiple theatres of action. The later Continuations, however, focus on a single protagonist (Perceval). The 'centripetal' and 'centrifugal' forces which shaped the vast narrative cycles of the period are thus also visible in the Continuations as a whole.

Hinton's chapter on scribal rubrics in the manuscripts of the Continuations is particularly original and interesting. As he shows, in positioning the rubrics the scribes seem to be responding to and reinforcing the self-reflexively 'bookish' moments of the text: their rubrics are often triggered by explicit mentions of *l'estoire* (especially when found in rhyme with *memoire*). Changes in authority formulas also reflect the increasing bookishness of later medieval textuality. In the twelfth-century romances the *conte* is the aural story we are listening to; in the thirteenth century reference is made to the *livre* as the handwritten book that medieval readers would have had in view. Hinton plausibly suggests 'that this tendency for thirteenth-century vernacular manuscripts to represent the text as a *livre* may be linked to an increase in the production of manuscripts for lay audiences in this period' (p. 81). The tradition of Arthurian verse romances after Chrétien de Troyes provides a point of comparison for some of the thematic concerns which Hinton highlights. The search for vengeance preoccupied the Continuators and also allowed them to knit together narrative episodes. Gawain's reputation is another recurring narrative preoccupation of both the verse romancers and the Continuators; Hinton draws attention to the playful intertextuality of the episodes where Gawain's identity is questioned.

Hinton's argument could at times have been enriched if he had also looked outside French literature and French-centred scholarship (for instance, my own '*Sir Gawain and the Green Knight*' *and French Arthurian Romance* (Oxford: Clarendon Press, 1995) and J. A. Burrow's 'The Poet and the Book' (*Genres, Themes, and Images in English Literature from the Fourteenth to the Fifteenth Century*, ed. by Piero Boitani and Anna Torti (Tübingen: Narr, 1988), pp. 230–45) are both relevant to his arguments). However, this is a substantial and wide-ranging book as it stands, based on an extensive programme of reading and research.

UNIVERSITY OF BRISTOL   AD PUTTER

Colonizer or Colonized: The Hidden Stories of Early Modern French Culture. By SARA E. MELZER. Philadelphia: University of Pennsylvania Press. 2012. 320 pp. £49. ISBN 978-0-8122-4363-5.

Sara Melzer's intriguing study depicts a conflicted early modern France as it sought to reconcile two different 'colonial' narratives about itself. The first concerned the resurgence of ancient Gaul in France's historical consciousness, a troubling, barbarous presence refracted through the narratives of the ancients, while the second perpetuated an image of France embarking on its own 'civilizing' endeavours as it sought to colonize the New World.

Melzer furnishes a nuanced application of postcolonial theory to early modern France, caught in a 'memory war' (p. 36) as it struggled with the greatness of the Roman heritage; this was a cultural model that implied the relegation of France's own intellectual elite to the camp of the colonized *other*. She characterizes the quarrel between the ancients and the moderns as a site of conflict between two radically different visions of the history of France. The moderns privileged a Gallic, pre-colonial but potentially barbaric past (p. 44), while the ancients understood French history as essentially beginning with Roman colonization. In this context, Du Bellay's *Défense et illustration de la langue française* (1549) is less a '[self-confident] manifesto' (p. 168) than a return to a vision of a pre-colonial Gaul, and an avowal of France's continuing cultural inferiority.

However, these interrogations about France's relationship to its former colonizers arose during the era in which France was itself attempting to implant its own colonies in the Americas. Melzer situates the *relations de voyage* of this era within the context of the Catholic Reformation and of France's colonial impetus in Canada. Here, a strategy of assimilation was threatened by the fear of 'regressing into barbarism' (p. 115) born from the interactions between French and indigenous peoples; these were contacts in which the maintenance of French cultural boundaries was often problematic.

Bringing both strands together, Melzer considers the role of representations of the Amerindian *sauvages* in mediating the relationship of France with the ancients. She analyses the theme of imitation, drawing interesting links between its manifestations in the Latin-based French education system and the frequent depictions by ecclesiastics of Amerindians mimicking French traits. The classical aesthetic, in turn, is considered as a postcolonial response to the ancients; this, for the author, explains the virulence of the *Querelle du Cid*, which resonated with deeply felt anxieties about the very nature of French identity. She also explores the potential of classicism to further the assimilation of Amerindian peoples, through a discourse emphasizing their transformability. For Melzer, the *sauvage* functions as a 'lever' to break the bind with antiquity, or a 'lens' through which to look at the past, encouraging the foundation of a 'new logic' based on the concept of progress (p. 135).

Melzer summons an impressive breadth of sources from the more familiar commentators, such as Du Bellay, Pasquier, or Fontenelle, to lesser-known missionaries in the Americas, such as Claude d'Abbeville or Paul Le Jeune. Despite an isolated editorial oversight (an extract between pages 151 and 152 is repeated, in large part, between pages 194 and 195), she offers a rich interrogation of the crossovers between early modern France's views of itself as colonizer as well as *other*. This book constitutes an original contribution to the study of early modern aesthetics and colonial history, as well as inspiring reflection on France's present-day cultural narrative.

UNIVERSITY OF WARWICK   MICHAEL HARRIGAN

La Librairie de Montaigne: Proceedings of the Tenth Cambridge French Renaissance Colloquium, 2–4 September 2008. Ed by PHILIP FORD and NEIL KENNY. Cambridge: Cambridge French Colloquia. 2012. x+236 pp. £15. ISBN 978-0-9554905-1-4.

This enticing, immaculately produced book contains twelve chapters, nine in French, three in English; they are preceded by an informative introduction in English providing abstracts of each. The colloquium from which they stem marked the generous gift to Cambridge University Library of the books relating to Montaigne assembled by Gilbert de Botton.

Montaigne described his own library (*Essais*, III. 3), claiming to own about a thousand volumes. These were dispersed after his death; only around a hundred works have been positively identified as having belonged to him. Paul Nelles considers how Montaigne assembled his library in Bordeaux, 'one of the outermost reaches of the European communications system' (p. 2). He gives an illuminating analysis of the stock of the Bordeaux bookseller Étienne Thoulouze, much of it from presses in Lyon. He also surveys Simon Millanges's output. Philip Ford, whose recent untimely death leaves a great void, writes about Montaigne's knowledge of Greek, his Greek books, and the use he made of them; Richard Cooper considers his numerous Italian volumes. Marie-Luce Demonet assesses the position in Montaigne's study of two minor philosophers, the methodical Pichot (a doctor interested in the relations between physical and mental illness) and the now more famous La Primaudaye. Alain Legros and André Tournon focus in independent chapters on Lucretius. Legros looks at Lambinus's edition of the Latin poet, which Montaigne owned and annotated, in Latin and later (Legros maintains) in French. He provides illustrations of Montaigne's notes. Tournon examines the ways in which Montaigne describes Lucretius's text, expressing surprise and criticism, and reinterpreting the poet in order to grasp his meaning. Tournon adduces interesting legal material to clarify some of Montaigne's remarks, and gives several lengthy footnotes providing additional perspectives. Catullus, especially the Catullus found in the closing lines of 'Sur des vers de Virgile' (*Essais*, III. 5), is the focal point of Emily Butterworth's chapter, which skilfully suggests how mourning and desire are simultaneously held in suspension by Montaigne thanks to intertexts. John O'Brien returns to his interest in Anacreon, demonstrating how the editor of the *Anacreontea*, Estienne, advocates licence in the use of sources, and how this recommendation casts light on Montaigne, who rarely uses the edition of the Greek lyric poets by Orsini that sat on his shelves: he 'suspends or even just discards hierarchy, rigid genealogy and the organisation of sources around a central principle that authorises or authenticates' (p. 151). (It would have been helpful to translate the snippets of Greek in this chapter.) In analysing the impact of Cicero's *Tusculan Disputations* upon Montaigne, Michel Magnien produces a fundamental reassessment of Montaigne's debt towards the Latin statesman and writer, suggesting, for instance, that he is gradually won over 'par l'énergie des phrases, des formules ou des sentences qu'il lit et relit chez Cicéron' (p. 173). Magnien provides a valuable appendix of passages from the *Tusculan Disputations* used in the *Essais*. Jean Balsamo argues that there existed a copy of Montaigne's work designed to assist with the production of a new edition and containing additions and corrections. Philippe Desan considers Montaigne's reading and rereading of others and of himself, distinguishing between 'livres de proximité' and 'livres de la périphérie' (p. 205). Finally, Patrick Boyde, in a chapter peppered with personal revelations, appraises Montaigne's reaction to Lucretius and provides a checklist of Lucretian quotations in the *Essais*. The contributions to this volume are of an extremely high standard, displaying a rare blend of erudition and clarity and teaching one about Montaigne's reading and writing. A theory as to which books Montaigne took with him on his travels would have been a welcome addition.

BIRKBECK, UNIVERSITY OF LONDON   JEAN BRAYBROOK

Penser l'ordre naturel, 1680–1810. Ed. by ADRIEN PASCHOUD and NATHALIE VUILLEMIN. Oxford: Voltaire Foundation. 2012. x+266 pp. £60. ISBN 978-0-7294-1052-6.

This collection of essays grouped around the theme of natural order between 1680 and 1810 provides stimulating and diverse snapshots of the topic across a range of subjects. The editors specifically adopt an interdisciplinary approach, with a focus on scientific/philosophical and literary/aesthetic subjects, to the exclusion of economic/political aspects of natural order. The papers deal with well-known individual thinkers such as Diderot, La Mettrie, and Sade as well as with the themes of physico-theology, the Alps, artificial procreation, descriptive poetry, and less-studied scientific writers such as Lazzarro Spallanzani and Michel Adanson.

The lengthy introductory chapter by Nathalie Vuillemin outlines the history of the concept of natural order, tracing a line from Linné to Laplace via the *Encyclopédie*, and providing helpful bibliographical details of existing scholarship on the subject. The central point of Vuillemin's introduction is to emphasize the tension between the observation of regularity and the presupposed human theoretical framework behind this observation. This is the tension between the observer and what is observed—the 'construct' of experience—a key insight for many of the contributions. The general presentation does not properly introduce the book's other articles, which inhibits any sense of balance or unity across the volume. This is partly explained in the conclusion by Adrien Paschoud as evidence of the equivocality of the concept of natural order. Without any editorial guidance, the articles by Aurélie Luther on eighteenth-century discourse on the Alps and by Vanessa de Senarclens on Diderot's *Salon de 1767* seem out of place as they do not obviously pertain to the book's theme. There are, however, a number of impressive articles.

The first contribution, by Andreas Gipper, deals with French and German physico-theology. It is a sound introduction to the topic, with detailed readings of the thought of Christian Wolff and Abbé Noël-Antoine Pluche. Gipper uses the concept of natural order to show both the originality and the underlying contradictions (finalism) within the physico-theology movement. The key argument of Wolff and Pluche was to show that God demonstrates a divine freedom by transcending the necessities of mathematics and scientific logic. Gipper's close reading establishes the interconnected nature of Wolff's and Pluche's discourse with the central tenet of aestheticization of nature—seeing beauty in nature as a proof of God.

Paschoud's treatment of La Mettrie's little-known *L'Homme plante*, which is here labelled a 'pendant' to the infamous *Homme machine* (p. 53), perceptively establishes the essentially linguistic and polemic basis of La Mettrie's texts and their 'vertiges lexicaux' (p. 64). Paschoud identifies La Mettrie's polemics as a philosophical strategy to provoke critical thought. Claire Jaquier's contribution examines the descriptive poetry of Jean-Antoine Roucher and Jacques Delille from 1770 to 1810, showing how the two, in differing ways, retained the postulates of natural theology (despite the arguments of the *Encyclopédie*) and managed to harmonize the view of nature as both a God-made spectacle for man and a system of scientific processes into which man is integrated.

Joël Castonguay-Bélanger's chapter on artificial procreation is an excellent survey of the ideas on animal breeding and their impact on human eugenics from Maupertuis to Cabanis, culminating in analysis of literary discourse on interracial reproduction, with particular focus on Rétif de la Bretonne and Robert-Martin Lesuire. Geneviève Goubier provides a useful critical analysis of the flawed scientific reasoning about reproduction employed by the priest Spallanzani, whose ideological presuppositions meant that his observations could only ever serve to furnish proof of an established divine order and preformationism.

In summary, the usefulness of this volume lies in the individual contributions on their specific themes rather than as a comprehensive introduction to the theme of natural order in the period.

University of Manchester   Nick Treuherz

Un commerce pour gens ordinaires? La Rochelle et la traite négrière au XVIIIe siècle. By BENOÎT JULLIEN. (Exhibition catalogue) La Rochelle: Archives départementales de la Charente-Maritime. 2010. 80 pp. €15. ISBN 978-2-9176-8813-7.

Être noir en France au XVIIIe siècle (1685–1805). By ANNICK NOTTER, ERICK NOËL, OLIVIER CAUDRON, and BERNARD GAINOT. (Exhibition catalogue) La Rochelle: Musée du Nouveau Monde. 2010. 51 pp. €8. ISBN 2-9516743-7-6.

La Rochelle, l'Aunis et la Saintonge face à l'esclavage. Ed. by MICKAËL AUGERON and OLIVIER CAUDRON. Paris: Les Indes savantes. 2012. 340 pp. €42. ISBN 978-2-84654-247-0.

La Rochelle is not inclined to political correctness. Historians and those interested in the transatlantic slave trade and its literary fallout are all the better served. Shame has to be set aside, just as it might be by those involved in prostitution… except that the slave trade was legal and open, 'un commerce pour gens ordinaires'. The municipality was among the first in France to acknowledge its slave-trading past, opening the Musée du Nouveau Monde in 1982. Leading researchers in the area started by taking the broad view before focusing on the role of Nantes, Bordeaux, Le Havre, etc. The 'loi Taubira' of 10 May 2001 recognizing slavery and the slave trade as crimes against humanity led to action on various fronts, broadly educational in nature, to ensure a duty of memory in an increasingly multicultural society. La Rochelle brought together all its relevant bodies in 2010 to create several exhibitions and related cultural manifestations in the town. These catalogues and this book (which subsumes much of the former's visual contents) are handsomely produced and vividly illustrated with colour facsimiles of period documents and paintings which bear lasting witness to major aspects of those activities.

The role of La Rochelle was second only to Nantes among French ports in the eighteenth century dealing in the triangular trade, in despatching 427 slave ships between 1717 and 1793; it took first place in the last third of the century, the traffic peaking at 39 in 1785–86. Some seventy shipowners from the town were engaged in the trade, but as with any major commerce, hundreds of others, from shipwrights to bakers, from sailors to insurers, were involved. The book makes an even more substantial contribution than its 340 pages might suggest: it is large (245×220 mm) and printed in two columns. Over thirty contributors, including such well-known scholars as Jacques de Cauna, Jean-Michel Deveau (whose 1990 book on *La Traite rochelaise* is a founding work alongside the books of Serge Daget and Gabriel Debien), Marcel Dorigny, Pascal Even, Bernard Gainot, Benoît Jullien, as well as the editors of the volume, offer some forty articles in four sections: '"L'infâme trafic" (Voltaire): routes, réseaux et acteurs', 'D'une rive à l'autre: la société esclavagiste et la métropole', 'La longue route vers les abolitions', and 'Les héritages contemporains: mémoires et commémorations pour ne pas oublier'.

Commercial networking in La Rochelle often involved Protestant families, interested intermarriage, and associations with like-minded Dutch traders. The 1685 Revocation of the Edict of Nantes, depriving them of access to many official posts, encouraged their engagement in trade, that involving slaves becoming for a time the most lucrative. From that date, captains were required to keep a daily log, a mine of information. Detailed instances are given of families retaining a base in France and implanting a branch in the West Indies to ensure maximum trust and benefit, providing fascinating background information for those interested in the resulting literature. For them, the unpublished first-person account by an African princess taken into slavery (Augeron and Caudron, p. 53) and substantial extracts from Henrion de Ponsey's *Mémoire pour un Nègre qui réclame sa liberté* of 1770 (pp. 208-14) will have particular resonances. As will the passing mention (p. 96) of a slave ship called *Duc de Duras*, especially as no mention is made in these volumes of the little Senegalese girl Ourika, who landed at La Rochelle in August 1786 as she was being taken to Paris by the Chevalier de Boufflers as a gift to his aunt... and a consequent gift to literature through Mme de Duras's eponymous novella. A recent historical novel, *L'Affaire de l'esclave Furcy* by Mohammed Aïssaoui (Paris: Gallimard, 2010), relates to a (non-)slave on whom the historian Sue Peabody has written substantially and who may have as yet uninvestigated links with the Furcy family from Charente which gave rise to a place name in Haiti (p. 285), since ships from La Rochelle also went to Bourbon (Réunion). A host of connections can be made on the basis of these magnificently produced and fascinatingly rich works.

Trinity College Dublin   Roger Little

Correspondance littéraire. By Friedrich Melchior Grimm. Ed. by Ulla Kölving. Vol. vii: *1760*. Ed. by Sigun Dafgård Norén. Fernay-Voltaire: Centre International d'Étude du xviiie Siècle. 2012. liii+396 pp. €130. ISBN 978-2-84559-095-3.

The editors of this excellent edition of Grimm's issues of the *Correspondance littéraire* have had to cope in the previous three volumes with the fact that their primary source, the manuscript of the copy sent to the Duchess of Saxe-Gotha, is the only one to survive, causing obvious problems where there are issues missing from it. The year 1760 causes no such problems, as the manuscript of the copy sent to Louise-Ulrique of Sweden, a new subscriber that year, also survives, and, despite some differences between the two, plugs the gaps. This year sees Grimm back in Paris after his long absence in Geneva in 1759, and exercising the newly acquired role of representative of the city of Frankfurt to the French court.

This is the year of Palissot's *Les Philosophes*, which combines its ridicule of the *philosophes* in general with personal attacks on friends of Grimm. Grimm's own article on the work begins by suggesting that he is discussing it only because he has to: the issue for 1 June begins as follows: 'Vous voulez, sans doute, que je vous parle de la fameuse comédie des *Philosophes* qui a tant occupé le public depuis six semaines' (p. 126). Since the play did not receive its first performance until 2 May, that figure of six weeks is significant; perhaps it is intended to include two weeks of anticipation before the premiere; perhaps the issue was simply late; but it does seem to be a signal that the play is simply not important enough for Grimm to be in any hurry to discuss it. This is, however, belied by Grimm's article, which, while it quite rightly dismisses the play as derivative and artistically negligible, makes a rather more serious attack on the mentality which not only produced it, but made of it a popular success. And subsequent issues also show that Palissot had scored a palpable hit against the camp of the *philosophes*, as attacks on it in the form of both epigrams and more extended texts continue to appear up until October. Particularly interesting are three letters from Voltaire to Palissot included in the issue for 15 August, which, despite their injured tone and defence of the victims of Palissot's satire, also show a determination to remain on civil terms with the satirist of which Grimm clearly disapproves.

It is not without irony that in the very same issue as Voltaire's criticism of Palissot's attack on the *philosophes*, we find his own uncompromising attack on another of the *anti-philosophes*; for this is the year of *L'Écossaise*, in which Fréron is pilloried in the character of Frelon. Grimm had already reported on the publication of the play in the issue for 15 June, when, in an otherwise appreciative review, he saw this character as badly written. So when, in his review of the first performances in the issue for 15 August, he reports, not without a certain irony, that a change of the character's name to Wasp forced on Voltaire by the authorities to protect Fréron had no effect, he also implies that they would have done better to ban the character altogether. But it is above all the series of biting epigrams called *Les Frérons*, which separate Grimm's review from Voltaire's letters to Palissot, that most call into question Voltaire's right to criticize anyone else for indulging in personal satire. Presumably, despite the closeness to Voltaire he seems to have built up during the previous year, this juxtaposition cannot have been accidental on Grimm's part.

The themes that emerge during the course of the year and the juxtapositions in Grimm's text continue to fascinate as this series progresses, and, as ever, the introduction and notes are invaluable.

SWANSEA UNIVERSITY   DEREK CONNON

Germaine de Staël: Forging a Politics of Mediation. Ed by KARYNA SZMURLO. Oxford: Voltaire Foundation. 2011. x+312 pp. £65. ISBN 978–0–7294–1024–3.

This welcome new collection of essays on Madame de Staël responds to, and furthers, recent trends in scholarship on a writer whose significant achievements in a variety of fields are receiving ever-increasing recognition. As is pointed out here, Staël featured for the first time in 2000 in the crucial French examination, the *agrégation*. The collection focuses primarily on Staël as a writer and agent in the political world, and as a figure who engaged in various kinds of literary, cultural, and personal mediation. It also situates her firmly within her historical and literary context, with several articles relating Staël's writings to those of her contemporaries and predecessors.

This political focus has been assisted by the new editions of Staël's political works published over the last thirty years, including an English translation by Aurelian Craiutu of her most extended study, *Considérations sur la Révolution française*

(Indianapolis: Liberty Fund, 2008). In the first half of this collection, 'Revolutionary Engagements', Craiutu contributes a valuable essay on Staël's advocacy of moderation: how she steered a path between Jacobinism and Napoleonic rule via her conception of balanced but co-operative powers in the state. Concentrating on Staël's case against Napoleon, Susan Tenenbaum shows how she draws on French history to present the emperor as an ersatz Louis XIV, only more baneful and dangerous. Meanwhile Chinatsu Takeda highlights the commitment to a second parliamentary chamber evident in *Considérations*, and argues that the book is a pioneering liberal interpretation of the Revolution as a political rather than an economic or social movement. Focusing on the treatment of exile and return in Staël's works, Jean-Marie Roulin emphasizes how, unlike some other writers, she gives the topic a political inflection, 'linking the constitution of one's personal identity to the necessary political refoundation' (p. 149). From a less theoretical standpoint, three other essays examine Staël's networks of communication and interventions for specific ends: Marie-Ève Beausoleil explores how letters among Staël's vast array of correspondents and her published works combined to further her political aims, while Paul S. Spalding and Catriona Seth, respectively, examine her role in freeing Lafayette from imprisonment and her efforts to avert the guillotining of Marie Antoinette.

The second section, 'In Space and Time: Cultural Cross-Currents', opens with one of the most fascinating articles in the collection, Ann T. Gardiner's reappraisal of the celebrated 'Groupe de Coppet'. From research on the extensive comings and goings at Staël's estate, Gardiner showcases the sheer number of people from different fields and with divergent purposes who visited: rather than accommodating a stable group of distinguished thinkers, the estate was a place of rich variety, but as much a stopping-place for exiles and travellers as a centre of intellectual resistance to Napoleon.

Other essays in this section revisit the terrain of Staël's most studied work, her 1807 novel *Corinne*, but in ways that stress its subtitle, *ou l'Italie*. Both Clorinda Donato and Robert Casillo question Staël's treatment of Italians therein: Donato through the lens of Ugo Foscolo, a writer whose important novel of 1798, *The Last Letters of Jacopo Ortis*, Staël overlooked, and Casillo from the perspective of Stendhal. Countering this sceptical approach is Paola Giuli's argument for the career of improviser Corilla Olimpica as an important context for *Corinne*, and Nanora Sweet's generous account of how recent critics have complicated our understanding of the novel's representation of Italian poetry.

All of these sixteen essays—including those not covered here—are of value. The collection is, however, clearly one for Staël specialists: the essays are all in English, but there are no translations of any of the many quotations from French.

UNIVERSITY OF AUCKLAND JOANNE WILKES

De l'abject et du sublime: Georges Bataille, Jean Genet, Samuel Beckett. By CLAIRE LOZIER. Oxford: Peter Lang. 2012. vii+319 pp. £45. ISBN 978-3-0343-0724-6.

In examining the work of Bataille, Genet, and Beckett in the light of the abject and the sublime, Claire Lozier's book both carries out valuable comparative work and illuminates two important theoretical concepts whose treatment can be uneven. In scrutinizing the encounter of the abject and the sublime, Lozier does much to refine our understanding of the negative pleasure of the sublime, a sensation which derives from formlessness or vertiginous scale, and of the interpretative possibilities of the figure. Lozier traces the sublime back to its origins in classical rhetoric, where it is related to *deinos* ('le terrible, le redoutable et le véhément' (p.13)) and, stylistically, to *deinōsis*, associated with stylistic exaggeration and the indignation of the listener. The close readings are sure-footed and incisive throughout, and recontextualize all three authors significantly. As Lozier notes, the standpoint vis-à-vis the abject and the sublime in Beckett's work is arguably the most distinctive, as it is largely implicit, rather than (as in Genet and Bataille) explicit. In this chapter there are valuable insights into Beckett's invocation, in *Malone meurt*, of Kaspar David Friedrich and of Lucretius. The suggestion that Beckett's mathematics owe something to Kant's mathematical sublime is a valuable one, and merits further exploration. As Lozier suggests, 'cette forme de sublime se manifeste à travers l'évocation, non de l'infiniment grand, mais de l'infiniment petit' (p. 197); given the vast textual apparatus devoted to the problem in Beckett, the implications of Lozier's argument could be taken further still. What, in particular, are the implications of Beckettian *deinōsis* for the collision of the abject and the sublime, and the tortured confrontation with the limits of the expressive which characterizes so much of Beckett's work? Lozier undertakes a persuasive analysis of the importance of the postmodern sublime, focusing in particular on Beckett's writings on art: there is rigorous work here on the classical sources of Beckett's 'vanité', which Lozier now links to the sucking stones episode and the larger question of the famous 'syntax of weakness'. The second part of the analysis of the poetics of Beckett's sublime centres on the important debates on the unrepresentable unleashed by Lyotard's work. Lozier quotes relatively recent studies such as those of Gary Adelman and Andrew Slade here, and once more the approach is careful, detailed, and never less than scholarly. Essays such as those of Slade and Adelman are sometimes juxtaposed with those of key thinkers such as Giorgio Agamben (quoted immediately after Adelman), and at times one might wish for a framework which allows for further evaluation of their relative importance. After considering Agamben's work on unspeakability and the Muselmann, Lozier considers the posthuman (in the sense of post-nuclear catastrophe), and takes *Worstward Ho* as a post-catastrophe parable before initiating a fascinating argument on *Breath* as a still life which engages with the Vanitas tradition. Lozier touches on the *October* debates on the *informe* before returning to *Le Dépeupleur* and the plays in the context of the dilemma of unspeakability, so problematically and provocatively aligned, in

Beckett, with the idea of 'l'innommable'. The attention to the text is, once more, truly rigorous, and Lozier establishes herself here as an exemplary, critically aware reader of this transgressive trinity of authors. This, then, is a rich and valuable resource for scholars of Beckett, Genet, and Bataille, and those concerned with the troubled figures of abjection and the sublime: immensely rich, scholarly, and provocative, Lozier's book will undoubtedly bring new insights to the study of the abject and the sublime for some time to come.

UNIVERSITY OF EXETER   DAVID HOUSTON JONES

The Pleasures of Crime: Reading Modern French Crime Fiction. By DAVID PLATTEN. Amsterdam and New York: Rodopi. 2011. x+269 pp. €54. ISBN 978-90-420-3429-7.

David Platten's study is a diachronic account of key moments in the development of French crime fiction from its inception in the mid-nineteenth century to the early years of the twenty-first century. Platten seeks to explore 'the attraction of reading crime fiction in its various guises', and to examine 'the impact on French cultural life that the genre has had at various stages in its history' (p. 17). The first chapter establishes the literary, social, and political factors that led to the consolidation of the new genre in the late nineteenth century in the work of Émile Gaboriau and Maurice Leblanc. In the second chapter, on Georges Simenon, Platten persuasively argues that though Simenon's novels eschew political commentary, they contain profound meditations on social environments which can be seen to prefigure the 'interventionist modes' (p. 45) of subsequent *noir* fiction. The exemplars of early French *noir* here (Chapter 3) are Francis Ryck and André Héléna: Platten examines their work as examples of the ways in which *noir* combines a 'mythic mode', privileging character archetypes and narrative closure, and a 'contingent mode' permitting a critical examination of post-war French society (p. 92). In Héléna's Occupation novels, Platten argues, 'we find an uncanny match of history, the misery of the Occupation, with genre, the bleak amorality of the *noir* ethos' (p. 83). The heirs to Héléna are the *néo-polar* authors of the 1960s and 1970s, notably Jean-Patrick Manchette and Jean Amila, the subjects of Chapter 4, 'The Aesthetics of Commitment'. Along with Didier Daeninckx, these writers turn crime fiction to polemical ends, excoriating the systems of advanced Western capitalism, and, in Daeninckx's case, the corruption and abuses of power in recent French history. Platten skilfully uses the theories of Marcuse and Althusser here to contextualize the *néo-polar*'s aims. Indeed, a major achievement of this study is the instructive ways in which it deploys critical theory in order to illuminate the social and political significance of the primary texts. Thus Platten analyses the plague-outbreak plot of Fred Vargas's *Pars vite et reviens tard* (2001) by using Baudrillard's theory of the simulacrum (pp. 234–35). The final chapter is entirely devoted to Vargas, a writer who has benefited from the increased literary respectability of the crime genre brought about almost single-handedly by Daniel Pennac's 'Saga Malaussène' series (Paris: Gallimard, 1985–99). In his sixth chapter, on 'Modern and Contemporary French Crime Fiction', Platten examines the importance of Pennac as well as Tonino Benacquista and Jean-Claude Izzo in contributing to the 'retour au récit' in recent French fiction.

Two thematic chapters further enrich Platten's exegeses. Chapter 5, 'The Scene of the Crime', examines the built environments in which crime narratives are set. It is a truism of crime-fiction criticism that 'a city-less crime novel is inconceivable' (p. 135). Platten departs from this, producing fascinating readings of the social and geographical structures of the provincial town, of the countryside, and of HLM estates, as they function respectively in the work of Pierre Siniac, Pierre Véry, and Jean Vautrin. Chapter 7 focuses on the importance of youth culture to the French *roman noir*.

In his conclusion, Platten suggests that the 2007 'Pour une littérature-monde' manifesto may, in its critique of the modes of cultural hegemony, have positive implications for perceptions of genre fiction. This accessible and well-documented study makes a strong case for the relationship of crime fiction to the literary mainstream having shifted in recent years to become 'one of difference in equality' (p. 253). In such a changed landscape, Platten's study will be inspirational in helping to shape the future modes of crime-fiction scholarship.

UNIVERSITY OF KENT   LUCY O'MEARA

Women, Language and Grammar in Italy, 1500–1900. By HELENA SANSON. Oxford and New York: Oxford University Press for the British Academy. 2011 xii+ 417 pp. £85. ISBN 978-0-19-726483-6.

Helena Sanson's book, based partly on existing studies published between 2005 and 2010, stands out for its thorough coverage and its rigorous use of documentary evidence. The complex evolution of the Italian language is assessed across four centuries, and considered from the specific perspective of female education and culture, or rather the relationship between grammar and women. Intended as a 'key to knowledge', *grammatica* reveals its many layers of symbolic meaning. The metaphorical charge that the discipline acquired via classical and medieval iconography (particularly in the figure of Nicostrata-Carmenta) is the starting-point for Sanson's research: 'As in the visualization of the nine Muses, the grammatical gender of the Latin *grammatica* lends itself naturally to an iconographical representation of the subject as a female figure captured in a range of poses, in combination with a variety of—at times contradictory—attributes' (p. 2).

It is known that in Italy, more so than in other Romance areas, the historical status of the vernacular was long subjected to the supremacy of Latin. The situation changes naturally with the spread of the printing press. From the early sixteenth century there is an ever wider circulation of vernacular books, and thus the need for a common standard is felt more keenly. It is not by chance that the development of the printing press coincides with a substantial increase in the production of vernacular grammars. With this in mind, of particular interest is Sanson's overview of the first grammars aimed at women, such as Lodovico Dolce's *Dialogo della institution delle donne* (Venice, 1545), reprinted several times in the latter half of the sixteenth century. Sanson considers it in relation to other grammars of the time, highlighting its pedagogical approach and ideological stance. So it is that women assume a considerable role in the history of the Italian language, not merely from a literary point of view, through a temporary rebalance of rights which influenced even the discussion of grammar dedicated to 'Hiparca' offered by Rinaldo Corso in his *Fondamenti del parlar toscano* (Venice, 1549).

The end to political stability and the gradual foreign dominance contribute to the obliteration of the temporary linguistic development which was brought about at a supra-regional level in the course of the sixteenth century. A series of competing factors left Italy with a linguistic evolution that differed markedly from other European countries. An understanding of the peculiar case of Italy is dependent on seeing the language first and foremost as a political, rather than cultural, entity. Indeed, political fracture is reflected in the fracturing of everyday language: in other words, the language of conversation based on exchanges between various speakers and reciprocal contamination. Faced with such a crisis, a solution of the literary sort is practically unavoidable, and backed fervently by the Jesuits, who became unchallenged as the sole providers of educational establishments and practice. In the specific case of female education, a return to highly conservative or traditionalist tendencies can be seen. This much is confirmed by the beliefs of Orazio Lombardelli, professor of rhetoric, who in his short treatise on grammar (*I fonti toscani* (Florence, 1598)) situates 'the female sex on a par with children: two categories associated, according to contemporary ideas, by their limited intellectual and linguistic abilities' (p. 113).

By now Bembo's model was gaining favour, and subsequently the seventeenth century too increasingly turned its back on modern Florentine. Inroads made on the social front as well, in the Counter-Reformation period, gradually came to an end, thus reducing the position of women in the context of intellectual life. 'In the Seicento, in contrast with the more philogynistic Cinquecento, women were also displaced from their role as privileged recipients of polite literature, against the background of a returning misogynistic literary production' (p. 115).

Sanson rightly insists that 'in the linguistic history of Italy, the Settecento represents a turning point' (p. 129). The use of dialect remained widespread, as shown by Maurizio Pipino's *Gramatica piemontese* (Turin, 1783), which Sanson analyses with accuracy and originality. It is certainly no surprise that in the 'Century of women', steeped as it was in Enlightenment culture, female education sees an improvement in quality. Italian, albeit in its various regional incarnations, nevertheless remained the language of the elites, as Giuseppe Baretti observed with characteristic foresight. One of the book's strong points, therefore, is the attention Sanson devotes to handbooks for women during this period, foremost among which must be the *Trattato degli studi delle donne* (Venice, 1740) by the Sienese scholar Giovanni Niccolò Bandiera, where an objective change in mentality can clearly be felt with respect to previous centuries. Sanson observes: 'Educating women could, according to Bandiera, bring only positive effects to the institution of marriage and the family as a whole, as well as to the whole of society and the political system'

(p. 153). Against this backdrop of partial emancipation stand the figures of Aretafila Savina de' Rossi, Laura Bassi, Elisabetta Caminer Turra, Diamante Medaglia Faini, and Rosa Califronia (author of the *Breve difesa dei diritti delle donne* (Assisi, 1794)), each of whom Sanson portrays briefly but discerningly. Naturally, language teaching remained closely connected to literary learning. Gian Vincenzo Gravina in his *Regolamento degli studi di nobile e valorosa donna* reiterated the view that the literary tradition constituted a resource for language learning. Even in the eighteenth century 'knowledge of the Italian language had then to be reinforced by reading linguistically sound literary works' (p. 163).

Only with Manzoni does the shift take place in Italy from the written to the spoken language. A substantial section of the book is indeed given over to linguistic debates during the nineteenth century. The supremacy of Florentine as sought by Manzoni in fact represented a breakthrough that was by no means straightforward. Sanson is exhaustive in reconstructing the disputed process of the nation's linguistic codification, providing moreover an original apparatus of documentary evidence. In the varied regional or even municipal context of Italy in the early Ottocento, the defence of a single language for the entire country represented an extremely arduous undertaking. Sanson considers Emilia Luti's contribution crucial for contextualizing Manzoni's proposed solution. It is certainly commendable to assign a central role to the woman who became a linguistic adviser to Manzoni during the revision of his novel, though occasionally Sanson exaggerates her importance in providing grammatical advice. (Manzoni and Emilia met only in the summer of 1839, when the definitive edition of the Quarantana had already been completed. Emilia was twenty-four at the time.)

On this basis, Manzoni replaced a purely literary or rhetorical vision of the language with a more complex and progressive outlook. So it was that for the first time in the history of the Italian language the social element became part of the equation. Links between Florence, the 'cradle' and centre for the divulgence of the national language, and other cities in the peninsula became ever closer, while the establishment of a set of common rules seemed an attainable goal. Sanson examines the intimate connections in nineteenth-century Italy between the question of national unification and the language question. In the Risorgimento the concept of 'mother tongue' takes on a decidedly political meaning, with language being an integral part of a nation. And while the disputes around language do not lead to a promotion of the dialects, it is true that obsolete forms of the literary tradition tend to be forgotten in favour of establishing a readily identifiable code of orality. Therein lies the strength of Manzoni's vision: in avoiding hybrid forms and mixtures of various dialects, he saw in the spoken Florentine of the 1820s the language to bequeath to the unified nation. Not an ephemeral and artificial reality (such as the fourteenth-century language proposed by Bembo), but a dynamic and well-defined phonetic substance. The connection between mother and tongue thus became more pressing: 'To summarize the essence of the Question debates of the time, one could say that the core of the problem was how to make Italian effectively a *mother tongue*, in the sense of the language that a mother would use with her children and, conversely, the language that a child would learn naturally in the first years of life' (p. 261). Such notions fit perfectly with the figure of the *maestra*, a 'second mother', to which Sanson devotes one of the book's most successful sections (pp. 274–84). Moreover, the *lingua materna* is to be learnt from one's earliest years, as Dante prophetically declared: 'a language is natural when it is learnt from the mother in childhood, without any effort or rules' (p. 350).

Università di Bologna   Francesco Sberlati
                                                    (translated by Paul Howard)

Dante's 'Commedia': Theology as Poetry. Ed. by Vittorio Montemaggi and Matthew Traherne. (The William and Katherine Devers Series in Dante and Medieval Italian Literature) Notre Dame: University of Notre Dame Press. 2010. xii+388 pp. $40. ISBN 978-6-268-03519-8.

This volume publishes the proceedings of the conference held in Robinson College, December 2003, that brought together Dante scholars and theologians to discuss the *Commedia* as theology. This reviewer has just completed another review, for *Approaching the Holy Mountain: Art and Liturgy at Saint Catherine's Monastery in the Sinai*, ed. by S. E. J. Gerstel and R. S. Nelson (Turnhout: Brepols, 2010), similarly conference papers and for an exhibition, held at the Getty Museum in 2007, where the participants dialogued and whose essays now lead from one to the other harmoniously, all participating in the editing and presentation in print. I noted their failure to reference John G. Demaray's and Carol Kaske's observations that Mount Sinai is Dante's Mount Purgatorio. But they discuss admirably early Christian theology's use of typology, an aspect the volume under review largely lacks (Auerbach gets one reference only). This volume mainly sees Dante through the prism of modern theology and modern literary criticism, not his own. Its essays are mostly discreet, created within boxes separated from each other, the multidisciplinary dialoguing of the Cursor Mundi series not having been encouraged to flower.

In their introduction Vittorio Montemaggi and Matthew Traherne, as editors, discuss the crux of the 'allegory of the poets' as fictional and distinct from the 'allegory of the theologians', which is truthful. In *The Pilgrim and the Book: A Study of Dante, Langland and Chaucer* (New York: Peter Lang, 1987), now in Italian as *Il Pellegrino e il libro: uno studio su Dante Alighieri* (Florence: Centro studi romei, 2012), I present the argument that because Dante places himself within his pilgrim text as within a flesh-and-blood parallel to Adam's exile and to the Gospel-writer Luke's pilgrimage, his poetry becomes theology, his allegory typology; it is incarnational.

Robin Kirkpatrick's essay, 'Polemics of Praise', asks that the theme be approached with greater closeness to text and context, in Dante's own first-order discourse, rather than our scholars' second-order one, and sees theology more as liturgy, as priests' poetry. Peter S. Hawkins's 'All Smiles' reflects on Dante's laughter, like Troilus's on glimpsing this puny globe at the Cosmos's centre/periphery, reflected in Beatrice's smile, on the Eckhartian laughter in the Trinity, and on the humility/joy at admitting error, the *metanoia* from them. Montemaggi discourses on 'Unknowability as Love', specifically in the Ulysses and Ugolino cantos, two episodes that are rather lacking in love. Piero Boitani's 'Poetry and Poetics of Creation' discusses the *animula* of the Dormition of the Virgin (one splendid example of which is by Arnolfo di Cambio in the Opera del Duomo and which perfectly explains 'figlia del tuo figlio') and other examples of the soul as child, of farmers at vintage, of the eagle, of the folly of the theologians who get it wrong, thereby eliciting a smile, of God's 'coursing' over the waters at Creation, of angels, ringing the changes on Hebraic and Hellenic paradigms, in Dante's text. Matthew Traherne discusses 'Liturgical Personhood' in the *Commedia*, an essay which could have benefited from recalling Kirkpatrick's juxtaposition of Dante as secular poet to Hopkins as priest-poet, while noting Dante's scraps from the liturgical Office and the Mass, from Penitence to Praise, the reflected Glory of God in Creation, seen as the 'smile of the universe'. Traherne speaks of the absence of the Sacraments in the *Commedia*, not mentioning that medieval exile went hand in hand with excommunication, that being Dante's state unless he were to be reconciled, as he desired, in the Ceremony of Penance in the Baptistery of Florence.

Next, among the theologians now, Oliver Davies discusses the *Commedia* and the Body of Christ, both in pre-modern and modern terms, as ubiquitous glory, though for us no longer cosmological. Theresa Federici discusses Dante as David, both sinners, particularly with Psalm L, and God's scribe. Paola Nasti's 'Caritas and Ecclesiology in Dante's Heaven of the Sun' cites Boccaccio on theology as the poetry of God, next discoursing on the Church as Christ's Bride. Douglas Hedley discusses 'Neoplatonic Metaphysics and Imagination in Dante's *Commedia*' as resulting in the Romantics' appreciation of him, themselves espousing Neoplatonism. Christine Moevs's 'Il punto che mi vinse' discusses the knowledge of oneself and God, beyond time/space. Denys Turner, who studies his namesake, pseudo-Dionysius, in Julian of Norwich, here discusses Dante, Aquinas, and Eckhart and their theological rhetoric, particularly as regards vernacular poetry.

Two afterwords follow, by John Took and David Ford. Indexes give references from the *Commedia* and the Bible.

In all these essays there is an undertow of submeanings, on love, on light, on word, on speech, on silence, on body, and on gesture, but too little on medieval theology's continuum of the Alexandrian allegorical readings of the Bible (*figura/typology*), which are likewise Dante's; much of Aquinas's *Summa* but none of Ong's incarnational understanding of Aquinas's lyrics. We moderns, if scriptural, are Antiochene. It is among the critics that the theme of humility comes forth, not among the theologians.

UNIVERSITY OF COLORADO, BOULDER   JULIA BOLTON HOLLOWAY

Il saggio, il gusto e il cliché: per un'interpretazione di Mario Praz. By DAVIDE DALMAS. Palermo: duepunti. 2012. 208 pp. €18. ISBN 978-88-89987-71-1.

Davide Dalmas's recent book is a masterful examination of Mario Praz, the literary critic most responsible for the vibrancy of English studies in Italy between the 1930s and 1960s. Dalmas shows that Praz continued to put forward daring and original interpretations of literature and cultural history until his death in 1982, challenging the later association of Praz's *gusto* with mere cliché. The last chapter ends with an open question about Praz's own technique of turning faded images into parody in search of his taste, in Italian *gusto*; the author seems to wonder if Praz, whose narrative often created a junction between enthralment and disillusion, finally aimed to resurrect the spirit of the past in order to make his observations on artistic tastes more animated. Dalmas maintains that Praz's critique, seen as a history of taste, allows readers to become acquainted with their own times and with the dominant cultural taste. Particularly interesting is Praz's brief gloss about classics, which are interpreted by modern readers as such. However, according to Praz, moderns read classics in search of their anxieties and expectations, without considering their belonging to an inaccessible past as a limitation or an obstacle.

As Dalmas notes, the final republication of Praz's œuvre by the prestigious Italian publishing house Adelphi was a sign that a re-evaluation of his work would not be long in coming. As he puts it, 'Praz è proposto definitivamente non solo come critico ma come grande scrittore del Novecento, come un classico moderno' (p. 162). Another was the 2002 translation and republication of Praz's perceptive introduction to Charles Lamb's *The Essays of Elia* (republished in the *Charles Lamb Bulletin*), which can also be taken as a sign of growing international interest in Praz's career in the UK. Charles Lamb, observer of the birth and consolidation of what we now consider characteristically eccentric British urbanity, was Praz's favourite essayist, one of his role models for style.

With great skill, Dalmas condenses and narrates Praz's literary career, which began with a titanic study on Romanticism, *La carne, la morte e il diavolo nella letteratura romantica* (published in 1930 and in an English translation by Angus Davidson as *The Romantic Agony* in 1933). As Dalmas points out, according to Frank Kermode, Praz's most renowned text became a classic 'che va annoverato tra i libri che hanno il potere di cambiare la visione che il lettore ha della storia della società in cui vive, e persino della sua stessa storia personale' (p. 64). *La carne* was built upon his previous works, *Poeti inglesi dell'Ottocento*, *La fortuna di Byron in Inghilterra*, and *Secentismo and marinismo in Inghilterra*. Like others in his generation, including Gabriele Baldini, Elémire Zolla, Giorgio Melchiori, and Agostino Lombardo, Praz was inspired to pursue English studies by Emilio Cecchi, whose pioneering *Storia della letteratura inglese del secolo XIX* was published in 1915. The scholarship that this group produced between the wars has rightly led to its being considered the golden age of Italian *anglistica*.

The exploration of the Roman academic milieu to which Praz belonged is one of the strongest aspects of Dalmas's book. He was also a visitor for longer and shorter periods in England itself. In 1933 Praz spent some time in London, where he read Aby Warburg's studies and met the director of the Warburg Institute, Fritz Saxl. It was in London that Praz established the philosophy of furniture—a concept invented by Poe and deepened by Baudelaire—as an instrument for interrogating and investigating the fictional and private self in literature and the visual arts. The following year he published *Studi sul concettismo*, an elaboration of his interest, which he shared with T. S. Eliot, in the English metaphysical poets. Dalmas looks closely at Praz's relationship with the anglophone literary world—for example, his friendship with the English expatriate Vernon Lee, recorded in their letters. He is mentioned in Edmund Gosse's private correspondence and in Derek Patmore's *The Italian Pageant* (1949). Admitted to the Pen Club in 1949, and by that time considered an international authority, he was knighted in 1962.

In his later books, *Il patto col serpente* (1972) and *Il giardino dei sensi* (1975), continuity with the Italian tradition of English studies was especially strong. His final books, *Voce dietro la scena* (1980) and *Il mondo che ho visto* (1982), exemplify what Dalmas refers to as Praz's constant attention to time appearances, echoing the title of his book *I volti del tempo* (1964) (p. 155); here, Praz's nuanced *gusto* is finally open enough to allow the reader glimpses of autobiography. The title of Dalmas's book, *Il saggio, il gusto e il cliché*, suggests the triangle of writing components or literary forms that Praz shaped and developed in his works, and that, later, Edmund Wilson and other critics recognized as his main literary talent: 'La ricerca di Praz non andava in direzione della poesia in prosa ma verso la creazione di una personale rielaborazione del saggio moderno di tradizione anglosassone' (p. 128). Dalmas's book acts as a kind of encounter between Praz and his most beloved authors (Lamb, Proust, Henry James, among others) and stands as a homage to Praz. Praz, and Dalmas writing about Praz, both manage to walk the line between the biographical essay and critical insight. Dalmas's book is an ambitious endeavour to place Praz and his idiosyncratic views of literature and society at the centre of the scholarly world once more.

ROYAL HOLLOWAY, UNIVERSITY OF LONDON   ILARIA MALLOZZI

The Fiction of Juan Rulfo: Irony, Revolution and Postcolonialism. By AMIT THAKKAR. Woodbridge: Tamesis. 2012. 181 pp. £50. ISBN 978-1-85566-238-4.

Almost sixty years after the publication of *El llano en llamas* (1953) and *Pedro Páramo* (1955), Amit Thakkar's reading of Rulfo's fiction as an exercise in irony is thoughtful and illuminating. If a critique of the Mexican Revolution and the post-Revolutionary state will be noted by any diligent reader of Rulfo, Thakkar explains in painstaking detail the different levels on which this stance is formulated. The discussion is anchored on the crucial function of irony and aided by postcolonial theories such as those put forward by Homi Bhabha. Upon finishing the book, the reader can only agree that without an understanding of irony, some of the power of Rulfo's work would be lost (p. 40).

The book follows an approach based on the dynamics between two forms of irony: centripetal (or internal, between 'form and content') and centrifugal (or external, between 'text and context') (p. 2). Thakkar's methodology proves productive, for it allows him to elucidate the ironic subtexts of short stories such as 'Nos han dado la tierra' and 'El día del derrumbe' in a continuum that goes from certain elements internal to the stories, such as the title, to a critique of the context, in this case the rhetoric of the post-Revolutionary state. Throughout the book, the reader is captivated by Thakkar's exercise of close reading and his penetrating analysis of Rulfo's works against the discourse of the post-Revolutionary state in speeches, newspaper articles, essays, and murals. Read against this background, Rulfo's words acquire an additional weight.

Thakkar argues that the way in which the central pre- and post-Revolutionary regimes in Mexico engaged with the country was comparable to a form of neo-colonial domination (p. 73), a suggestion that some readers may find debatable. And yet one of the most compelling analyses is that of the teacher in 'Luvina' as an in-between figure grappling with the contradictions of the competing discourses of colonialism and egalitarianism in the post-Revolutionary rhetoric. Equally lucid is the discussion of Father Rentería in *Pedro Páramo* as a character that undermines both the state's 'fetishistic stereotype of evil' and the Church's martyrological images during the Cristero war (p.116). In Thakkar's reading, the priest is both a victim of his own flaws and a pawn trapped in the complexity of the relations between state, Church, and a tradition of rural *caciquismo* that draws on the colonial legacy. There is also a discussion of *caciquismo* from a historical perspective, which again produces a lucid analysis of Pedro Páramo's ironic ambivalence. Ultimately, Thakkar posits and demonstrates that irony is a strategy which encourages an inquisitive mode of reading: by noticing 'centripetal' irony, the reader is prepared to undertake an interpretative task where the awareness of 'centrifugal' irony results in the full appreciation of the political meaning of the texts.

There are aspects of the book that some readers will not find convincing: the argument of 'cosmic irony' in Pedro Páramo's relationships with women does seem dangerously close to justifying rape, as Thakkar himself notes (p. 142). Similarly, was there such an unproblematic continuity in the 'colonizing' discourse of pre- and post-Revolutionary regimes in Mexico? The author seems aware of 'the risk of conflating different forms of colonial experience' (p. 86), and yet at times his discussion seems to overlook such difference. Finally, a future edition would do well to correct the typos in the Spanish quotations. All this notwithstanding, Thakkar's remarkable insight and scholarship render this book essential reading for anyone interested in deepening their understanding of Rulfo's works.

Royal Holloway, University of London   Olivia Vázquez-Medina

The Cambridge Introduction to German Poetry. By Judith Ryan. (Cambridge Introductions to Literature) Cambridge: Cambridge University Press. 2012. xii+238 pp. £17.99. ISBN 978-0-521-68720-1.

Judith Ryan's superb new introduction to German poetry is to be welcomed on any number of fronts: it is unimpeachable in its treatment of major texts from the German-language lyric canon, presenting these with a richness and verve which should appeal both to the conventional readership of an 'introduction' and to those with a serious existing interest in German poetry; it combines formidable scholarship—ranging from medieval to contemporary poetry—with an admirable lightness of touch; it witnesses to a refreshing willingness on the part of a major press still to publish works on subject-matter which some of us may have feared was edging towards being viewed as recondite (the same press, it should be added, which published Ronald Gray's valuable *An Introduction to German Poetry* (1965), with which Ryan's text bears some comparison). Poetry is cited in German throughout, with accompanying prose translations.

Ryan's *Introduction* serves both as an account of defining themes of German poetry as they recur in a wide historical spectrum from the Middle Ages to the present, and as a sensitive guide to the questions which might animate a critical response to any given text or grouping. Her main chapters mark out a broadly historical scheme whose terms none the less allow Ryan considerable flexibility in moving between different thematic areas: 'Poetic Roles in Early Song-Lyrics'; 'Devotional Poetry'; 'The Rhetoric of Passion'; 'Classical Antiquity and Modern Experience'; 'Romantic Poetry and the Problem of Lyric Unity'; 'The Self and the Senses'; 'Modernism and Difficulty'; 'Poetry after Auschwitz'; 'Political Poetry'. One of the most skilful aspects of Ryan's exposition is the way she conveys the historical moment of these various constellations while also using them to make connections which a purely chronological account would find much harder to substantiate. Thus the chapter on devotional poetry begins with a consideration of the Lutheran 'Kirchenlied' and finishes, entirely convincingly, with an account of Celan's 'Tenebrae'. The intellectual force underlying such a conjunction belies this book's 'introductory' status.

Students who turn to Ryan for help with critical appreciation will find themselves well catered for. Even though the book implies very serious claims about the character and historical determinacy of German poetry, it grounds all of this in exemplary close readings, which it unfolds with scrupulous explication of prosodic effects and different metrical forms. At the back of the book there is a helpful glossary of poetic terms, a guide to German metrics, and some advice on 'working on the text' and 'writing up your close reading'. This should make it a fixture on reading lists for courses on the German lyric. It should be added that Ryan—thankfully—reads all her texts in the spirit of a traditional practical criticism, and draws out complexity and ambiguity without any recourse to fanciful theoretical vocabularies. Nor does she exhibit that revisionist hubris which would foist on the reader 'previously unknown' writers who should almost certainly remain unknown. Rather, she addresses herself with outstanding tact and critical acumen to the major names of the German lyric, and has produced a book which deserves the largest possible readership among all who have interests in the subject, be their needs more or less introductory.

UNIVERSITY OF KENT   IAN COOPER

Die Lebenszeugnisse Oswalds von Wolkenstein: Edition und Kommentar. Vol. IV: *1438–1442, Nr. 277–386*. Ed. by ANTON SCHWOB and UTE MONIKA SCHWOB. Vienna: Böhlau. 2011. xxiv+352 pp. €39. ISBN 978-3-205-78631-3.

This is the fourth of five volumes in an edition which will bring together all known documents associated with Oswald von Wolkenstein, the most innovative and perhaps also the most colourful late medieval poet in German. He gives us an example of late medieval autobiography, with a strong first-person perspective which encourages the reader to piece together the author and his life's experience behind the persona of the singer. It is therefore of prime importance that Oswald, unlike his predecessor Walther von der Vogelweide, can be traced through a multiplicity of documents as a historical figure, allowing us to read the historical record alongside the literary construction of a self in the songs.

Three themes dominate the documents of the current volume: local and imperial politics; a series of lawsuits about property rights; and a strong sense of family in all its complications. Despite the fact that Oswald had left imperial politics to return to more provincial Tyrol after being reconciled with Count Frederic of Tyrol, he continues to play a part in the larger political scene as well as at home: we learn how Oswald is called to arms when the peace treaty between Trent and Venice is on the verge of collapse yet again (pp. 89–90); we see him acting as mediator on behalf of Count Henry IV of Tyrol between two parties of burghers from Nuremberg (pp. 162–63); he receives accounts of political events in Brixen and their echo in the empire from fellow citizens (pp. 216–17); and he is consulted by another friend about tactical voting at the upcoming diet in Meran (pp. 248–49). As in the previous volumes, the often turbulent family relations can be extrapolated from the many documents relating to property transfers and disputes about ownership rights: the castle of Hauenstein had been apportioned to Oswald in 1407, but the documents in this volume remind us that although Oswald had been resident there, on and off, since 1417, the fief was held by his older brother Michael (p. 30)—a cause of occasional strain between the brothers, though in this period the dominant impression is one of pride in familial bonds strengthened through property held in common between a number of (male) members of the family. The largest group of documents, however, relates to a local scandal: a bitter and long-drawn-out dispute between the neighbouring communities of Ritten and Villanders over rights of pasture and access. Schwob's commentary is exemplary in giving us a context in which to read events, and he reminds the reader that conflict here is not so much the result of personal wrongdoing, or of particularly litigious individuals, but a consequence of social structures in which communal use is long established but not clearly regulated. The sequence of proclamations and legal exchanges allows us to see social conflict escalation in all its complexity: Oswald, denounced by the opposing party as someone with a record of trouble-making himself, wades into the dispute, skilfully uses the fact that the opposing party had employed a spy to the advantage of his side, and causes a stir through a series of public proclamations in Brixen—sufficient for the news of the dispute to travel well beyond Brixen and reach the King. Yet Schwob's collection also reveals that it is the diplomatic skill of the elder brother, Michael, which brings about a peaceful resolution.

The volume thus offers historians an insight into the circumstances of a particular individual, but also a much broader picture of the social networks, economic circumstances, and institutional organization of late medieval society in Tyrol. Historians often prefer normalized editions in which the use of modern orthography offers greater ease of reading. Schwob aims to offer the best of both worlds: his decision to retain the orthography of the originals allows scholars of German an equally important assessment of a writing language in transition, while the meticulous commentary which precedes each document gives contextual information and summarizes the content. The fact that seemingly dry legal documents make fascinating reading is thus tribute to Oswald von Wolkenstein, whose voice emerges as distinctly from his letters as it does from the songs—but tribute also to the achievement of the editors, because it is their scholarship and meticulous presentation which brings those facts to life.

SOMERVILLE COLLEGE, OXFORD ALMUT SUERBAUM

Johann Joachim Eschenburg und die Künste und Wissenschaften zwischen Aufklärung und Romantik: Netzwerke und Kulturen des Wissens. Ed. by CORD-FRIEDRICH BERGHAHN and TILL KINZEL. (*Germanisch-Romanische Monatsschrift*, suppl. 50) Heidelberg: Winter. 2013. 464 pp. €58. ISBN 13: 978-3-8253-6091-7.

Johann Joachim Eschenburg (1743–1820), if he is known at all outside specialist circles, is remembered perhaps best as a victim of Goethe's and Schiller's *Xenien* and the subject of Schiller's contempt as a representative of 'das Elende'. This is perhaps a good place to begin. Goethe and Schiller saw themselves (and few others) as an elite, set apart from the common herd, touching only significant themes and forms and investing these with substance through organic processes derived from nature. Their writings and endeavours in the 1790s have to do with sifting the essence from the superficial and the merely inclusive—and discoursing on their own superiority.

Not surprisingly, they had little time or patience for one whose poetic model was still Horace's *Ars poetica*, who was a close friend and collaborator of the much-hated Friedrich Nicolai; one who saw literary form as subject to rules essentially devised generations earlier; for whom literature and its practitioners adhered to the same order and system that applied in all spheres of knowledge; who believed in inclusivity—of the good and the less good—in the pursuit of an all-encompassing account of human intellectual endeavour. All this, too, from a professor at the Collegium Carolinum in Brunswick, who had produced a *Handbuch der klassischen Litteratur* (first 1783), *Entwurf einer Theorie und Litteratur der schönen Wissenschaften* (first 1783), *Beispiel-Sammlung* (1788–95), and *Lehrbuch der Wissenschaftskunde* (first 1792). It seemed to Goethe and Schiller that, instead of being singled out for excellence, they had in Eschenburg's account been accorded the same treatment as Cronegk or Ramler or Lichtwer or any number of 'also rans' in the poetic stakes.

They were aware, of course, that Eschenburg had produced the first complete prose translation of Shakespeare (1775–77, 1782), but did not advertise the matter. Goethe also knew that Eschenburg had been a friend of Karl Wilhelm Jerusalem, the model for Werther, but that was a sensitive subject. They were certainly not interested at all in his systems of knowledge and aesthetics; they did not care about his interest in the 'Singspiel'; his many translations of significant English works on the aesthetics of music and painting left them cold; they did not share his interest in the whole of Shakespeare that found expression in his huge compendium *Ueber W. Shakspeare* (1786) (although they dipped into it, while it became a bible for the young Romantics, August Wilhelm Schlegel and Tieck). Lessing was for them a rival, but now safely out of the way: Eschenburg had been his close friend in the last years of his life in Wolfenbüttel. One could go on.

The twenty-two contributions to this excellent volume discuss all of these subjects and some more besides. The authors know their eighteenth century and recognize that it cannot be seen merely as the sum of its challenges and transformations. It has also to be understood in terms of the continuities, generational overlaps, norms, models, and prescriptions that most accepted and only some rebelled against. This is a discourse that centres on Brunswick, Leipzig, Hamburg, Berlin, not Weimar. The contributors also show how much remains to be discovered and how uncertain many of our assumptions are. Thus Eschenburg emerges not just as the first real German expert on Shakespeare but as a significant disseminator of all things English, older (who knows that he effectively discovered Chaucer for the Germans?) and also contemporary.

We also have glimpses of Eschenburg the friend, the correspondent, the family man, and see contemporary images of him. The volume contains the most comprehensive bibliography of his works to date and holds many surprises. It is a major contribution to eighteenth-century studies.

TRINITY COLLEGE, CAMBRIDGE   ROGER PAULIN

Luise Gottsched the Translator. By HILARY BROWN. (Studies in German Literature, Linguistics and Culture) Rochester and New York: Camden House. 2012. vii+248 pp. £55. ISBN 978–1–57113–510–0.

Luise Adelgunde Victorie Gottsched, née Kulmus (1713–1762), is remembered by literary historians primarily as a dramatist in her own right and as a literary skivvy for her husband, the celebrated Leipzig professor Johann Christoph Gottsched (1700–1766). She was, however, a prodigiously diligent translator, a side of her work which has hitherto been largely neglected, even scorned: Hilary Brown cites critics as labelling her Molière translation 'a failure', her Pope 'a triumph, with limitations', and her renditions of philosophical and historical tracts as being 'competent' but requiring 'no further comment'. Against such a background, the appearance of this ground-breaking study, happily coinciding with the tercentenary of her birth and the sestercentennial anniversary of her death, is welcome indeed.

The plan of the book is straightforward. Chapter 1 surveys the growing importance of translation in seventeenth- and eighteenth-century Germany, especially in the wake of Martin Opitz's *Buch von der Deutschen Poeterey* (1624), where it was argued that translation was a necessary step towards raising the standard of the vernacular. Brown describes the place of translation in the German Enlightenment, focusing on the work of Johann Christoph Gottsched and especially on the role of eighteenth-century women among the ranks of translators. In assessing Luise Gottsched's position in this scenario, Brown asserts—against the *communis opinio*—that she 'appears to have thrown herself willingly into her translation projects and not to have doubted the importance of her undertakings' and that there is 'no evidence to suggest that she would have preferred a career independent of her husband or that she harboured other more "literary" ambitions that her husband stifled' (p. 38). This thesis is persuasively argued in the subsequent six chapters, in which Brown carefully assesses Luise Gottsched's translations in the areas of philosophy and religion, journalism, drama, poetry and literary prose, and science and scholarship. In the field of philosophy she planned (though apparently did not execute) translations of Shaftesbury and Berkeley, and made translations of, for example, Bayle, Leibniz, and John Eachard's criticism of Thomas Hobbes. The most interesting part of Chapter 2 is that dealing with the Gottscheds' sympathies for Deism and their courageous criticism of Pietism. A central role in the latter was played by Luise Gottsched's satirical piece *Die Pietisterey im Fischbein-Rocke* (wisely published anonymously and allegedly in faraway Rostock), an adaptation of Guillaume-Hyacinthe Bougeant's anti-Jansenist play of 1730, *La Femme docteur*. Chapter 3 is particularly important: it explores Luise Gottsched's under-researched role as a (co-)translator of English moral weeklies, the *Tatler*, the *Spectator*, and the *Guardian*. She translated over half of the *Spectator*'s 635 issues and, singlehandedly, the whole of the seven-month run of the *Guardian*. Moreover, she translated several issues of the *Free-Thinker*, one of the first English journals to cater specifically for women's interests. Brown rightly stresses what a remarkable achievement it was, at a time when English was not at all well known in Germany, for her to have coped so extraordinarily well with translating the diverse range of material to be found in these journals; in doing so she made a real contribution to promoting a refreshingly non-Latinate style of German, modelled on the English of Addison and Steele. She translated direct from English, whereas earlier attempts at translating the *Spectator* into German had relied on French translations of the original. Luise Gottsched was a skilful translator, as is evident from the sample of her rendering of Dryden's verse quoted by Brown. Just as her play *Die Pietisterey* was a risky undertaking, so too she claimed that her aim in translating some of the somewhat subversive and satirical material from the *Guardian* was to prove that not all the English were 'Freygeister und Wollüstlinge'; her espousal of such writing, though not uncontentious, served to promote Enlightenment ideas in Germany. As for drama (Chapter 4), Brown cites recent critics as opining that Luise Gottsched's translations in general are devoid of formal and linguistic subtlety and that, for instance, the language of her version of Molière's *Le Misanthrope* is 'common, blunt and jarring'. Yet, she persuasively argues, this is to fail to appreciate that Gottsched's choice of texts and approach to translation were part of her and her husband's deliberate cultural programme to revolutionize German theatre. Transposing French comedies in which characters 'dance attendance on the Court, flatter each other's sonnets, strut around in blond periwigs and frilly rhinegrave breeches' (p. 117) into a German context was inevitably going to be a far from straightforward task, yet it was a challenge to which she rose successfully. The Gottscheds' work showed the Germans that they needed to take the theatre seriously. Chapter 5, on poetry and literary prose, discusses her translations of Horace and Lucian—amounting to little more than dabbling on her part, yet foreshadowing developments in German literature later in the century—and, much more significant, her skilful verse translation of Alexander Pope's *Rape of the Lock*, which played a major role in establishing his reputation in Germany. With this translation she seems to have aimed to promote Pope's poem as a model for satire, and more generally in embracing the work of British authors she was helping to open up German literature to influences other than French. Luise Gottsched also had wide interests in natural sciences and scholarship generally: among her many translations in these fields were, for example, twelve volumes of papers from the Académie Royale des Inscriptions et Belles-Lettres in Paris. This activity on her part was not a dilettante pastime; rather, it was 'a self-assured display of erudition' (p. 165) which aimed to foster a culture of scholarship and debate in Germany, her translations proving invaluable to any Germans who wished to inform themselves about wider European developments in various fields of scholarly endeavour. Finally, in Chapter 7, Brown discusses the relation between Luise Gottsched's translation work and her 'original' writing. She shows that the distinction between 'translation', 'adaptation', and 'original writing' is fairly meaningless in Gottsched's case: even in her own 'original' plays such as *Die ungleiche Heirat*, *Die Hausfranzösinn*, and *Das Testament* she was consciously following foreign models, so that there is in effect little difference between a work she adapted while translating, and an 'original' work shaped by a foreign model. For her, the prime concern was the ideas contained in the texts and the applicability of these ideas to contemporary Germany.

All told, this is an excellent study. It opens up a woefully neglected aspect of research into Luise Gottsched and points the way to the need for further exploration of early women translators and indeed of the scope and role of translation more generally. Brown's book is admirably succinct: of its 248 pages more than one hundred are taken up with notes (at the end of each chapter), illustrations, an appendix listing Gottsched's translations and adaptations, a bibliography of primary and secondary literature, and an index. Her publisher, Camden House, has served her well, provided one disregards the Americanization of 'Haymarket Theater' (p. 88) and several unfortunate German word-divisions.

LONDON, INSTITUTE OF GERMANIC AND ROMANCE STUDIES   JOHN L. FLOOD

Die Aufklärung ist weiblich: Frauenrollen im Drama um 1800. By ELKE PFITZINGER.
    (Literatura: Wissenschaftliche Beiträge zur Moderne und ihrer Geschichte, 26)
    Würzburg: Ergon. 2011. 248 pp. €38. ISBN 978-3-89913-811-5.

'Frauen sind der blinde Fleck der Aufklärung'—Alexander Košenina's pithy observation sums up a consensus of scholarship on the German Enlightenment (*Literarische Anthropologie: Die Neuentdeckung des Menschen* (Berlin: Akademie Verlag, 2008), p. 117). Even for Kant, the complaint in *Was ist Aufklärung?*—that the 'fairer sex' is entirely and deliberately kept dumb—was an exception rather than the rule. Elke Pfitzinger's study sets out not only to analyse the female characters in selected dramatic texts, but to demonstrate through them the tensions underlying the Enlightenment project. The female characters, Pfitzinger argues, are a good barometer of such tensions precisely because women were not the Enlightenment's central concern. Women, perceived as 'natural' beings, challenged the rational precepts of the Enlightenment, and—following Adorno and Horkheimer—the dramas' engagement with them reveals the proximity of Enlightenment to myth.

Pfitzinger analyses three broad areas of Enlightenment thought. Mothers (Cezilie in Goethe's *Stella* and Elisabeth in *Götz von Berlichingen*) and the women in *bürgerliches Trauerspiel* are shown to contrast with the positive image of feminine domesticity in the pedagogy of the time. Second, Schiller's Maria Stuart and Kleist's Kunigunde von Thurneck are read, in the context of Schiller's 'schöne Seele', as positive and negative models of aestheticized womanhood. The discussion of the 'schöne Seele' is inconclusive, but Pfitzinger rightly shows that Maria imperfectly matches Schiller's definition, as she is calculatingly image-conscious to the end. Third, the study tracks the nuances of 'Vernunft' through a series of prominent examples: Minna von Barnhelm; Lessing's Orsina and Goethe's Adelheid von Walldorf as 'Machtweiber' who are rational but not reasonable; Iphigenie and, finally, Penthesilea as case studies in the Enlightenment's close interrelationship with myth. This is a productive discussion, although its conclusion on *Iphigenie*, in direct emulation of Adorno—'im Moment ihrer höchsten Idealisierung bekennt sich die Aufklärung nicht mehr zu sich selbst' (p. 194)—is unduly sceptical.

This study gives a valuable account of female characters in contemporary contexts, and it perceptively points out differences between philosophical theories and the imaginative practice of literature. Its thematic approach emphasizes characters and character traits that are otherwise easy to ignore. Adelheid's rationality is one of these, and another is Minna von Barnhelm's visual fit—'im Negligee'—to the 'Traditionslinie der Buhlerinnen und Machtweiber' (p. 131) that is inherent in her forthright personality. Pfitzinger is also right to insist on the difference between literary and other discourses, though she has also been reluctant to press the logic of this distinction further. By organizing the figures according to thematic fit, the discussion isolates them from the economies of the individual plays, and even from full comparison with other women in the same work. Elisabeth and Adelheid in *Götz* are treated separately; Marwood and Orsina are focal points, but Sara Sampson and Emilia Galotti are not; Maria Stuart's beauty is analysed with little discussion of her antagonist, Elisabeth. Similarly, little attention is given to differences between authors, or across the study's broad time-span, from *Miß Sara Sampson* (1755) to *Das Käthchen von Heilbronn* (1810). The claim underpinning this thought-provoking study—'In der Literatur ist die Aufklärung weiblich' (p. 228)—will continue, however, to invite students and researchers alike to work on the blind spot of the Enlightenment.

UNIVERSITY OF BRISTOL   STEFFAN DAVIES

Ludwig Tieck: Leben — Werk — Wirkung. Ed. by Claudia Stockinger and Stefan Scherer. Berlin and Boston: de Gruyter. 2011. xvii+845 pp. €169.95; $238. ISBN 978-3-11-021747-6.

Following the publication in the previous year of *E. T. A. Hoffmann: Leben — Werk — Wirkung* under the editorial direction of Detlef Kremer, de Gruyter have produced the second author-based handbook of its Lexikon series, *Ludwig Tieck: Leben — Werk — Wirkung*. The result by co-editors Claudia Stockinger and Stefan Scherer is an 845-page 'Tieck-Handbuch', the purpose of which is to offer a 'Gesamtüberblick über Leben und Werk Tiecks, über die Traditionen und Kontexte, in denen beides zu situieren ist, und nicht zuletzt über Tiecks Wirkung' (p. xi).

The book's logical organization of material into five main sections, which contain an astonishing number of essays (51 in total), allows for a comprehensive and surprisingly deft historical and literary overview. The volume concludes with three additional sections: (1) a timeline that begins with Tieck's birth in 1773 and ends in 1920 with the publication of *Das Buch über Shakespeare: Handschriftliche Aufzeichnungen von Ludwig Tieck*, (2) a bibliography with divisions based on genre, motifs, and individual works by Tieck, and (3) a varied selection of images (portraits and busts of Tieck, musical notations by Schubert's predecessor, Johann Friedrich Reichardt, and works by Runge and Friedrich), all of which speak to Tieck's prolific literary career and friendships, non-literary influences, and the intertextuality of his work.

When confronted with Tieck's œuvre—his poetry and comments about poetry, his translations of Cervantes and Shakespeare, his many dramas, novels, and shorter works, his literary criticism, editorial output, and indeed his 'Kunsttheorie, Kunstgeschichte, Kunstbeschreibung, Kunstgespräche und poetisierte Kunst' (the title of Helmut Pfotenhauer's contribution)—one is struck by the manner in which Tieck's writings are adeptly diffuse. When coupled with his long life, itself an anomaly among his early Romantic contemporaries, classification becomes elusive. Gustav Frank explores issues surrounding Tieck's 'Epochalität' and his ability to either inhabit or reflect multiple literary modes of being from the late Enlightenment to early Realism. Additional contributions in the first two sections help to clarify the constellation of personal and professional relationships that mattered for Tieck, as well as the historical context(s) that gave rise to his work.

While Tieck was not as inclined to philosophical speculation as a number of his contemporaries, especially Novalis and the Schlegel brothers, the third section admirably explores Tieck's extensive theoretical engagement with poetry, the visual arts, and literary criticism. As a result, this section has perhaps the most to offer to those for whom Tieck's corpus is either familiar or foreign. Quite unknown even among Tieck specialists, for example, is his interest in sublimity. Matters of aesthetics seem to have occupied the youthful Tieck at least as early as his university years, when he penned a fragmentary essay on the sublime (under the influence of Grosse and Moritz). Antonie Magen's concluding essay of the section considers Tieck's role and understanding of himself as an editor of works by numerous contemporaries (e.g. Novalis, Maler Müller [Friedrich Müller], Kleist, and Solger) and thereby explores the implications of Tieck's philological self-awareness within the German literary tradition of the nineteenth century. The fourth section shifts the focus from Tieck's theoretical to his poetic works and proceeds chronologically from his earliest writings as a student to his late prose. The final section then maps Tieck's effect on both his contemporaries and his successors within literature, the visual arts, music, and the theatre, before concluding with Heidrun Markert's essay on 'Tieck-Forschung' from 1900 to the present. After approximately seven hundred pages, Markert's rather concise essay allows the reader to step back in order to consider not only the specificity of the works themselves but also the evolution of their scholarly reception.

Naturally, a review of this nature must be selective and rather broad in its approach. In the first instance, *Ludwig Tieck: Leben—Werk—Wirkung* serves as an indispensable reference manual for researchers concerned with Tieck's life and works. It is a formidable work of scholarship and will surely be one of the primary reference works for Tieck specialists as well as for Germanists with an interest in eighteenth- and nineteenth-century German culture in general. However, there is something of the vertigo of lists (to borrow from Umberto Eco) with edited collections of this nature, especially one that treats a polymath such as Tieck. Amidst the profusion, there is at times a tendency towards congestion and even indeterminateness. One wonders whether, after almost eight hundred and fifty pages of text, this lingering, if unintended, ambiguity surrounding Tieck's status and works is precisely the point.

UNIVERSITY OF WARWICK   BRIAN HAMAN

Weltliteratur: Modelle transnationaler Literaturwahrnehmung im 19. Jahrhundert. By PETER GOSSENS. Stuttgart: Metzler. 2011. xiii+457 pp. €49.95. ISBN 978-3-476-02305-6.

Studies of the term *Weltliteratur* tend to begin with Goethe's handful of late-life remarks on the emerging age of world literary circulation and then skip to Marx and Engels's famous pronouncement in the *Communist Manifesto* on the globalization of not only material, but intellectual production. While these two striking examples make obvious candidates for an anthology (see, for example, *World Literature: A Reader*, ed. by Theo D'haen and others (London: Routledge, 2012)), they leave out a fascinating, under-researched slice of history that the first part of Peter Goßens's book sets out to document, namely the complex reception and diverse use of Goethe's term in the decades after his death. Goßens's history includes both the lead up to 1848 and its aftermath, describing in turn the humanistic, utopian, Socialist-leaning aspirations with which *Weltliteratur* was first imbued, and the nationalistic, comparative, canon-building work with which it was tasked in the wake of political disappointment. In so doing, he reads Marx's pronouncement on world literature not as a utopian vision but as the theoretical endpoint of the term itself. If, in Goßens's assessment, Marx saw *Weltliteratur* as nothing less than a means for the bourgeoisie to exploit the world market, after 1848 the term itself contracted from political to merely literary-historical tool, detached from its cosmopolitan and humanistic associations as it constructed a national German identity against a transnational background.

Goßens's comprehensively researched book is divided into three sections, the first situating Goethe's term within the discourse of cosmopolitan humanism around 1800, the second tracing the reception of *Weltliteratur* from Goethe's death up until 1848 within the circles of Karl August Varnhagen von Ense, the Young Germans, and German Socialists, and the third following the fate of the concept in transnational literary histories from 1848 to 1888, books that would help to establish comparative literature as an academic discipline. While studies of world literature tend themselves to be pointedly transnational in scope, Goßens focuses almost exclusively on the fate of the word in Germany, identifying this as a subfield almost entirely ignored by scholarship (p. 124) and concluding that up until about 1870 the word existed predominantly as a German phenomenon (p. 401). While scholars in France, for example, were laying the groundwork for the study of a *littérature comparée*, they did so without recourse to the German concept until late in the century.

The topic of Goßens's first section has received the most research; Goethe's meaning of *Weltliteratur* has been extensively explored ever since Fritz Strich's monumental *Goethe und die Weltliteratur* (1946), with excellent recent studies by Hendrik Birus, Anne Bohnenkamp, Manfred Koch, John Pizer, and Dieter Lamping, among others. Goßens's contribution is to read Goethe's term not just as an interest in the circulation of foreign literary works (an idea he sees better represented by Goethe's neologism *Weltpoesie*, p. 23), but rather as a 'model of moral and ethical exchange' of knowledge as such (p. 30), transnational cultural communication in the service of a utopian vision of universal perfection. Goßens situates Goethe's ideas within a larger discourse of cosmopolitan humanism around 1800, which he sees supported by an older tradition of the *historia litteraria*, or the encyclopedic tombs of the knowledge of the world. As these histories began around 1800 to focus specifically on the literary production, they became the model for works such as Friedrich Bouterwek's *Geschichte der Poesie und Beredsamkeit* (1801–19), Johann Gottfried Herder's projected *Allgemeine Geschichte der Literatur*, and the increasingly transnational lectures of Friedrich and August Wilhelm Schlegel in Berlin and Vienna. These divergent models of world literature all took telescopic historical views going back to antiquity. Goethe, as Goßens reminds the reader, operated at the end of his life in a changed and in some ways foreshortened media landscape, one where he could receive tri-weekly copies of *Le Globe* from Paris, or Thomas Carlyle's newly published Schiller biography from England; the experience of this increased literary traffic and circulation impacted on his own understanding of *Weltliteratur*.

Goethe's death in 1832 was experienced as a national tragedy. In the wake of this crisis, Karl August Varnhagen von Ense's posthumous essay on *Wilhelm Meisters Wanderjahre* offered an influential reading of Goethe as utopian visionary.

The Berlin salon of Varnhagen's wife Rahel Levin had close ties to Goethe's Weimar, but beginning in 1830 also actively explored Saint-Simonism. Goßens reads Varnhagen's reception of Goethe, along with his growing interest in foreign literatures (especially Russian), in the light of these sympathies in order to argue that Varnhagen modelled a 'weltliterarisches Denken' (p. 175), one markedly Socialist and humanist. This socio-political agenda is echoed with nuanced variations in the writing of Varnhagen's contacts in their statements on *Weltliteratur*—Moritz Veit, a Hegelian philosopher turned book publisher, Young Germans such as Ludolf Wienbarg, Karl Gutzkow, Heinrich Laube, and (in radicalized forms) Socialist critics such as Georg Herwegh and Karl Grün. Goßens's detailed research traces the network of connections between various groups: Berlin's salons and philosophy departments, Weimar intellectuals, the German book-publishing market, political journalism, Prussian and Austrian bureaucracy (Varnhagen was stymied by both in his attempt to found a Goethe Society). He also demonstrates the range of responses to the concept of world literature, including nationalistic reactions from Wolfgang Menzel and Theodor Mundt. His reading of Marx and Engels shows them rejecting world literature as a bourgeois construct in part for tactical reasons, as an implicit rejection of its champions, such as Karl Grün.

The failure of the revolution of 1848 can be heard in Johannes Scherr's wistful foreword to his *Allgemeine Literaturgeschichte* of 1851, where he recalls the 'idea of cosmopolitanism' (p. 363) that had defined German classicism, a sentiment missing from his later editions. Scherr is one of a number of literary historians and anthologists who sought in the later nineteenth century to define the parameters of *Weltliteratur*, reworking the model of the *historia litteraria* from a nationalistic as well as pedagogical perspective. Goßens discusses both serious academic books, such as Hermann Hettner's study of the eighteenth century's intellectual exchange between England, France, and Germany, as well as the many popularizing literary histories that hammered out competing canons of great works. He ends with 1888 at a moment when this literary rather than socio-political thinking had come to fruition in the institutional foundation of comparative literature, with Moritz Carrier's research and Max Koch's newly established *Zeitschrift für vergleichende Literaturgeschichte*.

Goßens fills holes in scholarship of the term *Weltliteratur*, detailing unique historical circumstances that affected its meaning in the nineteenth century, but the discussions he unearths also almost inadvertently sound contemporary. Comparing Herder's ethnological inclusiveness as editor of *Stimmen der Völker* (1807) with the aesthetic selectiveness of Friedrich Schlegel takes one right into the debates of current editors of the Norton or Longman Anthologies of World Literature. Reading the deeply utopian, cosmopolitan aspirations of *Weltliteratur* in 1832 reminds one how much the term continues to be weighted with political hope, mobilized anew in the last decade as a response to the attacks of 9/11 with a vision of a better-educated, communicative global community. As such Goßens's book reveals continuity in the history of this complex, forward-looking term

UNIVERSITY OF ILLINOIS AT CHICAGO   ANNA GUILLEMIN

Space in Theodor Fontane's Works: Theme and Poetic Function. By MICHAEL JAMES WHITE. London: Modern Humanities Research Association. 2012. viii+ 190 pp. £19.99. ISBN 978-1-907322-29-7.

One of the newer advances in the progress of literary theory is, as I have heard, the 'spatial turn'. This would seem to be a capacious topic, if one may say so, since spatial representation is a fundamental component of literature, especially of realist literature. For the purposes of his study of Theodor Fontane's prose works, Michael James White defines space as the world beyond the subject (p. 2) and his procedure as asking 'how space and literariness are linked, what the relationship between space and the literary text as a symbolic art form is, and how an analysis under the general heading of "space" leads to fresh insights into the individual text' (pp. 2–3). White distinguishes between focalization, the way space is perceived by characters or the narrator, and structure, the relationship of space to other images in the text.

His painstaking readings and refined detail, accompanied throughout with articulate awareness of methodological considerations, cannot be summarized in this brief space; I will just touch upon some characteristic results. He begins with the first section of *Die Wanderungen durch die Mark Brandenburg*, 'Die Grafschaft Ruppin', showing how the description of manor houses and interiors characterizes the Prussian military nobility as modest and unpretentious; 'spatial representation serves a rhetorical purpose' (p. 28). The contrasting rooms at Crown Prince Frederick's Rheinsberg retreat relate to contrasting elements in his character and their unification, while the subordinate place of Prince Henry is indicated by the layout of the building. In *Vor dem Sturm* spatial multiplicity reinforces the variety of attitudes towards the historical situation, the inner complexity of the characters, and the episodic rapidity of events. With *Schach von Wuthenow* and *Graf Petöfy* White turns to the spatial representation of awareness. The sequence of spaces illustrates Schach's growing understanding of himself from a rather dim perceptivity to a more complex sense of complication and contradiction. The opposite is shown to be true of *Graf Petöfy*, where the spaces reflect Adam and Franziska's drift into delusion. The symbolism of left and right corresponds to a contrast of the (French) west with the (Slavic) east. The deft interpretation has the effect of elevating the aesthetic value of the sometimes slighted story.

An aesthetic view of life is also implied in *Irrungen Wirrungen* and *Unwiederbringlich*. One might think the former well suited to this enquiry with its significant spaces, such as Lene's workplace, Hankels Ablage, or the cemetery, but White concentrates on the market garden and Botho's ride to the cemetery. The issues concern subjectivity and imagination; Botho's memories of the market garden 'grant him access to values beyond those he encounters in his own life'

(p. 111). Given the opportunities in the novel, this section strikes me as somewhat compressed. *Unwiederbringlich* exhibits contrasting landscapes in Germany and Denmark with similarities between them. Both Christine and Holk have problematic relationships to their surroundings; 'the representation of space [...] clearly functions as a means of illustrating Holk's psychology' (p. 117). White's longest chapter is appropriately devoted to Fontane's longest novel, *Der Stechlin*, which is built around a space. The interior spaces distinguish Stechlin and the Barbys from the other characters. Adelheid's space, with its large furniture in a small room, indicates delusions of grandeur. The contemplative quiet and isolation of Stechlin are contrasted with the modern bustle of Berlin, but these spaces are not monolithic and contain layers of meaning. For example, the Stechlin manor house is a relatively new building, replacing an old castle. White rightly, I think, denies that the lake can be a symbol of revolution, but he has a little difficulty coping with its alleged responsiveness to current upheavals, and he several times stresses the choice of traditional continuity over the hectic modern as enacted by Woldemar's move from Berlin to Stechlin. Throughout the book there is much more that is illuminating and persuasive. Ultimately White is concerned not just with the analysis of spatiality but with claims of the ways spatial representation serves aesthetic effect and awareness.

One question that can arise in contemporary literary study is whether the abstruse theoretical superstructure is necessary to the results achieved. White actually adverts to the theoreticians of the 'spatial turn' rather sparingly. Instead, the meticulously probing close readings, the pursuit of symbolism, sometimes a bit forced, the search for paradox and ambiguity, formulations such as 'harmony, unity, multiplicity, and paradox' yielding 'a timeless power' (p. 123), and the disclaimer of any 'attempt to examine the text as a cultural artefact or as indicative of wider social practices' (p. 2) are reminiscent of the New Criticism of yore. Indeed, in White's resources we encounter a number of very old friends: Cleanth Brooks, Brooks and Warren, I. A. Richards, René Wellek, Wellek and Warren, Wimsatt and Brooks. There are also occasional allusions to the Russian formalism influential when I was a student. This seems to me somewhat unusual today, and while I think that it contributes to the strength of the interpretative achievement, one consideration troubles me a little. Congruent with the abstinence towards social and political context is White's strong endorsement of Fontane's principle of *Verklärung*, which he takes not as euphemistic avoidance of reality but as a kind of aesthetic surplus value, perceiving beauty in the real and raising realism to a poetic height and intensity, as though art could not be made out of distress and the awareness of injustice.

The book is exceptionally well written, precise, compact, and lean. It has been well edited with very few faults. In one place a conflation of Karl Friedrich von dem Knesebeck with his great-grandfather might be confusing to the reader (p. 26). Once in a while it might be more appropriate to render *Schloß* as 'manor house' rather than 'castle'. The book appears to assume a prior familiarity with Fontane. It is not exactly written for specialists, but it will be of most use to those who know Fontane's texts well. However, there are many of these.

YALE UNIVERSITY   JEFFREY L. SAMMONS

Memory, Metaphor, and Aby Warburg's Atlas of Images. By CHRISTOPHER D. JOHNSON. (Signale: Modern German Letters, Cultures, and Thought) Ithaca, NY: Cornell University Press and Cornell University Library. 2012. xviii+286 pp. $35. ISBN 978-0-8014-7742-3.

Aby Warburg (1866–1929), the art historian whose Kulturwissenschaftliche Bibliothek, founded in 1925, later migrated to London as the Warburg Institute, is an important figure for the study of cultural memory. He was especially interested in how *Pathosformeln*, visual formulae expressing intense emotion, were adapted from their pagan origins during the Middle Ages and the Renaissance. He increasingly saw art as helping to liberate humanity from primeval fears by transforming images, as when the ancient Saturnian demon is humanized as Dürer's *Melencolia*, and as providing a symbolic dimension that saves us from confronting too directly the nakedly factual universe revealed by science. Memory, as E. H. Gombrich explains in *Aby Warburg: An Intellectual Biography* (2nd edn (London: Phaidon, 1986), pp. 221–22), thus has a dual role in preserving the mythic images into which early humanity projected their terrors while locating these images within our law-governed universe. But progress is not inevitable: the past holds out the lure of atavism, and primitive violence can always return.

Christopher Johnson deals with an ambitious project in cultural memory which was unfinished at Warburg's death. This was his *Mnemosyne*, consisting of sixty-three wooden boards to which Warburg attached photographs of images, in order to illustrate the changes undergone by images of the Greek gods and by ancient *Pathosformeln*. The panels no longer survive, but the 971 photographs that make up the third version of this *Bilderatlas*, as Warburg also called it, have been published in Volume II/i of Warburg's *Gesammelte Schriften*, edited by Martin Warnke (Berlin: Akademie Verlag, 2000). These juxtaposed images invite comparison with modernist montage and particularly with Walter Benjamin's unfinished *Passagen-Werk*.

Although Johnson's dense, rich, often digressive book defies summary, it is centrally concerned with *Mnemosyne* as a work of cultural memory based not on metonymy, like modernist montages, but on metaphor. Its implicit history of culture moves from primitive anthropomorphism to modern abstraction, but with no sense of triumphant progression, for Warburg deplored not only a relapse into primitive terror but also any advance into sterile abstraction. For him, metaphor served to create distance from experience and hence a *Denkraum* or intermediate space of reflection. He feared that in modern machine civilization such inventions as the telephone and the telegraph impoverished life by abolishing such distance.

Warburg's *Denkräume* recollect the past in the form of visual metaphors which preserve intense emotions with sensuous immediacy but also with reflective distance. Thus the tragic scene in Dürer's *Death of Orpheus* moves us without overwhelming us. Warburg identified his *Pathosformeln* with the 'engrams' or 'mnemic traces' hypothesized by the zoologist Richard Semon in 1904. In turn, they helped to inspire Ernst Robert Curtius's concept of 'topoi' or literary commonplaces handed down through the centuries. Warburg also borrowed a term from Goethe in calling his formulae 'Urworte leidenschaftlicher Dynamik' (quoted by Johnson, p. 62).

Although Johnson's large claims for the supreme importance of metaphor to Warburg may not altogether convince, he does much both to illuminate the *Mnemosyne* project and to place Warburg in the larger context of philosophical and critical thinking about metaphor. He suggests an affinity with Vico, for whom poetry and reflection originate with metaphor, and with thinkers indebted to Vico, notably the classical philologist Hermann Usener, whose encyclopedic *Götternamen* (1896) traces the metaphorical origins of ancient religion. He contrasts Warburg's understanding of metaphor with Ernst Cassirer's theory of the symbol and with the account of all language as dead metaphor in Nietzsche's posthumously published essay 'Über Wahrheit und Lüge im außermoralischen Sinn' (though Johnson curiously fails to notice that Nietzsche's theory is anticipated by Jean Paul in a passage quoted by Warburg and reproduced here on p. 38). There is, however, a close affinity with Hans Blumenberg, for whom metaphors are not the expression of thought but above all a means of thinking and hence share the fluidity of Warburg's *Pathosformeln*. Johnson's final chapter asks why Warburg, in the last year of his life, was so enraptured by reading Giordano Bruno, and concludes that Bruno's passionate allegories made him for Warburg 'an archetypal figure who heroically, ethically, and, in the end, tragically dedicates his life to taming astrological superstition and associated monstrous imagery' (p. 211).

THE QUEEN'S COLLEGE, OXFORD   RITCHIE ROBERTSON

Das emotionale Wirkungspotenzial von Erzähltexten: Mit Fallstudien zu Kafka, Perutz und Werfel. By CLAUDIA HILLEBRANDT. (Deutsche Literatur: Studien und Quellen, 6) Berlin: Akademie Verlag. 2011. 331 pp. €89.80. ISBN 978-3-05-005196-3.

This monograph combines cognitive poetics, narratology, and reader-response theory. It is divided into two halves. The first half sets out a detailed methodological apparatus for analysing the potential emotional effects of narrative fiction. The second half applies this methodology to three German-language novels of the 1920s written by authors from Prague: Kafka's *Das Schloss* (1926), Perutz's *Der Meister des Jüngsten Tages* (1923), and Werfel's *Verdi: Roman der Oper* (1924). In the case of each novel, Claudia Hillebrandt uses the first published reviews in order to test her interpretative hypotheses empirically in terms of the text's reception by contemporary readers.

Hillebrandt proceeds with caution. She deliberately excludes certain categories of emotional response from her investigation. She concedes that the evocation of mood resists classification (p. 62); and she also rules out associative emotions which do not lend themselves to narratological analysis because they require extensive contextualization (p. 301). Hillebrandt therefore restricts herself to an analysis of empathy, sympathy, suspense, surprise, and disorientation (p. 300). She calls these five emotions 'diegetic' because they correlate closely to textual factors in the narrated world. The methodological half focuses on elaborating methods designed to assess the reader's emotional attachment to fictional protagonists. Hillebrandt's aim is to identify the qualities of a text which invite emotional reactions such as empathy, sympathy, 'Mitleid', or 'Mitfreude' (p. 70). There follows a detailed classification of the textual markers which (explicitly or implicitly) elicit emotional responses from the reader (pp. 78–84). Hillebrandt is particularly interested in identifying qualities which point towards underlying moral or ideological value systems. The aim is to reconstruct the value systems of the protagonists, or even that of the narrator, although Hillebrandt admits that determining the value hierarchy of an entire literary text tends to be 'problematic' (pp. 96–97). She makes the doubtful claim that reliable moral value judgements are important in order to elicit the reader's sympathy (p. 100), although she grants that this does not apply in the case of Kafka. She does not consider the possibility that the reader might feel sympathy for an amoral or immoral protagonist, or the possibility that a protagonist might be simultaneously sympathetic and unsympathetic to the reader. It is unfortunately characteristic of this book that the terms 'irony' and 'ambivalence' are not to be found in the 'Sachregister' at the back. The methodological half of the book also shows that suspense, surprise, and disorientation are linked to the ways in which a text transmits or withholds information. We are informed that 'Lust' is not an emotion but merely a 'Fortsetzungsimpuls' (p. 131); this is too reductive for me. 'Angstlust' (pp. 131 and 211) sounds more interesting but receives scant attention. There is also a brief discussion of 'artefact-based emotions', translated as 'Artefaktemotionen' (p. 129), which relate to much wider questions of reception and canonization, and which therefore exceed the boundaries of text-based analysis.

The second half of this study is much to be preferred. Kafka's *Das Schloss* is a daunting prospect for any critic, but Hillebrandt engages adeptly with the recent secondary literature, suggesting that it may be possible to find a few isolated instances in *Das Schloss* in which an implicit value scheme can be found (p. 158). According to Hillebrandt, this occurs most notably in the portrayal of Amalia: whatever else we (or the other characters) may think about her, Amalia's rejection of the written summons sent by Sortini inspires our admiration (p. 181). The predominant reader response to the interpretative openness of *Das Schloss* is, however, disorientation (p. 190). Hillebrandt's empirical analysis of early reviews of *Das Schloss* bears out Emily Troscianko's thesis that Kafka's texts tend to disorient readers in order to invite speculative cognitive responses from them (*Kafka's Cognitive Realism* (London: Routledge, 2013)).

The analysis of Perutz's *Der Meister des Jüngsten Tages*, a classic thriller, seems excessively concerned with the fictional editor's afterword, which insinuates that the first-person narrator, Yosch, is unreliable. Hillebrandt focuses mainly on the effects that this revelation is likely to have on subsequent rereadings. What I missed here was a detailed analysis of narrative suspense; there is insufficient realization that

Yosch's narration serves to heighten suspense because of his bewildered reactions, which invite readers to share in his bewilderment. Hillebrandt does successfully demonstrate, though, that *Der Meister des Jüngsten Tages* elicits emotional effects in line with Todorov's theory of the fantastic.

Werfel's *Verdi: Roman der Oper* centres on the artistic rivalry between Verdi and Wagner, incidentally the subject of a recent book by Peter Conrad (*Verdi and/or Wagner* (London: Thames and Hudson, 2013)). Werfel's novel fascinated Thomas Mann, who read it in June 1924; indeed the novel sheds some light on Mann's own development at this time. Hillebrandt argues that the emotional style of *Verdi* is justified by the operatic theme of the novel (p. 258), and she shows that this novel contains structures analogous to those of a libretto. In conclusion she returns to her preferred theme of sympathy, noting that Werfel's novel is designed to make us sympathize with the eponymous protagonist (p. 296).

Hillebrandt's concluding claim that the reader's sympathy depends mainly on the moral values of the protagonist in question (p. 304) seems to require further refinement. Surely in many reading experiences we care about characters despite (or perhaps even because of) their moral failings. And, as Hillebrandt herself concedes in the case of *Das Schloss*, it is precisely K.'s opacity which invites readers to bring their own emotions to bear on their interpretation of the character (p. 302). Aside from the minor reservations mentioned here, this study certainly succeeds in offering a differentiated technical description of a very small number of emotional effects elicited by fictional texts. In doing so it makes a decent, if ultimately rather modest, contribution to the field of cognitive narrative poetics.

UNIVERSITY OF GLASGOW   ERNEST SCHONFIELD

Kafka und die kleine Prosa der Moderne/Kafka and Short Modernist Prose. Ed. by MANFRED ENGEL and RITCHIE ROBERTSON. Würzburg: Königshausen & Neumann. 2011. 299 pp. €49.80. ISBN 978-3-8260-4029-0.

At times it can strike a reviewer that the metaphor of the curate's egg was perhaps devised with collections of scholarly essays by various hands in mind. This meticulously edited and well-conceived volume of essays, by contrast, prompts only admiration for its cohesiveness and the consistently high quality of the individual essays, some of which are exceptionally fine. As one might expect from a volume conceived in the Oxford Kafka Research Centre, Kafka's short prose receives more attention here than that of any of his contemporaries, but the comparative and contextual character of many of the essays ensures that new light is thrown on his many experiments with short prose forms, which in turn serve to illuminate, through likeness or dissimilarity, the intellectual, narrative, and stylistic contexts in which they are analysed.

The volume opens with some prefatory reflections on the genres or subgenres that make up the general type 'kleine Prosa', followed by two further essays of a general character, one by Dirk Göttsche on 'Minimalisierung und Funktionalisierung des Erzählens' around 1900, and one by Rüdiger Zymner on Kafka's short prose in relation to the 'klassische Moderne', here understood rather broadly and taken to include writers as diverse as Kleist, Flaubert, Kierkegaard, Hamsun, Wagner, Strindberg, Nietzsche, Döblin, and Joyce. Section II offers five essays analysing Kafka's short prose, including two by the editors of the volume, one from Ritchie Robertson on Kafka's use of singular and collective narrators and the other from Manfred Engel on narrative integration and fantasy in 'Beschreibung eines Kampfes'. Also in this section are Julian Preece on the tradition of the 'Brautbrief', as instanced by Kafka's correspondence with Felice Bauer; Carolin Duttlinger on the dialectic of 'Aufmerksamkeit' and 'Zerstreuung', a theme present from his earliest published prose work ('Betrachtung') to his last story ('Der Bau'); and one of the highlights of the volume, a fascinating analysis by Gerhard Neumann of generic fluidity in the evolving drafts of a tiny prose fragment ('Die Welt ist ein stinkender Hund'), which situates Kafka's approach to writing on a continuum somewhere between pure 'Schreibprozess' and completed, self-contained work of art, a perpetual 'Zögern vor der Geburt'. Section III opens with a bravura reflection by Stanley Corngold on 'Aphoristic Form in Nietzsche and Kafka'. As if modelled on the danger-defying trapeze and high-wire artistes beloved of both Kafka and Nietzsche, the essay leaves the reader (or at least this reader) with head spinning from the effort of following one intellectual *salto mortale* after another; as with so much of Corngold's work, these highly condensed thoughts demand (and will certainly repay) repeated reading. Most of the other essays in this section consider Kafka in relation to a selection of individual contemporaries (Robert Walser, Döblin, Benn, Musil, and Broch), but two of the contributors (Moritz Baßler and Andreas Krämer) take on the particularly vexed question of how Kafka's work should be seen in relation to Expressionism. Given the fact that the essays interconnect with one another in many ways ('Zerstreuung' is an important topic for both Duttlinger and Anne Fuchs, for example), it is a pity that the volume is not provided with a topical index.

UNIVERSITY OF BIRMINGHAM   RONALD SPEIRS

Hermann Hesse: Das Leben des Glasperlenspielers. By HEIMO SCHWILK. Munich and Zurich: Piper. 2012. 432 pp. €22.99. ISBN 978-3-492-05302-0.

The volume opens with an account of the young Hesse's determined attempt, on 7 March 1892, to abscond from the prestigious Maulbronn seminary, an institution with which Heimo Schwilk is familiar, having been a pupil there himself. This potentially self-destructive act is commonly regarded as signalling the birth of anti-authoritarian liberalism in an author who remained something of a house-trained anarchist throughout his long career. 'Im Seminar fingen meine Nöte an', Hesse writes in his *Biographische Notizen* of 1923. Schwilk relates many of his subsequent dilemmas to this attempted breakout and thus to the factors that provoked it, notably a strained relationship with his parents, both of whom, as ardent Protestant Pietists, exuded missionary fervour. Letters to and from home are cited as evidence of the vehemence with which the adolescent Hesse rejected their world-view and their well-intentioned advice—for example, when Frau Hesse was moved to warn him not to read Novalis in the mistaken belief that he was a Roman Catholic. Hesse refused to attend his mother's funeral and it was many years before he became reconciled with his increasingly senile father, who, like Hermann Kafka, could rarely bring himself to voice a positive comment on his son's publications.

It is no coincidence that much of the new material in this biography is derived from Hesse's vast corpus of letters, some still kept under wraps. Three marriages cannot fail to provide the biographer with tantalizing material, but some of the big questions still remain unanswered. Was Mia Bernouilli's depressive passivity the product or the cause of Hesse's offhand treatment of her? The milestones on the road to marital breakdown are enumerated in detail, but readers are left to draw their own conclusions as to its causes.

And so it is with other controversies. His enthusiastic support of the German position at the start of the First World War is understandable given his dislike of the British, French, and Russians, whom he believed to lack true spirituality or 'Geist'; his ambivalent attitude towards Nazi Germany can be put down to lingering hopes that he might exert influence by continuing to be published there—but why did he refer to émigré writers as a 'pack of swine' ('Saupack', p. 349)? Although Hesse was quicker than Thomas Mann to spot the menace of Fascism, he was less willing to condemn it outright, even after Germany's defeat. And what was it that bound him so very closely to his psychoanalyst, Josef Bernhard Lang? Their friendship endured for thirty years and provides some of the most illuminating insights into Hesse's private preoccupations, his disturbing dreams and gross fantasies, his hypochondria, drug dependency, and suicidal inclinations. The doctor, a fellow depressive who was himself in serious trouble with the authorities for breaking Swiss anti-abortion laws, provided advice, companionship, and narcotic substances that would have been impossible to obtain through other channels.

Schwilk examines each of Hesse's novels in the light of his personal development. The texts are found to reflect less in the way of real experiences and more in the way of latent desires and ambitions. The theme of suicide recurs with surprising frequency; letters to close friends indicate that it was rarely far from the author's thoughts. Shortly after his second wedding, he was found unconscious beside an empty phial of the sedative drug Veronal, having smashed the glass door of a hotel in a fit of rage, and Schwilk concludes: 'Hesse sucht nicht das Glück, sondern den Schmerz [. . .]. Ich leide, also bin ich' (pp. 267, 276). Anyone who assumes that the mature Hesse ever attained the balanced serenity of an enlightened Siddhartha must soon realize that this was far from the case. He was tormented by demons every bit as powerful as those that threaten to destroy the 'Steppenwolf', and by yearnings for metamorphosis such as those that force Goldmund and Josef Knecht to step out of their sheltered microworlds and face the challenges of an unpredictable, often chaotic, reality.

Hesse as seen by Schwilk emerges in many guises, foremost perhaps that of the chameleon, at times a kleptomaniac, masturbator, manipulator, counter-cultural genius: forever restless, solitary, irascible, unloving to the point of abuse, capable of oscillating between bucolic provincialism and an Orientalism of his own manufacture, experimenting with self-chastising vegan Naturism à la Monte Verità while equally drawn to masked balls in urban night clubs. This man may well have possessed not one, not two, but a thousand souls, 'tausend Seelchen', in Ruth Wenger's assessment (p. 263). A small segment of each is competently placed before the reader in this well-researched biography.

UNIVERSITY OF KENT   OSMAN DURRANI

Du 'fatum' au divin: le mythe dans l'œuvre d'Alfred Döblin (1935–1957). By CATHERINE GOURIOU. (Contacts: Études et documents) Bern: Peter Lang. 2012. 483 pp. €78.85. ISBN 978–3–0343–0664–5; ISSN 0933–6095.

There is a particular sort of trap into which scholars can easily fall when interpreting the works of Alfred Döblin. Intent upon extracting the textual evidence that supports their thesis about his devotion to psychoanalytic theory, for instance, or about his commitment to Catholicism in his later years, they fall through the intricate fabric of Döblin's narratives and end up sitting in an intellectual pit of their own creation. Catherine Gouriou does not entirely avoid such pitfalls. In her discussion of Döblin's last published novel *Hamlet* (1956) in particular, she identifies allusions to mythical figures that she can associate with Jungian archetypes, but without discussing *which character* makes such attributions and why; and she highlights the moments at which the main protagonists entertain manifestly Christian ideas without considering *in what spirit* each of them does so at a particular stage of the action. But her book, which is an elaborated version of her Strasbourg doctoral dissertation of 2008, nevertheless deserves notice for its systematic and comprehensive presentation of the issues associated with the role of myth in Döblin's writing and thinking during the last two decades of his life.

Thomas Mann's remark to Karl Kerényi in 1941 about the need to wrest control of the power of myth from the hands of the Fascists by psychologizing it has long provided a cornerstone for the analysis of the novels that he published after the rise of Hitler. Gouriou draws attention to an earlier letter from Mann to Kerényi, dating from 1934, in which Döblin is mentioned as a prime example of the emergence of a mythic tendency in the modern novel. Mann refers in particular to what he calls Döblin's 'Marduk-Roman', i.e. *Babylonische Wandrung* (1935), which Gouriou rightly presents as a relatively straightforward example of Döblin's disillusioning treatment of mythic pretentions: his Babylonian god descends to earth, only to have his sense of his own importance undermined and dashed. It is in her discussion of Döblin's subsequent fictions that Gouriou reveals the wide range of functions that myth actually fulfils in his writings. In *Amazonas* (1937–48) it provides the medium for his elaborate critique of modern European civilization as it expands into South America; in *November 1918* (1939–50) she detects the reappropriation of myth in the use Döblin makes of the stories of Faust and Antigone; and in *Hamlet* she distinguishes between two kinds of potential in myth: its capacity to obscure the truth and delude the members of the Allison household who participate in the storytelling that forms the bulk of the narrative on the one hand, and its function as a 'bridge to the divine' on the other.

Gouriou's analyses explore the connections between Döblin's narrative practice and the assessments of the workings of the German mind to be found in his letters and essays of the period after 1933, helpfully providing the full German text of the quotations on which she bases her judgements in her footnotes; and she situates Döblin's thoughts on the role that mythic structures play in the human imagination in relation to the thinking of his contemporaries—Ernst Cassirer, Hannah Arendt, and Horkheimer and Adorno, as well as C. G. Jung. In the process she also sheds light on the seemingly oblique relationship in which Döblin's fictions often stand to the historical world in which he was writing, highlighting the strong sense of moral purpose that underlay his decision to return to Germany in 1945 and to contribute as best he might to the post-war re-education process. It is in that perspective that the complex entanglement of mythic representations in *Hamlet* can be recognized as the necessary preparation for the experience of demythification—as a detoxification of life and its possibilities—that the reader shares with the protagonist Edward when he finally emerges from his 'long night' as an individual capable of independent moral judgement.

St John's College, Cambridge   David Midgley

Joseph Roth: Europäisch-jüdischer Schriftsteller und österreichischer Universalist. Ed. by Mira Miladinović Zalaznik and Johann Georg Lughofer. (Conditio Judaica, 82) Berlin and Boston: de Gruyter. 2011. x+358 pp. €94.95. ISBN 978-3-11-026505-7.

Were evidence still needed to confirm Joseph Roth's standing in the mainstream of academic debate, it was provided by the organization of no fewer than four symposia in 2009 to celebrate the seventieth anniversary of his death. Almost irrespective of his renown as novelist, journalist, and travel writer, Roth today attracts attention because central to all his writings are issues of such topical scholarly concern as identity, space, dislocation, deracination, and migration. Appropriately, the present volume originated in an event held in Slovenia, once a province of the Austro-Hungarian Empire dear to Roth for its loyalty to the Habsburg throne and famously celebrated in what remain probably his most widely read novels, *Radetzkymarsch* and *Die Kapuzinergruft*. Not surprisingly given its provenance, the volume provides fresh and interesting material on Roth's reception in Slovenia, as well as a sensitive examination of his relationship with Poland, the reborn Slavic nation state into which Roth's native, multi-ethnic Galicia 'disappeared' after the dissolution of the monarchy.

Like many conference-inspired publications, this collection contains the odd contribution that would not have made it into a peer-reviewed journal. That said, the standard is generally very high indeed, and the volume as a whole reflects the breadth and depth evident in Roth scholarship today. Although it appears in the series Conditio Judaica, Jewish issues are not central to the collection. In the three contributions exclusively devoted to Roth and Judaism, Roth's essentially negative attitude towards Zionism is stressed, but only Klaus Zelewitz musters the courage to ask why, amidst the plethora of work devoted to the subject, so little attention has been paid to Roth's observation, made in a letter to Stefan Zweig in 1935, that: 'Ein Zionist ist ein Nationalsozialist, ein Nazi ist ein Zionist' (p. 43). Perhaps inevitably, even in the context of a volume highlighting the resonance today of many of Roth's views—e.g. on the question of a 'European' identity—Zelewitz elects not to pursue the issues raised by this incendiary claim. Thankfully (at least in the opinion of this reviewer), despite its reference to Roth as an 'österreichischer Universalist', the volume is not obsessed with the extent to which Roth is to be considered an 'Austrian' writer. That work examining Roth's often less than endearing treatment of the women in his life should form the other major biographical strand in the volume is not unexpected, but all the contributions here are strong, especially that by Helen Chambers on 'Sex und Behörde' in Roth's reportage from the 1920s.

The sections entitled 'Zwischen Kulturen und Orten', and more especially 'Soziales und Geschichtliches', contain often disparate material ranging from Ulrike Zitzlsperger's excellent essay on the significance of cafés, stations, and hotels as 'semi-public spaces' to Jon Hughes's thoughtful reflection on 'Generationsdiskurse und Geschichte(n)' in Roth's œuvre. Of particular note here is David Horrocks's elegant and urbane essay examining the very divergent notions of 'cosmopolitanism' to be found in Joseph Roth and his 'friend', admirer, and financial backer Stefan Zweig. As Horrocks observes, although the two refugees from Hitler may often be regarded as linked by a nostalgia for the Habsburg past (a truism this volume goes some way towards dispelling as far as Roth is concerned), the difference between them is profound: Zweig's cool cosmopolitanism is essentially abstract, relating to 'Menschheit' in its generality. Roth's on the other hand is warmer, more immediate, and always specific to the individuals he meets in the street, in the café, or on the train. Sadly, David Horrocks died in 2011. It is fitting that this substantial volume, containing many other first-rate contributions which only constraints of space prevent me from discussing, is dedicated to his memory.

UNIVERSITY OF EDINBURGH ANDREW BARKER

Briefe. By THOMAS MANN. Vol. III: *1924–1932. Text und Kommentar in zwei Bänden*. Ed. by THOMAS SPRECHER, HANS R. VAGET, and CORNELIA BERNINI. (Große kommentierte Frankfurter Ausgabe, 23.1, 23.2) Frankfurt a.M.: Fischer. 2011. 674 pp. (text), 861 pp. (commentary). €95. ISBN 978-3-10-048372-0.

Bekenntnisse des Hochstaplers Felix Krull: Der Memoiren erster Teil. By THOMAS MANN. Ed. by THOMAS SPRECHER and MONICA BUSSMANN. 2 vols. (Große kommentierte Frankfurter Ausgabe, 12.1, 12.2) Frankfurt a.M.: Fischer. 2012. 446 pp. (text), 900 pp. (commentary). €80. ISBN 978-3-10-048343-0 (vol. I), 978-3-10-048344-7 (vol. II).

The Große kommentierte Frankfurter Ausgabe of Thomas Mann's works, a major and welcome scholarly undertaking that also offers much to the general reader, is now well advanced. At the time of writing, seven volumes of fiction, three of letters, and three of essays, plus *Betrachtungen eines Unpolitischen*, have appeared. With the diaries, there will be thirty-eight volumes altogether.

This edition differs, to its advantage, from many scholarly editions of complete works. Too often they are white elephants, affordable only for libraries, with extensive apparatus that can interest only a few specialists. By contrast, the GKFA offers clean, readable texts, and commentary volumes full of helpful annotations and extracts from relevant biographical and source materials. The commentaries can provide lovers of Mann's work with considerable pleasure as well as instruction.

The latest collection of letters—more than half of which were previously unpublished, or published in relatively inaccessible places—covers nine years of Mann's life in the Weimar Republic. They deal with the completion and reception of *Der Zauberberg*, with his work on what became the *Joseph* tetralogy (though as late as 1932 Mann contemplates only three volumes), with his attempts to build up the literary section of the Preußische Akademie der Künste by recruiting Hauptmann, Hofmannsthal, and Hesse (all unavailing), with the award of the Nobel Prize in 1929, with the increasingly nationalistic atmosphere of the later Republic, and of course with travels, lectures, meetings, translations, and family matters. Thus they convey a rounded picture of Mann's varied and arduous life.

Der Zauberberg was received with much incomprehension. Readers found it coldly intellectual, boring, formless. To several correspondents, Mann summed up the point they were missing: 'Es handelt sich letzten Endes um Kritik und Überwindung der als Todesfaszination verstandenen Romantik zugunsten des Lebensgedankens und eines neuen Humanitätsgefühls' (p. 183). The novel's detractors included the chairman of the Nobel Prize Committee, Fredrik Böök, so when Mann was eventually awarded the Prize in 1929, it was ostensibly for *Buddenbrooks*. He was then beleaguered by extraordinary claims that the Prize should really have gone to Arno Holz, but for Holz's death on 26 October that year, and that Mann ought to have shared the prize money with Holz's two widows. Another issue *Der Zauberberg* raised was Mann's use of Gerhart Hauptmann as a model for Peeperkorn's memorable idiosyncrasies. We know that Hauptmann himself recognized the resemblance (see Peter Sprengel, *Gerhart Hauptmann: Bürgerlichkeit und großer Traum. Eine Biographie* (Munich: Beck, 2012), pp. 586–87). In this volume we find Mann first professing amazement that anyone could imagine a similarity (p. 96), then admitting that a fortnight in Hauptmann's company may have left some traces (p. 113), and finally writing Hauptmann a convoluted letter of apology (pp. 142–45).

As Mann works on his next novel, *Joseph und seine Brüder*, the letters record a darkening atmosphere. He is used to sniping from the *Münchner Neueste Nachrichten*, but around 1930 he finds himself increasingly exposed to nationalist and National Socialist attacks from many quarters. Mann gives a suitably firm reply to a correspondent who tries to persuade him of the merits of National Socialism (pp. 568–72), deplores the growing cult of the irrational, and laments in 1932: 'Die patriotische Reaktion ist heute in vollem Siegen begriffen' (p. 643). His many dire forebodings would fall far short of reality, as the next volume of letters will confirm.

The 523 letters are of course only a selection from Mann's voluminous correspondence. Other letters are quoted in the commentary to illuminate those in the main text. In giving a broad picture of Mann's life, this volume is not in competition with previously published volumes devoted to individual correspondences, such as those with Josef Ponten and Hermann Hesse. Mann's peculiar relationship with the tactless and patronizing Ponten, in particular, needs to be followed in the extensively annotated *Dichter oder Schriftsteller? Der Briefwechsel zwischen Thomas Mann und Josef Ponten 1919–1930*, ed. by Hans Wysling (Bern: Francke, 1988). Letters to others, however, offer sidelights on these relationships, as when Mann tells Hans Reisiger, after a visit to the Hesses, that their marriage looks shaky because he is such a difficult husband and she does not share his passion for skiing (p. 607). (A tiny flaw in the otherwise immaculate editing is that 'Ninon Hesse' and 'Ninon Dolbin' are listed separately in the index, though they are the same person, and that the commentary fails to mention that in this case Mann's forebodings were unjustified, as Hesse's third marriage lasted till his death in 1962.)

The editors of *Felix Krull* first provide a minute account of the novel's genesis, which goes back to the first decade of the twentieth century; examine the literary and factual texts which gave Mann material and stimulus; trace the novel's reception; and then offer a separate introduction to each of its three parts, followed by a 'Stellenkommentar'. The paralipomena include the original version of the Eleanor Twentyman episode, in which not only Eleanor but both her parents make sexual advances to 'Armand', and we then have extensive quotations from Mann's source material, including an illustrated newspaper article about the workings of a luxury hotel, stories about hotel thieves, and evocative pictures of Lisbon and of an Italian actress whom Mann imagined as the model for Senhora Kuckuck. All this is invaluable for the understanding and appreciation of Mann's comic masterpiece. The editors also write in a light and graceful style which is a pleasure to read.

Occasionally one might query the editors' emphases. Following Hans Wysling, they make great claims for the overwhelming influence of Schopenhauer's theme of illusion. But the novel's tone is far removed from Schopenhauerian pessimism: Krull approaches the world with discriminating enjoyment. The idea that the world is an illusion hiding an unpleasant reality, forcefully expressed in the Müller-Rosé episode, soon recedes into the background. For Krull, the world is all surface, and life is a performance, in which he is equally authentic in performing Armand or Venosta. It was to this aspect of the novel—the presentation of the world as surface—that some moralistic reviewers responded by complaining of its 'Welt ohne Transzendenz' (p. 191). Now, after the 'performative turn', Mann seems to have been far ahead of his time.

The detailed survey of immediate critical reactions is followed by a very short 'Forschungsgeschichte', which might better have been omitted. It is little more than a list of titles, not all of which appear in the bibliography, and it ignores important publications in English. Donald L. Nelson's *Portrait of the Artist as*

Hermes (Chapel Hill: University of North Carolina Press, 1971) deserved mention, at least for taking the mythical interpretation to its limits, and when placing the theme of 'Hochstapelei' amid the plutocracy of the *belle époque*, the editors should have referred readers to Ernest Schonfield's *Art and its Uses in Thomas Mann's 'Felix Krull'* (London: Maney, 2008). Nevertheless, the commentary volume is an invaluable quarry of information which readers will use with gratitude.

THE QUEEN'S COLLEGE, OXFORD   RITCHIE ROBERTSON

'Lieber und verehrter Onkel Heinrich'. By KLAUS MANN. Ed. by INGE JENS and UWE NAUMANN. Reinbek bei Hamburg: Rowohlt. 2011. 304 pp. €19.95. ISBN 978-3-498-03237-1.

Researchers dealing with Klaus Mann have frequently claimed that the relationship between the writer and his uncle Heinrich was close, and at any rate closer than that with his father Thomas Mann. Indeed, Klaus and Heinrich shared many thematic interests and topics of conversation—and also stylistic features in their writings—both during the Weimar Republic and during their exile from Nazi Germany. In the second half of the Weimar Republic, both the young novice writer Klaus Mann and Heinrich, a well-established, leading intellectual, stood for a left-wing political and cultural internationalism, for detailed knowledge and love of French culture, and last but not least for slightly scandalous, sexually explicit writings. In the light of the similarities and the many private and public points of contact between these two writers, it is surprising that the intellectual and personal exchange between them has hitherto remained largely unexplored. In *'Lieber und verehrter Onkel Heinrich'* Uwe Naumann, who has a commendable history of (re)publishing all aspects of Klaus Mann's œuvre, and Inge Jens set out to fill this gap. Divided into four sections, the volume assembles all private and public texts preserved which the two writers wrote to and about each other, including letters, Klaus's diary entries, literature reviews, and excerpts from memoirs and autobiographies.

The table of contents for the volume reveals that the title's focus on Klaus is accurate in so far as Heinrich Mann only ever once published an official statement on his nephew, and this text—the uncle's contribution to the memorial book *Klaus Mann zum Gedächtnis* (section three of the volume)—was published after Klaus's suicide following extensive revision by Erika Mann (see pp. 223–24). The first section of the volume, however, paints a much more balanced picture. It contains the writers' letters to each other, many of which are here published for the first time. These were written both in the context of family relationships and in the writers' official capacities as leading figures of the German exile movement: Klaus, editor of the exile journals *Die Sammlung* and *Decision: A Review of Free Culture*, writes to Heinrich, patron of the former and contributor to the latter. The letters contain short notes on most of the big debates and scandals of the early exile years, from the public withdrawal of several contributors from *Die Sammlung* to the foundation of the Deutsche Volksfront and the Deutsche Freiheitsbibliothek, the PEN meeting in Barcelona in 1935, and the disputes surrounding Leopold Schwarzschild's *Das*

Neue Tage-Buch and Gottfried Bermann-Fischer's leadership of the Fischer-Verlag. In nearly all of these debates at least one of the two writers played a central part, and they exchange opinions and give each other advice and solace.

Altogether, the letters present a friendly and respectful intellectual exchange between equal partners. However, especially the interrelation between these letters and the excerpts from Klaus's diaries published in the second section (which contains all Klaus's public and private statements on his uncle) provides a deeper insight. Klaus's diary entries show how much diplomatic care and strategic acumen underpinned the exchange with Heinrich. This can be seen, for example, when Klaus dreads to write an 'arge[r] Brief' to persuade his uncle to exchange an unwanted contribution to *Die Sammlung* for a better one (p. 112) or when he sends his seemingly heartfelt but actually hypocritical condolences after the death of Heinrich's wife in 1944 (pp. 66–67, see also pp. 218–19). Most importantly, though, the letters and diaries prove that there was indeed an intellectual and aesthetic symbiosis between the two writers. Both the open conversation and the private notes contain benevolent, approving, and in some cases enthusiastic responses to their respective writings. Heinrich reacts positively and passionately—and with considerably more warmth than father Thomas Mann—to Klaus's exile novels, and the nephew reads, rereads, and admires Heinrich's works and concludes that he has been '[s]tilistisch [. . .] viel mehr von Heinrich beeinflusst als ich wusste' (p. 138). Moreover, the frequently observed links between Heinrich's *Der Untertan* and Klaus's *Mephisto* are confirmed by the nephew's enthusiastic reception of his uncle's novel as 'meisterhaft' during the period when he was writing his *Roman einer Karriere* (pp. 126–27).

In a knowledgeable epilogue, the editors attempt to contextualize and interpret the texts presented in the volume. However, this section provides little more than an overview of the two writers' lives with a focus on their personal and intellectual points of contact. A discussion of themes, structures, and motifs of *Der Untertan* and *Mephisto* promises to offer an interesting starting-point for a deeper comparative analysis of Heinrich's and Klaus's œuvre, but it remains sketchy. The strength of this volume lies mainly in the collection and juxtaposition of the material presented, even though the individual parts of this material are not in all cases exceptional or interesting (see, for example, the many diary entries in which Klaus simply notes that he wrote a letter to uncle Heinrich). The editors reach the conclusion 'dass die oft behauptete besondere Verbundenheit von Onkel und Neffe mehr intellektueller als persönlicher Art war' (p. 220), but the questions repeatedly raised (not only) in this volume concerning 'wo Klaus Manns Werke vom Denken und Schreiben des Onkels beeinflusst sind, wo sich Parallelen, vielleicht auch literarische Fortführungen oder gar Verschärfungen [. . .] finden lassen' (p. 208) once again remain mostly unanswered.

Johannes-Guttenberg-Universität, Mainz   Karina von Lindeiner-Stráský

Bloch-Wörterbuch: Leitbegriffe der Philosophie Ernst Blochs. Ed. by BEAT DIETSCHY, DORIS ZEILINGER, and RAINER ZIMMERMANN. Berlin and Boston: de Gruyter. 2012. xxv+744 pp. €149.95; $210. ISBN 978-3-11-025671-0.

This edited volume offers an encyclopedic reconstruction of the philosophy of Ernst Bloch. Contributors contextualize and explain Bloch's most significant concepts from *Antizipation* to *Zeit* in the form of individual essays, with the aim of providing a complete systematic overview of his thought. As the editors explain in their introduction, the reception of Bloch was problematic during his lifetime and has been insufficient since his death (p. v). Both his obstinate, unorthodox Marxism and his Marxist-inflected reception of classical German philosophy made a scholarly engagement with Bloch's thought difficult on both sides of an ideological divide in the context of which it matured. Times change, however, and the editors see the contemporary intellectual climate as an opportune moment in which to reappraise Bloch's philosophical enterprise as a whole. The volume promises to become the standard German-language reference work on Bloch, of use to newcomers and specialists alike.

Although a critical perspective is not lacking, the work is primarily conceived in terms of an exposition of Bloch's main ideas. Each entry begins with a short paragraph summarizing the relevant term as it appears in Bloch's work, followed by a genealogical history of the concept before returning to a more detailed perspective on the use and place of the term in Bloch's thought. This structure means that one does not need to be a philosopher, much less a Bloch scholar, to benefit from the text, which contains potted histories of ideas from dialectic to substance and beyond. As always with a volume like this, one could quibble about composition. In general, though, the entries are well balanced, thematically speaking, with the editors avoiding the danger of painting Bloch simplistically as a 'metaphysical' or 'Marxist' thinker.

Bloch's true philosophical innovation is his central operator 'Noch-Nicht' or not-yet, which expresses the fundamental idea that the world is unfinished and is striving towards its completion. As Johan Siebers points out in his entry on 'Noch-Nicht' (pp. 403–11), the concept has no obvious terminological predecessor—Bloch himself called the not-yet his first and only original thought. If Heidegger's insight that every thinker thinks only one thought identifies the mark of a great philosophy, Siebers shows how this applies to Bloch by demonstrating that all the themes of Bloch's philosophy relate to the dimension of the not-yet. This entry is therefore essential reading for those unfamiliar with Bloch as well as those seeking a deeper understanding of his work.

Another entry which deserves special attention is Hans Heinz Holz's piece on 'Spekulativer Materialismus' (pp. 483–508). The volume is dedicated to Holz, an erstwhile student of Bloch's in Leipzig, who sadly passed away before its publication, but who is rightly credited with contributing significantly to a fuller understanding of Bloch's thought (p. vii). In particular, Holz is the only one thus far to have devoted significant attention to Bloch's philosophy as a speculative materialism, a term the coinage of which Holz attributes to Bloch (p. 490). Since speculative and materialist thinking are—both respectively and in intersection the one with the other—once again in the limelight of European philosophy, Holz's entry highlights the relevance of Bloch's work also in the contemporary context.

UNIVERSITY OF SHEFFIELD   CATHERINE MOIR

Memorialization in Germany since 1945. Ed. by BILL NIVEN and CHLOE PAVER. Basingstoke: Palgrave Macmillan. 2010. xvi+421 pp. £65. ISBN 978-0-230-20703-5.

This impressive volume describes and analyses Germany's 'phenomenal memorial activity' since 1945 (p. 2). It takes 1945 as a 'decisive turning point' following which traditional, nationalistic forms of public commemoration and memorialization were called into question (p. 5). The notion of memorialization is potentially very broad, even more so in the light of Pierre Nora's concept of *lieux de mémoire*, but the editors mark out specific parameters for their survey: this is interested in memorialization as a 'conscious process', which leaves 'marks on the physical and temporal landscape'. In other words, it examines the 'visible, tangible markers of memory' (p. 6). Following the work of James E. Young, the volume is particularly attentive to the counter-memorial, i.e. the decentralized, horizontal modes of public commemoration, which oppose the central, vertical forms of traditional memorials. While this might seem to introduce a contradiction—the counter-memorials of the 1980s as provocatively *inconspicuous* markers of memory (e.g. Jochen Gerz's invisible monument in Saarbrücken, *2146 Steine*)—Niven claims that a 'second generation' of alternative memorialization has proven 'insistent, importunate, and intrusive' (p. 7). Above all, by focusing on the signs and processes of post-1945 memorialization, the volume resists treating memorials merely as static objects, considering also the role of Germany as a society that partakes of memorializing practices on a public, political, and institutional level.

Niven and Paver present a rich collection of thirty-seven essays, bringing together a wide variety of analyses from a range of contributors (those working closely with memorials and museums, as well as academics). They emphasize that this is not an exhaustive list but rather a series of studies showing 'typical and emerging patterns, together with models for understanding and evaluating them' (p. 7). While the different subjects covered might seem too disparate to be assembled in useful or meaningful ways, the editors do a good job of guiding readers through the material. Firstly, the volume is clearly divided into five sections: the first three are concerned with how the different experiences of different groups are remembered ('Remembering German Losses', 'Remembering Nazi Crimes, Perpetrators, and Victims', 'Remembering Jewish Suffering'); Section IV focuses on 'Socialist Memory and Memory of Socialism', and Section V on 'Memorializing Germany's Ambivalent Legacies'. Secondly, their lucid introduction sets out the terms of the survey, indicates shared concerns, and offers a useful framework for reading. And beyond this, Paver's own chapter, neatly positioned near the middle of the volume, integrates a helpful summary of arguments made so far; Niven's succinct conclusion, meanwhile, usefully draws together the many threads in suggestive but non-prescriptive ways. In this sense, the volume does what it sets out to achieve, resisting the imposition of false categories and engaging precisely with the 'messy complexity of memorial activities as they are lived out' (p. 8).

One of the principal merits of the collection is that it looks 'beyond Berlin' (Beattie quoting Rosenfeld and Jaskot, p. 328), and thus produces a more wide-reaching and representative image of the memorial landscape in Germany as a whole. It considers other regions (Urban on Bavaria's peculiar status in National Socialist history), other cities (Lotz on the history of street signs in Dresden and Mainz), less prominent, smaller towns (Beattie on the memorialization of Torgau's 'double past', Dittrich on memory tourism in Peenemünde), and even other countries (Livingstone on the work of the German War Graves Commission in foreign territories). The volume also moves very deliberately beyond the debates that surround Berlin's much-maligned Memorial to the Murdered Jews of Europe (only one essay looks at this specifically (Sion), and a few others more peripherally (Tomberger and Rickard)). In so doing, it discusses examples of memorialization which are less familiar, or which have garnered attention recently, for instance the Memorial to the Homosexuals Persecuted under the National Socialist Regime (Haakenson), as well as attempts to commemorate the Rosenstraße Protest (Potter), the White Rose (Rickard), the victims of the euthanasia programme at Grafeneck (Knittel), and Rosa Luxemburg (Bavaj). The volume also takes a long view historically speaking, using the benefit of hindsight to observe the effects of memorialization in a divided Germany from a post-Unification perspective; as such, it reveals what Niven calls the 'cross-fertilization' of East and West, that is, the emergence post-1990 of gestures perceived as taboo in the GDR and BRD respectively (p. 5).

Individual contributions are necessarily short in such a wide-ranging volume, which has its advantages and disadvantages. In some essays the brevity is frustrating; with only limited scope to explore their ideas, it seems authors have had to compromise either in terms of the material they could present, or in the framing and development of their argument. That said, the best contributions strike an impressive balance between conciseness and depth—the excellent essays by Scharnowski, Paver, Saunders, and Knittel are succinct but insightful and thought-provoking. On the other hand, the short essays provide very useful introductions to a reader either wishing to gain an overview of Germany's contemporary memorial landscape, or else seeking leads to follow. Perhaps all the chapters do what Nagel claims for his own, namely, offer an initial outline of the topic, thus 'paving the way for further research' (p. 135). Perhaps brevity also inevitably restricts the extent to which authors can use theoretical approaches: the vast majority of the essays assess their chosen memorials and memorial sites using specific data (visitor numbers, media coverage, government policy, community initiatives), and the arguments which attempt a degree of theorization remain rather tantalizing (Haakenson's use of Walter Benjamin, Sion's mention of Freud), or do so merely implicitly (Tomberger's use of 'phallic signifier'). But, again, a reader looking for more in-depth, sustained theoretical discussions can be guided by the bibliographical references gathered here.

Overall, the wide range of examples addressed, together with the guidance provided by the editors' introduction, provide a very informative introduction to, and overview of, memorialization since 1945. Niven and Paver's volume will be essential reading for any course on post-war German identity and memory culture, as well as an indispensable point of reference for scholars working in these fields.

UNIVERSITY OF EDINBURGH   DORA OSBORNE

Die Poetik des Gedenkens: Zu den autobiographischen Romanen H. G. Adlers. By THOMAS KRÄMER. Würzburg: Königshausen & Neumann. 2012. 271 pp. €39.80. ISBN 978-3-8260-4825-8.

The question 'Why are H. G. Adler's works not more widely known?' was asked by friends and colleagues of the writer even before his first major works were published in the 1950s. Thomas Krämer's densely argued and thoroughly researched monograph not only briefly addresses this question, but, more importantly, provides a comprehensive argument for *why*, a hundred years after his birth, Adler's novels deserve a much wider audience. Although this work results from a dissertation conducted by the author in Berlin, the significance of Krämer's achievement goes far beyond that of the standard reworked doctoral dissertation. Krämer has produced the first monograph on the novels of the long-neglected writer, sociologist, theologian, musicologist, psychologist, and polymath H. G. Adler (1910–1988). His innovative approach is grounded in archival research on Adler's three published autobiographical novels—*Panorama* (1968), *Eine Reise* (1962), and *Die unsichtbare Wand* (1989)—and retains a literary focus while drawing on contemporary theories of trauma, memory, and autofiction. This approach yields more than a first comprehensive introduction to Adler's fiction: *Die Poetik des Gedenkens* develops a systematic theory of Adler's poetics of trauma and offers signally new insights into Adler's complex works.

Krämer interprets Adler's autobiographical novels as works of therapeutic memory that serve to recreate a damaged sense of self in the wake of the experiences of deportation, concentration camps, and bereavement through the murderous actions of the National Socialists. For Krämer, Adler's novels are works that reflect on the constructive process of *Gedenken*, meaning both active memory and commemoration. However, Krämer's work is not simply an application of contemporary theory (Assmann, Langer, Laub, and Weigel are all referenced) to novels written fifty years earlier; Krämer draws on Adler's magisterial work of sociology, *Theresienstadt 1941–1945: Das Antlitz einer Zwangsgemeinschaft* (1955; 2nd edn 1960), to read Adler's fiction in the light of his own wide-ranging critique of modernity. Crucially, Krämer shows the importance of Adler's diagnosis of the sickness of 'mechanical materialism' in contemporary European society, his commitment to a conservative *Sittlichkeit*, or traditional morality, and his theologically informed belief that divine grace is the only way for humanity to overcome both original sin and the catastrophe of modernity. Krämer also situates Adler within the context of European Jewish thought, putting into critical perspective Adler's idiosyncratic conceptions of truth, testimony, and the dignity of the individual. This context strengthens Krämer's argument for the centrality of the autotherapeutic function to Adler's poetics; for Adler, even in the abyss of the camps, the individual can retain the dignity required to resist the soul-destroying mechanisms of Nazi administration. Adler's novels, in Krämer's account, become a way to strengthen and amplify that individual's voice.

Krämer aligns his subsequent readings of the three novels with the theoretical framework worked out in the first section of the monograph, analysing each as a 'model of remembrance', then on the macro-structural level, then on the level of content, noting in each case the novel's handling of the key themes of *Sittlichkeit*, administration, and mechanical materialism, before analysing the stylistic features of each. This extremely schematic approach makes the novels seem to have rather more in common than they in fact do; each of the novels has its very distinct poetic voice and aesthetic strategy. While drawing out the commonalities of a large body of work must necessarily be the task of the monograph, at times Krämer's analysis borders on the repetitive. But this observation is a minor quibble, compared with the important and timely achievement that *Die Poetik des Gedenkens* represents. Krämer's close textual analysis teases out many of the trickier aspects of Adler's poetics (particularly in *Eine Reise*) and provides countless original and useful insights into questions of language, memory, and identity in the novels. This monograph provides an excellent starting-point for anyone interested in Adler's thought as well as his fiction, and constitutes an invaluable resource for the growing field of Adler scholarship.

UNIVERSITY OF LEEDS   HELEN FINCH

German and European Poetics after the Holocaust: Crisis and Creativity. Ed. by GERT HOFMANN, RACHEL MAGSHAMHRÁIN, MARKO PAJEVIĆ, and MICHAEL SHIELDS. (Studies in German Literature, Linguistics and Culture) Rochester, NY: Camden House. 2011. 310 pp. £40. ISBN 978-1-57113-290-1.

In the field of post-Holocaust poetics—an area as well rehearsed in some respects as it is under-researched in others—there is always a risk that in revisiting 'discussions of the hows, ifs, and shoulds of Holocaust testimony, representation, and rememoration', we get too caught up in these 'old debates' to gain new ground (p. 1). The present volume is evidently well aware of this risk and proposes in its introduction that, while the individual contributions to the volume are to be understood as 'merely the latest realizations' of these discussions, 'our anxious returns to the Holocaust debates of the past are being restoked' by the anticipation of a 'dawning age of post-remembrance' (p. 1). With this second 'major sense of caesura', 'arguably even more radical than that first Zero Hour', upon us, the editors suggest, we have gained a 'certain historical distance' that 'allows new questions to be asked' (pp. 1, 8). Given, not least, the still speculative nature of this second caesura, it is perhaps inevitable that the main body of the volume does not quite keep step with the ambitious agenda set by the editors and largely remains, as the back-cover blurb puts it, 'embedded in the discourse triggered by Adorno' (p. 1). Read in terms of the latter, however, this volume constitutes a thorough and thoughtful engagement with poetological developments after the 1945 rupture (or lack thereof) and an excellent source of in-depth, nuanced readings of Adorno himself.

A first section comprising six essays sets out to investigate the 'Poetics after Auschwitz' developed by individual authors, with contributions on survivors Nelly Sachs, Paul Celan, Rose Ausländer, and Ilse Aichinger, and also on Ingeborg Bachmann, thereby offering a comprehensive overview of post-Holocaust poetry from the immediate post-war period. Elaine Martin on Sachs, Gisela Dischner on Celan, and Annette Runte on Ausländer read especially nicely in conjunction with each other as a complex reflection on the absence or presence of a 1945 watershed, and the poetic shifts that did or did not occur as a result. Hans-Walter Schmidt-Hannisa's piece on Charlotte Beradt's exploration of the subversive potential of dreams and their ability to express the inexpressible stands out both for its less well-known subject-matter and for the fact that it is the only essay to cover prose writing in the first two sections.

Part II, on 'Tradition and Transgression', is concerned 'with the wider discourse on postwar poetics', although with two out of six essays devoted to Gottfried Benn and two to Heiner Müller, the discourse is perhaps not as wide as it might have been, even if the perspectives adopted on the material are diverse and thought-provokingly contradictory (p. 10). The first two contributions, by Rüdiger Görner and Stefan Hajduk, on Benn's later œuvre attest to his impact on post-1945 poetics, whereas Chris Bezzel's piece on Concrete Poetry as an 'extension' of avant-garde artistic production since the 1900s dismisses him as 'a nostalgic reprieve' (p. 165). Renata Plaice and Barry Murnane on Müller make for an excellent pairing, writing from opposite yet interestingly complementary angles. In the light of the volume's contemporary aspirations, this reader would have welcomed more material on recent authors, though there is a strong contemporary piece by Aniela Knoblich on Thomas Kling.

The third and final section, 'Comparative Explorations in European Poetics', places the debate in a broader European context. However, it consists of only three substantial contributions on Sartre, Malraux, and the Yugoslav writer Danilo Kiš, and a shorter concluding piece by editor Gert Hofmann on Claude Lanzmann's *Shoah*. As the editors acknowledge, it could either have done with being more extensive, or have made way for additional material from the German context. In particular the inclusion of more contemporary German-language authors might have allowed for further reflection on the premiss of a present sense of caesura as posited in the volume's introduction. Having said this, as Knoblich, citing Wilfried Barner, has pointed out, 'any experience of epochs is necessarily a question of perspective' (p. 200), and the editors are to be congratulated on raising timely (perhaps too timely?) and important questions, even if all of the answers to these questions are not (yet) forthcoming.

MERTON COLLEGE, OXFORD   KIRSTIN GWYER

New Directions in German Cinema. Ed. by PAUL COOKE and CHRIS HOMEWOOD. London and New York: IB Tauris. 2011. xii+308 pp. £16.99; $29.50. ISBN 978-1-84885-907-4.

In his seminal essay 'From New German Cinema to the Post-Wall Cinema of Consensus', Eric Rentschler charts the rise of a new generation of German film-makers who rejected the auteurist approaches of Fassbinder and his contemporaries, and looked instead to popular cinema and, above all, to Hollywood for their inspiration (in *Cinema and Nation*, ed. by Mette Hjort and Scott Mackenzie (London: Routledge, 2000), pp. 260–77). Building on Rentschler's analysis of the state of German cinema from the perspective of the year 2000, *New Directions in German Cinema* traces the next decade of film production in the Federal Republic and considers the ways in which recent German films have engaged not only with the consensualist agendas of the 1990s comedies, but also with the more introspective, socially critical legacy of the New German Cinema.

The editors Paul Cooke and Chris Homewood have produced a volume of essays that focus on landmark productions released between 2003 and 2008. In the course of their thought-provoking introduction, the reader is reminded of the sheer diversity of film output in Germany during the past decade and—in the context of an increasingly globalized industry—how problematic the notion of a German national cinema has become. As the editors point out, the comedies of the 1990s have been superseded by a much more critical engagement with discourses of national identity in the Federal Republic. For while the legacy of DEFA and East German film culture prior to 1990 provides a lens through which to view the problematic impact of reunification, the transnational turn in German cinema—as exemplified, above all, in the films of Fatih Akin—has brought the situation of the Turkish diaspora in the Federal Republic ever more sharply into focus. Likewise, questions of German-Jewish identity, German–Polish relations, and the current valency of 'Heimat'—that most loaded of concepts—have been critically probed in films by Dani Levy (*Alles auf Zucker!*, 2004), Hans-Christian Schmid (*Lichter*, 2003), and Edgar Reitz (*Heimat 3*, 2004).

As Cooke and Homewood argue, the renewed emphasis on the complexity of socio-political structures in the Berlin republic has been accompanied by a revival of interest in formal experimentation. In the case of directors such as Oskar Roehler, Fatih Akin, and Christian Petzold, they discern an attempt to follow in the footsteps of Fassbinder and to 'create aesthetically challenging cinema that can also indulge audiences' desires for popular genres' (p. 6). Likewise, the slow-paced reflective aesthetic so prominent in some of the productions of the so-called 'Berliner Schule' has, as they point out, been hailed in some quarters as a 'Nouvelle Vague Allemande' for the next millennium. In the final part of their introduction the editors turn their attention to the genre of the heritage film and the emotional power of mainstream cinema—Dennis Gansel's *NaPolA — Elite für den Führer* (2004) and Oliver Hirschbiegel's *Der Untergang* (2004) are perhaps the most obvious examples—to produce identificatory narratives that some have condemned as deeply reactionary. Nevertheless, as they argue, to dismiss such productions out of hand is to ignore the ways in which, as Alison Landsberg has argued, such films allow the spectator to 'inhabit other people's memories *as* other people's memories [...] thereby respecting and recognising difference' (*Prosthetic Memory: The Transformation of American Remembrance in the Age of Mass Culture* (New York: Columbia University Press, 2004), p. 14). Indeed, one of the great strengths of Cooke and Homewood's introduction is the way in which they demonstrate that the relationship between mainstream cinema and the prevailing discourses of memory in the Federal Republic is much more complex than many commentators have been willing to acknowledge.

With the sole exception of John Davidson's chapter on Alexander Kluge's avantgarde 'Minutenfilme', the chapters in the volume are devoted to studies of some of the best-known films to have emerged from Germany in the last decade, including *Sophie Scholl — die letzten Tage* (2005), *Das Leben der Anderen* (2006), *Der Baader Meinhof Komplex* (2008), *Die fetten Jahre sind vorbei* (2004), *Yella* (2007), *Wolke 9* (2008), *Gegen die Wand* (2004), and *Heimat 3* (2004). The contributions to the volume are grouped around several distinct clusters: the legacy of the Nazi past in contemporary Germany; the impact of reunification and the place of the GDR past in the Berlin Republic; the history of the post-war Federal Republic; the re-working of genre cinema and, in particular, the 'Heimat-film'; and the aesthetic legacy of the New German Cinema. Each chapter moves well beyond conventional textual readings and seeks to situate the work selected for detailed analysis within the wider context of prevailing aesthetic and political discourses. The volume has been conceived with the needs of non-German speakers in mind, and almost all of the films selected are readily available in subtitled formats. Moreover, while the individual contributions by some of the leading scholars in the field could function as stand-alone essays in their own right, when read in the context of the editors' introduction they coalesce into a persuasive narrative outlining the overall development of German cinema in this decade. One might quibble about the lack of suggestions for further reading at the end of individual chapters; but the volume as a whole does include an extensive bibliography. Clearly written and with a number of illustrations, *New Directions in German Cinema* seems set to become a key text for courses on contemporary German cinema at both undergraduate and postgraduate level.

University of Warwick   Seán Allan

Translating Sholem Aleichem: History, Politics, and Art. Ed. by Gennady Estraikh, Jordan Finkin, Kerstin Hoge, and Mikhail Krutikov. (Studies in Yiddish, 10) London: Legenda. 2012. xi+219 pp. £45. ISBN 978-1-907975-00-4.

Sholem Aleichem was one of the most important and popular Yiddish writers of the twentieth century, yet because of the murder of nearly the entire Yiddish-speaking population of Europe during the Holocaust, his work is known today mostly through translation. The superb new edited collection *Translating Sholem Aleichem* explores the topic of translating this canonical Yiddish master to raise broader questions about translation generally and the specific difficulty of translating Yiddish into English. The collection also offers several new and important biographical insights into Sholem Aleichem the man and unpacks the creative decisions behind several of his best-known stories. The volume's excellent introduction situates Sholem Aleichem's work in the broader currents of European culture and daringly suggests that Yiddish, far from being a marginal, uninteresting European language, existed at the nexus of East and West, and of modernism and traditional modes of storytelling.

Twentieth-century Yiddish literature is perhaps uniquely suited as a template for understanding how translation works because of its linguistic, historical, and political aspects. Yiddish, often referred to as an 'open' or 'fusion' language, is highly idiomatic, and Sholem Aleichem used this aspect to create extremely textured, multilingual, and layered narratives where wordplays between different linguistic elements are central. For translation theorists, his work is a playground for postmodern ideas about the issues inherent in multilingual texts. Gabriella Safran's wonderful essay 'Four English Pots and the Evolving Translatability of Sholem Aleichem' shows how English translators evolved in their notions of whether Sholem Aleichem's works were 'translatable' at all. As Safran delineates, the various attempts at capturing the essence of this author mark out the perceived limitations of English when working with a language that is so richly multilingual.

Historically, Yiddish literature carries the burden of direct association with the Holocaust, and the project of translating Yiddish writing evokes important questions concerning the issue of whether and how a literature can carry such a burden. As the introduction states, 'The reason for the discomfort among post-war translators of Yiddish is that, whatever the complexities of linguistic untranslatability, the loss of the culture and civilization which was built on the Yiddish language intensifies both the difficulty and the moral responsibility of translating the literary hallmarks of that civilization accurately' (p. 5). In other words, the project of translating Yiddish literature is profoundly important because these works are all that remain of a destroyed civilization.

Anna Vershik's essay 'Sholem Aleichem in Estonian: Creating a Tradition' discusses how the three Estonian translators of his work (one of whom is the author of the essay) grapple with the burden of creating his literary tradition in Estonian. Olga Litvak's stimulating essay 'Found in Translation: Sholem Aleichem and the Myth of the Ideal Yiddish Reader' examines how 'the debate about Sholem Aleichem's "translatability" implicates the reader in a conservative discourse about cultural decline' (p. 7). She brilliantly challenges the notion that before the Holocaust there was a sort of 'ideal reader' who understood Sholem Aleichem exactly as he intended himself to be understood, while the Holocaust ruptured for ever the connection between readers and some type of idealized 'pure' Yiddish. In this way Litvak undermines the idea that a language can be a sacred holder of an entire culture.

Translating Sholem Aleichem also discusses the question of how the ideological aims of different eras in Soviet and European history impacted on the manner in which his works were translated and understood. Mikhail Krutikov and Gennady Estraikh both give interesting and important accounts of how shifting Soviet ideologies about the role of the 'folk writer' played out in the manner in which Sholem Aleichem's works were canonized during different Soviet eras.

I would highly recommend this volume for a range of readers: those interested in issues of translation generally, those who wish to know more about the life and work of this central Yiddish writer, and those desirous of understanding the complexities of translating Yiddish.

MONASH UNIVERSITY   LEAH GARRETT

Early Modern Women in the Low Countries: Feminizing Sources and Interpretations of the Past. By SUSAN BROOMHALL and JENNIFER SPINKS. Farnham: Ashgate. 2011. 247 pp. £65. ISBN 978–0–7546–6742–1.

This is a complex, interesting book which does exactly what it says in the subtitle. While it is indisputably about women in the Low Countries during the transition from the Middle Ages to the period of wealth and stability known as the Dutch Golden Age, it refuses the reader the comfort of an overarching narrative of women's lives. And while its agenda of increasing women's visibility in historical representation may at first seem reminiscent of feminist historical work produced in the 1970s and 1980s, this book not only shows that a great deal of work still remains to be done but also demonstrates that the task needs to be approached in new ways.

An important strength of Susan Broomhall and Jennifer Spinks's co-written volume is its keen awareness of the constructedness of all historical accounts. Interestingly, it chooses to focus on those accounts that inform the wider public's enjoyment of historical places and spaces in the Low Countries. Through a series of detailed studies, Broomhall and Spinks investigate and question the use of historical sources both by historiography and by the heritage industry, and the choices made by those whose job it is to convey a sense of the past to visitors to museums, galleries, and tourist destinations in Flanders and the Netherlands.

The chapters are arranged in broadly chronological order and focus on a wide range of women in the Low Countries: elite women at the beginning of the early modern period; women textile workers in Leiden towards the end of the fifteenth century; Louise de Coligny, grieving widow of Willem I; well-to-do female owners of dolls' houses; and women associated with the Rembrandt House and the Rubens House. These chapters are followed by a further two dealing with the 'Uses of Place for Tourism, Heritage and History' and with what we might call 'heritage shopping', in which the authors investigate the dynamic between past and present, seeing the 'consumer desire to touch and to own objects that recall this past' as a form of engagement with history, rather than as a branch of shopping. They insist that taken as whole, such activities 'collectively testify to ever-changing ways of experiencing and apprehending the past' (p. 194). Some traces of the past discussed in the book, such as women remembered in restaurant names or statues, are disconnected from any historical narrative and I find these survivals all but meaningless, although I do concede that they leave open the possibility of a link to the past. All the same, the idea that all these ways of engaging with the past contribute to a collective experience is one I need to think more about and I am grateful to the authors for opening it up for reflection.

The chapters which focus on early modern women and their lives depend on a reconceptualization of the notion of egodocument, generally understood as personal documents such as letters and journals, which extends it to include such material objects as memorials, buildings, and miniature houses. Broomhall and Spinks demonstrate the ways in which these new historical sources can be used in order to inscribe women into the historical account of the period in question. For example, in the chapter on 'Memorializing Grief in Familial and National Narratives of Dutch Identity', they use prints and William's mausoleum with its depiction of him as head of both the nation-family and his own family to discuss the establishment of the Oranje-Nassau dynasty. Crucially, they suggest that through her demonstration of private grief and insistence on the importance of family in her letters to Willem's younger brother Jan, Louise de Coligny played an important part in the creation of the dynasty. Their conclusion displays the subtleties of their approach: 'we suggest that the Orange-Nassau also became Dutch through women's strategies, modes, and themes of persuasion: through letters and articulations of emotional states that also fashioned the national story' (p. 97). While conceding that such means are more difficult to present to museum visitors, Broomhall and Spinks point out that the resulting lack of representation is due to gendered memorialization processes, concluding that more attention to the personal dimension could redress the imbalance. They are thinking here of the story of Louise's own contribution to her husband's monument: that she placed Willem's heart in a lead box. Such a box was certainly found in the monument when it was restored in 2001.

UNIVERSITY COLLEGE LONDON   JANE FENOULHET

Wages of Evil: Dostoevsky and Punishment. By ANNA SCHUR. Evanston IL: Northwestern University Press. 2012. 241 pp. $45. ISBN 978-0-8101-2848-4.

The aim of Anna Schur's monograph on Fedor Dostoevskii is to subject the author's views on the question of punishment to a more systematic examination than has hitherto taken place. It is perhaps surprising that no such study has been undertaken before, given the centrality of the theme to Dostoevskii's œuvre, and the balance and rigour Schur brings to the subject are to be welcomed. The plurality of views and ambivalence regarding punishment she identifies in Dostoevskii's writing result in a study that is ultimately somewhat inconclusive, but in her rejection of the search for a single unifying idea, she avoids the limited and one-sided interpretations which sometimes afflict the field. As such, rather than advancing a particularly forceful argument, the main achievement of the book is to enlighten readers on the subject in detail. It will therefore be of considerable use to students, while also containing sufficient originality and complexity to engage scholars and contribute to Dostoevskii studies more widely.

In considering Dostoevskii's pronouncements on and depictions of questions of punishment in his journalistic work and his fiction, Schur focuses, for obvious reasons, primarily on *Notes from the House of the Dead*, *Crime and Punishment*, aspects of *The Brothers Karamazov* (in particular Dmitrii's trial), and a number of essays from the *Writer's Diary*, notably those concerning contemporary court cases. Although it is good to see interrogation of texts other than the usual suspects, one might suggest that space could have been found for more in-depth examination of both *The Idiot*, to which only a little over three pages are devoted, on the question of capital punishment (pp. 20–23), and *Demons*, which receives only one passing mention in an endnote; the absence of reference to Fedka the convict is perhaps particularly surprising. The thematic arrangement of the material around questions such as retribution and the need for punishment, guilt and intention, and the possibility of moral transformation, is coherent, but it means that certain works are frequently revisited. Moreover, the painstaking approach to interrogating these questions results occasionally in a tendency to reiterate similar points in different ways. This does not override the positive features of the study, but it presents the reviewer with a problem, as although the six chapters ostensibly have distinct focuses, their overlapping material means they are not particularly amenable to succinct formulation. For that reason the remainder of this review, rather than attempting to outline the specific chapter contents, will instead provide an overview, focusing on distinctive themes and ideas that emerge in the course of the work.

Schur positions Dostoevskii's writing on punishment generally to good effect in the context of contemporary criminology and debates on penal reform both in Russia and Europe, but the latter question is represented largely as a process of Russia looking to penal theory and practice abroad, when it would perhaps be more accurate to suggest that the traffic went both ways. For example, the British penal reformer John Howard visited Russia twice (and indeed died in Kherson in 1790), and later versions of his 1777 tract *The State of the Prisons in England and Wales* include a section on Russian prisons (4th edn (London: Johnson, Dilly, and Cadell, 1792), pp. 85–95). Some discussion of how (or whether) responses to Russian penal institutions affected the penal reform movement beyond Russia's borders would have been interesting, although that is, perhaps, the subject for another book. This minor omission notwithstanding, Schur successfully marshals her material to emphasize the difference in Dostoevskii's view of human nature and its malleability from that of both penal reformers and his radical opponents. Both Dostoevskii's notion of the impenetrability of the inner life of the individual (a subject on which more reference to *The Idiot* could potentially have been useful) and his conception of the abrupt and unpredictable nature of moral transformation indicate his belief that the human being is not amenable to systematic reforming influences. At the same time, Schur attests to Dostoevskii's acceptance of the need for punishment—in *Crime and Punishment*, for example, legal punishment is ultimately shown to be necessary, whatever the workings of Raskolnikov's conscience.

By bringing together different facets of the question, *Wages of Evil* reveals the complexities in Dostoevskii's position, and the hesitations (a key trope for Schur) and reversals that are apparent as he wrestles with the problem, presenting a picture that is a far cry from the dogmatic Orthodox moralist that sometimes emerges in studies of the author. As much as in its engagement with the specifics of the question of punishment, Schur's contribution lies in her nuanced approach, and for this she should be applauded.

UNIVERSITY COLLEGE LONDON   SARAH J. YOUNG

Tolstoy on War: Narrative Art and Historical Truth in 'War and Peace'. Ed. by RICK MCPEAK and DONNA TUSSING ORWIN. Ithaca, NY, and London: Cornell University Press. 2012. 256 pp. $24.95. ISBN 978–0–8014–7817–8.

The occasion that prompted this collection co-edited by Colonel Rick McPeak, Head of the Department of Foreign Languages at the United States Military Academy at West Point, was a conference 'War and Peace at West Point' held in April 2010. The relevance of Tolstoy's novel to today's cadets remains remarkably fresh, as McPeak explains in his report of their reactions to the discussions and debates at the conference. Their own training led them in particular to respond keenly to Tolstoy's views on leadership. The context of time and place does indeed determine the reader's response to *War and Peace*. Importance of context was rightly recognized by many of the speakers, such as Alexander M. Martin, who, in his contribution 'Moscow in 1812: Myths and Realities', drew attention to the particular social and political background of Russia in the 1850s and 1860s against which Tolstoy wrote his epic.

It is the universality of Tolstoy's vision, however, that is celebrated in a multi-disciplinary approach. As Donna Tussing Orwin argues in her introduction, literary critics, historians, social scientists, and philosophers have their own discrete insights. David Welsh is even able to consider Tolstoy as an 'International Relations theorist'. These various disciplines are all represented here and the collection's undoubted impact stems from the extent to which their respective insights illuminate each other.

Historians Dominic Lieven, Dan Ungurianu, Alan Forrest, and Martin have their say in the first four chapters. Although it is recognized that there was no deliberate distortion, there is a meticulous critique of Tolstoy's idiosyncratic use of the historical sources at his disposal. Military planning and execution were belittled in favour of highlighting the crucial role of the psychology of the common soldier in battle, his morale, motivation, and will. They share the objections of Tolstoy's contemporary military reviewers, as Orwin points out in her sympathetic account of their reading of the novel as it appeared. Yet, however wrongheaded Tolstoy's interpretations of such issues as the actual situation of 1812 Moscow or the role of partisans might appear to professional historians, they are obliged to recognize his forging thereby of an enduring national myth that has helped to form modern Russia.

How that myth was fashioned is the question tackled by the literary critics. Gary Saul Morson explores the use made of maxims, wise sayings, and aphorisms that grope for knowledge while recognizing that the expression of human experience is ultimately beyond the grasp of mere words. The importance of pithy folk sayings as mouthed by Karataev is also acknowledged by Jeff Love in his examination of the concept of the 'great man', a central question in War and Peace. Again it is his wise reticence that puts Karataev above Napoleon with his calculated, wordy expositions.

The interweaving of historical theory and literary artifice is perceptively examined by McPeak in his relating of the novel's duelling scenes to Clausewitz's attempt to interpret military violence through the metaphor of the duel. For Orwin, an understanding of Tolstoy's poetic devices is crucial to make sense of the philosophy of history and war behind his depiction of Borodino. Elizabeth D. Samet suggests that Tolstoy's conflation of the haphazard and contingencies may be related to the practice of contemporaries as diverse as George Eliot, Dickens, and Melville, and, informed by her experience as professor of English at West Point, speculates on how that quintessential Tolstoyan insight might have a bearing on the cadets' understanding of modern asymmetrical warfare.

This is an excellent co-operative study undoubtedly strengthened by the focus afforded by the symposium's location and audience.

BANGOR   W. GARETH JONES

Lydia Ginzburg's Alternative Literary Identities: A Collection of Articles and New Translations. Ed. by EMILY VAN BUSKIRK and ANDREI ZORIN. (Russian Transformations: Literature, Thought, Culture, 3) Oxford: Peter Lang. 2012. xiii+441 pp. £50. ISBN 978–3–03911–350–7.

The Soviet critic Lydia Ginzburg has been known to Slavists for over half a century as an incisive thinker who had something of substance to say at a time when most 'criticism' was merely repetition of Socialist realist truisms. Neither a dissident nor a political conformist, in the 1960s and 1970s she published a series of full-blown studies with the titles *On the Lyric*, *On Psychological Prose*, and *On the Literary Hero*. These established her reputation as a major scholar, albeit one overshadowed by the better-known figures of Iurii Lotman and Mikhail Bakhtin. During the decade before her death in 1990 and continuing thereafter, fragments of her literary, philosophical, and personal musings began to come to light. These notes stretched from her early years as a literary professional and former student of the Formalists to notes written during the height of Stalinism and, eventually, the demise of the Soviet Union. The most striking notes come from Ginzburg's first-hand experience during the Siege of Leningrad.

Ginzburg revelled in the analysis of transitions, in the very concept of 'inbetweenness'. The volume under review both analyses and represents this concept. It represents a movement away from the first generation of Ginzburg scholars, who typically focused on Ginzburg's large-scale studies and shared some of her life experiences or elements of her historical period. A number of them (including the author of this review) knew her and discussed her work with her as she wrote and reworked her texts. Her unrelenting mind and the dense complexity of her prose are often palpable in their work. On the other hand, a newer generation of scholars, represented in the present volume, generally came to 'Ginzburg studies' later on. They tend to focus on the notes that remained unpublished, or only partially published, during Ginzburg's lifetime. The lively immediacy of the earlier studies is lacking, but this generation has the benefit of distance, historical hindsight, new theoretical approaches, and above all, access to a wider range of Ginzburg's writings and a certain freedom of expression not available to their precursors. This transition, the historical conditions that gave rise to it, the 'types' or identities of the participants, and the ongoing discussion of what it all means could not be more fitting in terms of Ginzburg's own interests and world-view.

The volume contains an introduction with a definitive biographical sketch based partly on materials not available earlier, ten articles, and translations of six pieces of Ginzburg's writing. In relation to the earlier understanding of Ginzburg, the figure who emerges here is darker and more prone to deep-seated anxieties, more focused on her own and others' failures in the quest for a life of significance. In the introduction Andrei Zorin argues that Ginzburg's turn away from large studies to marginal forms was, in essence, an admission of failure. Sergei Kozlov concludes that Ginzburg suffered 'a colossal defeat' (p. 26). Emily Van Buskirk gives her contribution the self-explanatory title 'Varieties of Failure: Ginzburg's Character Analyses from the 1930s and 1940s'. These are very strong statements by the current leaders of Ginzburg studies. Other authors take a more neutral analytical stance, including Irina Sandomirskaia's article on discourse analysis, Stanislav Savitsky on reflection as an ethical value, Laurent Thévenot on *Notes of a Blockade Person*, Alyson Tapp on Ginzburg's 'rational impressionism', and Zorin now writing on Ginzburg as a psychologist. Still others offer exceptions to the generally sombre tone. These include essays that wrestle with more contentious issues, typically Ginzburg's perceptions of particular authors, or less reverential perceptions of Ginzburg by others. These include Alexander Zholkovsky's discussion of Ginzburg's focus 'between genres', Caryl Emerson's analysis of Ginzburg's relation to Tolstoy and Lermontov, Andrew Kahn's study of Ginzburg on Mandel'stam, and Kirill Kobrin's analysis of rituals in Ginzburg's blockade prose. As they leap over the anxiety of Ginzburg's influence, these contributors demonstrate the very joy of cognition that permeates Ginzburg's own work on even the most disturbing topics. This is the joy recognized by Kobrin as he describes the blockade person—a widely acknowledged stand-in for Ginzburg—as he 'broke the circle with new efforts of will and mind [. . .] analyzed his tragic experience [. . .] and achieved victory' (p. 262).

In spite of the clearly articulated theme of failure in this volume, the volume itself is nothing short of an acknowledgement of Ginzburg's victory. Its articles and translations provide a valuable tool in the ongoing analysis of one of the most important transitional thinkers of the twentieth century. Indeed, Ginzburg is a thinker whose ideas and experience are relevant in the wider arena of humanistic studies, including trauma and Holocaust studies, and, in their own idiosyncratic way, relevant to the concerns of poststructuralist theorists whose ideas emerged concurrently with hers, albeit at a considerable geographical, intellectual, and moral distance. The volume will be of use to a wide array of scholars and others concerned with major intellectual currents of our times.

UNIVERSITY OF SOUTHERN CALIFORNIA   SARAH PRATT

Soviet and Post-Soviet Identities. Ed. by MARK BASSIN and CATRIONA KELLY. Cambridge: Cambridge University Press. 2012. v+370 pp. £60. ISBN 978-1-107-01117-5.

The major achievement of *Soviet and Post-Soviet Identities*, an edited collection dedicated to the social institutions, attitudes, and practices that shaped collective identity in the former Soviet state, is to complicate our understanding of how national identities are formed. Emerging against a backdrop of studies that have focused on the macro-management of memory in post-Socialist communities, this volume is a welcome reappraisal of the relationship between state and subject, which foregrounds the role of Soviet citizens in shaping, understanding, and articulating the institutions, beliefs, and practices that framed their existence. The volume challenges the facile 'nostalgia' paradigm, which has come to function as a substitute for critical engagement with the ways post-Soviet communities engage with their pasts, providing instead a collection of 'snapshots' of post-Soviet reality, which reveal the various and at times contradictory roles that memory plays in shaping national identity. The result is a disconcertingly complex picture of shifting affinities and embedded identities, which, while defying easy synthesis, doubtless renders more faithfully than many studies of nation-building and historical revisionism the messy reality of national identity in the Soviet and post-Soviet contexts.

The introductory articles by Ronald Grigor Suny and Nancy Condee provide a theoretical foundation for the methodological thrust of the volume as a whole. Addressing the significance of emotion or 'affect' for national identification, Condee asserts the need to move beyond the limits of constructivist analyses of 'imagined communities', to examine what being 'Soviet' actually meant to the people who identified as such, and to explore the genuine affections and affiliations that emerged around the 'constructed' idea of nationhood. This preoccupation links a number of the most engaging contributions to the volume. Albert Baiburin's article (Part II, Chapter 5, 'Institutions of National Identity'), for example, offers fascinating insights into the ways in which the institution of the Soviet passport and its rituals of presentation informed citizens' sense of national identity and their perceptions of themselves as subjects of the Soviet regime. An article by Andrew Jenks (Part III, Chapter 7, 'Myths of National Identity') explores the implications of the Gagarin cult for ordinary Soviet citizens, arguing that it increased collective self-worth and promoted a sense of interconnectedness between citizens, the state, and celebrity. The role of the experience of deficit in creating a discursive community bounded by a 'special, almost cryptic knowledge inaccessible to those who did not share various food practices of the time' (p. 284) is the subject of a compelling article by Anna Kushkova (Part v, Chapter 14, 'Languages of National Identity'). In the concluding part of the volume, Alexander Panchenko (Part vi, Chapter 16, 'Creeds of National Identity') explores the resilience of vernacular religious practices in the face of official efforts to undermine religious life in the Soviet state, and the role played by 'religious consumption' in forming the official perception of religious identities and real social networks.

There is much to commend in *Soviet and Post-Soviet Identities*. The collection showcases some strikingly original research, by Russian anthropologists and ethnographers in particular, that will doubtless invigorate the at times stale debate on nation-building and memory politics in post-Socialist Eastern Europe. It is also gratifying to note the presence of regional case studies (Elista, Perm', and Novgorod, for example), the cultural specificities of which are explicitly recognized rather than whitewashed in an attempt to cast the local as microcosm of the national. The decision to structure the volume thematically rather than chronologically is effective inasmuch as it draws out connections between the ideologies and institutions explored in the case studies. This approach nevertheless produces some problems of focus. A number of the articles appear artificially 'stretched' into the post-Soviet era, and their reflections on changes to attitudes and behaviour patterns after 1991 sometimes serve as a coda to more substantial engagement with the Soviet period (Michael Gorham's and Catriona Kelly's articles are exceptions in this regard). The volume also privileges the Russian experience, and, while the editors reasonably justify their selection as an attempt to avoid 'a potted history of what happened to different republics under Soviet power' (p. 9), one occasionally wonders how translatable the volume's arguments are into the more peripheral territories of the former Soviet state (Moldova or the Baltic Republics, for example). In a volume already so broad in historical scope, territorial span, and disciplinary focus, however, this is perhaps an unreasonable criticism. Bringing into dialogue some of the most engaging and innovative new research on the construction of social identity in the Soviet and post-Soviet states, this volume is an impressive achievement and valuable contribution to the field.

UNIVERSITY OF ST ANDREWS   VICTORIA DONOVAN

ABSTRACTS

'Tolle lege': Epiphanies of the Book   by Theodore Ziolkowski

The word '**epiphany**' is often applied so loosely that it has become useless as a critical term. To enhance precision, the phrase 'epiphany of the book' is introduced to designate moments of insight produced, not by a supernatural power as in revelations nor by a fleeting impression as in **Joyce**'s epiphanies, but by a passage in a book, as in **Augustine**'s *Confessions*, **Petrarch**'s account of his ascent of Mont Ventoux, **Kleist**'s 'Kant-crisis', and J. S. **Mill**'s 'awakening' by Marmontel's *Mémoires*. In contrast to bibliomancy, which applies only to the individual, these insights reflect epochal transformations.

Lacunary Knowledge in Sebald and Proust   by Edward J. Hughes

This article proposes a comparative analysis of **Marcel Proust** and **W. G. Sebald** and explores the representation of **knowledge** and **memory** in their respective works. It shows how with both authors, mental processes are often dramatically represented, notably in terms of the **fallibility** to which such processes give rise. In exploring the importance of the **epistemological** dimension of their writing, the article reflects on how **unknowingness**, often acting as a key narrative driver, lies at the heart of the sceptical view of knowledge in both corpora. The limitations of self-knowledge are seen to function at both private and collective/national levels.

'P.S.': The Dangerous Logic of the Postscript in Eighteenth-Century Literature   by Richard Terry

This article examines **postscripts** both as a feature of **eighteenth-century letters** and as a literary device. Although postscripts could be used for entirely banal purposes such as sending regards or expressing thanks for a gift, their fictional usage was governed by a more specialized set of conventions. The main contention of this article is that the temporal lag between a letter and its postscript allowed novelists such as **Richardson** to explore new ways of manipulating **narrative time**. Henry **Fielding**'s spoof novella *Shamela*, with its numerous postscripts, can be seen as an ironic reflection on that aspect of Richardson's novelistic practice.

Ruins and Visions: Stephen Spender in Occupied Germany   by Florian Alix-Nicolaï

Stephen Spender's testimony on **post-war Germany** constitutes an original, informed account of living conditions in the British occupation zone. The English poet's nuanced narrative combines detailed portraits with aphorisms, and non-fiction with representative, semi-fictional episodes, thereby disrupting the illusion of objective **reportage**, while still adhering to the **ethics of witnessing**. A staunch liberal, Spender criticizes **book censorship** and the theory of **collective guilt**. He also provides a literary analysis of **Goebbels**'s works, though he fails to attend to Nazi propaganda techniques. Pessimistic over Germany's future, Spender nevertheless wishes that the defeated nation would reintegrate into the European family.

Henri-Georges Clouzot's *L'Enfer*: Modern Cinema at the Crossroads of the Arts   by Marion Schmid

Based on surviving rushes and screenplays for the film, this article reconstructs **Clouzot**'s unfinished *L'Enfer* (1964) and appraises the artistic influences that shaped the project. Contrary to the **Nouvelle Vague**, whose members sought to establish cinema as an autonomous art form, Clouzot seeks new possibilities of cinematic expression through **interart dialogue**. After discussing the influence **Proust**'s *Recherche* had on Clouzot's unconventional treatment of time and memory, the article examines how he appropriates the experiments of the historical avant-garde, **kinetic art**, and experimental music before analysing the film's afterlife in Clouzot's *La Prisonnière* (1968) and **Chabrol**'s *L'Enfer* (1993).

ABSTRACTS

Michel Tournier and the Virtual Essay   by Christy Wampole

This study considers the œuvre of **Michel Tournier** through the lens of the essayistic. While recognized primarily for his early novels, such as *Vendredi, ou les limbes du Pacifique*, *Le Roi des aulnes*, and *Les Météores*, Tournier enlisted the **essay** unremittingly as a means to blur the line between fact and fiction and to complicate the notion of authorial voice. From his explicit statement that he wished to use **Paul Valéry**'s essayistic narrative *Monsieur Teste* as a model for his own writing to his tendency towards digressive meditation and philosophical departures, Tournier embodies a provocative articulation of **Montaigne**'s original writerly attempts.

The Power of Woman's Words, the Power of Woman's Silence: How the *Madrastra* Speaks in the Thirteenth-Century Castilian *Sendebar*   by Andreea Weisl-Shaw

This article analyses the function of the ***madrastra***'s stories within the narrative construct of the **thirteenth-century Castilian *Sendebar*.** The bad wife is successful to a point in her **debate of exempla** with the King's advisers, despite the lesser narrative quality of her tales. I argue that this happens because, in accordance with the medieval discourse of **misogyny**, the **power of the woman's words** resides not only in their content, but in their very utterance, and, by extension, that the **power of woman** herself derives from her very presence and from her ascribed status as troublesome and destructive element.

What Do We Say When We Say 'Juan Gelman'? On Pseudonyms and Polemics in Recent Argentine Poetry   by Ben Bollig

Juan Gelman is perhaps **Argentina**'s best-known living poet, a Cervantes Prize winner and a name mentioned annually in literary circles as a Nobel candidate. The question explored here is at once simple and complex: why do polemics and polemicists seem attracted to Gelman? The article seeks an answer in Gelman's **poetry**, focusing on a long-standing tendency in his work, namely his publication of poems under names other than his own, and the links between his **pseudonymous poetry** and **apocryphal translations** and political shifts in his work.

Hölderlin on Tragedy and Paradox: 'Die Bedeutung der Tragödien [. . .]'   by Charles Lewis

This article considers one of the most enigmatic texts of **Hölderlin's poetics**, the fragment on the 'The Meaning of **Tragedies**'. Despite the currently accepted later dating (1802–04), the text is often read in terms of the concept of metaphorical expression found in the earlier Homburg poetics. However, I suggest that if the concept of **metaphor** is present, it is in the form of two limiting extremes, corresponding to the terms 'das Lebenslicht' and 'das Zeichen=0' respectively. If the former corresponds to an extreme of non-figurative expression, the latter corresponds to an opposite and paradoxical extreme of figurative presentation.

'Das Land, in dem das Proletariat [nur] genannt werden darf': The Language of Participation in Heiner Müller's *Der Lohndrücker*   by Michael Wood

The workers in **Heiner Müller**'s *Der Lohndrücker* (1956–57) lack a language with which to discuss their reality and a voice with which to change it. However, the gaps in their language stimulate creative responses from the **theatre audience**, and thus create the possibility for a participatory democracy to emerge in the auditorium. Previous studies of *Der Lohndrücker* barely discuss Müller's language, and therefore pass over its productive capabilities. They also consider the play only in relation to the **1953 Uprising** and international matters in 1956, but this article demonstrates the relevance of the **GDR**'s domestic situation in 1956.

'Long Live Poland!': Representing the Past in Polish Comic Books   by Ewa Stańczyk

This article discusses **representations of the past** in **Polish comic books** from the last decade. It suggests that, particularly in the period from 2005 to 2010, **graphic narratives** portraying **national** history were largely dependent on state funding and as such were subservient to the official **politics of memory** promoted by the conservative Law and Justice Party. It also discusses alternative comics which indicate a shift towards **personal and local histories** that are no longer grounded in the national myth of martyrdom fostered by a large portion of the political establishment in contemporary Poland.

Looking for the Creator: Pelevin and the Impotent Writer in *T* (2009) and *Ananasnaia voda dlia prekrasnoi damy* (2011)   by Sally Dalton-Brown

Pelevin's novel *T* and prose collection *Pineapple Water for the Beautiful Lady* (*Ananasnaia voda dlia prekrasnoi damy*) explore the **(post)modern** notion of **fallible authorship**. **Foucault**'s formulation of the **author function** as an interpretative construct implies the **author figure** as both cause and effect, arising from the text and imposed upon it. In *T* Pelevin posits the character and reader as co-creators of the text, existing with the author in an endless and solipsistic creative loop without origin. In *Ananasnaia voda* Pelevin attempts to look outside this 'vicious circle' towards a Creator, a point of **narrative origin**.

www.ingramcontent.com/pod-product-compliance
Lightning Source LLC
Chambersburg PA
CBHW072123290426
44111CB00012B/1753